Living in the Eighth Day

Princeton Theological Monograph Series

K. C. Hanson, Charles M. Collier, D. Christopher Spinks,
and Robin A. Parry, Series Editors

Living in the Eighth Day

The Christian Week and the Paschal Mystery

Steven Underdown

PICKWICK *Publications* · Eugene, Oregon

LIVING IN THE EIGHTH DAY
The Christian Week and the Paschal Mystery

Princeton Theological Monograph Series 234

Pickwick Publications
An Imprint of Wipf and Stock Publishers
199 W. 8th Ave., Suite 3
Eugene, OR 97401

www.wipfandstock.com

PAPERBACK ISBN: 978-1-62564-186-1
HARDCOVER ISBN: 978-1-4982-8851-4
EBOOK ISBN: 978-1-5326-4629-4

Cataloguing-in-Publication data:

Names: Underdown, Steven

Title: Living in the eighth day : the Christian week and the paschal mystery / Steven Underdown.

Description: Eugene, OR: Pickwick Publications, 2018 | Series: Princeton Theological Monograph Series 234 | Includes bibliographical references.

Identifiers: ISBN 978-1-62564-186-1 (paperback) | ISBN 978-1-4982-8851-4 (hardcover) | ISBN 978-1-5326-4629-4 (ebook)

Subjects: LCSH: Spiritual formation | Education (Christian theology) | Divine office | Monastic and religious life | Easter | Spiritual life | Church year

Classification: BV4490 U52 2018 (print) | BV4490 (ebook)

Manufactured in the U.S.A.   08/02/18

I dedicate this work to my wife Mary.

Jesus Christ yesterday and today,
the beginning and the end,
Alpha and Omega;
all times belong to him and all the ages;
to him be the power and the glory for ever and ever. Amen.[1]

1. Prayer at the blessing of the Paschal candle in the Easter Vigil of the Roman Rite, *Sunday Missal* (1975) 209.

Contents

Part II: Towards a Theology of Liturgical Time

Preface

THIS IS A STUDY in applied theology. It falls into four sections. A prologue outlines the historical context in which the research was undertaken, principally the life of the parish community in the Church of England but also the life of an Anglican contemplative monastic community. Part One then explores the idea that the ultimate concern of Christian education is *personal formation*. Central here is the belief that personal maturity is best understood in relation to the paschal mystery: only insofar as anyone is willing to be incorporated into the paschal mystery can that person attain maturity and become able to share in the life of the eternal Kingdom.

Part Two explores ways in which the Church might so order its use of the regular temporal cycles of the day, the week, and the year as to facilitate the personal growth of its members. It is argued that this way of growth has, as both its ground and its goal, creative, dynamic relationship with the persons of the Trinity—while growth towards fullness of relationship with the persons of the Trinity will go hand in hand with growth towards fullness of personal relationships within the Christian community itself. My particular focus will be a weekly pattern of life—I call it the "Pattern of the Week"—in which each week is observed as kind of Holy Week in miniature. I present this weekly pattern as providing a series of *covenanted occasions of creative encounter* between the divine persons and the worshipping community. In order to demonstrate that there is nothing in the history of the Christian use of time which might undermine my suggestions about the way the Church might understand and use its seven-day cycle, I briefly recount and discuss the history of the Church's use and understanding of the seven-day week.

In the final chapters of Part Two I set out what I believe is an original theology of time. I call it an "iconographic theology of time." I present the unfolding temporal cycles (again, the day, the week, and the year) as the context for inherently personal (and inherently paschal) encounters between God and man, encounters in and through which men and women can come both to direct knowledge of the divine persons and to participation in their shared life.

This book began life as an academic dissertation. It was successfully submitted as a PhD thesis at Kings' College, London, in 2002, under the title "The Christian Week and the Paschal Mystery: A Study in the Theology of Liturgical Time, Personhood, and Christian Education." The text of this book is substantially that of the thesis, although passages in Greek have been transliterated and some of the more technical discussions removed. The bibliography has been updated.

The title adopted for this book, *Living in the Eighth Day*, looks to an early Christian designation for Sunday. In the nascent Church, the day that now, without a second thought, we call Sunday was variously the Lord's Day or the First Day of the Week; and yet this day soon this day also became known as the Eighth Day. As such it was seen as standing beyond "natural time," beyond ordinary history, and the customary seven-day cycle. It was seen as the first day of a radically new week and of a new aeon, a new creation, a new way of being. As the *Epistle of Barnabas* (c.130 CE) has it; "the eighth day is the commencement of a new world; and this is why we celebrate the eighth day with joy—the same day on which Jesus rose from the dead . . ." (15). The eighth day is a day both in time and beyond time. It represents *eschatological time:* it sees the coming together of the life of this world and the life of the End, the Eschaton. *The Eighth Day* points to the fact that the life of the Church is always both a life in this present world and also a life in communion with the End, the ultimate goal of all existence. For indeed, the life of the Church is always, at heart, a life lived in dependence upon and in communion with the risen and glorified Christ. This book looks to explore what this means and how this is possible.

Acknowledgments

MY INTEREST IN THE Christian understanding of time and in the Church's weekly pattern of life began in the 1980s when I first encountered Fr. Alexander Schmemann's *World as Sacrament*. Subsequently I would find much of value throughout Fr. Alexander's other writings. I owe Fr Alexander a great debt of gratitude.

During the early years of my work on the book I received uncomplaining support from the members of the monastic community of which I was then a member, and especially from Fr Colin CSWG, who is now Superior of the Community. I should also express thanks to Fr Alan Sharpe, Vicar of St Patrick's, to his late wife Susan, and to the people of St Patrick's, Hove.

In the final preparation of the thesis Fr John Musther and the late Wendy Hay offered much support. In the preparation of the final text of this book Andrea Burgess and the Revd Dr Jo Drew offered invaluable help. My wife, Mary, offered advice and unfailing encouragement. I am very grateful.

The library staff at King's College, the Institute of Classical Studies, Dr Williams's Library, and the (much lamented) Sion College Library were all very helpful.

I must also thank Professor Andrew Walker, supervisor of my PhD at King's College London, for his support and long-suffering patience.

Dr Robin Parry, my editor, offered much helpful support and advice.

The system used for bibliographic references follows *The Chicago Manual of Style, 16th edition, 2010*. Footnotes are cross-referenced to the bibliography. References to patristic sources is by author and title; for convenience the title is sometimes abbreviated these abbreviations are expanded at the end of the bibliography (pp. 315–18 ff.)

A list of general abbreviations is given on pp. xiii–xvii.

For references to online resources I follow the guidelines in *The Chicago Manual of Style, 16th edition, 2010*.

In quotations, all italics and emphases are in the original texts, except where I indicate that they have been added.

Unless specified otherwise, biblical quotations are from the New Revised Standard Version, ©1989, the Division of Christian Education of the National Council of the Churches of Christ in the United States of America.

Please note, I apologize if at times I cause offense by using the term "man" to designate not just male humans but humans of either sex. Were I able to find an easy-to-use alternative, without sexist connotations, I would happily use it. But the term "man" has a positive advantage over any alternative I can find, since at one and the same time it can designate not just the individual human person but corporate humanity. A sentence such as "Man was made for something better" speaks simultaneously of each human person and of corporate, collective humanity. No alternative term or expression does the same.

Abbreviations

ABD   *Anchor Bible Dictionary* (6 vols.), ed. David Freeman, *et al.* (NY: Doubleday, 1992)

ACW   Ancient Christian Writers (New York: Paulist Press)

Bib   *Biblica* (Rome: Biblical Institute Press, 1920–)

B-G   *The Œcumenical Documents of the Faith*, ed., T. H. Bindley, 4th ed.; revised with introduction and notes by F. W. Green (London: Methuen, 1950)

CCP   Celebrating Common Prayer: A Version of the Daily Office SSF [The Society of St Francis] (London: Mowbray 1992).

CBQ   *Catholic Biblical Quarterly* (Washington, DC: Catholic Biblical Association of America, 1939–)

CCL   Corpus Christianorum, Series Latina (Turnholti: Typographi Brepols, 1953–)

CREP   Concise Routledge Encyclopedia of Philosophy (London: Routledge, 2000)

CSEL   Corpus Scriptorum Ecclesiastoricorum Latinorum (Vienna: Geroldi, 1866–)

CSWG   Community of the Servants of the Will of God (An Anglican monastic community based at Crawley Down in East Sussex, UK)

DACL   *Dictionnaire d'archélogie chrétienne et de liturgie*, ed. F. Cabrol. 15 vols (Paris: Letouzey et Ané, 1907–1953)

DBI   *A Dictionary of Biblical Interpretation*, ed. R. J. Coggins and J. L. Holden (London: SCM, 1990)

Dies Domini	Keeping the Lord's Day Holy: Apostolic Letter Dies Domini of the Holy Father John Paul II to the Bishops, Clergy and Faithful of the Catholic Church on Keeping the Lord's Day Holy (London: CTS, 1998)
DS	*Dictionnaire de spiritualité, ascétique, et mystique*, 20 vols in 16, (founding ed.) Marcel Viller (Paris: Beauchesne, 1937–94 [1932])
DTC	*Dictionnaire de théologie catholique*, 30 vols in 15 (founding ed.) A. Vacant, (Paris: Letouzey & Ané, 1909–50)
EB	*Encyclopaedia Britannica*, 14th edition (Chicago: Encyclopaedia Britannica, 1971) 24 volumes
ECQ	*Eastern Churches Quarterly* (London, 1945–64)
EEC	*The Encyclopedia of Early Christianity*, ed. Everett Ferguson, 2nd ed. (New York and London: Garland, 1998)
EECh	*The Encyclopedia of the Early Church*, ed. Angelo Di Berardino, tr. Adrian Walford (and W. H. C. Frend) (Cambridge: James Clarke, 1992)
EH	Ecclesiastical History
EJ	*Encyclopaedia Judaica*, ed. Cecil Roth (New York: Macmillan, 1971)
EOT	*Encyclopaedia of Theology*, ed. Karl Rahner (London: Burns and Oates, 2nd imp. 1977)
Ep.	Epistle(s)
ERE	*Encyclopedia of Religion and Ethics*, ed. James Hastings (Edinburgh: T.&T. Clark, 1908)
ET	English Text
HBS	Henry Bradshaw Library
HUCA	*Hebrew Union College Annual* (Cincinnati, Ohio: Hebrew Union College Press, 1924–)
HE	Historia ecclesiastica
JBC	*Jerome Bible Commentary*, ed. R. E. Brown, J. A. Fizmyer, R. E. Murphy (London: Chapman, 1968)

JBL	*Journal of Biblical Literature* (Atlanta, GA.)
JPE	*Journal of Philosophy of Education* (Dorchester-on-Thames, UK: Carfax)
JSNTSS	*Journal for the Study of the NT: Supplement Series* (Sheffield)
JTS	*Journal of Theological Studies*, New Series (Oxford)
LS	*Greek-English Lexicon*, eds. Liddell and Scott, 9th ed. (Oxford: Oxford University Press, 1940)
LMD	*La Maison-Dieu* (Paris: Les Éditions du Cerf, 1945–)
LXX	Septuagint version of the Hebrew Bible. See *Septuaginta, id est Vetus Testamentum Graece iuxta LXX interpres*, ed. Alfred Ralfs. 2 vols (Stuttgart: Deutsch Biblegesellschaft, 1980)
MC	P. E. More and F. L. Cross, eds., *Anglicanism* (1935)
Mishna	*The Mishna*, tr. H. Danby (London: Oxford University Press, 1933); also *The Mishna, a New Translation*, Jacob Neusner (New Haven and London: Yale University Press, 1988)
NCE	*New Catholic Encyclopaedia* (Washington DC: Catholic University of America, 1967)
NPNF	*The Nicene and Post-Nicene Fathers of the Christian Church*, eds. Philip Schaff and Henry Wace (Grands Rapids: Eerdmans, 1979 [Oxford, 1892])
NJBC	*The New Jerome Biblical Commentary*, eds. Raymond Brown, Joseph A. Fitzmyer, Roland E. Murphy (London: Chapman, 1989)
OCP	*The Oxford Companion to Philosophy*, ed. Ted Honderich (Oxford: Oxford University Press, 1995)
OCCT	*The Oxford Companion to Christian Thought*, ed. Adrian Hastings (Oxford: Oxford University Press, 2000)
ODCC	*The Oxford Dictionary of the Christian Church*, 3rd ed., eds. F. L. Cross and E. A. Livingstone (Oxford: Oxford University Press, 1997)
par.	and parallel(s)

Philokalia	*The Philokalia, The Complete Text* compiled by St Nikodemos of the Holy Mountain and St Makarios of Corinth, tr. and ed. G. E. H. Palmer, Philip Sherard and Kallistos Ware (London: Faber and Faber: 1979–) 4 vols. to date
PG	*Patrologie cursus completus. Series graeca,* ed. J. P. Migne (Paris, 1857–66) 161 vols.
PGL	*A Patristic Greek Lexicon,* ed. G. W. H. Lampe (Oxford: Clarendon, c.1961)
PL	*Patrologie cursus completus. Series latina,* ed. J. P. Migne (Paris, 1844–64) 221 vols.
PW	*Paulys Real-Encyclopädie der classischen Altertums-wissenschaften,* August Friedrich Pauly and Georg Wissowa (Stuttgart: Metzler, 1893-1978)
RBén.	*Revue Bénédictine* (Maredsous, 1884–)
SB	*Kommentar zum Neuen Testament aus Talmud und Midrash,* H. L. Strack and P. Billerbeck, (Munich, 1922–)
SC	Source crétiennes, ed. Jean Daniélou et al. (Paris: Cerf, 1940–)
SCMCS I	*Christian Spirituality:* vol. 1, *Origins to the Twelfth Century,* eds. Bernard McGinn, John Meyendorff, and Jean Leclercq. (London: SCM, 1987)
SCMCS II	*Christian Spirituality:* vol. 2, *High Middle Ages and Reforma-tion,* ed. J. Raitt; B. McGinn; J. Meyendorff. (London: Rout-ledge and Kegan Paul, 1987)
SCMCS III	*Christian Spirituality:* vol. 3, *Post Reformation and Modern,* ed. Louis Dupré and Don E. Saliers, in collaboration with John Meyendorff (London: SCM, 1989)
SCMJS I	*Jewish Spirituality,* vol. 1, *From the Bible through the Middle Ages,* ed. Arthur Green. (London: SCM, 1985)
SCMJS II	*Jewish Spirituality,* vol. 2, *From the Sixteenth Century to the Present,* ed. Arthur Green. (London: SCM, 1988)
SEC	Studies in Early Christianity, ed. E. Furguson. 18 vols. (NY: Garland, 1993)

Schürer	*History of the Jewish People in the Age of Jesus Christ (175BCE–135CE)*, Emil Schürer, ET. trans. Géza Vermès and Fergus Millar, Organizing Editor Matthew Black, rev. ed. (Edinburgh: T. & T. Clark, vol. I, 1973, and vol. II, 1979).
SL	*Studia Liturgica* (Notre Dame, IN: Societas Liturgica, 1962–)
ST	*Summa Theologica*, Thomas Aquinas (London: Blackfriars, 1964–)
SVS	St Vladimir's Seminary
SVTQ	*St. Vladimir's Theological Quarterly* (Crestwood, New York: SVSP)
TDNT	*Theological Dictionary of the New Testament*, 10 vols., G. Kittel and G. Freidrich, eds., tr. and ed. G. W. Bromiley (Grand Rapids: Eerdmans, 1964–76) English version of Kittel, *et al.*, eds., *Theologisches Wörterbuch zum Neuen Testament* (Stuttgart, 1933–)
TMAM	Thomas Mar Athanasius Memorial Orientation Centre (Manganam, Kottayam, India)
TSL	*The Study of Liturgy*, Cheslyn Jones, Geoffrey Wainwright, Edward Yarnold, SJ, eds. (London: SPCK, 1987 [1978])
TSS	*The Study of Spirituality*, Cheslyn Jones, Geoffrey Wainwright, Edward Yarnold, SJ, eds. (London: SPCK, 1986)
ZAW	*Zeitschrift für die alttestamentliche Wissenschaft* (Berlin)
ZKT	*Zeitschrift für katholische Theologie* (Verlag Herder Wien 1877–)
ZNW	*Zeitschrift für die neutestamentliche Wissenschaft* (Berlin: de Gruyter, 1900–)

Prologue

THIS IS A STUDY in applied theology and Christian education. It is rooted in a particular historical setting. In 1985 Dr Eric Kemp, Bishop of Chichester, invited an Anglican monastic community to send six monks to found a monastery in a run-down parish under his care. I was one of those six monks. The community was CSWG, the Community of the Servants of the Will of God, an Anglican contemplative community dedicated to prayer and the recovery of the Church's unity. Its base was a secluded monastery on the outskirts of the village of Crawley Down in the north of the bishop's diocese. The parish was St Patrick's, in Cambridge Road, Hove, on the south coast of England, some thirty miles from Crawley Down. The Bishop's hope was for the renewal of Christian life in an area where ordinary patterns of Church life had long since broken down and people had no expectation that the Church had anything to offer that might either help meet their immediate needs or help to give sense and direction to their lives. Over the next ten years my involvement with St Patrick's—and especially my involvement in its ministry of teaching and spiritual formation—helped to shape the ideas developed in this book. In turn, as my ideas developed so I was able to suggest ways in which the life of St Patrick's might be further advanced and the parish become a more effective setting for Christian formation.

The life at St Patrick's was at a very low ebb when the Bishop invited CSWG to become involved. This meant that those looking to its renewal found themselves confronted with fundamental questions about the nature of the Church, the nature of the Christian vocation, and the relationship of the contemporary Church to those traditions of life, prayer, and worship to which it is heir.

The centrality of education and formation in the life of the Church became clear: people attending the church had little or no Christian background. But at the same time, it was obvious that it would never be enough simply to offer teaching about Christ and the Christian tradition and not enough merely to offer moralizing exhortation. The teaching ministry in the church must look to encourage and facilitate the spiritual (or personal) formation and growth of its members. Catechesis and discipleship must go hand in hand.

But how was this educational and formational work to be accomplished? What does it mean for the Church to be enabling spiritual growth? In this book I explore just such questions. In particular, I examine the way a weekly pattern of life focusing on the paschal ministry might support spiritual growth.

Because sharing in the life at St Patrick's was so influential for the development of my proposed answers, it will be useful to describe something of the history of St Patrick's and of CSWG.

My account of the early history of St Patrick's is based on the standard local histories;[1] my account of the parish's more recent history is based largely on anecdote and personal recollection, though I allow Bishop Eric to speak for himself in explaining his hopes for the St Patrick's venture,[2] and I draw also on a description of a visit to St Patrick's made incognito by Michael De-la-Noy in 1992.[3] My account of the history of CSWG leans heavily on the Community's own publications. No doubt that history might be presented rather differently by people outside the community; but because the Community's willingness to be involved in the work at St Patrick's can only be understood in relation to its self-understanding I have been content to allow the Community to speak for itself.[4]

St Patrick's, Hove

St Patrick's was founded in 1856 when Brighton and Hove were highly fashionable. St Patrick's was to be part of an extravagant new development, the Brunswick Estate, later Brunswick Town.[5] Grand five-storey Regency-

---

1. Faulkener, *St Patrick's*, in *Hove Encyclopedia*, Vol. 12, part 1, 134–141.

2. CSWG, St Patrick's.

3. De-la-Noy, *Church of England*, 206–13.

4. See CSWG, Introducing CSWG.

5. See Dale *Fashionable Brighton*; Middleton, *Brunswick Town*. The church itself was built as a proprietory chapel by Dr James O'Brian (1810–84), a wealthy Anglo-Irish priest of Protestant persuasion (see Middleton, *Brunswick Town*, 33). This means that it was church he owned and ran himself, gaining an income from pew rents, marriage and funeral fees, and various other sources. (An Act of Parliament was normally needed before a proprietary chapel could be built, but none was granted in the case of this church.) Pew rents and other fees secured Dr O'Brian a substantial income. On his death one of his nephews inherited the church. The parish was subsequently made over to the diocese (1885). Steadily through the early decades of the twentieth century a succession of vicars moved St Patrick's towards High Church tradition. See Faulkner, "St Patrick's" *Hove Encyclopedia*, Vol. 12, part 1, 139–141.

stucco houses were built along wide avenues and around lawned squares. They became town-houses for the wealthy of Britain and Continental Europe. Brunswick had its own police and fire services, and its own Town Hall. For some fifty years congregations at St Patrick were large and there was no shortage of wealthy patrons.

During the early decades of the twentieth century, however, things began to change. Brunswick fell from fashion and the wealthy moved away. By the late 1940s the majority of the grand houses were in multiple occupation, divided into flats or bed-sits. Conditions in many were squalid.[6] There was no stable community. Very few saw the Brunswick area as their long-term home. People came and went. Outwardly Brunswick retained a certain grandeur, but the impressive facade hid much deprivation. Local Government statistics revealed an almost complete absence of family life, and show a large proportion of people living alone. Drug abuse was rife and alcoholism common. Through the post-war period attendance at St Patrick's steadily declined. By the 1970s the huge church building was in considerable disrepair and the congregation numbered a mere handful.

Faced with either closing St Patrick's or initiating a scheme for renewal Bishop Kemp chose to be radical. He brought a new Vicar to St Patrick's, but he also looked to involve in his initiative both a theological college and a religious community. The new priest, Fr. Alan Sharpe, arrived in 1983. He came with his wife, Susan, their five children (aged nine to seventeen), and also two young men preparing for the priesthood. Before long, groups of students from Chichester Theological College also began to spend time in the parish on pastoral placement. The bishop's hope was that one of the college's lecturers could be based in St Patrick's, so that theological study and training in pastoral ministry might go forward hand in hand.[7] As for the involvement of a religious community, the bishop looked first to a women's community with long experience in parochial ministry; when plans for their participation fell through he turned to CSWG.[8]

---

6. There was talk of demolishing Brunswick Square or of turning the central garden area in to a car park. Attitudes changed and in English Heritage granted Brunswick Square Grade 1 listed building status (24th March 1950.)

7. The Principal of the Chichester Theological College, Fr John Hind, had long been a regular visitor to Crawley Down. He subsequently become Bishop of Horsham (1991) and Bishop of Gibraltar in Europe (1993). In 2001, following the retirement of Eric Kemp, he was appointed Bishop of Chichester, and bercame Episcopal Visitor to CSWG. He retired in 2012 as Bishop of Chicheser.

8. The women's community was the Society of St Margaret, East Grinstead. See Anson, *Call of the Cloister*, 336–55; SSM, *Doing the Impossible*; Catherine Louise, *Planting of the Lord*.

The Community of the Servants of the Will of God had come into being through the 1940s and 50s.[9] The founder and first Superior, Fr. Robert
Gofton-Salmond (1898–1979), can be counted among those wealthy and
well-connected Anglican priests who, after the pattern of the slum priests
of the Tractarian Movement, sought a ministry among society's most needy
and disadvantaged.[10] After almost twenty years of service as a parish priest
in the slum areas of London's East End, and somewhat exhausted by his
ministry, he looked to found a place of retreat and refuge where those involved in similarly demanding work might find spiritual refreshment.[11] He
moved to Crawley Down (West Sussex) in 1938, settling in a simple holi-
day chalet, hidden away in dense woodland. Although Fr Gofton-Salmond
seems to have envisaged some kind of religious community coming into
being he seems not to have had any clear idea about what kind of community that might be.[12] Through the 1940s men came to join him, but few
stayed for long and the life was slow to take shape. From the outset he had
looked for advice and inspiration to two men who had also worked in the
London slums. Fr. Gilbert Shaw (1886–1967) was a married priest who had
worked in the East End during the inter-war years. Well-known as a spiritual director and an advisor to religious communities, Fr Shaw's involvement
with CSWG reached back to its very foundation: he had even helped Fr
Gofton-Salmond choose Crawley Down as the site for his venture. Gilbert
Shaw would remain a friend and advisor to CSWG until his death.[13] Both
Fr. Gofton-Salmond and Gilbert. Shaw had known and admired Fr William
Sirr (1862–1937), an Anglican Franciscan who, after long years of pastoral
ministry in London and elsewhere (including three years as founder-di-
rector of England's last leper colony) felt himself called to help re-establish
within the Church of England something absent since the Reformation:
the enclosed contemplative monastic life.[14] He spent the final twenty years
of his life in seclusion at Glasshampton in Worcestershire, converting an

9. See Anson, Call of the Cloister, 214–17; CSWG, Introducing CSWG.

10. Rowell, *Vision Glorious*, 116–40, et passim..

11. CSWG, *Introducing CSWG*, 12–17.

12. CSWG, *Divine Office*, 13–14.

13. CSWG, *Introducing CSWG*, 10–12; CSWG, *Gilbert Shaw*; Hacking, *Such a Long
Journey*. Also Arthur Royall, *Gilbert Shaw and The Sidney* http://www.royall.co.uk/roy-
all/gilbert-shaw-sidney.htm (May 2000).

14. Shaw, *Father William*; Curtis, *William of Glasshampton*; William, *Franciscan
Revival*, 60–62. For Fr Sirr's theology of the religious life see Sirr, *Whatchman*, 17–19,
35–36, 43. See Thorndike, *Works* 5, 570–73 (ch. 37), where monastic life is presented as
being essential to the church: "[S]eeing it [monastic life] is a perfection to Christianity,
it is certainly a blot in the reformation which we profess, that we are without it."

abandoned stable-block into a monastery and looking to establish a community. During his lifetime no community came into being, but Fr Shaw and Fr Gofton-Salmond were among those who visited, found inspiration, and were able to learn from his experience.

Importantly, these three men, whom CSWG now accounts its joint-founders, not only shared a common experience of ministry among the disadvantaged and marginalized, they also shared the conviction that it was the specifically *spiritual* dimension in Christian life that was most in need of renewal. A saying attributed to Fr Sirr has been seen as encapsulating their common belief: "The mission of the Church is weak because its prayer is weak."[15] Only through the renewal of the Church's mystical and ascetic traditions—that is, its vision of God and its tradition of conversion of life—could the life and witness of the Church be renewed.

Significantly, although each of these three men was committed to a high doctrine of the incarnation and the sacraments and was inclined to align himself with Anglo-Catholic tradition, each also tended to stand somewhat apart from the triumphalism which today is often identified as a feature (and a weakness) of the Anglo-Catholicism of the 1920s and 30s, that is, during the period when the movement was at the peak of its popularity and influence.[16] Fundamental was their realization that the Church itself is always under judgment. A favorite text of Gilbert Shaw was, "Judgement begins with the household of God" (1 Pet 4:17). And before him, William Sirr had seen his call to contemplative monastic life in relation to his conviction that the Church of his day was under judgment and failing in its essential purpose. The Church was leaving the great mass of the population unaffected, and all too often it was offering *religion* rather than *renewal* to those it did influence.[17] He saw the call to the renewal of the Church's prayer as a call to repentance, a repentance that would both open the way for the renewal of the Church's vision of God and provide a basis for appropriate response to God's loving initiative on humanity's behalf, a response that would issue in the radical renewal and redirection of human life. It could not be enough for the Church to perpetuate the patterns inherited from its immediate past. In

15. Although this saying is attributed by CSWG to Fr Sirr and has long served as a community motto for CSWG, I cannot find it anywhere in Fr Sirr's own writings. Those who knew Fr. Gofton-Salmond and Fr Shaw say that both of them attributed it to him. Cf. the words of one of Fr Sirr's advisors, Richard Meux Benson SSJE, "The slowness of mission work makes us realize how very little prayer is really being made by Christendom to God," "More prayer and less preaching would I believe do more for the Church both at home and abroad." Longridge, *Further Letters,* 42, 231.

16. Cf. Pickering "Anglo-Catholicism," 154–58.

17. Curtis, *William of Glasshampton,* 128–29.

each and every age the Church must be *coming alive* with the life that Christ gives. This will always be a life "once given" to the Church (and essentially unchanging) but a life which must be appropriated anew in each and every generation. The Church is only being itself when it is becoming itself.

Something of the same conviction underlay the decision of both William Sirr at Glasshampton and Fr. Gofton-Salmond at Crawley Down to resist the temptation to adopt wholesale those patterns of monastic life—Benedictine, Cistercian, Carthusian, or whatever—which many in the Western church assumed to be normative. Both men were convinced that patterns of life appropriate in the medieval era might be of limited value in the very different social and cultural conditions of a post-industrialized world. Gilbert Shaw, more of an intellectual than either of his associates, played an important part in the development of their thinking. He emphasized the need for the Church always to be entering into a "prophetic view" of the historical era in which it is living, and not least, *a prophetic view of the Church's own life, ministry, and culture.* Significant in Gilbert Shaw's own formation were conversations he had, not only with William Sirr and Fr Gofton-Salmond, but with members of the Orthodox Churches, most notably Fr Sophrony (Sakharov), 1896–1993, who, after surviving the catastrophes that befell his native Russia in the first two decades of the twentieth century, successively became a monk, hermit, and spiritual director on Mount Athos before founding an Orthodox monastery at Tolleshunt Knights in Essex.[18]

Gilbert Shaw's principal concern became the renewal of what he termed the Church's "one great tradition" of prayer, life, and witness. He never defined exactly what he meant by this phrase, but it is clear that he saw the content of that tradition as essentially a *life*—not simply a body of doctrines or a system of practices.[19] First and foremost, he saw this tradition as grounded in the very life of Christ: his divine-human life lived in loving service of the Father and in total dependence upon the Holy Spirit but lived also for the sake that his human brothers and sisters might come to know fullness of life in and with him (cf. John 10:10). And since there is only one Son, who has ever one and the same life, there can but be essentially only *one Christian tradition.* There can be much variety in the expression of this tradition—for there can legitimately be much variety in human culture, and

18. See e.g., Hacking, *Such a Long Journey*, 99–101, 128. Curtis (*William of Glasshampton*, 130) records that Lev Gillet and William Sirr talked about the possibility of an Anglican-Orthodox ecumenical monastic community; cf. Behr-Sigel, *Lev Gillet*, 203. On Fr Sophrony see Louth, *Modern Orthodox Thinkers*, 303–14.

19. His collected sermons and retreat addresses are held at Crawley Down and by his literary executors at Fairacres in Oxford.

each human person is utterly unique in his or her distinct personhood. But as Gilbert Shaw would see it, the saints of both East and West, for all their diversity and variety, belong to and witness to this one tradition: to the one life that is theirs in Christ.

Importantly, then, the Church can draw on and learn from all that has gone before. Gilbert Shaw gladly acknowledged the value of the work of the Church historians of the nineteenth and early twentieth centuries. He was also a keen amateur student of the human sciences, of psychology and the like. And although he insisted that the essential content of the tradition of the Church is a *life*, he was also keen to stress the value of what might be termed the "secondary" aspects of that tradition. He saw the theological and mystical traditions as bearing witness to the life that Christ shares with the world. The ascetic tradition he saw as giving guidance on how that life can be appropriated. And the Church's tradition of worship he saw as looking to the celebration of the life of Christ—and as a vehicle through which people can participate in that life. In Gilbert Shaw's vision these different aspects of Christian tradition belong together. All are grounded in the (one) life of Christ, but that is a life *known* and *lived* by the saints each in his or her own distinct way.

Looking to see the renewal of the Church in its essential tradition— its living knowledge and experience of God—Gilbert Shaw insisted that the Church must be willing not only to draw on all that is authentic in the past but to forsake any practices or devices by which it might be muting or masking the fundamental challenge—anything which might, for instance, be subverting it into quietism, ritualism, intellectualism, or emotionalism, even pastoral over-activism. (There are many possibilities!) In particular, he insisted on the need for Church to learn to take its place in what he termed the "spiritual conflict," i.e., the work—essentially Christ's work— of overcoming everything, whether in the human heart or the world at large, that would obscure or distort the Church's vision or divert it from its essential purpose.

What came, then, to be established at Crawley Down was a contemplative community for men. It was Fr Gregory CSWG (Leslie Dudding), who became Superior in 1966—and who remained Superior until shortly before his death in 2009[20]—who gave material form and expression to the ideas and ideals of the three founders. With Gilbert Shaw's help and after discussions with Fr Sophrony, Fr Gregory revised the Community Rule.[21]

20. See   http://www.crawleydownvillage.co.uk/personalities_view.php?per_id=6. Accessed July 2017.

21. See CSWG, *Monastic Rule*.

Subsequently he set about developing the community's liturgical life, revising both the Eucharistic rite and the Daily Offices. This work took many years (and continued under the direction of Fr Colin CSWG, Fr Gregory's successor at Superior[22]). Influential in all this was the community's contact with contemporary Orthodoxy. However, Fr Gregory, like Gilbert Shaw before him, came to believe that the Orthodox Church, even if in many respects it can be seen as standing uniquely close to the heart of the Christian tradition, is, nevertheless, also under judgment. It too is challenged to enter into a prophetic understanding of its vocation and to see how it is to relate redemptively and re-creatively to contemporary culture. The Church will be failing in its ministry if it simply stands apart from contemporary culture and condemns it.

Gradually the community's vocation, the aim and purpose of its life, became clearer. CSWG came to see itself as called, first and foremost, to rediscover itself as a *eucharistic community*, that is, as a community which not only celebrates the Eucharist but is learning to live the whole of life within the divine Son's eucharistic relationship to the Father: receiving everything directly from the Father's hand (by the Spirit), living all of life in grateful dependence upon him, and offering everything that belongs to this world back to him as a gift of love (by the same Spirit), a priestly oblation, one in and through which the world is being redeemed, renewed, and gathered into its ultimate destiny. To this end the Community sought to establish itself as a "community of nurture," i.e., a community which would be able to offer practical, prayerful support to its members while they were learning to cooperate with the Holy Spirit and the Father's re-creative work going on within them; in other words, while they were coming to recognize God's ever-present action in their lives and learning to take their place in the Son's life and work. It is *participation* in Christ, not *imitation* of him that constitutes Christian life. Convinced of the value of Gilbert Shaw's understanding and insights, Fr. Gregory came to emphasize the centrality of the spiritual conflict in Christian life. The argument runs thus: a rebellious world cannot be gathered into Christ's redemption except that it goes by way of the redeeming passion of Christ, wherein it will be purified and regenerated, so that all is made new; but importantly—and this is an idea which I have been at pains to develop and which features in this book—no one can come to that fullness of personal maturity which God wills unless that person is not only willing to allow God's re-creative work to go on within, but is also willing to take his or her part in Christ's redemptive, re-creative, self-sacrificial work on behalf of others (and of the world at large). To be mature is to be

---

22. Hope, "True Vision with Praise."

like Christ. To be like Christ is to be sharing his work. Christ himself would want nothing less for anyone.

It was after Fr Gregory had served as Superior for almost twenty years and the community's membership had grown to fifteen that Bishop Kemp invited CSWG to be involved in the Hove venture. The bishop (perhaps without realizing it) was inviting CSWG into an environment which was a late twentieth-century equivalent to the East End slums in which its three founders had ministered during the early decades of the twentieth century. Whereas the founders of CSWG had witnessed extreme poverty and material deprivation, now, in the 1980s, Brunswick bore witness to a multitude of problems typical of urban life in the post-industrial Western world. Most obvious, perhaps, were problems with drink, drugs, and vagrant homelessness. But alongside these lay more fundamental disorders: an almost complete lack of stable social structures, a widespread breakdown of family life, and an underlying malaise—a sense that life is ultimately meaningless, purposeless. Where, perhaps, London's East Enders had once felt themselves forgotten by God and neglected by the Church, many in the late-twentieth-century inner-city had dismissed the Church and religious faith as irrelevant to their needs and hopes.

So it was that in June 1985 six members of CSWG moved to Hove.

The Life and Worship at St Patrick's 1985–95

Preaching at the inauguration of the monastery (5th June 1985), Bishop Kemp explained,

> What is being attempted here is something new and it is being attempted by three old and well-tried instruments of God, a parish, a community, and a theological college. For each of these there will be some breaking of past moulds so that the new may develop, and this requires of each a maximum degree of openness to the Holy Spirit in patience, in understanding, in sympathy and above all in vision and in love.

The Bishop's hope was far-reaching:

> The ... aim of this enterprise is to *give*, to give hope to the people of this parish, to give hope to the whole Church. There is the hope of discovering a new dimension of the monastic life and helping towards that renewal of it that the Church of England so sorely needs. There is the hope of finding new dimensions of training for the ministry so that the priests of the future may know more deeply the spiritual basis of their ministry . . . .

He continued:

> Above all it is our hope to give an example of a parish and con-
> gregation devoted to the praise of God the Father, Maker and
> Master of the universe, searching and caring for God the Son in
> the hearts and minds and bodies of every person, conscious of
> the Holy Spirit leading them in prayer, showing them the vision
> of God's calling and inspiring their wills to follow it. This could
> be an example of service, a service of hope to the whole Church
> of God.[23]

From the day of their arrival, the monks joined the parish community
each day for some of the worship in the parish church. Soon the monastic
community was involved in the work of teaching and spiritual direction.
But living under a strict rule of enclosure, the monks were not involved in
parish visiting or works outside the monastery.

During the next few years the life of the parish changed dramatically.
In the winter of 1985–86 the worship area in the church building was re-
organized. Out went the pews, rank upon rank of them facing a far-distant
high altar. Now the congregation was seated in a horse-shoe shaped arc, no
more than two rows deep, around a central altar,[24] with the sanctuary area
marked out by large free-standing icons of the Virgin and Christ-child,
and of Christ the Word, while, as a focus for the worship, behind the altar
hung a large copy of Rublev's celebrated icon, the so-called Trinity icon.[25]
(See fig. 5, cf. fig. 3.)

Not only had the seating been rearranged but the space in the main
body of the church was now used differently. Significantly, except when
actually ministering at the altar, the celebrant now sat at the West End of
the horse-shoe; that is, *among* the congregation, as one of them, not at the
East End, facing them (after the pattern of a Roman magistrate in a law
court). Both the Eucharist and the Offices included much movement to and
from the altar: of the Bible from altar to lectern—signifying the coming of
God's Word to his people; of a processional candle each evening at Evening
Prayer—signifying the coming of Christ as light to a world in darkness; of
the Gospel book from the altar to the centrally-placed lectern—signifying
Christ coming as Word and Wisdom to a world caught in error and confusion; and after the proclamation of the gospel, the Gospel book would be

23. See CSWG, *St Patrick's*.

24. More accurately, the altar stood not at the center of a circle but at the far focus
of an ellipse. See fig. 5.

25. More properly, "The Hospitality of Abraham." For history and theology of this
icon see Bunge, *Rublev's Trnity*.

processed around the congregation so that people might venerate it—as they might venerate Christ himself coming into their presence to speak to them. Notably, the entire congregation would gather with the priest at the altar for the offering of intercessions at Evening Prayer and Morning Praise, and for offering of the Eucharistic Prayer at the Eucharist itself. The Eucharistic Prayer, while, in some sense, properly the prayer of the priest (who says most of the words) is also the prayer of the whole people. This gathering of the community for the offering of the Eucharistic Prayer demonstrated that the priest is leading the community in its work as a priestly people.[26] (The priest *leads* the people, he does not substitute for them or simply act on their behalf. There is appropriate structure and hierarchy in the Christian community, but this notwithstanding, the entire community shares a common vocation, a common dignity, a common baptism.)

All this movement, coupled with the use of icons and incense (great clouds of it!)—all this can all help to demonstrate or reveal the *dynamic and all-encompassing nature* of Christian worship. It indicates that a *work* is going on whenever the community offers worship: there is movement from God towards the community and the community responds to the divine initiative. And it indicates that this work of God has many dimensions: it involve the whole created nature of each member of the community: body, intellect, emotions; and it involves them in their relationships to one another too. It gathers all that belongs to the past (a past extending back to the origins of creation) and it looks to the future—even to the final consummation of the End. (Indeed, I adopt the view—a view I shall explain and explore later, that somewhat paradoxically, the End is the starting point for Christian worship: Christian worship is never in essence a human initiative reaching out towards God; it is a response to the End, to that fulfillment of all things which God in Christ has already accomplished and which he now unceasingly opens up to human participation.)

At the very time these liturgical changes were being introduced, a major work with the homeless also began. It began almost accidentally. One evening a homeless couple who had taken refuge in the church through the day were allowed to remain in the building overnight. The next evening they came back—and brought their friends. Within a few weeks upwards of a dozen men were being accommodated nightly in

---

26. I think of the priest at the altar as principally *calling down* God's blessing on an offering which *all* the people, precisely as a *priestly* people, are making. This is an offering of remembrance and thanksgiving: remembrance of and thanksgiving for God's loving work through the ages on behalf of his people, a work fully realized in Christ and now opened up to the world in and through him.

unused store-rooms.[27] (It was at this time, however, that the theological college withdrew from the St Patrick's project, claiming that the demands of the situation left too little time for study.[28]) This work with the homeless would eventually become widely known. In 1993, in recognition of this ministry, Bishop Kemp appointed Fr Sharpe a non-residentiary canon of Chichester cathedral. In the mid-1990s, a multi-million pound project to re-house and rehabilitate the homeless began.[29]

Michael De-la-Noy records a visit to St Patrick's in the early 1990s, during what would have been a typical mid-week evening:

> I . . . wandered into church at 6.45. An assortment of tramps, alcoholics and the mentally ill were all jumbled up with parishioners in pews arranged around a free-standing altar in the nave, and vespers was underway, the plainchant being led by a young estate agent. Father Sharpe, in alb, sat in the centre. . . . No account of the liturgy could by itself convey the unselfconscious devotion of the service. . . . [For] the consecration everyone gathered in a strange intimacy around the altar, within feet of the celebrant. A home baked roll was consecrated; the paten and chalice were modern earthenware. Yet there was nothing folksy about the occasion. At the peace . . . everyone moved round to kiss or shake hands. . . . Everyone, including many of the down-and-outs . . . received communion. It was a gentle, moving experience, which seemed by the nature of those present—unwashed, wearing mittens, unpatronised and essentially unimpressed and at home—to offer a glimpse of what worship may have been like in the Middle Ages, a rediscovery of a marriage of reverence, impressive ritual and sensible simplicity.[30]

De-la-Noy remarks: "What seems to have happened is that the spirituality emanating from St Patrick's sparks a response in people who are often tragically disoriented."[31] He quotes Fr Sharpe,

---

27. The development of this work is not well documented.

28. The college would close in 1993.

29. As part of the millennium celebrations the unitary authority of the "towns" of Brighton and Hove was granted city status. In March 2001, as part of the city's celebrations, Queen Elizabeth II visited. St Patrick's was one of only two projects in the city she visited. See *Daily Telegraph*, 30 March 2001.

30. De-la-Noy, *Church of England*, 211f.

31. De-la-Noy *Church of England*, 212. De-la-Noy also describes (206–10) his visit to the Hove monastery. The account is inaccurate in a number of details but not without value.

Many [in the parish] have no family backgrounds. A lot . . .
are in very, very difficult circumstances; financially, spiritually,
morally, everything you can think of. I'm not altogether sure
who lives next door [to the vicarage]. It is all tiny rooms, and
people sometimes come here just to get lost.[32]

De-la-Noy attributes the growth of the parish to "placing a tiny religious community in the street"[33]—which is to under-estimate the contribution of Fr Sharpe, his family, and the parishioners. But in fact during their
first few months in Hove the monastic community had sometimes tem-
porarily accommodated a few homeless people in the monastery, and this
initiative can be seen as preparing the way for Fr Sharpe to begin his much
larger and more demanding work in the church building. And as well as
undergirding the whole redevelopment of St Patrick's with prayer, the Community also made considerable contributions to the liturgical revisions. De-
la-Noy quotes Fr Sharpe:

We have adopted many of [the monastery's] patterns of worship, which has been very helpful. They've given us a sort of
stability, I suppose, in an area that is *very* unstable. They have
helped us develop the prayer life in the parish, which I think is
of paramount importance. . . . What has occurred is a remarkable revival of worship, largely among people who had never
been to church before. In 1983, there might have been fifteen
at the Sunday parish Mass. On a Sunday, there are now at least
100, and during the week . . . a congregation of thirty is a regular
occurrence . . . .[34]

Among elements adopted from the monastery's liturgy were such
things as a daily lamp-lighting at Evening Prayer, the use of incense—lots
of it!—at every Eucharist and all major Offices, the liturgical use of icons,
and regular sacramental anointings. Drawing on resources made available by the monastic community, steps were also taken to make prayer
resources available for home use: abbreviated forms of Evening Prayer
and Morning Praise, booklets on the Christian theological and spiritual
tradition, leaflets suggesting forms of grace at meals, and so on. Candles,

32. De-la-Noy, *Church of England*, 212; cf. 210–13; 314; 315. De-la-Noy misnames
the Vicar, Fr *Alan* Sharpe, as Fr *John* Sharpe and his account contains other similar
inaccuracies. (John Sharpe was, in fact one of the monks, and appeared in *Crockfords's*
as such, though he was always known in the Community as Brother Mark.)

33. De-la-Noy, *Church of England*, 212.

34. De-la-Noy, *Church of England*, 210f.

prayer-ropes and mounted icon-prints from the monastery's workshops were on sale in the parish.

In adopting these features from the monastery's liturgy, the parish had unwittingly adopted—rather paradoxically—many elements of what had once been part of the so-called Cathedral Liturgy.[35] CSWG had introduced such things in the wake of Vatican II, which opened the way for radical liturgical revision not only in the Roman Church but in the Anglican Church too. A particular influence for CSWG had been its contact with a French Capuchin, Frère Jean-Claude Tromas. He had founded a hermitage (or skete) in Normandy. Many French religious communities of that time were exploring liturgical renewal and were looking for inspiration to early Church tradition and contemporary Orthodoxy. Frère Jean-Claude Tromas did pioneering work in this area. CSWG came to adopt from him forms of daily worship much richer than those it had previously been using.[36] Always the aim was not simply to introduce forms which were merely more "correct"—or more entertaining. The new patterns were looked to facilitate or foster spiritual formation. The use of a rich selection of biblical and extra-biblical texts and the incorporation of much "action"—including lamp-lightings, processions, incense, etc.—all this was intended to lead the worshippers not just towards an abstract appreciation of God's action on behalf of his people but into direct *encounter* with him.

Importantly, by its very nature, any such encounter will be essentially *spiritual*, and as such will impact upon the worshipper's entire being: body and soul, mind and emotions. Though, that having been said, different people will experience this essentially *spiritual* action in different ways, according to their particular psycho-physical makeup. Some, for example, will feel deeply moved—they will be impacted emotionally. For others, namely those who tend to relate to the world intellectually rather than emotionally—"with the head rather than the heart"—the impact of the spiritual encounter may be the emergence of a new understanding, of new insights and ideas. With yet others, the predominant impact may be physical; it may be felt, for example, as a surge of energy, spurring to activity.

Ultimately and essentially, however, the impact is spiritual. And however such encounter is initially experienced, the impact will always, in some measure, be *transformational*. The worshipper will be brought not just to a new understanding or to novel experience but will be opened up to a new

35. See Mateos, "Divine Office," 477–85; Taft, *Liturgy of the Hours*, esp. 32–33, 192–217, 345–65; Guiver, *Company of Voices*, 54–59. Note the music in the CSWG liturgies is basically Western. (See CSWG, *Divine Office*, 13–15; Hope, "True Vision with Praise"; Peers, "Schools of Prayer," 50–51).

36. Peers, "Schools of Prayer," 12–17; CSWG, *Divine Office*, 11–17.

way of life—indeed, to new life and a world of new relationships. The mature Christian is not someone who knows everything about Christ or someone who experiences powerful emotional (or physical) responses to Christ, but as someone who shares Christ's relationship to the world. In other words, the mature Christian is someone who participates fully—body, soul, and spirit—in Christ's life and work, his loving and redemptive relationship to his human brothers and sisters, and to creation more generally.

One of the most important features adopted by the parish from the monastery's life was something I had taken to calling—I believe the expression is original to me—the "pattern of the week." This is a weekly pattern of worship and extra-liturgical events in which each week is observed as a kind of Holy Week in miniature. In the late 1970s, at the suggestion of Frère Jean-Claude Tromas, CSWG adopted the practice of giving a theme to each day of the week. (The pattern is set out in Table 3; above, p. 282) The pattern owes something to some of the mediaeval patterns of votive masses (see Table 2; above, p. 281), but its basic theme is the paschal mystery: the resurrection is the principal theme of Sunday, and the story of Christ's passion is unfolded from Thursday onwards. Later, in the mid 1980s, and largely at my suggestion, CSWG began to refine and develop its use of the liturgical week. As part of this, the paschal theme was further emphasized in worship, and, more generally, some of the liturgical themes commemorated in the weekly pattern were given expression outside of formal worship. For example, the Community introduced an evening Eucharist on Thursdays, preceded by a preparatory meal which included lamp-lighting and an expanded grace—after the pattern of the events in the Upper Room (but with no attempt simply to re-enact those events, as might be done in, say, a TV docu-drama). Saturday came to be observed as a rest day, a Sabbath at the end of the working week where manual work was kept to a minimum, and time could be given, not only to enjoyment of the day itself (and to the enjoyment of God's goodness) but to preparation for Sunday, the day of new life.

When CSWG became involved with St Patrick's I proposed that some such pattern be adopted in the parish. My hope was that this might help to give shape and direction to the parish's life and make it a more effective context for personal growth. Fr Sharpe supported my proposals. The necessary liturgical material was prepared and I drew up a set of leaflets explaining the pattern of the week and suggesting ways in which parishioners might make use of it. A version of these leaflets is available for download from the website linked to this book.[37] Significantly, the parish community were able

37. Website: LivingInThe8thDay.co.uk. Also available for download at this site are booklets setting out the eucharistic liturgy which came to be used in St Patrick's is and the form of the Pre-Sanctified Rite celebrated early each Friday evening. Also available

to introduce elements which the monastic community at Crawley Down, with its strict timetable and firmly established patters of life, could not see its way into incorporating into its own programme. For example, in St Patrick's each Thursday evening after the Eucharist, the parish community, along with the monks, stayed together for a time of teaching and a vigil of prayer, after the pattern of the prayer of Jesus and his disciples in the Upper Room and the Garden of Gethsemane. Similarly, after their midday Eucharist on Saturday, now kept as a day of rest, the parish community, along with the monks, shared a simple meal and discussion-time together. See further chapter 18 later in this work (esp. 221–227).

The remainder of this book will explore themes implicit in the use of the Pattern of the Week: namely, the nature of the Christian vocation and the nature of the educational ministry of the Church and questions relating to how the liturgical cycles (and most especially the seven-day week) can be used to provide a setting for Christian growth and Christian formation.

---

is the form of grace used at parish meals on Friday evenings (after the Pre-Sanctified) and on other special days.

I

The Structure of the Book and the
Theological Frame of Reference

In Part One I explore, first of all, the idea that the nature and character of the Church's educational ministry will be misunderstood wherever there is an inadequate appreciation of the goal of that ministry or—and this is part of the same problem—where there is an inadequate anthropology, i.e., doctrine of humanity and humanity's relationship to God. I will argue that Christian education must be concerned, at heart, with *personal* formation, that is, with the development and formation of the human person *qua* person—and that means as *person with capacity for fullness of personal relationship to God, to other people, and to creation more generally*. In other words, to be fully human is to have appropriated, and to be using well, the God-given capacity for personal relationship, a capacity imaging the capacity (so to speak) of the divine persons themselves, and a capacity which human person realize in and through the Holy Spirit, the very Spirit who himself mediates (as it were) and bears within himself, as his life, the love of the Father for the Son, and of the Son for the Father.

Judaeo-Christian tradition considers man as created in the divine image. In constructing my theory of Christian education, I look to claims that the most fundamental truth about the divine life is that it is a *personal life*: the mystery of God is essentially the mystery of *who* the divine persons are, not of *what* they are; and I shall argue that therefore the most fundamental truth about man will be that he exists *as person*. Personhood is the primary—and, indeed, the ultimate—ontological category. But while each of the divine persons is eternally perfect and complete in his personhood, the human person has personhood only (so to speak) in potential.[1] He or she has it both as

---

1. Here it needs to be noted that mainstream Christian tradition holds that Jesus, though fully a human *being*, was not a human *person*. At the incarnation the Son took to himself all that belongs to human nature while yet remaining *who* he had always been, i.e., the Second Person of the Trinity. Only because he was divine, i.e., a divine person, could the Son restore true life to created humankind. See Meyendorff, *Byzantine Theology*, 32–41; Meyendorff, *Christ in Eastern Thought*, 14–19. For a brief but brilliant account of these matters see McIntosh, *Mystical Theology*, 187–208.

gift and as calling, and has a work to do if he or she is to attain to fullness of personhood. I shall argue that classical mainstream Christianity has seen the ultimate goal of the Church's educational ministry as nothing less than the entry of the disciple into direct knowledge of the divine persons and communion in their life—with all that that entails for his or her relationships with other people and with the created order in general.

Central to my argument is the idea that personal maturity is to be understood in relation to the paschal mystery. The divine persons live eternally in relationships of self-giving love, relationships that are, I hold, essentially *paschal*. There is no eternal or abiding life outside of the paschal mystery. The work of the incarnate Son was to bring his adopted humanity into fullness of conformity with his eternal divinity, and that meant, above all, conforming his adopted humanity, body and soul, to the paschal mystery. This he accomplished through his obedience, that is, through bringing his human will into conformity with the divine will. And yet this was something he had to accomplish progressively. In his created humanity he had to *grow*. As his humanity matured and his life unfolded, so the demands made upon his obedience grew. In a fallen and rebellious world, this way of growth inevitably led to suffering. The incarnate Son had to overcome all that resisted or fought against the divine purpose. The temptation to turn from his vocation reached its limit at his passion. But there, not diverted from his purpose even by the worst of death's threats, he completed his work. Through his willing acceptance of death he brought human *nature* to unprecedented maturity. He brought it into fullness of communion, fullness of right relationship with his divine *personhood*. Thereby, in his own person, he brought created human nature, and all that belongs to human nature, into fullness of communion with the divine nature. Thus, he completed the vocation set before him at the incarnation—the same vocation which had always been set before man but which no one before him had accomplished. Resurrection is to be seen as the natural fruit of the Son's obedience.

Open to die into the Father's hands, the Son was open to receive from the Father all that he had ever wished to give to man: life eternal.[2] Before the Son, nobody had been able to enter into the resurrection life because no-one had had the necessary openness, the necessary faith, the necessary trust. Following his resurrection, however, the Son chose to open his resurrection life to others. Thereby he revealed his love, his generosity of heart, in all its fullness.

---

2. The resurrection was in no sense a reward or recompense for Christ's sufferings. It was the natural outcome of his openness.

The educational ministry of the Church and the task of the Christian educator must be concerned, then, with enabling people to live within this new and eternal resurrection life—something they can only do *as persons*. But if Christ offers his human sisters and brothers the possibility of living the divine life, no one can share that life unless he or she *chooses* to do so, chooses, that is, to accept the gift that Christ offers. This means that no one can only attain to fulfillment in Christ except that he of she uses his or her freedom (that very freedom which is itself a divine gift) to appropriate the life of Christ, and this he or she does insofar as he or she is willing to acquire the dispositions which are offered in Christ.

These dispositions can be termed *virtues*. That is the traditional Christian designation. But to avoid misunderstanding in what follows, I would suggest here that it is vital to recognize that the Christian virtues have *positive content*. They have about them what might be termed a positive *drive* or *energy*. It is too easy to imagine, for example, that honesty is the absence of dishonesty, that courage the absence of fear (or perhaps the refusal to be governed by fear), and that self-forgetfulness is the absence of self-concern. But such thinking renders the virtues rather sterile. In truth the virtues have energy. Just as in biblical terms *peace* is not simply the absence of noise and conflict but the (positive) presence of fullness of life and of a desire to see others know fullness of life, so with all the virtues: inherent to each is a positive energy—such that, for example, *purity of heart* is not a sterile lack of pollution or impurity but a positive *wholeness of heart* or *fullness of integrity*, within which lies a positive drive towards wholeness or integrity.

That having been said, we can turn to a well known patristic comment of John Damascene on virtue and the Christian vocation. Looking to Genesis and the claim that humanity has been made in the divine image and likeness, he writes: "The expression 'according to the image' indicates rationality and freedom, while the expression 'according to the likeness' indicates assimilation to God through virtue."[3] Ultimately, all the Christian virtues (indeed all human virtues) involve that selflessness or self-loss which belongs to the paschal mystery. Personhood, freedom, the paschal mystery, participation in Christ, eschatological fulfillment—these belong together. The mature human person is someone who has appropriated the relationships, dispositions, and virtues that belong to the glorified Son— and to the paschal mystery. It is not simply *through* the paschal mystery that the human person has access to fullness of life; it is *within* that mystery that fulfillment is found. The cross is not only the gateway through which humanity must pass to attain final glory. The cross is *within* the glory.

3. *Orth. Faith* 2:12 (PG94: 920b).

Cross, divine glory, paschal mystery, eternal fulfillment—these co-inhere. They are mutually defining.

Since self-giving, paschal love not only represents the gateway to the resurrection but *defines* the resurrection life, no one can share the resurrection except insofar as he or she is willing to live in and by paschal love. It is deeply significant that the Son, confronted with a fallen world, *labored for its redemption*. Only insofar as someone is willing to labor (in Christ and with Christ) for the world's redemption, and even for the redemption of his or her enemies, can he or she be in the divine likeness. The trials of life provide opportunities to learn to live by paschal love. (So, of course, in their own way do life's joys.) The divine persons have established the life of the Church to be a context in which human persons can learn to cooperate with the Holy Spirit's action on their behalf and so come to share the Son's life and work. The Church is not functioning effectively if it is not enabling this.

The educational ministry of the Church must look, then, not simply to teaching about the paschal mystery but to enabling people to participate in it. The divine persons are themselves ever at work to enable this, but the Church is called to help, to cooperate. This is why I explore the idea that if the ultimate goal of Christian education is to enable the disciple to live in fullness of right relationship with God, then its immediate aim is to *set the disciple free from all that prevents him living in such relationships*. Fundamental here is the idea that the Church's ministry of teaching (both its teaching about doctrinal matters and its teaching about morality) look to set the disciple free from the condition in which inevitably (if more or less unwittingly) he of she will have picked up as a consequence of growing up in a fallen world. Christian discipleship involves asceticism, but this is an asceticism not just of the physical appetites but also of the mind, of the thoughts and beliefs. To be free to respond to God in a fully personal way, the disciple's fallen habits of thought must be redeemed. These are those thoughts and patterns of thought which incline the human person to try to secure his of her own future and his or her own beatitude in disregard of (or in ignorance of) God's good purposes. Like the asceticism of the flesh, this asceticism of the mind looks not to the abolition, denial or negation of the disciple's createdness, but to its redemption and fulfillment. Our createdness, including our created mind, is destined to share the life of the End, but can do so only insofar as it has been brought onto the "new ground" of Christ's own relationship to the Father.

But there is more to setting disciples free from their fallen nature and from sin than freeing them from false beliefs. There is also the problem of the fallen human will. To enter into the promises of God the disciple must *choose* to live in conformity to the divine will. Knowing the divine will, and *choosing to do it* are different things. Ignorance is only part of the problem. There is something very naïve in the familiar claim, "I would have no trouble doing the divine will if only I really *knew* what it was." In the Scriptures, for example, the prophet Jonah is presented as someone who knew the divine will but was unwilling to do it (Jonah 1). Something similar can be said about Jesus in Gethsemane: he knew the divine will but found himself hesitant about doing it (Mark 14:32ff., par.; cf. Rom 7:14–25).

This is why I see it as important to explore what I see as a second aspect of the educational ministry of the Church, a dimension too often neglected, perhaps because educationalists have too often worked with an inadequate anthropology. This is the idea that the Christian educator (and the Christian community in general) have a responsibility not only to teach the truth about God, humanity, and the world, but also to offer such support as will help people to choose to *trust* God, to believe his promises, and to do as he commands. It goes without saying that those involved in the Church's educational ministry can offer support through words of advice and encouragement. But I shall suggest that they can also offer support in another, more profound, inward, and mysterious way. I shall explore the idea that there exists a mysterious ontological union between human persons, one which makes it possible for the Christian educator (insofar as he or she is living in and by the Spirit) to help enable the personal growth of those in his or her care. Importantly, just as the divine persons themselves unfailingly offer human beings support without ever violating their freedom or dignity, so too the mysterious support which the Christian educator can offer will never violate anyone's freedom or dignity. The choice to live by the divine will must always be a *personal* choice, freely made. This is why any attempt to coerce people into Christian belief or practice will be self-defeating. Any such attempt cannot but be grounded in a mistaken notion of the character of Christian life and God's purposes. On the other hand—and altogether more positively—precisely because of the profound and mysterious ontological union between all human persons, wherever one person is using his freedom in accord with the divine will he will be helping others to do the same. This is why it is important to explore this "second dimension" in Christian education.

It takes time for anyone to learn to live within the paschal mystery and attain personal maturity. Thus I link educational theory with a theology of time. This is the theme of Part Two.

Of course there is nothing new in seeing time as the context for human growth. Some theologians, however, have seen time not as homogeneous or uniform but as having a particular rhythm and content, a rhythm and content which render it an effective vehicle for growth in knowledge of God and in Christ-likeness. Of prime importance here is the way in which these theologians see time and history not only as providing a framework for the divine action but as vehicles of the divine presence. In Part Two I explore the idea that the essential "content" of time is the person and work of the eschatological Son. The argument is that since Pentecost the Son ever comes forth, moment by moment, in the power of the Spirit, from his place in the End with the Father. And this he does to make himself known and to be involved in the life of the world. The paschal mystery is again central: the Son comes forth from the End bearing in himself all the "states" or "stages" through which he passed or which he acquired during the time of the incarnation as he grew to maturity; and above all he comes bearing in himself paschal love. Indeed, he comes looking to share that love with others so that they may live by it too. Through learning to live in trusting, self-forgetful, paschal dependence on the divine love, created human persons can come to be personally present to the eternal divine persons, in image of the way in which the divine persons are ever present to humankind and the created realm.

I shall argue that the temporal cycles of the day, week, and year, and even the "mini-cycles" of the breath and heart-beat have a paschal rhythm, a rhythm of activity and rest, of engagement with death and of renewal. It is this that enables them to constitute an effective context for formative encounter with Christ.

Although in Part Two I am largely concerned with theological issues about the Christian understanding and use of time, included in this part of the book is a discussion of my "worked example," the Pattern of the Week as lived at St Patrick's, Hove. As background to this, I review the history of the seven-day week. I do so in an attempt to show that there is nothing in the traditions of either the Jewish or the Christian week that undermines or invalidates my proposals about how week might be used, indeed that much in this history supports these proposals. My review of the history of the week looks to and depends upon the historical research of others, and contains no original historical research. I believe, however, that my interpretation of this information is original. It includes what I term an "iconographic theology of time." This represents the final theological justification for the use of the Pattern of the Week. The book ends with some more general suggestions about the pastoral possibilities of the Pattern of the Week.

Sin

So far I have said little about sin. This is no accident. I see the work of Christ as being for humanity's redemption, as the answer for sin, but I see it also as being directed towards the final fulfillment of the human vocation. And I tend to put the emphasis on this second dimension (so to speak) of Christ's work. I see sin as always being concerned, at root, not with the breaking of rules or regulation, not even with breaking the commandments. I see it as being concerned with breaking relationships, indeed with breaking hearts, both the heart of God and the hearts of our human brothers and sisters. Through selfishness and self-concern, through pride and fear, through closing in on ourselves in disregard of the well-being of others, we damage our relationship with God, with our brothers and sisters, and indeed with creation itself. We cause suffering and hurt. And we fail in our vocation. Where God wills unity and communion we introduce distance, division, disharmony. Christ's sacrifice is the answer to this. His self-giving to his disciples at the Last Supper, to the Father on the cross, and also at Pentecost with the outpouring of his Spirit on the Church—these restore to humanity the possibility of fullness of relationship: fullness of relationship to God, to other people, to creation at large, and even to own created selves. The possibility of us living in this new order of relationships comes to us as a gift, but it a gift which we are called to appropriate freely and willingly. For although we are saved by God as a gift, and not by any efforts of our own, that gift must be appropriated personally, by our free choice. Only thus can we be restored and fulfilled in our personhood—which in God's generosity, in his love, is his will for us. (We cannot accept or receive the gift of *personhood* except by *our free choice*.)

Genre and Methodology: What Sort of Work is This?

This work is synthetic and expository rather than empirical/critical. If God is by nature personal, and if mainstream Christian tradition is grounded in and defined by personal experience of *who* God is and how he acts, then it is surely inappropriate to seek objective proof of God's existence and there is relatively little to be gained from analysis of propositions concerning *what* God is like. The tradition of the Church cannot be reduced to a series of logically-linked positions (although definitions of faith can help secure that tradition and hold it open for others to begin to share).[4] At the same time,

4. I would hold that this tradition, like the divine love, is inclusive rather than exclusive. Even insights from non-Christian traditions—religious, scientific, or

the personalist character of Christian tradition can secure its continuity and consistency through time: since the divine persons remain eternally who they are, and since their love for the world is unchanging, all those human persons who respond to the divine initiative enter into a *common* life, a *common* experience.[5] In this work I have chosen, therefore, to look to those who can *witness* to the experience of God's action in their lives and in the world at large.[6] I believe that such witnesses can be found throughout history and across the confessional spectrum. I look to the witness of canonized saints and to men and women not only of accepted intellectual accomplishment but of acknowledged integrity of life. I look to theologians from the early Eastern and Western Christian traditions, and also to members of the contemporary Roman, Anglican, Reformed, and Orthodox churches. (I look, in other words, to those who witness to Gilbert Shaw's "One Great Tradition"; see p. 6 above.) As will become evident, I am particularly indebted to Fr. Alexander Schmemann, but I hope that the fact that it is possible to draw on witnesses from a variety of ecclesial traditions lends weight to my case.

As I have said above, it is incumbent upon the church always to be transmitting its tradition and always to be *recovering* and *renewing* its tradition. Unless this is happening, the Church is failing to be what God wills it to be.

---

whatever—can be seen as belonging to Christ. All that is good or true or beautiful belongs, in some sense, to him (while he has no part in anything that is not of goodness or truth or beauty—except to work for its redemption and transformation).

5. Of course I would accept that the *interpretation* given even of a genuine experience can be so misguided or mistaken as to be dangerous. This is why the theological and liturgical traditions are called to exercise a corrective function—principally, so I would suggest, by keeping the fundamental truths of the Trinity, the incarnation, and the on-going activity of the Spirit at the center of the picture.

6. Schmemann (*Church, World and Mission*, 156, 188) argues that witness and experience, not simply argument, are integral to the theological tradition. "[T]heology, when reduced . . . to a self-sufficient rational structure, . . . becomes defenceless before secular philosophies. . . . It . . . cuts itself off from its sources, from that reality which alone makes words about God *theoprepeis* adequate to God . . . ." Cf. Thatcher (*Truly a Person*, 274): "Both propositional and personal forms of truth are essential to theology."

Part I

Towards a Theology of Christian Education

2

Christian Education—
The Task

IN AN EARLY WORK, Alexander Schmemann explains: "Christianity is neither a philosophy nor a morality nor a ritual, but the gift of a new life in
Christ."[1] Indeed—bewilderingly for those encountering him for the first
time—Schmemann insists that Christianity is not even to be seen as a
religion.

> Much that is true of God has . . . been revealed in the long his-
> tory of religion. . . . Christianity, however, is in a profound sense
> the *end of all religion*. . . . Nowhere in the New Testament . . . is
> Christianity presented as a cult or religion.[2]

Schmemann sees religion as necessary "where there is separation between God and man"[3]; but the gospel emphasizes that Christ has overcome

---

1. Schmeman, *Liturgy and Life*, 12. See Haitch for a biography. For an obituary see
Scorer, "Alexander Schmemann (1921–83)." For a provisional assessment of Schme-
mann's work see Plekon, "The Church, the Eucharist and the Kingdom," 119–43;
Fagerberg, *What is Liturgical Theology*, 9–10, 221–22, 256–68; also Meyendorff, "A Life
Worth Living." Also, more recently, Louth, *Modern Orthodox Thinkers*, 194–213.

A thirty-minute documentary about his life and work is published on Youtube under
the title *The Spirit of St Vladimir's* (https://www.youtube.com/watch?v=qycRfRzTo9Q).
Schmemann is not without his critics, especially among conservative Russian Orthodox, both in America and in Russia itself. See Pomazansk, *Essays*, 82–102; Chrysostomos, "Orthodox People Apart." Chrysostomos claims support for his view from,
amongst others, Georges Florovsky (Chrysostomos, "*Protopresbyter Georges Florovsky*."
The journal *Orthodox Tradition* has carried many other articles critical of Schmemann
(and of OCA in general and of other "Westernized," ecumenically-inclined Orthodox);
see for example, Chrysostomos: "I consider the theological spirit of these two men to
have been wholly perverted by their ecumenistic leanings and a Western mentality"
(see his "Schmemann and Meyendorff." While many in Russia admire Schmemann,
he is not without his critics there too. For a review and comment on some such criticism see Zolotov *Ecumenical News International*. For an indication of how Schmemann
himself might have answered the criticisms of these "ultra-Orthodox" see Schmemann,
For the Life of the World, 129–30; *Liturgy and Tradition*, 42–47, 84, etc.

2. Schmemann, *For the Life of the World*, 19.

3. Schmemann, *For the Life of the World*, 19.

all such separation (cf. Eph 2:11–22). To see Christianity as a religion is to misunderstand its very nature. Schmemann sees religion as helping man cope with life and even with death; that is, as helping "to restore his peace of mind, to endure the other—the secular—life, to accept its tribulations, to lead a wholesome and dedicated life, to 'keep smiling' in a deep and religious way."[4] But this is only to deprive ordinary, secular life of real meaning "save that of being an exercise in piety and patience."[5] Schmemann contrasts this "spiritualising tendency" in religion with an opposite but equally problematic tendency to "activism," one which looks to provide man with a sense of purpose by directing his service to the world. But he considers that this too leaves the ultimate question unanswered.

> Whether we "spiritualise" our life or "secularise" our religion . . .
> the real life of the world, for which we are told God gave his only
> begotten Son, remains hopelessly beyond our religious grasp.[6]

But what, then, does Schmemann see as the "purpose" of Christianity? Schmemann says he wrote *For the Life of the World*, an exceptionally influential work, to address the question, "What *life* is . . . the motivation, and the beginning and the goal of Christian *mission*?"[7]—and by implication of Christian education. The key question becomes: what is the Christian *life*? As we shall see, Schmemann wishes to define the Church in relation to the End, the eschaton. But this is not to spiritualize the Christian life; for the "eschatological nature of the Church is not the negation of the world, but is, on the contrary, its affirmation and acceptance": the world is "the object of divine love."[8] Key here is the character of that *life* which God offers in Christ.

For much of its history Christianity has indeed functioned as a religion—and Schmemann would be the last to deny it.[9] People have often looked to Christianity to help them either "cope with" life or "be of service" to the world. Christianity can also, of course, be interpreted sociologically, as a cultural phenomenon. Schmemann, however, wishes always to emphasize

---

4. Schmemann *For the Life of the World*, ch. 6, esp. 95–99, where the *religious* worldview is identified with a *death-centered* worldview. See also Hopko, "Two 'No's' and One 'Yes,'" 1–5.

5. Schmemann, *For the Life of the World*, 12.

6. Schmemann, *For the Life of the World*, 13. Cf. C. S. Lewis's comment (*Miracles*, 87): "If 'religion' means what man says about God, and not what God does about man [then it has] in the long run, only one really formidable opponent—namely Christianity."

7. Schmemann, *For the Life of the World*, 11f.

8. Schmemann, *Church, World and Mission*, 212.

9. Schmemann, *The Eucharist*, 12f. and *passim*. See esp. ch. 6.

the ontological and existential import of what God has done for man in Christ: the "triumph of the divine life" in the midst of created life, a triumph which so utterly transforms the world that through it a new creation is inaugurated, one which, while rooted and grounded in the old, is not conditioned or determined by it.[10] Preaching at Schmemann's funeral Thomas Hopko made just this point. He presented Schmemann's life as the rejection of secularism and of religion-as-therapy, and yet as the unequivocal affirmation of "the world as sacrament."[11] Because of what had been accomplished in and by Christ, the world exists, here and now, as the context for a living encounter with the eternal divine Kingdom.[12] Schmemann's entire theology, his entire worldview is built on this.[13]

Here Schmemann places himself in the theological tradition of St Paul and the New Testament in general.[14] Paul presents the life, death, and resurrection of Christ, not as patching up the first creation or making life in this world more bearable, but as re-establishing life on a completely new foundation. He sees baptism into Christ as bringing about a radical re-creation: "If anyone is in Christ he is a new creation; the old has passed away, the new has come" (2 Cor 5:17; 6:1–4). Incorporation into Christ may help Christians to bear the sufferings of this world and the New Testament bears witness to the many sufferings of Paul and the early Church; indeed, persecution was the context of the writing of most of the New Testament writings. But Christians have the capacity to endure such suffering primarily because they know themselves to be sharing in a completely new kind of life. Paul's faith in and commitment to Christ do not simply help him "cope with" life (or with death); they place him beyond fear of anything which life or death might bring (cf. Rom 8:38f.; Rom 6:9–11). He recognizes that the rupture in the relationship between God and man that was caused by sin and lead to death, has been overcome in and through the obedience, death and resurrection of Christ. Death has lost its sting (1 Cor 15:55; cf. Rom 6:9). The life in Christ which Paul both knew and wished to make

10. The phrase "triumph of the divine life" is from Schmemann, *Celebration of Faith* I, 105.

11. Hopko, "Two 'No's' and One 'Yes,'" 2–3.

12. Schmemann, *For the Life of the World*, 45–48. For his criticism of contemporary culture, including ecclesial culture, see Schmemann, "The Problems of the Orthodox Church in America: II," 166–69, 172–74, 183–85; Schmemann, "The Problems of the Orthodox Church in America: III," 175–86; Schmemann, *Journals, passim*.

13. See, e.g., Schmemann, *Liturgy and Tradition*, 98f., and the discussion in Plekon, *The Church*, 127.

14. Plekon mentions various theologians, not all of them Orthodox, who share, more or less, Schmemann's view. Plekon, *The Church*, 121–22, 124, 128, see 128 nn.31–32.

known was not a life "spiritualized" and removed from mundane secular life; it is one which enabled Paul and his co-religionists to live and work for the world's transformation and redemption (cf. 2 Cor 5:16f.).

The life and work of Christ reversed the effects of the fall, bringing all that belongs to the created order and to the life of this world—including all relationships and historical events—into fully positive relationship with God (cf. chapter 19 below). Within Christ, and within that new creation which belongs to him, even life's trials and tribulations can serve the divine purpose. Sin and the temptation to sin can now lead to repentance and humility, not to mere remorse or hardness of heart. Most amazingly of all, death itself is made life-bearing. This is the heart of the gospel. Sin, death, the devil—none has the final word. Schmemann writes,

> The Church is the entrance into the risen life of Christ; it is communion in life eternal . . . . And it is the expectation of . . . the fulfillment of all things and all life in Christ. In Him death itself has become an act of life, for He has filled it with Himself. . . . And if I make this *new life* mine . . . , mine the certitude that Christ is Life, then my very death will be consummated in Christ.[15]

Whether writing about the Church's history or about its current state, Schmemann makes the same point: the trials which inevitably occur as history unfolds are God-given opportunities for entry into communion with Christ—the *risen, eschatological* Christ.[16] Schmemann always sets the mission of the Church and its ministry of education, within this broader context.

For Schmemann, the new life which the Church experiences in its communion with Christ gives direction and purpose to human life. "The Church's fullness and its home is in heaven. But this fullness is given to the world, sent into the world as its salvation and its redemption."[17] That fullness, that salvation and redemption are nothing other than Christ's own life opened up to human participation.

It is the *reality* of this new life, the *experience* of it—not just the hope of some future redemption—which inspired the active ministry of the early Church. And that inspiration was more than an idealism. It bore its own energy. To share the Son's life is to live in and by the Holy Spirit. "[I]n Christ

---

15. Schmemann, *For the Life of the World*, 106. Cf. Schmemann's final homily (Schmemann "Two 'Nos' and One 'Yes'"); Plekon, *The Church*, 138ff.; cf. Thekla, *Mother Maria, Her Life in Letters*, 100–125.

16. Schmemann, *For the Life of the World*, 112–13.

17. Schmemann, *Church, World and Mission*, 213.

. . . the light of the world comes to us in the joy and peace of the Holy Spirit . . . ."[18] The Spirit empowers the Church to live and work in Christ's name. It does so principally, not by infusing the members of the Church with superhuman gifts and powers, but rather *by enabling their freedom*. The Holy Spirit acts *personally*. His action is grounded in his own free act of love, and has its end in the increasing personal freedom of those to whom he ministers. His work is directed towards enabling created human persons to share the *freedom* belonging to the eternal Son—a freedom always lying at the heart of the Son's response to the Father.[19]

Schmemann was a Christian educator: "first and foremost a teacher of the Church."[20] The same could be said of St Paul. His concern was to encourage the faith of his co-disciples and of those who looked to him for help. Frequently he reminds his correspondents of the nature of the gospel (e.g., 2 Thess 2:2; 2 Cor 11:4; Gal 1:6), and warns them against turning the gospel into a cult or system of practices—a religion (cf. Gal 1:6; 3:1–5, and *passim*; cf. Col 2:16). Again and again he is at pains to explain to his correspondents what has *already happened to them* through their initiation into the Church and their incorporation into Christ, reminding them that they now stand in Christ, on the *inside* of God's answer to the world's problems (cf. Gal 2:18–21).

Schmemann was similarly committed to what might be termed the "churching" (or "re-churching") of the Church. Plekon explains: "[The] bulk of [his] published work was a sustained effort in churchly restoration and spiritual renewal, a 'churching' of the Church."[21] Thus, the Eucharist was an important theme. Schmemann saw the Eucharist as the coming into time of the substance and ultimate reality of Christian life: the divine Kingdom. And he saw the Eucharist as the place in which the Son, gathering all the things of this world into communion with himself, offers everything back to their ultimate divine origin and goal and "hands over the kingdom to God the Father" (cf. 1 Cor 15:24).[22]

For Paul, what Jesus had accomplished in history was crucial. But Paul's primary concern was not to remember a departed hero. His letters show little concern with the detail of Christ's life and ministry, and even when insisting on the importance of Christ's passion and resurrection Paul

---

18. Schmemann, *For the Life of the World*, 106.

19. Schmemann, *Church, World and Mission*, 179–91, esp 185–89.

20. Plenkon, *The Church*, 127.

21. Plekon, *The Church*, 124. See Schmemann, *Church, World and Mission*, 147–57, 172ff.

22. Cf. Plekon, *The Church*, 125ff., 131ff.

is not interested in the details of what happened—beyond his insistence that the Son had indeed died and been raised.[23] Paul had, however, direct first-hand knowledge of Christ's death and the resurrection. He knows himself to have died with Christ. He knows that he has met the risen Christ. And he knows, above all, that the only life he now has is the life he has in Christ. (Cf. Col 3:3: "for you have died, and your life is hidden with Christ in God.") For Paul, the world has no significant future outside of that offered in Christ (Gal 2:20f.; cf. Eph 5:2). Schmemann believes the same:

> The historical reality of Christ was of course the undisputed ground of the early Christians' faith: yet they did not so much remember him as know he was with them. And in this was the end of all "religion," because he himself was the Answer to all religion, to all human hunger for God, because in him the life that was lost by man . . . was restored to man.[24]

Referring (no doubt) to his own experience he writes:

> [T]he person who opens his life to Christ (if only partially, if only occasionally) comes to know *another life*, another way of living, . . . freeing his soul for the reign of joy and peace in the Holy Spirit which no one on earth is able to give, but which all along has been here within us. We fall, we sin, we walk away from that Kingdom; but we can no longer forget it completely, so we repent and return. And once again we are embraced by that same life, that same light . . . .[25]

Here is a key point for understanding the nature of Christian education. The "spiritualizing" and "activist" tendencies against which Schmemann warns are an ever-present threat: the gospel can easily be subverted. Theological clarification can guard the gospel against distortion and corruption, but if the Church is to remain healthy and "alive" more is required than doctrinal orthodoxy. It is only when the Christian community is growing in *first-hand* knowledge of the gospel that the threat to the gospel diminishes.[26]

The process of Christian education involves the community and all its members. A community growing in a shared experience of life in Christ will be a community whose individual members will be able to learn to receive

---

23. On this notorious problem in NT studies see Dunn, "Paul's Understanding of the Death of Jesus as Sacrifice," 192; "Jesus Tradition in Paul," 169–89.

24. Schmemann, *For the Life of the World*, 20. Here Schmemann explains that *For the Life of the World* was intended to remind people that "in Christ life—life in all its totality—was returned to man."

25. Schmemann, *Celebration of Faith*, vol. 1, 107.

26. Schmemann, *Church, World and Mission*, 156, 188.

all that happens to them directly from the hand of God, recognizing that all life's events come with the Father's blessing upon them, even when first appearances suggest otherwise.[27] Where a Christian community is learning to enter into that flow and re-flow of love which characterizes the Son's relationship with the Father, then its life will be becoming eucharistic. And where this is happening, the community will both be witnessing to the goal of human life and training its members to live eucharistically. Its witness and mission can also be expected to prosper: it will have something worthwhile to offer the world.[28]

Life in Christ and the work of Christian Formation

If the fundamental task of the Christian educator is to help people know and share Christ's life, at least two important things follow. First, it must be accepted that the initiative in Christian education will always belong to Christ himself. It is he who sets the agenda and chooses how the work of Christian formation will proceed. Secondly, the many aspects of Christian discipleship and the many activities involved in the process of Christian formation—including the study of doctrine and Church history, the exploration of ethical and social issues, and the acquisition of dispositions and skills necessary for mature participation in corporate worship and pastoral ministry—these are only important insofar as they foster reception of and participation in Christ's life.

Schmemann again:

> To be a Christian, to believe in Christ, means . . . to believe in a transrational and yet absolutely certain way called faith, that Christ is the Life of all life, that He is Life itself and, therefore, *my* life.[29]

He continues:

> All the Christian doctrines—those of the incarnation, redemption, and atonement—are explanations, consequences, but not the "cause" of that faith. Only when we believe in Christ do all these affirmations become "valid" and "consistent." Nevertheless,

---

27. Schmemann, *Celebration of Faith*, vol. 1, 34–36; cf. Schmemann's "Final Sermon," and Staniloae, *Victory of the Cross*, 5–6. Schmemann, in "Two 'Nos' and One 'Yes,'" insists that the trials afflicting the Church always provide opportunities for growth.

28. Schmemann, *Eucharist*, 34–35, 45–46.

29. Schmemann, *Eucharist*, 104.

faith itself is not the acceptance of this or that "proposition" about Christ, but of Christ Himself, as the Life and light of life.[30]

But what characterizes Christ's life? The answer can only be that the Son's life is essentially a *personal* life. Nothing more profound can be said of the Son than that he is a *person*: he is *someone*—a unique someone with a unique relationship to the eternal Father, but essentially, he is *someone*, just as are the Father and the Holy Spirit. And those virtues which characterize the Son's life: unfailing generosity, joyfulness, compassion, willingness to suffer for the sake of the wellbeing of others, etc.—these belong to the Son *as person*. Love is always personal. Likewise those titles which belong to the Son: eternal Word, Alpha and Omega, and so on—these belong to him *personally*. Indeed, to be Son is to be in *personal relationship* (by the Spirit) to the Father. Sonship is not a role. It is a relationship. In turn, the challenge to the Christian is to appropriate the virtues or dispositions of the Son and to do so *personally*. The eschatological life can only be borne personally—by persons, whether divine, human, or angelic. So it is that the sacraments must be seen as operating personally. It is the *person* who is baptized, ordained, anointed, married, who shares celebration of the Eucharist, or receives communion.

I am not alone in believing that concern with personhood must be central in any theory of Christian education. Plekon records Schmemann's interest in the impact of modernity upon the human person.[31] Others have been similarly concerned.[32] Anglican philosopher-theologian Adrian Thatcher explores the idea that "to become educated is to *learn to become a person*"[33] and suggests that Christian teaching on personhood might contribute to educational theory. "Christian faith and theology have specific things to say about what persons can become."[34] This he sees as possible because "Jesus Christ is the definitive pattern of personalness for Christians."[35]

---

30. Schmeman, *Eucharist*, 105. Cf. Boojamra, *Foundations*, 73: "Correct doctrine is valuable not as an academic exercise, but as a model which arises from faith and which allows faith to happen."

31. Schmemann, *Church, World and Mission*, 193–208.

32. E.g., Maritain, *The Person and the Common Good*; Jenkins, *The Glory of Man* and *What is Man?*; cf. Berger, *The Homeless Mind*. For an outline bibliography of Berger's work see Plekon, *Church, Eucharist, Kingdom*, 124, n.12.

33. Thatcher, "Learning to Become Persons." Thatcher looks to develop ideas set out in Langford, *Philosophy and Education*, 60 and Langford, "The Concept of Education," 3. See also Thatcher, "Education and the Concept of a Person" and Langford "Reply to Adrian Thatcher."

34. Thatcher, "Learning to Become Persons," 521.

35. Thatcher, "Learning to Become Persons," 524.

He is "the authoritative model of personhood."[36] Thatcher insists that Christ is more than exemplar; he constitutes the "anticipation and embodiment of a new humanity, a new sort of personalness, known . . . in the present experience of the church . . . ."[37]

The Christian notion of personhood could prove even more significant than Thatcher suggests. Thatcher looks to provide "prescriptive or ideal concept of person, squarely based on acknowledged [Christian] beliefs and values,"[38] considering that this will provide a basis for the revision of educational aims, the curriculum, and teaching procedure. He argues that the student must be seen and treated not just as *res cogitans* but as a whole person whose moral, emotional, and physical being must be engaged in and transformed by the educational process.[39] All this is commendable. But my own concern is somewhat different. I seek to explore issues relating to the very nature and purpose of human life, particularly the idea that human fulfillment can be found only in and through participation in the life of the Son. Schmemann's one-time colleague John Boojamra states: "The aim of Christian life and nurture is to permit the growth of *theosis* through a life-long encounter with Christ."[40] "Only as person can we encounter Christ!"[41]

In the next chapter, I shall develop this idea that fulfillment is found through participation in the life of the Son by exploring the complementary notion that personal maturity is to be understood in relation to the paschal mystery. Since the divine-human incarnate Son participates fully

36. Thatcher, "Learning to Become Persons," 525. Unhelpfully (to my mind) in this and other works, Thatcher chooses to employ "person" in a somewhat idiosyncratic way. Wishing to avoid the risk of confusion between the theological notion of person and the modern notion of person-as-individual (and also to avoid the non-PC "man"), he chooses to speak of Christ as both a human person and a divine person. The argument is set out in Thatcher *Truly a Person, Truly God*, 80–93 (cf. Thatcher, "Learning to Become Persons," 522f.). It is, I think, an unhelpful proposal. There is nothing essentially unorthodox in Thatcher's Christology, but his novel terminology is liable to cause confusion rather than prevent it. Compare the insightful presentation of the orthodox position in McIntosh, *Mystical Theology*, 187–208, esp. 193–98.

37. Thatcher, "Learning to Become Persons," 525–26. What Thatcher means by experience is not made clear. He speaks of the experience of living within a form of life "that seems to be 'non-natural' . . . which fragmentarily occurs when men and women live together understandingly and lovingly" (526). But he makes no ontological or metaphysical claims.

38. Thatcher, "Learning to Become Persons," 524.

39. Thatcher, "Learning to Become Persons," 527–33. Cf. Francis, "Theology and Education," 62. Newman's comments on curriculum, etc., remain normative. See Newman, *The Idea of a University*. See also Webster, "A Spiritual Dimension for Education?"

40. Boojamra, *Foundations*, 72–73; cf. 31, 88f.

41. Boojamra, *Foundations*, 89.

in the paschal mystery—such that participation in this mystery more or less characterizes his life—the measure of any human person's maturity will be the measure of his capacity to live by self-giving love. Only insofar as anyone is willing to participate in the paschal mystery is he or she able to participate in the Son.

3

Christian Education—
The Metaphysical Foundation
Personhood

The Christian Notion of Personhood

THEOLOGIANS HAVE RECENTLY SHOWN increased interest in the notions of *person* and personhood.[1] Some have argued that the notion of personhood is

1. See Illingworth, *Personality*; also the papers in Schwöbel and Gunton (eds.), *Persons Human and Divine*, esp. Zizioulas, "'On Being a Person," 33–46, also Zizioulas, "Human Capacity and Human Incapacity"; Lossky, *Image and Likeness of God*. Gill, argues that the notion of person is absent from early Greek thought. "Is there a Concept of Person in Greek Philosophy?" 192f. See Rahner's analysis of the concept of person, *EOT* 1206–25. Thatcher (*Truly a Person, Truly God*, 6–10) outlines six senses of the term "person."

The nineteenth- and twentieth-century Anglo-Eurpoean Personalist movement exerted an enduring effect. The movement was diverse. Maritain talks of "at least a dozen" personalist doctrines, "which, at times, have nothing more in common than the term 'person," Maritain, *The Person and the Common Good*, 12ff.; Yandell speaks of the "myriad" senses of "personalism" (*CREP* 667b). For the history of the movement see, e.g., Mann, *NCT*, vol. 11, 172a–174a; Macquarrie, *Twentieth-Century Religious Thought*, 58–68; Sayre, "Personalism," 129–35; also Schwöbel in Schwöbel and Gunton (eds.), *Persons Human and Divine* 1, 4–7. Personalism had many proponents among Catholics, including Newman (see Tracy, *SCMCS* III, 144); von Hügel, *The Mystical Element of Religion* (cf. Holland, *Friedrich von Hügel: Selected Letters*; Dupré, *The Common Life*, 145ff.); Marechal, *The Psychology of the Mystics*; Mounier, *A Personalist Manifest*; Maritain, *The Person and the Common Good*; also Gilson, *Being and Some Philosophers*. More recently Taylor has sought to take this movement forward, insisting that a whole host of philosophical issues focus on the status of the self; see *Sources of the Self*, and Kalaushofer, "Taylor-made Selves"; also Taylor's 1999 Gifford Lectures, expanded and published as *A Secular Age*.

For Anglican contributions see, e.g., Jenkins, *The Glory of Man*, and the bold claims he makes for personhood, or "personalness" as he terms it. Thatcher (*Truly a Person, Truly God*) looks to build on the work of analytical philosopher Strawson (see *Individuals*); but note Zizioulas' comments on Strawson's inability to cope with an individualism or particularity not grounded in space-time categories (Zizioulas, "Human Capacity and Human Incapacity," 415 n.1).

Among modern Jewish thinkers both Heschel and Buber have been accounted fundamental to Christian theology and ontology. Some, following Lossky,[2] see the notion of personhood as itself a Christian innovation.[3] Zizioulas considers it *the* Christian theological and philosophical innovation:

> The person both as concept and as a living reality is purely the product of patristic thought.... Belief in creation *ex nihilo*—biblical faith— ... [needs to encounter] belief in ontology—Greek faith—to give to human existence and thought its most precious good, the concept of the person. This and nothing less than this is what the world owes to Greek patristic theology.[4]

Zizioulas's concern is with what he terms "the living reality" of the persons—the person as realized fact, as existent reality. He sees personhood as a fundamental, defining metaphysical or ontological notion.[5] At the most fundamental level of his being each person, whether human or divine (or even angelic), answers to *who?* and not to *what?* nor yet again to *which?*—for he is more than simply a particular representative member of a genus. If this is so, however, any account of the nature of Christian education must be grounded in an account of the notion of personhood.

---

personalists. See Silberstein, SCMJS II, 405–432. Heschel, *Man is Not Alone*; Buber, *Moses,* chs. 1–2. On Buber's *I and Thou,* see Vermes, *Buber,* 39–59.

    Recent work in ethics looks back to the personalism of Aquinas and pre-Enlightenment tradition. See especially MacIntyre, *After Virtue;* MacIntyre, *Whose Justice? Which Rationality?*; MacIntyre, *Three Rival Versions of Moral Enquiry.*

    2. Lossky, *Mystical Theology,* 53; but cf. Lossky *Image and Likeness,* 111–12. Among nineteenth-century Orthodox theologians Florensky is recognized as having helped to re-establish personhood as an ontological category. (Florensky, *The Pillar and the Ground of the Truth,* esp. 39ff. (cf. 284–330); see Robert Sleninski's review SVTQ 43.1 (1999), also Tkachuk, "Love from Knowledge." Orthodox theologians have come to exert considerable influence in the West; see Plekon, "The Church, the Eucharist and the Kingdom"; Nichols, *Theology in the Russian Diaspora.*

    3. See Zizioulas, *Being as Communion,* 27–65; Illingworth, *Personality—Human and Divine,* 8; Webb, God and Personality, 20; Rahner, *Teaching of the Catholic Church,* 1207.

    4. Zizioulas *Being as Communion,* 27, cf. 65. Zizioulas may here overstate his case. While the development of the concept of personhood may be attributed to patristic thought, the development of "the living reality" of the person is due solely to the life and work of Christ himself.

    5. See Zizioulas "On Being a Person," 33, 35 n.2, 42f., 45f., also Zizioulas, "Human Capacity and Human Incapacity," 1975, esp. 420ff.; Gunton, "Trinity, Ontology and Anthropology," 58. Contrast Prestige, *God in Patristic Thought,* 157–96. Prestige fails to acknowledge the possibility that with the Cappadocians *hypostasis* came to designate a primary *ontological* category.

The Person and the Individual

It is important to distinguish the notions of *person* and *individual*.[6] In everyday speech the two terms are often treated as synonyms, but theologians have commonly used them to designate two quite different concepts—two different realities. The person is taken to be, in essence, a relational being, with the term *person* functioning as shorthand for "being with the (realized or unrealized) potential for (personal) relationship." The term "individual," on the other hand, designates "isolated individual." Therefore, while the person is defined by capacity for relationship and communion, the individual is defined by separation—by his or her autonomy. In looking to explicate the task of Christian education, Boojamra, for example, insists that *the individual and the collective* must be distinguished from *the person and the communal*.[7] In few contemporary writings on philosophy, sociology or the human sciences is this important distinction adequately appreciated. Maritain suggested that the person/individual distinction is "difficult . . . for sociologists, who . . . wonder for what purpose they should . . . equip themselves as metaphysicians."[8] More recently Andrew G. Walker has identified in the social sciences a damaging neglect of the notion of the person.[9] (On the other hand, he has also suggested that social scientists have found "clues about personhood that theologians ignore at their peril."[10]) Maritain equated the distinction between person and individual with that between the physical and the spiritual aspects of the human composite.[11] I think it is preferable to see individuality as concerning, not directly the material, but

6. See, e.g., Lossky, *Mystical Theology*, 121–24.

7. Boojamra, *Foundations*, 34.

8. Maritain, *Person and the Common Good*, 14.

9. Walker, "Concept of a Person," 154, n.2: "There is . . . no coherent and widely agreed concept of person in the humanistic studies." (More generally, Walker, "Concept of a Person," 137–57.) Cf. Maritain, *Person and the Common Good*, 14 and ch. 5.

10. Walker, "Concept of a Person," 138; also 152. See also Staniloae, *Experience of God*, vol. 1, xvii. Brian Morris seeks to trace the concept of what he terms "the person," but in doing so uses the terms "person" and "individual" interchangeably (Morris, *Western Conceptions of the Individual; Anthropology of the Self*). He makes passing reference to the vital Christian contribution to the emergence of the notion of person (*Anthropology of the Self*, 3) but neither work contains any analysis or discussion of Christian anthropology, and neither shows any interest in ontology. In the exploration of the "way people are" and "aspects of being a person" in Stevens (*Understanding the Self*) "person" is understood in terms of embodied subjective experience (both conscious and unconscious) and (culturally conditioned) social relations (see 16–34), and there is no concern with ontology or with anything corresponding to what in classical Christianity would be termed the *spiritual* dimension in human existence.

11. Maritain, *Person and the Common Good*, 43, cf. 31–46.

all that belongs to what might be termed the "natural" or the unredeemed, including the unredeemed physical, intellectual, and emotional aspects of human life—all of which things can be redeemed and all of which things can function as vehicles of personal presence and action.[12]

As a primary ontological category, personhood cannot be defined or analyzed in other, more fundamental, terms or categories.[13] And it cannot be scrutinized scientifically. Sophrony states, "The person is beyond definition and incognizable from without."[14] Nellas writes: "[M]an remains and will remain a mystery to science. . . . [What] lies at his core, by reason of his very structure, is a theological being which falls outside of the scope of science."[15] The person can only be known *personally*. The person can only be known through personal engagement and relationship.[16] Zizioulas states that the person cannot be known or "approached" through his nature.[17]

Individualism is widely seen as lying at the root of numerous problems in Western society and the modern world. Individualism is grounded in an ontology of separation and leads to a sociology and politics of separation. Theologians working with a personalist ontology see the corporate dimension in human life as fundamental. But where the basic unit of human existence is assumed to be the isolated individual, then the centrality of the corporate dimension in human life is missed. Relationship is seen as an optional (if highly desirable) extra in human life—maybe one which is essential for psychological well-being; but it is not recognized as being integral to human existence *ontologically*.

Western individualism is widely considered to be a product of the Enlightenment and Renaissance. Some see it as having its roots much earlier, in the late mediaeval era—where, for instance, there is a move in devotion and piety towards a concern with the individual and his "inner-state," and the concern in eschatology becomes, not the restoration of all things in

12. Here, however, I am not drawing a distinction between the realms of nature and grace, as has commonly been done in Western scholastic theology. See Meyendorff, *Byzantine Theology*, 138–50, 225; Meyendorff, *Gregory Palamas*, 162–166; Lossky, *Mystical Theology of the Eastern Church*, 101–2. Cf. "Nature and grace do not exist side by side, . . . there is mutual inter-penetration . . . , the one exists in the other," Lossky, *Mystical Theology of the Eastern Church*, 126.

13. Cf. Gunton, "Trinity, Ontology and Anthropology," 44.

14. Sophrony, *His Life is Mine*, 43. Cf. Lossky, *Mystical Theology*, 53; Meyendorff, *Byzantine Theology*, 142; Zizioulas, "On Being a Person," 45.

15. Nellas, *Deification in Christ*, 30.

16. See Sophrony, *His Life is Mine*, 45; also see Illingworth, *Personality—Human and Divine*, Lecture 5.

17. Zizioulas, "Human Capacity and Human Incapacity," 407, cf. 402, 416; Zizioulas, "On Being a Person," 44f.

Christ, but individual salvation.[18] Whatever the origins of individualism—and even the fall can be seen as a move from personal/relational existence to individual/isolated existence—it was only relatively recently that a *culture of individualism* could emerge.[19] Pre-modern societies had little room for "individuals"—and those that there were came principally from the privileged classes. Only in the wake of the Renaissance and Reformation was the right to pursue individual fulfillment progressively conferred on everyone, regardless of class, sex, or race. Shoumantoff has argued that a culture of

18. See Morris, *Discovery of the Individual*, esp. 1–10, 158–66; McIntosh, *Mystical Theology*, 64–66. On the place of the Renaissance in the development of the notion of the individual see Burkhardt, *Renaissance in Italy*, esp. 143–74. Evans suggests that when speaking of man "[early] mediaeval literature, like that of the ancient world, describes the typical representative of a 'class'" (*Philosophy and Theology in the Middle Ages*, 123); men exist not in their individuality but as members of that class of the good, the brave, the wicked, the virtuous, the foolish or whatever, or as members of such classes as the benevolent ruler or wise philosopher. Biographic and hagiographic traditions developed in which accounts of the lives of historical figures and saints were written according to pre-existent models, often regardless of the particularities of the actual life lived. Storkey ("Modernity and Anthropology") sees modernity as having begun with a defective anthropology and as having ended with one yet more defective. Carroll sees individualistic humanism as having "carried within its [very] seed the elements of its [own] destruction" (see Carroll, *Humaninsm*, 6). For Western tradition more generally see Taylor, *Sources of the Self*; also Morris, *Western Conceptions of the Individual*. (Taylor's concern is especially with "self and morals" and conceptions of "the good," see Taylor, *Sources of the Self*, x, and 3–107). For conceptions of the individual in different cultures see Morris, *Anthropological Studies of Religion*; also Ingold, "Humanity and Animality," esp. 23–31. (On the Sophists and individualism see Ferguson *Backgrounds*, 8–9, 303–6.) For an exploration of the development of individualism, especially vis-à-vis the family, and most especially in Western culture, see Shoumantoff, *Mountain of Names*, 115–55.

19. MacIntyre charts the breakdown of the sense of moral *community* which previously provided the context for moral behaviour and moral discourse; MacIntyre, *After Virtue*, esp. chs 1–8. Thatcher traces individualism in British empiricist philosophy and French Rationalism and outlines anti-individualist tendencies in a succession of Continental philosophers and British Idealists, including Hegel, Heidegger, Bradley, and Whitehead (Thatcher, *Truly a Person*, 122ff.). Dollimore (*Death, Desire and Loss*) discusses the idea that the twentieth century saw the *death* of the individual, an idea also found in Foucault and owing much to his reading of Marx and Freud, and to Hegelian dialectic. Parfit (*Reasons and Persons*) wishes to dispense with the notion of person altogether; cf. the criticisms in Dancy, *Reading Parfit*. Wittgenstein has been seen as a key figure in countering the Cartesian notion that the discarnate individual is the basic form of human life and in re-establishing community (and the body) as indispensable to (or foundational in) human existence (Kerr, *Theology since Wittgenstein*, 7–10; 26f.; 84–90; cf. "What constitutes us as human beings is the regular and patterned reactions that we have to one another," Kerr, *Theology since Wittgenstein*, 65.

individualism could not emerge until a whole range of social, scientific, and technological developments had taken place.[20]

I would suggest that if God's ultimate intention was always to bring human persons to fullness of maturity, he will always have been at work to bring into being cultures in which personhood might be nurtured. That being so, we might expect to find in many cultures the *beginnings* of a recognition of the value of the person. Sometimes a concern with the individual has been a step forward, a step towards a concern with the person; at other times it has been a degenerate step, a step away from a concern with personhood.

Consider Josipovici's view of Paul's contribution to the emergence of a culture of individualism.[21] He identifies in Paul a novel concern with the individual, his salvation and spiritual well-being; but what Josipovici fails to recognize in Paul is a worldview in which the communal or corporate dimension in human life is central (cf. 1 Cor 13, etc.). Because Josipovici has failed to distinguish the notions of person and individual, he misreads Paul. Only through post-Reformation, post-Enlightenment eyes can Paul appear as a proto-individualist.

The culture of individualism and the culture of personhood are grounded in radically different ontologies. But if man is indeed constituted in such a way that he can find fulfillment only in personal relationships, then an individualistic culture will not be able to help him reach his intended fulfillment. An ontology of personhood, on the other hand, sees each human person as created in and for personal relationship—and that means in and for, and out of love. Zizioulas has sought to elucidate just such an ontology of personhood, of love.

> The expression "God is love" (1 Jn 4:16) signifies that God "subsists" as Trinity, that is, as person and not as substance. Thus, love ceases to be a qualifying—i.e. secondary—property of being and becomes *the supreme ontological predicate*. Love as God's mode of existence "hypostasizes" God, *constitutes* his being.[22]

This being so, all of Christian theology, including its anthropology and its the theologies of Christian discipleship and Christian education, must be rooted in this ontology of love. Zizioulas again:

---

20. See Shoumantoff, *Mountain of Names*, 121–28.

21. Josipovici, *Book of God*, 253: "Both autobiography and the classic novel emerge . . . directly out of Paul" (cf. ch.12 *passim*).

22. Zizioula, *Being as Communion*, 46. See also Zizioulas, "Human Capacity and Human Incapacity," 410, 414, 432.

[I]f we wish . . . to push . . . the ontological question to the ulti-
macy which it deserves if it is to be ontology at all, we can only
do that by making freedom a corollary of love and by regarding
love (and its freedom) as the ultimate ontological notions.[23]

Freedom and its relationship to love are key themes in chapters 5 and 6.
Here it might be noted, however, that modern commentators have sometimes
suggested that theological concern with the person has developed at just the
same time that the notion of the person—and the realized fact of the person—
came under grave threat.[24] The twentieth century saw personhood threatened
both by collectivism, on the one hand, and by individualism, on the other.
In an article written in 1917, "Russia and her Icons," and during the rising
storm of the Revolution, Russian theologian Eugene Trubetskoi describes
artists Ostroukov and Gurianov cleaning Rublev's Trinity Icon. They had to
remove "several successive layers of overpainting to reach the original ancient
painting, which luckily turned out to be fairly well preserved."[25] Trubetskoi
came to suggest that the recovery of the icon at this crucial point in Russian history should be seen as providential, as a divine gift intended to help
the Russian people cope with the sufferings which he believed were to befall
them. Trubetskoi argues that the recovery of this image of persons in communion would help the people withstand the pressures of depersonalizing
collectivism. It gave a vision of what life could be.[26]

Can the work of those nineteenth- and twentieth-century theologians
who elucidated the notion of the person also be seen as providential and
as serving to counteract those powerful social and political movements
which have tended to depersonalize man? Can they help to restore to man a
"vision" of what his life might be. Is this the hope that the Church can offer
the world and which the world awaits?

We live in changing times. Technological advances have brought
ease of communication, travel, and transport, and together these make
the world, in some sense, smaller and more united, the so-called global
village. But at the same time, the contemporary world is beset by cultural,
political and social divisions. Strife and conflict rage. Oppression, ex-
ploitation, and ill-treatment are rife. Extremist worldviews, religious and

23. Zizioulas, "Human Capacity and Human Incapacity," 432, n.1.

24. Cf. Maritain, *Person and the Common Good*, 11–14 and *passim*; Walker, *Enemy
Territory*, 81–85; Schwöbel, *Persons Human and Divine*, 6–7; and note MacIntyre, *After
Virtue*; Taylor, *Sources of the Self*; Macmurray, *Self as Agent*, 29 (cf. Aves, "Persons in
Relation," 120–21).

25. Trubetskoi, *Theology in Color*, 93f. Further and more successful cleanings are
outlined in Sheredega, "Andrei Rublev."

26. Trubetskoi, *Theology in Color*, 71–98.

political, of both Left and Right see the "other," the "alien" as a adversary, a challenge to be defeated, a problem to be overcome. Routinely the other, the alien, the outsider is blamed for the problems of society and the ills of world. "*You* are the cause of my problems." Whether with the Nazis, the Soviet-era communists, or any subsequent self-interested, self-satisfied totalitarianism, the other, the alien, the "problem" is either to be exploited, excluded, or simply eradicated.

But at the heart of a worldview grounded in self-forgetful, self-giving love lies something quiet different. The incarnate Son worked for (and suffered for) the redemption and even the ultimate beatitude of the "problem person," even his own persecutors. No one was exclude from this goodwill. The divine goodwill extends to all: "You have heard that it was said, "You shall love your neighbor and hate your enemy.' But I say to you. Love your enemies and pray for those who persecute you, so that you may be children of your Father in heaven; for he makes his sun rise on the evil and on the good, and sends rain on the righteous and on the unrighteous" (Matt 5:43–44).

St Silouan quotes Jesus: "I have come not to destroy but to save" (Luke 9:56[27]) and goes on to say, "Thus our one thought is that all should be saved."[28] Previously Silouan had said: "If a man thinks kindly of his brother, deeming that the Lord loves him . . . that man is close to the love of God."[29]

Sophrony writes: "This commandment of Christ's, 'Love your enemies,' is the reflection in our world of the Triune God's all-purpose love."[30] It constitutes, he says, the "cornerstone" of Silouan's teaching. It has significance for all of us; for perhaps all of us invariably seek, in the first instance, either to escape from or to eradicate our own sufferings. The Christian is called seek for and labor for, not the eradication of our problems, but their redemption.[31]

Here in this expression of Trinitarian love, this outworking that seeks to resolve conflict, not through excluding or annihilating the "problem" and the problematic, but through its redemption, healing, and incorporation into the goodness, the beatitude God intends—here we perhaps see something of what the Church in this age can (and should) offer the world. It could, indeed, be argued that unless the Church is doing this it is failing

27. It is a variant reading, but in keeping with the sense of the passage.

28. Sophrony, *Saint Silouan*, 379.

29. Sophrony, *Saint Silouan*, 373.

30. Sophrony, *Saint Silouan*, 232.

31. This true also for our personal "internal" problems. The call is, not that we should escape from or eradicate our problems or "issues" (say fear or anxiety or pride or self-obsession) but to work for their redemption, their transmutation into blessings.

to be what it is called to be and is failing fully to appropriate the blessings, the beatitude God is offering.

So it is that while Rublev's icon engages us in a vision of persons living in perfect communion, perfect unity, that vision must be held together with a vision of a love that reaches out into the world, and even to the alien, the "enemy," to gather that person into the divine love, the divine goodness. Here one of the many innovations in Rublev's icon is significant. Bunge suggests that in similar "Trinity" icons predating that of Rublev the head of the central figure (usually taken to designate the Son) is invariably vertical and his gaze is directed forwards, towards the onlooker. In Rublev's icon the head of the central figure is inclined to the left and his gaze is turned toward the left-hand figure (taken to represent the Father). But I would suggest that this gentle inclination of the Son's head speaks not only of the Son's loving relationship to the Father. It does something else too. For the inclination of the Son's head in Rublev's icon echoes the inclination of the Son's head in many Byzantine icons of the crucifixion. This is a point which Bunge does not suggest but is something, which I suggest, can be seen as significant. The self-offering of the cross, the death of the Son, is intimated in Rublev's Trinity.

4

Personhood and Nature

The Emergence of the Christian Perspective

RECENT THEOLOGICAL CONCERN WITH personhood has demonstrated that for the Greek Fathers, particularly the Cappadocians, the fundamental reality of the divine existence is that God exists *personally*—more specifically as three divine persons, three *hypostases*, who have their being in their relation with one another.[1] (Importantly, they do not have their being *as* relationships; that would depersonalize them.) God answers to *who*—not to *what*.

The work of the Cappadocians is to be seen as crucial. Earlier Greek thought, deriving from Plato and Aristotle, had hinted at personhood, but the philosophical and cosmological preconceptions underlying Greek thought precluded the idea's full development.[2] So perhaps had various elements or factors prominent in the culture of the day: slavery, for instance.[3] Ontology was the primary concern for Greek philosophy. What is real? What has true and lasting existence? What *is*? All Greek traditions accorded ontological priority to the totality, the One, rather than to any individual, any particular. Particularity cannot be ontologically absolute. "[T]he many [i.e., the particulars] are always ontologically derivative."[4] Presupposing a pre-existing nature, inherently unified and allowing no division or separation, the assumption followed that anything tending away from this unity

---

1. See p. 37, n. 1, above.

2. See Brown, *Images of the Human*; Zizioulas, "On Being a Person," 35–37. For Plato see *Laws*, X 903c–d. For Aristotle see *De Anima*, II.1 412a–418, where it is argued that because the soul is a substantial form and not an individual substance existing its own right, the human soul is not immortal. For the soul as "form of the body," such that it cannot exist apart from the body, see *Metaphysics* 1070a 24–26. Cf. Hartman, *Aristotelian Investigation*; Barnes, *Aristotle*.

3. Westermann, *Slave Systems*; Wiedemann, *Greek and Roman Slavery*. Aristotle defined the slave as "living property" (*Politics* 1.2.4–5, 1253b) and a living tool (*Nic. Eth.* 8:11); cf. Varro's "articulate instruments" (*On Agriculture* 1.17.1). On Christian innovations, see *EEC*, 1066aff., with extensive bibliography.

4. Zizioulas, "On Being a Person," 36.

or separating from it was inevitably moving towards non-existence. Also fundamental was the concept of *cosmos*; that is, of an underlying, order or harmony (inevitably impersonal) which determines all subsequent or secondary existence.[5] Even the gods were constrained by the demands of this underlying order.[6] Man found himself subject to ruthless, impersonal forces and powers—hence the central role of fate in Greek drama.[7] In such a world there could be no place for absolute freedom, for anything beyond the demands of nature.[8]

Platonic ontology considered that absolute or abiding existence belonged only to the transcendent, noetic realm of eternal Forms or Ideas. The particular has only contingent and temporary existence. Aristotle took a different view and built his metaphysical system on the recognition of the existence of concrete, particular individuals; but his conviction that dissolution or death brought the irreversible end of the individual meant that no ontology of personhood could emerge.[9] Permanence or continuity of existence might be attributed to the species or type, but not to the individual. Humanity might survive, the individual human could not.[10]

The Cappadocians combined Greek concern with ontology with the biblical conviction of the absolute sovereignty of a personal God. Nowhere in the Scriptures is an ontology or philosophy of personhood developed, but the Scriptures bear witness to a personal God. The creation of the

---

5. See Guthrie, *Greek Philosophy 1*, 26; Barnes, *Early Greek Philosophy*, 17–19; Vogel, *Studies in Greek Philosophy*. "Greek thought in all its variations . . . operated with what we might call a *closed ontology*," Zizioulas, "Human Capacity and Human Incapacity," 403, n.1; cf. Zizioulas, *Being as Communion*, 29f.; Mascall, *Openness of Being*, 264f.

6. See, e.g., Eliade, History of Religious Ideas 1, 291.

7. See Kierkegaard, *Either/Or*, 42–162. Also Meredith "Fate," *EEC*, 423f.; Pelikan, *Christianity and Classical Culture*, 152–65. Compare, however, Jones, *Ancient and Modern*, 166: "[B]oth men and gods are one-hundred percent responsible for everything, all the time. Later Greek tragedians put this notion at the very centre of their tragedies." But do they have responsibility without power? Or is fate deterministic, not of *actions*, but only of their *consequences* (cf. pseudo-Plutarch *De fato*)? Fate and a deterministic understanding of man came to figure prominently in the various Gnostic systems. *EEC*, 60.

8. Josipovici explores Kierkegaard's account of the Greek understanding of the individual as embedded in "the substantial categories of state, family, and destiny," Josipovici, *Book of God*, 248–53.

9. Technically, "individual substances" or "first substances," see *Categories*, 2a11–14; 34–5; 4a10–13; 2b3–6; cf. *Metaphysics* 1003a, 2. On substance in Aristotle see Mackinnon, "Aristotle's Conception of Substance," 97ff.

10. On the survival, not of the individual, but of humanity—through the succession of individuals, see *De Anima* II.4 415b, 6–7. On the survival of *part* of the soul (the "active intellect") see *De Anima* II.4 430a17, 24.

world is presented as God's free act, not as an inevitable result or outwork-ing of his nature.[11] Creation has its beginning in the personal choice of God—in the "who" of the divine persons, not in the "what" of their nature. Similarly, the Scriptures present God as actively involved in the world's history. But this involvement is according to the divine choice, the divine will. God is not compelled or obliged to act as he does. (If we say that God is compelled by his own love, we are only saying that, being ever free, he always *chooses* to be concerned for the world's welfare, even when the world does not deserve that love.[12]) The doctrine of the Trinity derived directly from the Church's desire to remain faithful to the biblical account of God's action in and on behalf of the world. That the Cappadocians were able to give the inchoate trinitarianism of the earliest Christian centuries new and more profound articulation was possible precisely because they sought to remain faithful to biblical witness while yet also being willing to draw on insights from Greek philosophy.

In developing their trinitarianism the Cappadocians did not intend to give a systematic philosophically satisfying account of God's nature and being. Significantly, their account of the divine life and being uses non-tech-nical, everyday language.[13] Their aim, rather, seems to have been to prevent misinterpretation or misrepresentation of the understanding of God which they found in the Scriptures and early Christian tradition. They sought to adhere to biblical monotheism while yet acknowledging the personal par-ticularity of Father, Son, and Holy Spirit. They could not do otherwise and be faithful to Scripture.

Crucial to their formulation of Trinitarian doctrine was the acknowl-edgement of the distinct particularity of each divine person. Therefore they came to explain the divine unity in terms of personal communion, rather than identity of essence. Vital here was their decision to give new sense to the term *hypostasis*. Previously *hypostasis* had been used interchangeably with *ousia*. Both denoted "substance" or "underlying reality"—and generally designated physical (or quasi-physical) constituent nature.[14] Neither *hypostasis* nor *ousia*

11. See Florovsky, *Creation and Redemption*, 43–78. See May, *Creatio ex Nihilo*, esp. 166–68, 176.

12. Beginning in the Old Testament, the unfolding biblical story can be seen as an account of the discovery of who God is and of what he is like. A recognition that God is, in some sense, personal is present from the beginning, but quite what this means only emerges gradually.

13. Meyendorff, *Byzantine Theology*, 180–81.

14. Cf. Athanasius, *Letter to the Bishops of Egypt and Lybia* (PG26:1036b): "*hypostais* is *ousia* and has no other meaning apart from being (*to ōn*) itself. . . . For *hypostais* and *ousia* are existence (*huparxis*) . . . ." Also Zizioulas, *Being as Communion*, 36, n.23.

carried any personalist overtones. By using *hypostasis* to denote the *personal reality* of Father, Son, and Spirit, while yet allowing the term to retain something of its substantialist connotations, the Cappadocians opened the way for *person* to be recognized as the *primary*—i.e., most fundamental, most basic—ontological category. The implications of this philosophical breakthrough have yet to be fully explored or exploited.

If, on the one hand, the Cappadocians had to resist the substantialist, "naturalist" trend in Greek thought, they had, on the other, also to deal with a tendency in Roman thought producing a problem almost diametrically opposite. The Romans were little given to philosophical speculation. Their concerns were practical. Man was understood as a social or political being. He was defined therefore largely by his relationships. Ontology, permanence, substance—these were unimportant. But Roman interest in relationships provided no foundation for a personalist ontology. One individual might play many roles, consecutively or simultaneously. Being defined by these roles, he had little or no significant existence beyond them. It is to Tertullian, with a background in Roman law, that the first use is attributed in relation to God of the expression *una substantia, tres personae*.[15] But here the risk of functionalism remained. This terminology might be used in a modalist way, to indicate one God exercising three roles.[16] It was an awareness of just this risk that made the Greeks reluctant to adopt in theological discourse the Greek term equivalent to *persona*, namely *prosōpon*.[17] Both *persona* and *prosōpon* were in use to designate the theatrical mask (and by extension the theatrical role)—a usage without ontological implications.

Personhood and Nature

In their use of the phrase "one substance (*ousia*) and three persons (*hypostases*)" the Cappadocians opened the way for a specifically Christian doctrine of God. In emphasizing the ontological priority of personhood, they removed from their theology any suggestion that the divine life might be conditioned by a pre-existent (or ontologically prior) divine nature or

15. *Against Praxeas*, 11–12 (PL2:1670d).

16. Cf. Basil, *Ep.* 236:6 (NPNF 8, Second Series, 276); Zizioulas, *Being as Communion*, 37, n. 25.

17. "[*Persona*] did not meet with acceptance in the East *precisely because the term 'person' lacked an ontological content* . . . ," Zizioulas, *Being as Communion*, 37. As Zizioulas goes on to point out, if the meaning of *hypostasis* had not been modified away from a strictly substantialist (i.e., quasi-materialist) sense then *treis hypostases* might have been interpreted as suggesting tritheism.

substance—or by anything else. (It is often alleged that a major weakness in Western theology is that it gives nature priority over personhood.[18])

For Zizioulas, the origin and ground of the divine life rests in the *person* of the Father,[19] and not in some primordial generic nature. The divine persons have their being, not through participation in a common nature, but through loving communion with one another, that is, through the unconditioned and unconditional flow of love between them. The Father gives himself to the Son and Spirit fully and unstintingly, to each in a distinct way. And they in turn give of themselves to him—and to one another. In both "bearing" the Father's love and in answering to it, Son and Spirit have their being: they become who they are, they *are* who they are. But in returning the Father's love, the Son and Spirit do not return to him a "nature" that they possess: they *give themselves*. Within this flow and reflow of love, all that belongs to any one of the divine person belongs to all three, except that the distinct personhood of each (the *who* of each—the *mode* of being who they are) remains incommunicable.[20]

Importantly the divine nature (or substance) exists only as actualized in the individual particularity of one or other of the divine persons. As Zizioulas says, the divine nature does not exist "naked" or "without hypostases . . . , without a 'mode of existence.'"[21] Within the life of the Trinity, there is no conflict between the divine persons and their common nature—between who they are and what they are. To counter any suggestion that the divine nature might have priority over personhood, it would be safer to say that the divine nature "belongs to" the divine persons, rather than *vice versa*. The depth and perfection of the exchange of love between the divine persons

18. See Régnon, *la Sainte Trinité* I, 251f., 433f.; cf. Kelly, *Early Christian Doctrines*, 136. The approach is criticized by Congar, *Holy Spirit*, vol. 3, xviff., 72–78. But the tendency remains. For example, "[God] knows no constraint apart from his own nature . . . and *cannot* abuse his power" (Yarnold, *Time for God*, 27). It would show greater respect for the divine personhood and freedom to say that he *does not* abuse his power. Cf. Plantinga, *Does God Have a Nature?*

Significantly, Zizioulas points to a corresponding divergence in Christology: Cyril of Alexandria takes the *hypostasis* of the Son as the starting-point for Christology, the *Tome* of Pope Leo I begins from the "natures" or "substances" (Zizioulas, *Being as Communion*, 55).

19. Zizioulas, *Being as Communion*, 40f. Significantly, while the Father must be acknowledged as the source of the godhead, the co-equality of the three divine persons is evident in the way that each in turn is the "ground" of the communion (or the unity) between the other two.

20. Cf. John of Damascus, *Orth. Faith* 1.14 (PG94:859b).

21. Zizioulas, *Being as Communion*, 41ff. See the note, 41, n.37; also Zizioulas, "Human Capacity and Human Incapacity," 436. Cf. Basil, *Ep.* 38:2, (PG32:325ff.); Gregory Nyssa, *Eun.* 1 (PG45:337).

means, however, that each divine person can be said to possess the *whole* divine nature. But there is no gap between the divine persons, so that *all* that belongs to any one belongs also to each of the others (except for *who* he is—since the *who* is what he is, not something that belongs to him but *is* who he is). Crucially, the divine action is always seen as *one* action, so that each divine act belongs fully to each of the divine persons—though to each in his own way.[22] Because of the communion between the divine persons and the unity of divine action, each of the divine persons is God, not just a part or an "aspect" of God, nor just a representative of the godhead.[23]

The nature of personhood becomes clearer if we distinguish two kinds of relationship. First, there are relationships where one self-contained individual relates to others from within the security of (supposed) independence and self-reliance. Such relationships are limited by fear; in relating to others we risk what we already have (or what we think we have).[24] Contrast this with relationships grounded in self-giving love and self-sacrifice. Such relationships carry an inherent "risk."[25] The divine persons live in loving relationships of just this second "risky" kind. And it is into such relationships that they invite created human persons. Relationships of this second kind lead to what can be termed *communion*. (Note that individualism is a culture grounded in self-reliance and self-concern. A personalist culture is a culture of communion.) At the crucifixion the incarnate Son entered into fullness of "risky" relationship to the Father.

Important here is the notion of mutual indwelling, of coinherence (*perichōrēsis, circumincessio*). This term, first used in Christology to describe the relationship between the incarnate Son's two natures,[26] was subsequently used to describe the relationship between the persons in the Trinity.[27] But

22. Prestige, *God in Patristic Thought*, 257–60.

23. "When we ascribe divinity to the Father, Son and Spirit, the particular beings of Father, Son and Spirit are bearers of the totality of nature; in other words, each of the divine persons *is* God," Schwöbel, *Persons Human and Divine*, 14.

24. Cf. Schwöbel, "Human Being as Relational Being," 158.

25. On the importance of the way in which Christ makes himself vulnerable, with "no objectified security to rely on," see Zizioulas, "Human Capacity and Human Incapacity," 422.

26. Cf. Gregory Nazianzen, *Ep.* 101, 87c; [*Ep.* 101:6; (SC 208:38)]—though here only the verb (*perichōrēō*) is used.

27. Cf. Meyendorff, *Byzantine Theology*, 186f. Maximus was the first patristic writer to use the substantive *perichōrēsis*; he used it to speak of the relationship between the two natures of the incarnate Christ. It was only in the decades after Maximus that the anonymous writer known as pseudo-Cyril saw the value of the term *perichōrēsis* for describing the relationships within the Trinity (*Trin.* 9, 10, 23; PG77). Later John of Damascus sanctioned and popularized this theme (*Orth. Faith* 1.8; PG94:829a). But even

the concept is crucial for Christian anthropology. Some have already be-gun to explore the implications of this concept for ecclesiology—Florovsky, Zizioulas and Sophrony among them.[28] But more work needs to be done, especially in exploring its implications for the ordering of Christian com-munity life and for Christian education.

---

before the term came to be used with reference to the intra-Trinitarian relationships, the idea of co-inherence or mutual indwelling of the divine persons was developing: the Cappadocians adopted it from Athanasius, and Cyril developed it further. See Prestige, *God in Patristic Thought*, 282–99; Prestige, "'*perichōreō* and *perichōrēsis*,'" 242–52; Har-rison, "Perichoresis in the Greek Fathers," 35–65 and Stramara, "Gregory of Nyssa's Terminology," 257–63. Stramara shows that although Gregory does not use *perichōreō* or its cognates the *notion* is central to his thought. Similarly we can see that although the term does not occur in the New Testament, the notion of mutual indwelling is fundamental to the Johannine understanding of the Son's relationship to the Father—in this connection Gregory of Nyssa makes frequent reference to John 10:38 and 17:21 (see Stramara, "Gregory of Nyssa's Terminology," 258, n.10). In like manner the notion of mutual indwelling is as fundamental as any to the New Testament understanding of the Christian's relationship to Christ (cf. John 14:11; 15:9; Rom 12:5; Gal 5:13–14, etc.). Cf. the Johannine theme of the mutual indwelling of Christ and his followers, John 14:23; 15:4, etc.

28. Florovsky, "*Sobornost*," 55, 59, 61f.; Sophrony, *His Life is Mine*, 68f., 118; Zizioulas, "On Being a Person," 40, 46. Note Charles Williams interest in this theme (Williams, *Descent of the Dove*, 10, 162, 234–35 and *passim*. Indeed, *Descent of the Dove* is dedicated to "The Companions of the Co-inherence," a group of people inspired by William's vision. See Carpenter, *Inklings*, 103–7.

5

Personhood Human and Divine[1]

IN THE WAKE OF the development of the doctrine of the Trinity and the recognition of an ontological distinction between person and nature/substance, a doctrine of the incarnation emerged. Together these opened the way for the development of a specifically Christian anthropology.[2] A key issue in the age-long discussion about what it is to be man has been the interpretation of the biblical assertion that man is "in the divine image" (Gen 1:26–27; 5:1). I cannot attempt to recount the history of the debate around this issue.[3] But I would suggest that nothing is more fundamental to human make-up—and nothing more remarkable about man—than that he is a personal, hypostatic being. It is this, above all, that makes him "in the image."

---

1. In this chapter I repeatedly use the terms "man," "he," and "his" for the human person, using the terms in that inclusive sense which takes in all human person, male or female, adult or child (and sometimes collective humankind). While drafting the text I tried various alternatives; time and again, for example, spelling out "all men and women," "she or he," etc., but I felt this made the text unwieldy and unnecessarily confusing. I apologize if my use of "man" and "he" in this inclusive sense gives offence. (See also p. xii above.)

2. Anthropology here equates more or less to ecclesiology.

3. On the patristic theology of the image see Garrett, *EEC*, 561; also Cairns, *Image of God in Man*, chs. 1–8; Camelot, "Théologie de l'Image de Dieu"; Lampe, *PGL*, 410–16, esp. 413–14; Lossky, *Image and Likeness*, 125–39; Thunberg, *Microcosm and Mediator*, 120–39. Nellas explains that although the "image" theme does not exhaust every aspect of Orthodox anthropology, nevertheless, "the 'image' theme serves as an axis around which not only Orthodox cosmology but also Orthodox anthropology and Christology are organized," Nellas, *Deification in Christ*, 21f., cf. 22, n.6.

Note that I do not look here at that tradition, strong in the West and generally associated with Augustine, that has seen the *individual* human person as having been made in the image of the Trinity; see Louth, *Maximus the Confessor*, 211, n.120. When "in the image" is taken to refer to the individual human person being in image of the Trinity it can minister to just that individualism criticized above. I believe that the alternatives which I explore in this section have much more to offer the Church today (cf. Gunton, "Trinity, Ontology and Anthropology," esp. 49, 56, 58–61). Gregory of Nyssa sees "in the image" as applying to mankind as a whole, collectively (*On Man* 16:16f.; PG16:185b. See NPNF, Second Series, V, 406, esp. 406, n.6). Sophrony (*On Prayer*, 57): "[Prayer] shows us that . . . all mankind in its source and by its nature, is *one being, one man*."

In chapter 4, I outlined three aspects of the hypostatic existence of the Trinity. Each of these has significance for human existence and the human vocation: specifically, (i) each human person is uniquely and inviolably who he is; (ii) humanity as a whole is called to live one life, a life in which each person has his life and being, his joy and his hope, in each of the others; (iii) each human person has a capacity (and a calling) to embody all that rightly belongs to human nature: each is called to be *man* not just *a man*—though, somewhat paradoxically, each person will be *man* in a distinct way, unique to himself.[4]

But human personhood differs from divine personhood. In particular, although each human person is a unique and irreplaceable, a distinct "someone," he has his existence contingently—by divine gift, not by right.[5] And although the divine persons choose to give each human person an eternal destiny, the ontological gulf between the divine persons and created humanity is inviolable.[6] Moreover, the persons of the Trinity, as divine beings, eternally have fullness of personhood, while created human persons come into being only with what might be termed incipient (or potential) personhood. They are not in fullness of relation to God, to one another, to their own created nature, or to creation in general. And if they are to attain to such fullness, they have a work to do. Boojamra writes, "What we have in the patristic tradition is dynamic anthropology and personhood as the focus of history and salvation; personality development is foundational to Christian theology . . . ."[7] He adds later that nobody is born with "fully developed" personhood.[8] Meyendorff explains:

> [M]an, created in the image of God, is called to achieve freely a "divine similitude"; his relationship to God is both a givenness and a task.[9]

4. Cf. Lossky, *Mystical Theology*, 114–22; 1975, 188–89; also de Lubac, *Catholicisme*, 288.

5. Cf. Florovsky, *Creation and Redemption*, 45–47.

6. Athanasius, *Arains* 1:20 (PG26:55a); Maximus, *Cent. Car.* 3:25 (PG90:1024bc); Meyendorff *Byzantine Theology*, 129–31, 138.

7. Boojamra, *Foundations*, 118. Here he notes: "I think it is in the context of personhood that Orthodox pedagogues can make a genuine contribution to contemporary pedagogical issues."

8. Boojamra, *Foundations*, 119.

9. Meyendorf, *Byzantine Theology*, 2. Here Meyendorff also explains: "The central theme, or intuition, of Byzantine theology is that man's nature is not a static, 'closed,' autonomous entity, but a dynamic reality, determined in its very essence by its relationship to God." (Cf. Meyendorff, *Byzantine Theology*, 139–40). For man as poised in dynamic relationship to God, see Lossky, *Image and Likeness*, 139. All but the most reductionist views about human make-up suggest that to be a person is to be "in a

Clement of Alexandria, Origen, and Irenaeus all make just this point; while Gregory of Nyssa presents it in particularly subtle and sophisticated form.[10] Reflecting on Cabasilas' synthesis of these ideas, Nellas argues that the phrase "in the image" "implies a gift within man but also a goal set before him." It "constitutes man's *being*, but only in potentiality." He continues:

> The "in the image" is a real power, a pledge leading to a marriage which is hypostatic union, the unconfused but real and fulfilling mixture and comingling of the divine and human natures. Only then does the iconic being of man become real *authentic* being. Man finds in the Archetype [i.e., the Son] his true ontological meaning.[11]

The human vocation to personal growth, that is man's progress towards hypostatic union, must be accomplished within the opportunities which spatio-temporal life provides. This key point for a theology of Christian education can best be understood in relation to other aspects of what it means for man to be "in the image."

Human life, being hypostatic, is inherently relational and communal. The human person is created, not for self-sufficiency as an isolated individual, but to live in fullness of relationship with God and with the rest of humanity. Corporate humanity is called to image the perfect communion eternally existing between the divine persons. They are called to have their very life and being, their hope and their joy, in one another—just as the divine persons do. Fallen man is unable to live in such communion; he is unable even to imagine it. Paul, however, speaks of those in the Church not only as members of Christ, but as "members of one another" (Rom 12:5). This was already implicit in the "two became one flesh" of Gen 2:24. St Silouan held that the gospel command "Love your neighbor as yourself" carried ontological implications: in some sense, one's neighbor is oneself.[12] The one divine life is lived by three divine persons; and the (essentially) one human life is to be lived by myriad human persons.[13]

Where such perfect inter-personal communion exists the persons involved come to share all that belongs to their common nature—all that belong to each one. Christ in his risen glory, as both God and man and fully

---

process of becoming a person in the personal actualization of human possibilities" (see Schwöbel, *Persons Human and Divine*, 6).

10. See Muckle, "Gregory of Nyssa on Man as the Image of God."

11. Nellas, Deification in Christ, 37.

12. Sophrony, *Saint Silouan*, 371; cf. Sophrony, *On Prayer*, 57.

13. Cf. Gregory of Nyssa, *On Man* 5 (PG 44:185cd). Cf. Sophrony, "The Unity of the Church in the Image of the Trinity."

in communion with the Spirit, opens himself to be in communion with the members of the Church; insofar as anyone shares Christ's life so he or she shares all that belongs to Christ's divine-human nature, his divine-human life, and all that belongs to any other member of his body, the Church. Of the Eucharist, where the possibility of living in such communion with Christ and with others is opened up, Zizioulas explains: "There Christ is 'parted but not divided' and every communicant is the *whole Christ and the whole Church*."[14] Echoing Florovsky, Silouan, and Sophrony he writes:

> [T]he importance of Christ in this respect is that personhood is now objectively restored *not on the level of an individual* but *on the level of true personhood* which is capable of bearing *human nature in its catholicity*.[15]

It is only the fully mature human person, however, who can be in fullness of communion with Christ and all that is his.[16]

Fallen man inhabits a world of dualism, conflict, and tension. Fallen human beings find themselves divided from one another and divided within themselves. They experience neither themselves nor corporate humanity as unified wholes. But the saints perceive a different reality—one existing alongside, within or beyond the reality perceived by fallen man. United to the risen Christ they see that God's reign has already been established and that a whole new order of relationships *already exists:* it is one in which they already live. They find that through their willingness to be in communion with Christ they have been introduced into a life where all that belongs to this world has been rendered good. Even suffering can now serve a good purpose; it is the means through which they can be of service to the world and can make progress towards Christ-likeness. Labouring to reverse evil— even if only by not allowing it to drive them to despair—their communion with Christ is deepened. As they share more fully in his life, so they enter

---

14. Zizioulas, *Being as Communion*, 6of. Italics added.

15. Zizioulas, "Human Capacity and Human Incapacity," 435, italics added; see also 435 nn.1–2. Florovsky writes: "In catholic transfiguration personality receives strength and power to express [I would say to *embody*] the life of the whole," Florovsky, "*Sobornost*," 62. Cf. Mantzarides, *Deification of Man*, 154; Yannaras, *Freedom of Morality*, 266, n.1). For discussion of "catholic personality" see Schroeder, "Suffering Towards Personhood." For OT background see Robinson, *The Hebrew Conception of Corporate Personality*; Johnson, *The One and the Many*; *NJBC*, 77:69–74.

16. John Damascene explains that while the community and union of divine persons exists in reality, in men such community and union is only known to exist "by reason and reflection" (*Orth. Faith*, 1:8; PG94:828a). But this is not so for the saints, those who have so entered into the new life available in Christ. They see this communion realized (see Sophrony, *His Life is Mine*, 64).

into an experience of the communal, corporate dimension in human life quite inaccessible to those trapped in a fallen worldview and in the desire to perpetuate a separate autonomous existence. Silouan is said to have "prayed for the whole world as for himself,"[17] and his disciple, Sophrony, claimed *all* the sin of the world as his responsibility.[18]

Here it is important to look to another aspect of what it means for man to be created in the divine image. Human life images, not just the corporate life of the Trinity nor in some general sense the hypostatic life of the divine persons, but also specifically the hypostatic life of the Son. The Son's life is characterized by his grateful reception and loving *return* to the Father of all that the Father has given him. His life is characterized, in other words, by *eucharist*. It follows that mature human life, in image of the Son's life, will be characterized by loving gratitude for the Father's goodness and loving (self-sacrificial) service of his will.[19] The mature Christian stands, thus, as mediator between God and creation. Towards creation he ministers on behalf of God, manifesting, indeed "incarnating," the love that God has for all creation. At the same time he also ministers on behalf of creation by enabling and articulating creation's response to the divine initiative.[20] Standing thus in the Son's work—i.e., in that redemption and reconciliation which the divine persons ever wish to effect—he stands at that place where the Spirit is active and the divine love reaches out into the world. He stands, in other words, in the cross—and thereby he stands also in the divine glory.

Human Nature and the Human Person

Because the divine persons are perfect in their personhood there is no gap or interval, no tension or conflict between them and their nature. They are as persons all that their nature makes possible. It is not so for fallen man. Fallen man is not in command or control of his nature. He is not at one with it. The work of Christian formation—more generally, the work

17. Sophrony, *Silouan the Athonite*, see 222–28; 407ff., 493; cf. Sophrony, *On Prayer*, 17–19, 109–14 (cf. Matt 22:39; Lev 19:180; also Sophrony, *Wisdom from Mount Athos*, 15.

18. Sophrony, *On Prayer*, 115. Zossima in Dostoevsky's *Brothers Karamazov* says: "Make yourself responsible for all human beings and the whole world." In *Crime and Punishment* Dostoevsky writes: "Everybody lives in suffering and it is possible that in one specific person may live everybody's suffering." See Schroeder, "Suffering Towards Personhood," 254.

19. Cf. Farrer, *Brink of Mystery*, 20.

20. Cf. Ware in Staniloae, *Experience of God*, vol. 1, xxii.

of human growth—looks to bringing man into harmony (or *communion*) with his nature.

The divine nature exists only in (and as) its personal actualization in (and as) the divine persons. Similarly, human nature cannot exist apart from its actualization in (or as) distinct human persons. But, somewhat paradoxically, the principal locus of this nature is not in any human person, not even primordial, idealized, mythical Adam. The principal locus of this nature is the divine person of the Son—defined by his *sonship*. The Son was ever the model for man. (That is why he is ground of the unity binding humanity into one.[21]) The Son lived in fullness of harmony with his (created) human nature—as no one before him ever had. (And as no one since him ever has—except through participation in him.) He lived in fullness of harmony with his human nature at every stage of his life, even in his death. Indeed, in his death (and in the glorification that flowed naturally from it as its fruit) we see man in the fullness of his potential. Nothing is possible to man or to human nature that was not accomplished or realized by the Son.

But what did the Son realize or accomplish? It can only have been the attainment of *virtue*, of *love*—nothing else. The Son did not demonstrate artistic brilliance, mastery of differential calculus, or insight into the geological formation of mountains. He did not run a super-fast marathon, jump over high buildings, or flap his arms and fly. What he did do was attain maturity in virtue—those virtues, those dispositions, which enable mature human relationship, which collectively can be called love, and which, so we might say, constitute human maturity.

Insofar as anyone has come to share Christ's life, live by his virtues, share his dispositions, that person will no longer be conditioned or determined by the things which determined his life when he was caught in his fallenness and bound to his sin- and fear-conditioned nature. This means, more explicitly, that he will no longer be conditioned or determined by a desire to perpetuate an independent existence in disregard both of the needs of others and, ultimately, of God's purposes. (In other words, he will not be conditioned or determined by that self-love—Greek: *philautia*—against which the ascetic tradition of the Church rails.[22])

Importantly, the mature human person, that is, the human person fully united with Christ, will be at one with his or her created human nature. He of she will be at one with that nature *as that nature as God intends it to be—and always intended it to be.* Christ did not come to destroy human

---

21. Ziziouas, "Human Capacity and Human Incapacity," 440ff., esp. 441 (a), 442 (d–e).

22. See Hausherr, *Philautie.*

nature. He came to redeem and perfect it.[23] This he did by bringing his human nature into fullness of communion with his own divine nature; or to put the same thing differently, this he did by bringing his created human will into union with the eternal divine will. It was thus that he attained those virtues, those dispositions which make life in the kingdom possible. It was thus that he enabled his created human nature (and with it potentially all created human nature[24]) to become what it had always been intended to be: Spirit-bearing. In becoming Spirit-bearing, created human nature became "fitted for" or "appropriate to" the eternal life of the kingdom.

Since Pentecost, by the Son's gift, the Church can share in and live by that renewed, re-created nature. The person who appropriates that life, in the words of St Maximus, "while remaining in his soul and body entirely man by nature, . . . becomes *in his soul and body* entirely God by grace."[25] Such a person does not (of course) become a divine person, but he does come to share the divine life. He lives in and by the Holy Spirit, or, as Byzantine tradition has it, he lives in and by the "divine energies."[26] (The so-called *communicatio idiomatum.*[27])

Insofar as anyone lives by grace, or by virtue, or within the divine energies—these amount to the same thing—everything belonging to his nature (i.e., that particularization of human nature that is his particular body, mind, emotions, etc.) is opened to the work and action of the Holy Spirit.[28] His created nature becomes sacramental. Or we might say it becomes iconographic: it both discloses his personhood and acts as a vehicle, an instrument, or a medium of his *personal presence*. Indeed, his redeemed (but created) nature will disclose, not only the truth of his own existence, but the goal of all human life—since all human life has but one and the same goal. Mature created human life will disclose and mediate the divine life. It becomes the locus of convergence and communion between the created and the divine. What was first brought into being in the humanity of the incarnate Son now comes into being, by divine gift (grace), in the created

23. Cf. Lossky, *Image and Likeness*, 114.

24. See p. 55 above.

25. Maximus, *Amb.* 7 (PG91:1088c). Emphasis added.

26. Athanasius, *Arians* I.20 (PG26:55a); Basil *Ep.* 234.1 (NPNF 8, Second Series, 274). Also Meyendorff, *Byzantine Theology*, 130–32; Lossky, *Image and Likeness*, 126–37; Bobrinskoy, *Mystery of the Trinity*, 315–16; Musther, "Exploration into God," 68–71, esp. 70 n.28. Palamas is, of course, important; see Meyendorff, *Study of Gregory Palamas*, 202–27; Thunberg, *Man and the Cosmos*, 137–43.

27. See Meyendorff, *Christ in Eastern Christian Thought*, 24–27; Meyendorff, *Byzantine Theology*, 154–55.

28. Cf. Basil, *HS* 9.23 (PG32:109).

humanity of the Son's followers—and in all their diversity, for each is a unique expression of that humanity. The Son became man. He now enables his followers to become divine. As Irenaeus has it, in becoming all that we are he opened the way for us to become all that he is.[29]

I have said that the Son is the model for humanity, but some clarification is needed. Nellas explored the important idea that the archetype after which man was fashioned was always the *incarnate* Logos, or indeed, the perfected *eschatological* Christ *in his completion*—crucified and glorified and in fullness of right relationship to the Father.[30] But how could the incarnate or eschatological Christ be the archetype for created man when the incarnation had yet to take place? Nellas is among those who see the incarnation as part of the eternal divine plan, and not as something occasioned only by the fall and the need for redemption. The fall affected the character of the work required of the incarnate Christ, but was not the primary cause of the incarnation. "In relation to Christ man 'was made in the beginning as if to a standard or a pattern . . . so that he could receive God.'"[31] Quoting Cabasilas, Nellas explains:

> God created human nature with no other end in view . . . but this, that when he needed to be born he should receive his mother from that nature. And, having established human nature first as a necessary standard [in the person of the God-man, Christ], he then forms man in accord with it.[32]

The possibility of the incarnation is grounded in the fact that man has a *personal* life, and the foundation of the human vocation, what makes its fulfillment possible, is the fact that human persons are created as *persons*. But the fulfillment of the human vocation belonging to each and every (created) human person cannot be accomplished in or by anyone who will not

29. Cf. *Haer.* 5, prologue; cf. Athanasius, *Inc.* 54:3 (PG25:192b), also *Inc.* 8 (PG26:996c).

30. Nellas, *Deification in Christ*, 34ff.; cf. Manzarides, *Deification of Man*, 41f. Nellas looks to Nicholas Cabasilas (spelling the name "Kavasilas"), who makes this point in a decisive way: "It was for the new man that human nature was originally created; it was for him that intellect and desire were prepared. We received rationality that we might know Christ, desire that we might run towards him. We possessed memory that we might bear him in us. . . . For the old Adam was not the image for the new, but the new is a model for the old." Cabasilas, *Life* 6 (PG 150:680a), quoted Nellas, *Deification in Christ*, 34f. See especially the arguments Nellas presents on 37–39.

31. Nellas, *Deification in Christ*, 35f., quoting Cabasilas, *Life* (PG 150:560d). See esp. Nellas, *Deification in Christ*, 37.

32. Nellas, *Deification in Christ*, 36; quoting Cabasilas, *I Theomitor* (edited by P. Nellas, (Athens 1974) 150–52.

allow Christ to recapitulate in him the work of the incarnation. Each human person's principal work is to *allow* this to happen, or, in other words, to co-operate with God as this work which God wills and initiates moves forward. The very decision to cooperate with God—this itself can only be a personal work, a personal decision, grounded in God's will and realized through human cooperation with the divine initiative.

This is a key point for understanding both the tradition of the Church and the nature of the Church's educational ministry. For insofar as human persons allow Christ to recapitulate within them the way of growth which he accomplished through the course of his life on earth, they can know him from, as it were, the "inside." Thus, and only thus, can they know both what happened during the Son's incarnation and what his life is like now—his risen and glorified life. But participation in Christ brings human beings also to participation in one another's lives, i.e., participation in (or communion in) other peoples lives. The life of Christ is *one* life and those who are united to him share what can only ever be one and the same life. Therefore, as well as standing in Christ and within his life they also stand, so to speak, "inside" one another's lives—or simply "inside" one another. They are "members of one another" (Rom 12:5); "one flesh" (Gen 1:24)—while yet each human person remains eternally and inviolably who he or she is. (See what was said above about co-inherence; p. 51, n. 28.)

Freedom and Human Growth

Human persons can attain maturity and embody (or realize) human nature through freely choosing to live within the life offered by the Son; that is, through participation in that flow and re-flow of self-forgetful love that defines the Son's life.[33] The fact that man can act *freely* is crucial here. Growth towards maturity can be seen as growth towards fullness of freedom. Submission to the demands of fallen nature reduces the human being to something less than a person.[34] The challenge is to acquire the *freedom* offered by the Holy Spirit. "Where the Spirit of the Lord is, there is freedom" (2 Cor 3:17; cf. Rom 8:22). Christian asceticism looks to the acquisition of freedom. "Fasting is a test in which the personality [i.e., person] defies the self [i.e., the self-willed, un-free ego]. . . . [T]he self has to be forsaken by the whole being [= the person]."[35] Even the call to obedience has to be seen in these terms. Mere blind obedience can lead to the paralysis of the will;

33. Cf. Schwöbel, "Persons Human and Divine," 15.
34. See Zizioulas, "Human Capacity and Human Incapacity," 409f., 428–33.
35. Matthew the Poor, *Communion of Love*, 117.

Christian obedience, exercised within the ordered life of the Church, looks, not to the suppression of human freedom but rather to freeing the Christian from the demands of his fallenness—from the oppression and slavery that fallenness imposes.

Deification

The ultimate goal of Christian growth is sanctification or deification (*theosis, theopoiesis*), also termed *divinization*.[36] In the development and articulation of its doctrine of deification the Church looked back, in the first place, to various biblical texts, notably 2 Pet 1:4 (but also, for example, Rom 8; John 14–17), which says that those who are united to Christ become "partakers of the divine nature" (*theias koinōoi phuseōs*). The doctrine would subsequently undergo much development, but even in 2 Peter those who partake of the divine nature are said to have "escaped the corruption that is in the world because of passion" (*apophugontes tēs tō epithumia phthras*)— where *passion* can be interpreted as *subjection to nature*. Subsequent verses encourage ascetic discipline and the acquisition of virtue (vv. 5–11); for thereby the Christian comes "to confirm" (*bebaian*) the divine "call and election" (v. 10). Personal response to the divine initiative—a communion of wills—facilitates the inflowing of the divine life and the regeneration of human nature. Importantly it is primarily the human *person*, not human nature, who is the "object" of deification.[37] Man's nature can enter into and

36. Boojamra (*Foundations*, 31, 72) expressly presents theosis as the goal of all Christian formation. On theosis/divinization see Dalmais, *DS*, 1376–89; Gross, *La divinisation du chrétien*; cf. *Lossky, Image and Likeness*, 97–110; Lossky, *Vision of God*, 80–83, 108–10, 124–37; Lot-Borodine, *Déification de l'homme*; Louth, "Mahood into God"; Mantzaridis, *Deification of Man*, esp. chs. 1 and 5; Mantzaridis, *Orthodox Spiritual Life*, ch. 16; Meyendorff, *Gregory Palamas*, 175–78; further refs. *EEC* 338a–340b. See also Banks, *Deification in Eastern Orthodoxy*.

The doctrine of deification developed more fully in the East, but is by no means unknown in the West. For Western tradition, Dalmais, *DS*, 1370–76; Bonner, "Augustine's Conception of Deification"; Morris, *Discovery of the Individual*, 154–57; Dicken, *Crucible of Love*, 358ff, 368, 374. For Anglican tradition see Keble, *Letters of Spiritual Counsel*, 39; 1888, esp. xciv and xcix–c; also Allchin, *Participation in God*.

I would also refer to a lecture by Thomas Hopko in which he states that much of the literature of the Western Church, especially that of its monastic and ascetic tradition, "has to do with real deification." Among others, he mentions John of the Cross, Teresa of Avila, and Jan van Ruysbroeck. "I could easily write an essay proving that the real functioning theology of someone like John of the Cross was absolutely compatible with Palamism. And in fact he taught divinization," Hopko, TH795A.

37. Of course, the human person does not become a *divine* person; he remains a created person, but he shares (personally) in the divine life. See Maximus, *Thal.* 61:16 (PG90:44d); *Amb.* 10 (PG91: 1144c).

appropriate that transformation won for it by Christ, but only insofar as the human person chooses to allow that to happen.

Lossky, commenting on Maximus, writes: "[F]rom the first stage onward the way of Christian perfection . . . is the way of deification enabling us to transcend by grace the limitations of nature."[38] Fallen man is determined by his nature—that is by his past and his culture. And fallen man's (misplaced or mistaken) hopes, fears, joys, and griefs work together to maintain the *status quo*—that is, help to perpetuate his *fallenness*.[39] Ultimately, what determines fallen man is death and fear of death (cf. Heb 2:17; Rom 8:1). For fallen man death represents failure and loss. It is the ultimate defeat. It is a commonplace, however, that for the saint death is but the gateway to life.[40] Paul sees the Christian as called to appropriate Christ's victory over death. And, as Mother Maria Gysi says, if "Christ did not die from the seed of corruption inside him" but "purely . . . as a self-offering to God,"[41] then there is an abiding, enduring dimension to his death. Christian perfection lies beyond death. Being in Christ's victory places the Christian "inside" Christ's death, where he will share Christ's perpetual self-giving, his perpetual dying "into the hands of the Father." Death is integral to the divine life. Bouyer writes,

> [T]he death that is necessary for redemption after sin is only . . . one manifestation of that death to self which is ineluctably present at the heart of every possible participation of the creature, even intact, in a love, a life which are the very life and love of God.[42]

This is Paul's "wisdom of the cross" (1 Cor 2:6ff.; Rom 6:9, etc.). Insofar as the Christian shares Christ's life—a life eternal, a life beyond threat of death or destruction—he will not only be unafraid of death but will not need to seek to secure his own future or perpetuate an independent existence. In other words, *he will feel no need to sin.*[43]

38. Lossky, *Image and Likeness*, 109. See also Staniloae, *Experience of God*, vol. 1, 20, 25f.; *Experience of God*, vol. 2, 191–200.

39. See Mantzarides, *Orthodox Spiritual Life*, 149–50.

40. In traditional mainstream Christian thought, death is not seen as an *escape* from life, an escape from a suffering "natural life" to a pain-free "supernatural life," but as the *fulfillment* of natural life in the new life of the Kingdom. See, for example, Schmemann, *O Death*, passim (especially, 89–115 = *For the Life of the World*, 95–106).

41. Gysi, *Realism of the Orthodox Faith*, 91.

42. Bouyer, *Christian Spirituality*, vol. I., 435; also Balthasar, *Kosmische Liturgie*, 191ff.

43. Cf. Heb 2:17 (and Rom 5:12 as explicated by Meyendorff, *Byzantine Theology*, 144), also Irenaeus, *Proof: see* Behr, *Apostolic Preaching*, 98. Ignatius, *Rom* 4:1–2; 6:1–8. Meyendorff writes, "There is . . . a consensus in Greek patristic and Byzantine traditions

Like Christ, the saints, have not "abandoned" or "escaped" their nature—neither their individual make-up nor their cultural background. But their openness to the End alters their relationship to the past and to their nature. They have become so "transparent" to the divine action that the Holy Spirit's redemptive and re-creative work can go forward in them and then extend through them, into the wider world—and even reach back, it is said, into the past.[44] It is just such transparency to the divine action that renders human nature "Spirit-bearing"—a vehicle of the divine presence. It also enables human nature to become a vehicle of the divine *action*: miracles can be worked through the saints.

Human Personhood and the Transformation of Human Nature

Zizioulas has distinguished three forms or "editions" of the human hypostasis—biological, ecclesial, and eucharistic. He defines the first two thus: "The *hypostasis of biological* existence is 'constituted' by man's conception and birth[45]"; "The *hypostasis of ecclesial* existence is constituted by the new birth of man, by baptism."[46] In seeking to define man's *sacramental or eucharistic hypostasis* Zizioulas suggests that the Epistle to the Hebrews uses the term *hypostasis* in the sense he intends—"as an ontology which has its roots in the future, in eschatology" (cf. Heb 11:1).[47]

Zizioulas' recognition that human existence passes through certain stages is useful. But some of his comments should be handled carefully. His account of a series of stages in hypostatic existence—each "constituted" in a unique manner—can be read as indicating that at each stage a new *person* emerges. He speaks of the hypostasis of ecclesial existence as "constituted' by the new birth at baptism."[48] In other writings, however, he speaks of "*the identification of the 'hypostasis' with the 'person.'*"[49] And surely, the *person* re-

---

[that] sinfulness [is] a consequence of mortality," *Byzantine Theology*, 145. Here Meyendorff makes reference to Theodore of Mopsuestia, Theodoret of Cyrus, John Chrysostom, Theophylact of Ohrida, Gregory Palamas and Maximus.

44. Sophrony, *His Life is Mine*, 69: "By virtue of the ontological unity of the human race, healing for us means healing for them, too"—namely, "our ancestors."

45. Zizioulas, *Being as Communion*, 50.

46. Zizioulas, *Being as Communion*, 53.

47. Zizioulas, *Being as Communion*, 58, see n.58. See *Being as Communion*, 49–65 for Zizioulas' discussion of the relationship between the three.

48. Zizioulas, *Being as Communion*, 53.

49. Zizioulas, *Being as Communion*, 36. The same point is expressly made at other places in the same essay (33, 35, 41, n.37, etc.). Cf. Zizioulas, "Human Capacity and

mains the same throughout the process of Christian growth. No new *person* comes into being at baptism. From the moment of his creation each human being is inviolably and eternally a person. Lossky states: "Personhood belongs to every human being by virtue of a singular and unique relationship to God who created him 'in his image.'"[50] Zizioulas may be making distinctions not accessible to people less competent than he in Greek. For example although *hypostasis* and *person* can be used synonymously—and we have seen Zizioulas do just that[51]—*hypostasis* means not simply "person," but something more akin to "*a mode of existence*, one which cannot be defined or identified other than as personal."[52] Thus, Zizioulas' "stages" could represent different modes (*tropoi* in the terminology of Maximus) of personal existence: first, man's creation as a person by divine fiat; secondly, the new mode of existence conferred on him at baptism; thirdly, his personhood fulfilled eschatologically through participation in the eucharistic life of Christ. Each created personal being remains for ever the same person, and ever exists in a personal mode of being—for this personal, hypostatic mode of existence is definitive, and as hypostatic being, the human person cannot be assumed into or combined with another hypostasis.[53] Each human person remains always and unchangingly a unique and distinct hypostasis. (Although by denying his personhood and by choosing to live in a less than personal way he can only fall into a state of quasi non-existence.[54]) We might say that his personhood—and the divine image within him—goes in and out of focus according to his willingness to live in dependence upon the divine will and in conformity to the divine purpose.

What, then, is the eschatological mode of being of which Zizioulas speaks? Through cooperation with divine grace, the human person can participate in the new humanity of the risen, glorified Christ. And whereas fallen man's relationship to his own created being and to creation in general is largely determined by the past—his genetic make-up along with the

---

Human Incapacity," 408–10.

50. Lossky, *Image and Likeness*, 137.

51. Amongst many others, Sophrony (*His Life is Mine*, 23), for example, does the same.

52. Cf. Zizioulas' comment that as a consequence of patristic theological innovation, personhood is no longer to be seen as "an adjunct to a being [but] *is itself the hypostasis of the being*," Zizioulas, *Being as Communion*, 39.

53. Cf. McIntosh's account (looking to Maximus) of how baptism, for example, brings man to a different mode (*tropos*) of existence—"another way of being *who* we are" (McIntosh, *Mystical Theology*, 195–98; cf. 56–62).

54. Cf. Walker, *Enemy Territory*, 34. On Satan as a "lapsed" or "non-person" see also Ratzinger, "Abschied vom Teufel," 233. On Sheol in the Scriptures see *JBC*, 77:170.

historical, social, and cultural circumstances of his upbringing, etc.—eschatological man is determined only by the End, that is, by Christ. And here he is "determined" only by love—which is not to be determined at all.[55]

True freedom is not the freedom to do what one wills;[56] it is, rather, the freedom *not to have to do what* fallen nature asks or demands. Fallen, sin-stricken man is inward-looking and self-obsessed; he is self-protective and ever fearful of loss. Man set free from sin is free to live in communion with others. His mode of being is hypostatic—personal. He also exists *ec*statically—he looks outward.[57] Living an ecstatic, outward-looking life, his existence becomes "catholic." He encompasses others, and is willing to be encompassed by them.[58]

---

55. Cf. Boojamra, *Foundations*, 87 F, where Elchaninov, *Diary of a Russian Priest*, 82, is quoted.

56. Cf. Zizioulas, "Human Capacity and Human Incapacity," 410, esp. n.1.

57. Cf. Zizioulas, "Human Capacity and Human Incapacity," 408–10.

58. Zizioulas, "Human Capacity and Human Incapacity," 408, n.3; 409.

6

The New Humanity, the New Creation

THE SON'S WORK RE-CREATED human nature. But this re-creation was not accomplished "naturally," through the uniting of his human nature with his divine nature. It was accomplished *personally*, through the use of his free will—his divine will and his human will; and it was accomplished *progressively*. As the Son's life unfolded and he suffered more and more of the torments and trials inevitable in a fallen, fearful, and sin-stricken world, so always he continued to choose to surrender himself to the divine will. In the process he brought his adopted humanity, step by step, into fullness of conformity with his eternal divinity. The process was completed on the cross. It was as he "gave up his spirit" and surrendered himself into the hands of the Father that he overcame the last major obstacle preventing human communion in the divine life—namely fear of death and of personal annihilation. The so-called hypostatic union—i.e., the Son's uniting in himself of the divine and human natures—was only fully accomplished or realized in his death, a death undergone freely and willingly, in the fullness of human maturity.[1]

The vocation of each human person is to allow Christ to recapitulate within him or her the way of growth Christ himself pioneered. Each human person is to become all that Christ became. But we begin from, so to speak, the opposite end to that from which the Son began. He began as God; we begin as human. The human vocation can indeed be accomplished, but not through human self-willed effort. Our human vocation is only accomplished by grace—that is, through our cooperation with the divine initiative taken on our behalf. More specifically, for each one of us our vocation is only accomplished through our active, on-going trust in the goodness of God's will towards us—though our choice (again and again and again . . .) to surrender to (and cooperate with) the divine will. Salvation is God's work in us, but it is accomplished only with our consent.[2]

---

1. Meyendorff, *Byzantine Theology*, 153–65; Meyendorff, *Christ in Eastern Christian Thought*, passim.

2. On this theme in Maximus, see, e.g., Thunberg, *Microcosm and Mediator*, 240–42.

The Mystery of Love and Death, the Mystery of Sacrifice and Communion

In 1989 Bouyer published a work exploring the notion of mystery in Christian spiritual theology. In his introduction he writes:

> [A]t all times the human spirit has confusedly realized that the meaning of life can be found only in some mysterious meeting . . . between love and death.[3]

Bouyer demonstrates that these two mysteries are united and reconciled in the mystery of sacrifice, most especially in the perfect sacrifice of the paschal mystery. The paschal mystery exists first of all within the life of the Trinity. And in that life there is what can be seen as perfect sacrifice. Bouyer writes, "There is no doubt that . . . sacrifice . . . is a divine reality, the supreme divine activity."[4] A century earlier, F. D. Maurice had written: "There is the ground of sacrifice in the divine nature . . . it is implied in the very origin of the universe."[5]

At heart, sacrifice is not to be understood either as the surrender or loss of one thing that we treasure (perhaps a lamb, perhaps a son) for the sake of preventing some greater loss (perhaps the whole flock, perhaps a kingdom); nor is it a method for securing some benefit (a successful harvest) which would otherwise be withheld. Sacrifice begins with and in God. It begins in the life of the Trinity and in the eternal self-giving of the divine persons to one another. It finds expression in God's gift of existence to creation and in his gift of life to man, a gift which is costly to God—and puts him, so to speak, at risk. It finds fullness of expression in God's gift to man and to creation of *himself*—where indeed, in the incarnation, God suffers for having given man life. Insofar, however, as man responds to God's sacrificial self-giving by also living sacrificially, so he enters a new, more profound, and more fully *personal* relationship with God.[6] Within the self-sacrificial life of the Trinity are found both the *unity* of divine life (or nature) and the *distinction* of the divine persons.[7]

Man is created to live in a similarly self-sacrificial way. Only thus can man live *personally*. The cardinal virtues—faith, hope, and love—are

---

3. Bouyer, *Christian Mystery*, 4; cf. Bouyer, *Christian Spirituality*, vol. I, 435, Balthasar, *Liturgie cosmique*, 191ff.

4. Bouyer, *Christian Mystery*, 290.

5. Maurice, Doctrine of Sacrifice, 109, 118; cf. Ramsey, *Jesus and the Living Past*, 64–77.

6. Cf. Schmemann, *Eucharist*, 101–5.

7. See Ward, *Defence of the Soul*; Ward, *Gift of Self*.

integral to that self-giving which is the essence of sacrifice. And they are integral to personhood. This becomes obvious once we realize that *faith* equates to *active trust*. To believe in God, is not simple to hold a set of ideas (beliefs) about God; it is to trust God in the nitty-gritty of day to day life.

Similarly, the lack of faith which Jesus so often encounters in the New Testament stories is best seen as a lack of trust. So it is also that sin is not a matter of breaking rules or regulations, not even God-given ones. Sin, in its essence, is the failure or refusal to live by faith and trust and love. This means that there is always a *personal* dimension to sin. Sin always involves breaking (or damaging) relationships. We might even say it is about *breaking hearts*. We try to secure his own future in disregard of others, and at their cost.

Sin can be seen also in relationship to sacrifice. Just as sacrifice can be seen as *giving the best we have in order to establish or build relationship* (see above, 68–69), so sin can be seen as *the refusal to risk loss or to give of what we value*, and to do this at a cost to our relationships. Sin always involves the belief that we ourselves must secure our own future and that we cannot (or dare not) *trust anyone else for our wellbeing—not even God*. But in choosing self-reliance we inevitably deny ourselves our own beatitude. We shut ourselves off from the blessings (the life) God would share with us. (Which is also a life beyond our imaginings—as the resurrection life always will be to fallen man.) The Son opened himself to others and to his Father in his (sacrificial) self-giving at the eucharist and on the cross—and so was also open to receive new life, even the new life of the resurrection. Those rejecting the call to the self-loss implicit in sacrifice thereby close themselves off from the possibility of receiving new life. The hand (and the head and the heart) open to give is also open to receive. The hand (and the head and the heart) closed to giving is a hand (and a head and a heart) that cannot receive.

Life is about relationship and is found *within* that exchange which constitutes sacrifice. Personhood is realized in sacrifice.

But how can sacrifice restore wayward, fallen, estranged humanity to fullness of communion with its Creator? What could be offered from a damaged world? And how could a damaged world make a wholehearted offering? It was not possible for man to resolve his predicament; not until, that is, the incarnate Son in the upper room and on Golgotha offered himself, utterly and completely, into the hands both of God and of men. In the upper room, as *God*-and-man, he gave himself to his human brothers; on the cross, *man*-and-God, he gave himself to the Father. The Son's self-offering in the Eucharist and on the cross share the same dynamic and the same motive: they look to establish fullness of relationship, fullness of communion. Through his self-offering the Son restored communion between the divine and the human, the eternal and the created. Initially, so to speak, he restored these relationships *in himself.* He himself became the "place," the locus, of communion between God and man. Subsequently he called others to live within this communion; but this they can do only insofar as they are willing to participate in his self-sacrificial life. Participation in his life is through participation in his gift of himself to the Father and in his priestly, redemptive, self-sacrificial ministry on behalf of the world.

> [T]he Mystery [of love] is revealed and communicated in the mystical experience of believers as the eternal eucharist of the Son, giving back to the Father, in the Spirit, the love which is the very life of the Three, its living unity in their mutual and reciprocal gift, the unique sacrifice in which we are all offered and offerers in the unique offering consummated by the eternal Son at the climax of our history of sin and death, thus transfigured into that of our divine adoption.[8]

The gift of life in Christ must be appropriated. The Son himself had to *attain* to that human maturity which would allow him to offer himself fully to the Father. The call to the Christian is that he or she be transparent to the divine action—i.e., to be so undistorted by self-will and self-interest—that Christ has free rein to recapitulate within him or her the work of the incarnation. Only where this is happening can the Christian share the dying-and-rising-to-new-life which belongs by rights only to Christ himself and without which no human person can participate in the life of the Kingdom. The work of Christian growth (and of Christian asceticism) should be seen in these terms. Through asceticism the Christian detaches himself from the false hopes and fears, joys and griefs—in short, from false conceptions of himself, of God, and of the nature of life itself—which belong to his past conditioning and which prevent him from discerning and cooperating with the divine action.

Within the person of the incarnate Son, human love is perfected and death overcome. Death is not abolished—we shall still die—but it robbed of its sting. No longer does death lead to decay and loss. Where love is perfected, death is creative of life and personal relationship. That divine love which brought the world into being is itself a paschal love. In a sense, death lies at its heart. The divine persons die eternally into one another's hands. None "possesses" his life but, rather, each seeks to give life—to give his own life—and therefore each has his life as a gift. The Father both gives life and receives it back. The Son receives life and offers it back. The Spirit bears the gift of life from Father to Son, and from Son to Father, and he bears it,

8. Bouyer, *Christian Mystery*, 285f.

not as something apart from himself, but *personally*, as his *own* life. In a fully *personal* way, the Spirit is the flow and reflow of divine love, just as the Father is its source and the Son its fulfillment.

Human Freedom and the Human Response to the Divine Initiative

The redemption worked by the incarnate Son was accomplished only through his right use of the *human* freedom proper to his human nature. Although the Son's human will was always set on the Father's will, as he grew towards maturity so ever greater demands were made of him. Throughout this process, he always—that is, constantly or repeatedly—kept his human will united to the divine will. Something similar is required of each human person. To attain to maturity the human person has to learn how to use his will, how to use his freedom. "[We] cannot be saved *by* our own *will* [but] God cannot save us *without* our will."[9]

The Spirit is ever at work to enable human freedom. But man has to grow in freedom, becoming ever more free from the conditioning of his past. The human person will be given greater freedom insofar as he makes right use of the freedom he already has. The fall did not completely remove human freedom. Some capacity for response to God remained. Thunberg explains it thus, "What happens through the fall is that a *perversion* of man's capacity for self-determination takes place—not an annihilation of it . . . ."[10] The challenge for man is to use such capacity as he has for self-determination to acquire yet more freedom, yet more capacity for self-determination. An analogy: anyone wanting to be fit and healthy can only became so by making use of the health and fitness he or she already has. Exercise will increase the capacity for exercise; eating well will improve the physical system, including the digestion. The other side of the coin is that misuse of health or fitness will injure or impair them—a poor diet damages the digestion, the man who uses such fitness as he has only to take him to the pub, the drug dealer, or to the burger-bar will gradually loose such health and fitness as he once had. So it is that those who neglect or misuse the *freedom* they have will find that their freedom atrophies. Increasingly, they will find themselves determined by their circumstances, by what happens to them—and by their (fallen) nature. The same holds for freedom as it does for fitness: Use it or lose it. . . . But use it well and it will increase.

---

9. Cf. Maximus, *Cent.Car.* 3:25, 27 (*Philokalia* 2: 86, 87).

10. Thunberg, *Microcosm and Mediator*, 240.

The Gnomic, Deliberative Will

During the time of his incarnation, the choice confronting the Son was always simple. Pure in heart—in other words, with his heart unified and unconflicted—he discerned the Father's will and trusted in his goodness.[11] It is not so for those whose hearts and minds are divided. Insofar as we are self-obsessed we will not be able accurately to discern the divine will or recognize the divine goodness. We will see, rather, a multitude or complexity of conflicting possibilities. Zizioulas:

> In the fallen state of existence which is characterized by the dialectic of good and evil freedom has come to signify the possibility of choice between two things, and thus it has acquired rather an ethical significance. But the primary and true meaning of freedom is to be found in its ontological content . . . .[12]

In patristic anthropology, the capacity in fallen man to decide between the various options presented to him came to be designated the *gnomic* (or deliberative) will. This is to be distinguished from the faculty of self-determination proper to man. Maximus terms this the "natural will" (*thelēma pusikon*.) The ground of man's communion with God and the basis of the unity of all mankind lies in the right use of his natural (non-deliberative) will. All humankind is created for *one* life, a life it has in the one Christ— and that means, in the one, undivided divine will. But as Thunberg explains, fallen man lives not according to the divine will, but according to that perversion of it which involves him in deliberation and which tends to set one man (and his opinions) against another. "[The] fallen *gnōmē* . . . cuts the common human nature into pieces. . . . [I]t divides men from each other because of their different opinions . . . which instigate contrary actions."[13] This *gnomic* will represents a *habitus* for fallen man.[14] Neither unfallen man nor redeemed man needs to weigh the pros and cons of his actions. He lives a life of radical simplicity—of purity. In this he images the divine Son, who,

---

11. "[T]he divine person of the Word had no need to choose or decide by deliberation. Choice is a limitation, characteristic of our debased liberty . . . ." Lossky, *Mystical Theology of the Eastern Church*, 147. On the deliberative will see also Sherwood, *Maximus the Confessor*, 58–63; Thunberg, *Microcosm and Mediator*, 220–32; Louth, *Maximus the Confessor*, 61f.

12. Zizioulas, "Human Capacity and Human Incapacity," 428. In a note to this passage Zizioulas links the dialectic of good and evil with "the individualisation and fragmentation of being."

13. Thunberg, *Microcosm and Mediator*, 241; cf. Maximus *Ep.* 2 (PG 91:396d).

14. See Thunberg, *Microcosm and Mediator*, 224, 240. On the *gnomic* will in pre-Maximan theology see Thunberg, *Microcosm and Mediator*, 227–28.

according to Maximus did not engage in deliberation, but "kept his free will (*gnōmē*) in impassibility and peace with nature."[15] Louth offers useful clarifications here:

> The idea that Christ did not deliberate . . . seems very strange, since deliberating between different choices is what we are accustomed to think that freewill is all about. In the course of her criticism of current trends of moral philosophy in *The Sovereignty of Good*, Iris Murdoch at one point observes that "freedom is not strictly exercise of the will, but rather the experience of accurate vision which, when this becomes appropriate, occasions action." From this point of view deliberation is what we fall back on when our vision is clouded or confused: it is the measure of our lack of freedom, not the signal of our exercise of freedom.[16]

Louth continues:

> [Murdoch] maintains that "one of the main problems of moral philosophy might be formulated thus: are there any techniques for the purification and reorientation of an energy which is naturally selfish, in such a way that when moments of choice arrive we shall be acting rightly?" . . . That is a good way of formulating the approach of Byzantine ascetic theology . . . .[17]

Providentially, the *gnomic* will gives the human being a certain (limited and imperfect) freedom. Thus it can serve as a temporary expedient to help man cope with his fallenness and even provide a way out of that fallenness.[18] Mosaic Torah, for example, offers opportunities to lay aside self-will. Through obedience to the Torah progress is made towards the transcendence of his fallen nature. But the fulfillment of Torah (and of all Law) is personal trust in God. Insofar as the deliberative will is exercised in faith and love—i.e., is exercised personally—the way is opening up for God to give a renewed vision of himself and of his will for mankind. Whenever

---

15. *OrDom.* (PG 90:877d). Cf. Maximus, *Ep. 2: On Love* (PG 91:392d–400c), *Opuscule 3* (PG 90:45b–56d), e.g., "Evil consists in nothing else than [the] difference of our *gnomic* will from the divine will."

16. Louth, *Maximus the Confessor*, 62, quoting Murdoch, *Sovereignty of Good*, 67. (Cf. Bonhoeffer, *Ethics*, 1, 30, 56.)

17. Louth, *Maximus the Confessor*, 62, quoting Murdoch, *Sovereignty of Good*, 54.

18. Victorian novelist and theologian George MacDonald took this idea further: "[God] gave man the power to thwart His will, that by means of the same power [of will], he might come at last to do His will in a higher kind of way than would otherwise be possible . . .," MacDonald, *Unspoken Sermons*, "The Final Unmasking."

anyone acts in ways which he *believes* to be the will of God, he brings himself into such relationship with God as will hold him open to God's re-creative action. Even where someone's faith is still imperfect, that faith holds him open to be led out of the confusion and complexity belonging to the realm of the *gnomic* will. Where someone is open to being led, God will draw him into closer relationship with himself, until eventually he comes to share the perfect freedom of the sons of God (Rom 8:21).

Where someone is growing in faith, his *vision* of the divine goodness and the divine will can be renewed. Insofar as anyone surrenders (or transcends) the false (*gnomic*) freedom, so that person will be acquiring true freedom. Self-reliance and self-will, on the other hand, bring their own punishment. Of Satan in *Paradise Lost*, Lewis writes: "[A]ll his torments come, in a sense, at his own bidding."[19] To those who will not say to God *thy* will be done, God eventually says, "have your own way—*thy* will be done." Not a happy prospect! For in our fallenness we do not know what is good for us.

Perhaps both freedom and personhood, like prayer and love, cannot properly be understood except by those who have made some progress towards personal maturity. The immature will perceive little or nothing of either their true nature or the divine goodness.[20]

Before ending this chapter, I should acknowledge that the strongly realist philosophy I have adopted in this work would be rejected by many today. No one would deny, however, that philosophical realism has always been assumed in mainstream Christian tradition. I believe such a view is still philosophically sustainable.[21] The epistemological or hermeneutic circle inherent in this view finds its resolution, as I see it, in the raw reality of every-day life—and above all in the brute fact of death, which puts speculation in its place. This circle can also be ended, I would suggest, by the in-breaking of the divine life and the experience of divine mysteries. Like death, these carry an authority, an "absoluteness," that renders speculation redundant. Of course, not everyone will want to believe claims about mystical experience. Anyone can, along Kantian lines, question what elements in any experience were in any sense real or objective. (We can do it, to some extent, even if the experience was our own.) But why give absolute priority to the mind and to Cartesian doubt? Those who adopt a personalist

19. Lewis, *Preface to Paradise Lost*, 99.

20. Commitment to a reductionist metaphysics might lead someone to discount evidence which others would accept as supporting an ontology of personhood.

21. For a review of recent thought on the realist/anti-realist debate see *TPM* 8 (1999). Contrast Rorty, *Truth and Progress*, 63–83 with Searle, *Mind, Language and Society*. Searle does not seek to defend *theological* realism, but his arguments apply, *mutatis mutandis*, to the theological realm.

ontology and who see Christian tradition as a *tradition of life* are entitled to question the conceptual presuppositions of any non-"realist" metaphysics. The hungry man eats his bread. The contented man smiles.

7

Christian Education—
Personhood and the Human Vocation

I HAVE WORKED WITH the assumption that human maturity is realized in inter-personal communion. In the next two chapters I shall consider what it is in human make-up that enables such communion. First I look at some background issues.

The Make-Up of the Individual Human Person

Within the Mediterranean and Middle Eastern cultures in which the Church came into being various views of the make-up of the human individual emerged. Four of them I outline here. I designate them the materialist, dualist, synthetic, and holistic. Each is still influential today.

PRELIMINARY CONSIDERATIONS

First it is worth noting that the philosophical and theological discussion of human make-up is complicated by the fact that there is no agreed nomenclature: one man's *soul* is another's *spirit*, another's *mind*, and so on. The problem is not new. Usage was inconsistent in the philosophy of the Classical and Hellenistic periods. It is inconsistent in the New Testament writings. Terminological variation added to the problems at the early Christian Councils.[1] In modern writings on Christian anthropology and asceticism there is widespread and confusing terminological variation. So far as possible I adopt in this work the lexical stock employed in the modern English translation of the Greek *Philokalia*.[2]

I also need to explain that my argument looks to a distinction identified by Guthrie in even the earliest Greek philosophy. To the question "What is

---

1. On the problem in early Greek thought, see Everson, *Companions to Ancient Throught 2*, esp. 1–12. See also *TDNT* 3:609; 9: 616–17.

2. See, e.g., *Philokalia*, Vol. 1, 357ff.

this?'" he detects two conflicting approaches. He terms them the "material-ist" and the "teleological."[3] On the one hand, the question can be interpreted as requiring an account of the material from which the thing in question is composed; on the other, as requiring an account of the end or purpose or goal towards which that thing is tending. When asked, for example, "What is this painting?" the materialist might suggest that "really" or "ultimately" it is nothing more than an arrangement of shapes and colors, and if pressed, might work through a list of ever more basic constituents, ending per-haps—depending on his scientific sophistication—with pigments, minerals, molecules, atoms, sub-atomic particles, and so on. (And he might include something about the "coding" which determines how those constituents are ordered.) The teleologist would approach things quite differently. His is not with the constitution of the materials, nor their arrangement, but with the artists intention; not, that is, with what the art-work is made *from*, but with what it is made *for*. (Cf. Aristotle's *material cause* and *final cause*.) He might answer by suggesting that the painting is not only an image of (say) the art-ist's daughter but an attempt to express eternal truths, perhaps, for example, his profound love for her.

But how would either answer the question "What is man?" The mate-rialist might answer along the lines: "He is a species of ape, an animal, and although it cannot be denied that he is a social animal, living in a network of relationships and with sophisticated hopes and aspirations, in the final analysis, he is nothing more that an ape, and ultimately, beyond that, he is nothing but an assortment of chemicals and a genetic coding, a particular arrangement of (lifeless) matter." A scientifically sophisticated twenty-first-century materialist will, of course, give an answer very different in detail from that possible to anyone from an earlier generation. But whatever the degree of scientific sophistication, the underlying concern of the materialist will be with what things are made *from*. The teleologist, on the other hand, looks to see what things—man among them—are made *for*, and more gen-erally with how they function. A non-religious teleologist working within this-worldly parameters might, for example, simply see man as worker, wage earner, husband, father, etc. A Christian teleologist might want to insist that the most *basic* truth about man is his potential to partake in the divine glory and become a son of God by grace.[4] Whatever the precise details of his ac-count, the teleologist will be concerned with what man is made *for*.

3. Guthrie, *Greek Philosophy*, 21.

4. Such is clearly the view, for example of St Theophan. Cf. Williams, "Theology of Personhood," 15–17. Cf. Zizioulas, "Human Capacity and Human Incapacity," 420f.

Perhaps it is important to ask is whether people can move from one view to the other. Many hold, for example, that modern secularism encourages reductionist materialism. Is it part of the work of the Church, part of its educational ministry to enable its members to move towards a teleological outlook, wherein they see all that happens in relation to God and his purposes? Is it, indeed, the work of the Church to enable its members to see things, not just teleologically, but *eschatologically*—that is in relation to Christ the realized End of all God's purposes? Paul presents the task of "putting on the mind of Christ" as central to Christian formation (cf. Rom 12:2; cf. Eph 4:23).[5] Is learning to see things eschatologically part of that task and something the Church should be helping its members to do? Does it go hand in hand with the work of enabling the members of the Church to take a *prophetic* view of their times—that is, for seeing how God is working out his purposes through history and drawing the world to himself?

The distinction between materialism/reductionism and teleologism/eschatologism has wide application. Contrast, for example, the idea that the meaning of biblical notions or institutions—say, of Kingship or the Sabbath—can be discovered by looking into their historical origins with the very different idea that the real meaning of any such notion or institution will be one *towards which it is tending* (notwithstanding the possibility of a word's misuse). It is widely accepted today that words have meanings only contextually, and that the meaning of a word can never be discovered through enquiry into its etymology or early usage.[6] More generally, we might see the meaning of a word as the one which the person using it *is intending it to have*. In a similar way, to understand the Israelite institution of, say, the Sabbath it is necessary to look, not back to primitive social conventions about "taboo-days" and the like, but forward to the fulfillment of the Sabbath in the Kingdom of God. This is to look to the meaning which God himself *intends* the Sabbath to have.

If this is so, then the place to discover the meaning of the Sabbath, or of any other biblical institution or concept, will be the life of the Church; for God has established the Church to be the place where man can receive and enter into his revelation of ultimate truth.[7] All elements in this revelation ultimately have their meaning in relation to the person of the eschatological Christ. It is only when Christ the End is in view that the purposes and

5. Exactly this point is made by St Theophan; see Williams, "Theology of Personhood."

6. Hebraist James Barr has exposed the error of the etymological approach (cf. Barr, *Semantics of Biblical Language*, 107–60, 206–62; cf. Barr, *Biblical Words for Time*, 113–116, 127, 153–62), and no one trained in linguistic philosophy would give it credance.

7. Cf. Meyendorff, *Byzantine Theology*, 28f.

patterns of history and the real significance and meaning of all that belongs to this life can be discerned. Neither historical research nor scientific enquiry can, in and of themselves, lead to such an understanding.[8]

Historical research is not, of course, without value. It can help to correct mistaken beliefs and keep speculation under control. "History . . . prevents faith becoming fantasy."[9] But I would suggest that it is important to recognize that it is the End that gives meaning to history. It is right that the Church should look to the past for insight into how its life might be ordered today. But when it looks to the past it should be doing so in the hope of discovering *what it might mean for the Church of today to be in communion with the End.* The significance of the Cappadocians, for example, lies not in the fact that they managed to establish within the Church ideal patterns of life which we would do well to reproduce, but that they witnessed to the possibility of the Church living in communion with the life of the End. Similarly, St Paul is a valuable witness, not because he lived close to the time of Christ's sojourn on earth, but because he lived *close to the End* and knew the *eschatological* Christ. Even the Gospels can be seen in these terms. They witness, not simply (or primarily) to the historical Jesus or the events of his life, but to the eschatological Christ and his Kingdom (even though that Kingdom was being realized through those events). It is always Christ himself who constitutes the abiding treasure of the Church, its pearl of great price. Nothing in the history or tradition of the Church, neither any body of practices nor any set of doctrines, can be of more than secondary value or significance. Practices and doctrines can be vehicles of the divine presence and action and can help serve to enable growth both in knowledge of Christ and in response to his initiative, but they do not constitute the treasure. Indeed, where they become ends in themselves they hinder growth in living relationship to God.

There is another difference between the materialist and the teleological/eschatological outlooks. In looking to account for things by reference to their origin, materialism looks to discover a simple, "economical" explanation for the world, an account with no loose ends.[10] A teleological/eschatological outlook, however, can allow for the world to be essentially *unpredictable* and unfathomable. Not all teleologism will be open in this way. Some teleologists will want to define what the end of all things will be. But Christian teleologism, insofar as it sees the goal of life as participation

---

8. Cf. Wright, in Borg and Wright, *Two Visions,* 14–27.

9. Wright, in Borg and Wright, *Two Visions,* 26.

10. Cf. Barnes, *Early Greek Philosophy,* 17f. Also, Everson, ed. *Ancient Thought 2,* 5f.

in the divine love, can rest content with the acceptance that the End cannot be fully known or described. The person is essentially unknowable and inter-personal relationships will always be to some extent mysterious. This is especially true of relationships with the divine persons.

The notion of personhood is crucial. The worldview I am presenting here considers the person as a primary reality and a possible fact of experience. In dialogue with materialism the Christian need not be diffident about this starting point. Reductionist materialism is no less theory-laden than teleologism or an eschatologism.[11]

The two worldviews (the material and the eschatological), grounded as they are in different ontologies, give different accounts of the purpose, goal or meaning of creation. To the questions, What is the world about? What is it for? What is the significance of what is happening in the world or in our own lives?—to all such questions the materialist can only answer that in the final analysis the world is a system of mechanical processes and that although these might be extraordinarily complex and might be open to any number of interpretations (chemical, biological, sociological, historical, etc.) there is nothing of *enduring* significance in the world. Of course the materialist might give life an immanent purpose: to increase joy and limit suffering, for example. But ultimately it comes down to this: we're here, let's make the most of it, then move on—or, rather, disappear. (The materialist might even suggest that the question itself is meaningless, ill-founded, or unhelpful.) Classical Christianity, rooted in an ontology of personhood and a providentialist understanding of history, would answer that the universe exists for the sake of coming into being of perfected created persons, each of whom, by God's gift, has an eternal destiny. Through the study of the material realm and the historical process we can learn about the context within which man is to work out his purposes, and something too about divine providence.[12]

These considerations help to explain why I have sought to link an account of the nature of Christian education with an account of the history (and theology) of the Church's use of the seven-day week. For I believe that a well-ordered week can help to make the life of the Church an effective context for people to come to personal maturity. It can also help them come

11. See Taylor, *Sources of the Self*, 324–25.

12. One of the great challenges facing the contemporary Church is to see how the insights of science, which are progressing so quickly in so many areas (not least in the areas of genetics, evolutionary biology, neurobiology, physics and cosmology) can be held together with a personalist theology. Our growing knowledge of history (human and pre-human) presents a similar challenge for a providentialist understanding of history.

to a teleological/eschatological understanding of the things of this world, including their own lives, and a prophetic understanding of history, both of world history and of their own personal histories.[13]

Materialism and Human Make-up

A materialist understanding of human make-up is one in which, broadly speaking—

> Persons, personal identity, freedom, communion and consciousness are ultimately seen as the random products of physical processes on high levels of organization whose true character is disguised by treating persons and personal phenomena under a category *sui generis*.[14]

The Ionian pre-Socratics (sixth century BCE) are usually accounted the first materialists. Democritus (460–371 BCE), the early atomists, and later the school of Epicurus (341–270 BCE) took materialism forward.[15] Since the Renaissance, materialism has had many champions, among them Francis Bacon (1561–1626), Thomas Hobbes (1588–1679), T. H. Huxley (1825–95), Francis Crick (b. 1916) and Richard Dawkins (b. 1941).[16] The term "materialist" is applied somewhat inaccurately to the pre-Socratics. As Guthrie has demonstrated, in pre-Socratic times there was no clear distinction between the realms of matter and spirit (or intellect), or between empirical investigation and philosophical speculation.[17] But the evidence does indicate a concern among the pre-Socratics to discover and account for the principle (*archē*) from which things derive their being and characteristics and to find

13. Cf. John Damacense's account of the way all learning (secular and religious) can come to serve the single purpose of growth in depth of communion with God—God and his kingdom come to be seen in all things. See Armitage, "Knowing and Unknowing," 7–20, esp. 10–11.

14. Schwöbel in Schwöbel and Gunton (eds.), *Persons Human and Divine*, 4.

15. See Democritus, *de Anima* 406b17–22, 24–5. No original works of Epicurus survive; but for near-contemporary references see Nicholson, *Body and Soul*, 167, nn.16–17; cf. Annas, "Epicurus' Philosophy of Mind." For a review of classical thought on the soul-body-person issue see Irwin, *Classical Philosophy*, 197–224 (Democritus, 201f; Epicurus, 221); also Sorabji, "Soul and Self."

16. See *OCP*, 530b–532b, also 679a–680a, *OCP*, 93b; Horgan, *End of Science*, 159–190. Also Hobbes, *Leviathan*, esp. chs. 1, 34, 42, 44; Huxley "Animal Automatism" in *Collected Essays*, vol. 1 (1893), see Flew, *Body, Mind, and Death*, 196–20.

17. "[The] matter which was the sole and unique fount of all existence was itself regarded as endowed with spirit of life," Guthrie, *Thales to Aristotle*, 33; cf. Cornford, *From Religion to Philosophy*, 7; Barnes, *Early Greek Philosophy*, 12–18.

this, not in divine or mythological categories, but in their "nature" (*physis*).[18] The question "what is this?" becomes "what is this made from?"[19]

Today materialism appears in various forms.[20] Much of the sympathy for materialism derives from the success of experimental science. The recent claims of some that genetic inheritance explains, and perhaps determines, much in human behavior have sometimes been seen as draining the notion of the person of almost all its traditional meaning.[21] Recent work in neuro-psychology has shown the intricacies of the human brain-body complex and demonstrated something of the relationship between brain-function and certain mental states.[22] Brain damage or drug-induced psychosis can bring about such changes in personality that those who suffer them no longer seem themselves.[23]

At the same time, it is not always clear which problematic issues in the mind-body-person question will be resolved by empirical (biological, psychological, sociological) investigation and which by philosophical enquiry, i.e., clarification of the concepts involved.

If hard-line materialism is correct, then the Christian worldview falls. But reductionist materialism has been challenged on various grounds. Many philosophers have argued that brain states and mental states belong to different categories, such that the concepts required to describe and discuss brain states are not those required to discuss the *experience* of pain or love or

---

18. Cf. J. Barnes, *Early Greek Philosophy*, 20. Barnes also explains that *physis* has two meanings; rather like the English "nature." Cf. Collingwood, *Idea of Nature*, 45f. Note that *physis* has a strongly dynamic sense.

19. Cf. Morris, *Anthropology of the Self*, 24. For a critique of reductionism see Cassim, "Reductionism and First-Person Thinking."

20. For the diversity in materialism see *OCP*, 573a–b, 301b–302a, 569b–570b; also Irwin, "Aristotle's Philosophy of Mind," 57, and 57 n.2. For critical appraisal see also Hamlyn, *Metaphysics*, 161–86; Atkins, "Purposeless People," 12–36; Ward, *Defence of the Soul*, 134–52; and Nicholson, *Body and Soul*, esp. 22–48.

21. Among materialists, both those coming from the scientific community and those from the philosophical background, there are many who hold that, the fact of materialist reductionism notwithstanding, human beings should be treated with dignity and respect. Some have sought to construct non-realist, non-absolutist ethical systems. See *OCP*, 798a–b.

22. Greenfield, *Human Brain*; Greenfield, "Soul, Brain, Mind"; also Lycan, *Consciousness*; but see Horgan, *End of Science*, 258–65. I believe the treatment of mental illness would progress if it were better understood whether a particular patient's problems were grounded in (i) biological disorder (i.e., organic disorder), (ii) psychological problems (deriving from life experiences), (iii) spiritual issues (i.e., concerned with the meaning or purpose of life). I believe that although there is interplay between these three areas they are essentially distinct.

23. See Horgan, *End of Science*, 32–36.

anxiety. This objection applies equally to some of the proposed alternatives to materialism, including behaviorism (the belief that behavior indicates and equates with mental state),[24] functionalism (the view that what makes a mental state what it is, e.g., an experience of pain or joy, is the functional role which it occupies),[25] and anomalous monism (the belief that the mental and the physical are two irreducible ways of describing the same objects and events).[26] Against all of these it can be argued that *in practise* everyone, even the avowed materialist, works on the assumption that the human mind is more than (or other than) any of these reductionist views suggests.

Another objection sees materialism as logically inconsistent. The materialist explains all human behavior in terms of (material) *causes*, and not in terms of (logical, argued) *reasons*. To say that X believes Y is simply to say that X has brain-process Y, leaving no scope for any talk of the *reason* behind X's belief. The notion of reason becomes redundant. Beliefs are taken to be grounded in mechanical *causes*, not logical *reasons* (rather as computers produce results, not by reason or argument, but as an outworking of material causes). But what does this say for the belief in materialism? If it can be explained in terms of causes, not reasons, then there is no *reason* for believing in materialism. Indeed, the possibility of *reasoning* towards *any* belief, whether materialism or anything else, disappears. Materialism as a philosophical theory self-destructs.[27]

All materialist (and quasi-materialist) views of the mind or the person must address the widespread reluctance to accept the human being as merely a sophisticated biological machine. Despite understandable confusion in extreme cases—is the person in permanent vegetative state (PVS) still a person?—there is a popular conviction about continuity of personal identity through time; and despite obvious differences, Edward as ten-year-old child and fifty-year-old adult are taken to be the same person. Consider the experience of those who live and work with the exceptionally impaired. In the 1960s, Jean Vanier founded the first of his L'Arche communities where able-bodied "assistants" live in community with, in Vanier's phrase, "people with mental handicaps" (sometimes termed "core-members"). Vanier has

24. See *OCP*, 81. Ryle, *Concept of Mind* is generally taken to represent the standard presentation of philosophical behaviorism. Ryle himself frequently denied, however, that the work propounded behaviorism. G. W. Warnock suggests, "it both did and did not, in different passages," *OCP*, 789b. See also Thatcher, *Truly a Person*, 54–57.

25. See Fodor, *Psycholigcal Explanation*; but see Putnam, *Representation and Reality*.

26. Davidsion, "Mental Events."

27. Nicholson, *Body and Soul*, 29–48. Cf. Lewis, *Miracles*, ch. 3, on which see also the Introduction to Anscombe, *Collected Philosophical Papers* II; Mitchell, "Reflections on C. S. Lewis," 8–12, and Lucas, *Freedom of the Will*.

often expressed his conviction that many core-members have an unusually profound awareness of God and show uncommon sensitivity to the emotional and spiritual needs of others.[28] The former Bishop of London, Richard Chartres, has spoken of the significance in the development of his own religious commitment of the "extraordinary quality of happiness" possessed by his brain-damaged brother, Stephen.[29] An extreme case is recorded by John Bradburne (1921–79), an Englishman killed by local security forces while supervising the Mutemwa Leprosy Settlement in Rhodesia. The personhood of a blind, deaf, mute leper was not destroyed—and hardly diminished—by his disabilities.[30] Some women claim awareness of a *personal*, not just physical presence, within them during pregnancy. And in times of crisis—near death or birth, for example—the objective reality of personhood is commonly perceived more easily. Similarly in times of grief and loss people frequently wish to have someone present with them—not to have them offering words of comfort or practical help, but simply to be present, as a silent, sympathetic presence (cf. Mark 14:32).[31] I would hold that the person is directly perceptible—in philosophical terms, the person is a percept—but is perceptible only insofar as we ourselves are functioning as persons.

Any claim about direct perception of the person can be dismissed as wishful thinking or misinterpretation of a phenomenon explicable in other terms. If *all* such claims can be discounted, then the argument of this thesis would fail, as would classical Christianity. But any attempt to discount *a priori* the direct perception of the person will itself be grounded in metaphysical presuppositions that are open to question.

Even for someone with many gifts and accomplishments, the most important fact about him is not those gifts *per se*, but rather the *person* he has become through the use of them. In and of themselves, good works can be less than personal. The problem with Pharisaism is that upright, high-minded, morally correct behavior need not involve the *person*. It may be the result of conditioning. "[I]t is possible for someone to keep the whole of the Law without managing to free himself from his biological ego, from corruption and death."[32]

---

28. See the community's "Principles" as presented in L'Arche "Charter." Principle 4, for example states: "Weakness and vulnerability in a person, far from being an obstacle to union with God, can foster it." For a complementary Jewish perspective on personhood and disability see Sacks, *Faith in the Future*, 214–24.

29. *Guardian*, December 23, 2000.

30. Dove, *Strange Vagabond of God*, 229–30, 243 (cf. 211–50).

31. Cassidy, "Towards a Theology of Hospice Care," 10–11, 40, 85–86.

32. Yannaras, *Freedom of Morality*, 96; cf 24–27, 78–79.

If the essential vocation of the human person is to become that unique person he was created to become, then nothing matters much except to become that person. Everything else must be set within this context. Whatever anyone's particular gifts, the principal challenge facing him will be to grow in personal maturity. The way of growth will ordinarily involve the use of natural aptitudes and abilities and will take place within a framework of social relationships. Within this world people express and realize themselves through thought, words, and actions. Meanwhile, relationships develop between people and among groups through every-day interactions, physical, intellectual, and emotional. It is characteristic of fallen humanity, however, to identify people with their capacities and powers, with what they do and think—even with what they possess; but an ontology of personhood insists on the priority of the person over all such things.

A counterpart to the statement of John of the Cross and the ontology of personhood outlined above is the claim made by Sister Helen Prejean, well-known campaigner against capital punishment. Befriending a series of death-row prisoners (even witnessing their executions) has brought her to a conviction of the transcendent value of the person. "There is more to everyone than even the worst thing he has done."[33]

To suggest that the person (or the "soul") is somehow separate and distinct from the body, from the natural aptitudes and capacities, would be to adopt the kind of view commonly termed psycho-physical dualism.

Psycho-Physical Dualism I

Psycho-physical dualism has long represented an alternative to materialism. It is grounded in the conviction that there exists a radical divide between the realms of matter and intellect or between body and soul. Adherents of dualism—henceforth I shall use "dualism" in the sense of "psycho-physical dualism"—see the human person as constituted of body and soul, and as existing in (or belonging to) two distinct (but inter-acting) realms (the physical and the mental). Here it is the soul that, as a conscious substantial entity, provides the ultimate reference-point for distinct (individual or personal) identity and constitutes the primary object of moral concern.[34] Plato

33. BBC interview, *Woman's Hour*, Radio 4, 22 October 1999. See Prejean, *Dead Men Walking*, also Prejean, "Giving in to Life," 16, and her comments in *Catholic Agitator* 27.5 (1997) 7.

34. For recent accounts see Swinburne, "Body and Soul"; Swinburne, *Evolution of the Soul*; Lewis, *The Elusive Mind*; Ward, *Defence of the Soul*, esp. ch. 7; Eccles and Popper, *The Self and Its Brain*; Eccles and Beck, "Quantum Aspects of Brain Activity"; Cooper, *Body, Soul*. For an historical overview see Brady, et al., *NCE*, vol. 13, 450a–459b,

is credited with developing and promoting dualism—in somewhat different forms as his thinking advanced.[35] Basically, he took the soul to be immaterial, imperceptible, and immortal—and a singularity; while the body he saw as being material, perceptible, mortal—and composite.

An Alternative : The Synthetic View

Aristotle took a markedly different view from his teacher. Set out principally in *De Anima*, his treatment is complex and sophisticated. It remains open to varied interpretation.[36] He has been seen as seeking to hold together Democritian materialism and Platonic idealism.[37] Strongly emphasizing the essential unity of the human being, he insists that the soul cannot be conceived in separation from the body.[38] They are one, as are "the wax and the image impressed upon it."[39] As Hicks suggests, "Soul and body . . . are not two distinct things, they are one thing presenting two distinct aspects."[40] In a more restricted sense and yet with a wider reference than is general today, *soul* for Aristotle enables the living being to be (or to function as) itself. The soul is the form of the body.[41] Thus, even plants have souls; but conscious mental states can only be attributed to animals. This hylomorphic understanding of the soul-body question removes the need to choose between identifying the soul

---

462a–464a. Ryle (*Concept of Mind*, ch. 1) sets forth criticisms of dualism.

35. *Apology* 29d–30b; *Crito* 47e–48a; *Phaedo*, 64c, 79a–81b. See Lovibond, "Plato's Theory of Mind." Note that Plato ascribes to the body some things that we would naturally ascribe to the soul-mind, e.g., irrational sense-impressions and desires. In later works Plato shows an awareness of some of the problem in the view set out in *Phaedo*. See *Republic*, iv. 608d–612 and *Phaedrus* 245c–246d. But he does not abandon his dualism. Cf. Irwin, *Classical Thought*, 98–101, 235 n.28. (Note too Plato's implicit recognition of an essential physicality in human existence at the conclusion of his re-telling of the Myth of Er. *Republic* 614b–615a.)

36. See Irwin, "Aristotle's Philosophy of Mind," 56–83.

37. Irwin, *Classical Thought*, 130–32; Irwin, "Aristotle's Philosophy of Mind," 59–61, 70–76. Aristotle gives a critical account of the views of his predecessors: *de Anima* I (ii): 403B20–404A9, 404A30–31, 405A19–20, and 405B1–3.

38. II (i): 412a1–412b22; 413a3–5. This is so notwithstanding the fact that many (including Aquinas and Descartes) have read Aristotle himself as hesitating to press this non-dualist view; immediately after having argued for non-dualism he seems to withdraw from it: "It is not obvious whether the soul is the actuality of the body as the sailor is of the ship," II (i): 413a6–9. But see Irwin ("Aristotle's Philosophy of Mind," 73 n.11) on this.

39. *De Anima* II (i): 412b6–7; cf. 412b8–9; *Met.* 1045b17–22. See Irwin, "Aristotle's Philosophy of Mind," 70.

40. Hicks, in *Aristotle, de Anima*, xliii–xliv.

41. See Irwin, "Aristotle's Philosophy of Mind," 66–68.

(or mind or personality) with the radical alternatives of either some kind of material phenomenon or some non-material reality. Instead, the possibility appears of predicating mental (or psychic or spiritual) actions and activities on a subject, a person who is identifiably corporeal and physical—though the mode or manner of interaction between soul and body remains for Aristotle (as for philosophy in general) an enigma.[42] It is significant that Aristotle can be seen "look[ing] on life as a biologist"[43]—an empiricist, whose starting point is the world perceived by the human senses.

In the centuries immediately following his death, Aristotle's philosophical work exerted little influence. The Stoics, for example, adopted little from him.[44] At the dawn of the Christian era, his work enjoyed a revival, eventually influencing both Neo-Platonism and the Church.[45] But until the mediaeval period it was always his writings in logic and natural science that were considered the more valuable; Plato still dominated in philosophy. Insofar as Aristotle's philosophical work was known, it was generally at second hand and often in faulty transmission. He was even castigated for denial of the soul's immortality, and condemned as an "heretical" rationalist who had helped spawn Arius.[46] Only much later would Aquinas champion his cause and his composite model of human make-up—and that only after the study of his works, not long recovered in the West, had been banned at the Council of Paris in 1210. And even then, Aquinas looked to Augustine, with his Platonist background, to establish the possibility of a subsistent human soul and of human immortality.[47]

Psycho-Physical Dualism II

Throughout the early centuries of the Church, Platonism exerted a powerful influence, especially in the East. Origen was unusual in proposing, after the pattern of Plato, a dual creation,[48] but many early Christian

42. *De Anima* II (i): 406b15–25; Hamlyn, *Metaphysics*, 164–66; Thatcher, *Truly a Person*, 12.

43. Lawson-Tancred, *Aristotle, De Anima*, 13. Cf. Grayeff, *Aristotle and His School*, 30, 34.

44. Grayeff, *Aristotle and His School*, 49–68.

45. *OCP*, 50a–51a.

46. See for example, Tatian, *Or.* 2; 25; Athanagoras, *Leg.* 25; Gregory of Nyssa, *Eun.* 1.46; 2.411; 2.620. More generally, *EEC* 112b–114b.

47. *Summa Theologica*, IQ 75A2, where he refers not only to *de Anima* but to Augustine's *de Trinitate* X (vii).

48. See, for example, *Commentary on John* 20.22; see Crouzel, *Théologie de l'image de Dieu*, 148–53; *TSS*, 117. Origin's later writings are less influenced by Platonism (see

writings—especially those concerned with asceticism and the spiritual life—took for granted a psycho-physical dualism, as espoused by Plato.[49]

Descartes (1596–1650) gave new and compelling expression to mind-body dualism.[50] Psycho-physical dualism subsequently became so thoroughly integrated into the Western worldview that it long went more or less unquestioned. It became, in Ryle's words, the "official doctrine."[51] Eventually, however, shortcomings were recognized.[52]

For example, dualism so stresses the importance of the mind-soul in human identity that the physical and material component in human life loses all significance. This is more or less what happens with Plato, who not only identified the individual with the soul, but identified the soul with the rational, reflective intellect.[53] For Descartes, the essence of man is thought. He is *res cogitans*.[54] Such a view not only gives little value to man's physical make-up but also assigns little value to other aspects of his non-physical make-up: emotions, intuitions, aesthetic sense, etc.[55]

The identification of man with mind-soul-intellect has obvious implications for education, not least Christian education.[56] Importantly, while there is no need to doubt that the mind and intellect have a part to play in many aspects of human life, man's capacity to control his life and engineer

---

Rist, *Eros and Psyche*; Balthasar in Greer, *Origen*, xi).

49. See the section "Humans as Composite Beings" in Thunberg, SCMCS I, 294f.

50. See esp. *Meditations* 2, and *Objection* 5 (See Sorabji, "Soul and Self," 26, n.1).

51. Ryle, *Concept of Mind*, 13.

52. Thatcher, *Truly a Person*, 12–18; Braine, *Human Person: Animal and Spirit*, esp. 249–99, 447–79; Hasker, *Emergent Self*. Descartes recognized some problems himself (see *Mediations* 6).

53. See Irwin, *Classical Thought*, 99; Irwin, *Classical Philosophy*, 208–9; Sorabji, "Soul and Self," 12.

54. This is contrasted with the body, *res extensa*. In *Mediations* 6. Descartes sets out his belief that the mind or soul is "entirely distinct from the body and could exist without it." Cf. *Meditations* 2, and *Method*, pt.4. But note also that Descartes sometimes looked to counter or complement his psycho-physical dualism with a more unified view of what it is to be human In *Method*, pt. 5. he presents the soul "not [as being] lodged in the body like a sailor in a ship, but . . . more closely conjoined and intermingled with it to form a unit," Cf. Cottingham *OCP*, 191b; also Cottingham, *Descartes*.

55. Cf. Thatcher, *Truly a Person*, 14; cf. Thatcher, "Concept of a Person," 183–85; cf. Cottingham, *OCP* 191a; cf. Irwin, *Classical Philosophy*, 202–3, 208. Ward, for example, although he speaks of the necessity of seeing the soul as "both a spiritual and an embodied reality" (*Defence of the Soul*, 148), seems very much to identify the soul with the intellect.

56. The neo-Cartesianism which emerged in the late twentieth century acknowledged that mental states and individual personal acts might have (even must have) correlates in physical states, particularly brain states, but still took it for granted that the mind-soul is uniquely significant in defining the human individual.

his future—something which his proficiency in the understanding and management of the material world makes possible—also exposes him to what classical Christianity saw as a serious danger. He can use them to hide himself from the challenge of faith. Insofar as man trusts in his capacity to secure his own well-being, so he will fail to acknowledge his need for divine help—or for any relationship with God. But any *personal* relationship has to be grounded in faith. And while knowledge can complement and support faith, it cannot substitute for it. Insofar as man seeks to use his knowledge and skill to avoid the *risk* inherent in personal relationship, so he will miss out on those benefits, blessings, and joys which only personal relationships can bring—and for which he has been created.

A second major difficulty with mind-body dualism is its failure to see any significance or value in the communal, corporate dimension in human life. Thatcher, quoting MacIntyre writes, "With Descartes the foundations of 'that newly invented social institution, the individual,' are laid."[57] The effects were far reaching. Any sense that humanity shares a "common inheritance" and might look to a common future falls from view. Knowledge and expertise come to be seen as the "possession" of the individual, not as a common concern for all humanity. No longer is each person seen as both a participant in and as a contributor to the shared enterprise of humanity's on-going life and growth—an enterprise extending not only "horizontally" across social groupings but also "vertically" through the generations—instead he becomes an end-in-himself (what amounts to an *alternative* to corporate, collective humanity). As such he will tend to feel pressured to justify his existence through attaining some kind of success or distinction—by "making his mark." But thrown back on himself in this way—"I am what I have made myself, and nothing more"—he is vulnerable to feelings of isolation and the fear of failure.

The Synthetic View II

In the 1950s Strawson proposed a philosophy of the person which sought to correct both Cartesian dualism and materialist reductionism. He proposed that *person* is a complex unitary concept requiring "double-aspect" descriptions, i.e., mental and material.[58] Thatcher, suggesting that theologians have neglected Strawson's work, has sought to exploit his insights.[59]

57. Thatcher, *Truly a Person*, 122, quoting Macintyre, *After Virtue*, 212.

58. Strawson, *Individuals*. He generally identifies person with consciousness, after the model of Boethius (Strawson, *Individuals*, 87ff., but see 115f.). For a further attempt see Braine, *Human Person*.

59. Thatcher, *Truly a Person*, 18–22, 27–37; see 23f (n.30) for Thatcher's account of

Thatcher's work is valuable, particularly his development of the idea that "soul" and "heart" refer to "states of the person, not to things."[60] Everyday thought assumes that the *person* acts in human affairs: in everyday speech, the *person* is the subject of descriptions of human actions and mental states. It is not Bill's *brain* or even his *mind* that understands Pythagoras' theorem or knows the date of the Battle of Waterloo. It is Bill. Jane's body does not run for the bus or win the Olympic marathon—Jane does. Similarly, it is Jim who is anxious and Anne who prays; not his "nerves" or her soul.[61]

We can develop Thatcher's insights and see that many human actions, though attributable to a person (or individual) fail to be fully personal. Someone's thoughts, feelings, judgments, actions may be so conditioned by his social and cultural history, even by his genetic make-up, that he *as a person* almost disappears from the description of the action. He is driven by his conditioning. Indeed, this may even occur when someone is apparently functioning successfully and accomplishing a great deal. That too can be no more than the outworking of conditioning.

Returning to Thatcher, I would suggest that the weakness in his exposition is that while he looks to overcome a mentalist notion of personhood he does not really get beyond identifying the person with the mind. Notably he fails to discuss what it might be that enables human participation in the divine life. Significantly, he depends heavily on the idea that insight into the divine can be gained by working "upwards" from what is familiar in the human realm to the unfamiliar transcendent divine.[62] "If we are personal, then God, as perfect person, must be all that we are—and more. Our virtues: justice, love, compassion—these are but faint reflections of his." This, the so-called argument by analogy, has always been used by the Church. But Eastern tradition holds that this approach constitutes theology's "lowest and least reliable level."[63] Lossky writes, "Theological anthropology must be conducted from the top down, *beginning* from Trinitarian and Christological dogma."[64] Thatcher neglects the idea that the human person can enter into direct communion with the divine. In Eastern tradition such communion—seen as potentially

---

and reply to objections to Strawson's approach. Cf. Hasker, *Emergent Self.*

60. Thatcher, *Truly a Person*, 57, cf. 60–61. This looks to Strawson, *Individuals* and to Wittgenstein's discussion of "private language. " See Wittgenstein, *Philosophical Investigations*, §269ff.

61. See Climacus below, p. 94.

62. Thatcher, *Truly a Person*, 4, 5–6, and *passim.*

63. Cf. Meyendorff, *Byzantine Theology*, 9; cf. Sophrony, *Saint Silouan*, 161–2, 165–170.

64. Lossky, *Image and Likeness*, 185. Emphasis added.

open to everyone[65]—is precisely the ground of true knowledge of the divine and therefore of a more trustworthy and reliable theology.[66]

But if human persons can know the divine only through communion in the divine life, that communion can only be attained through *personal* response to the divine initiative and self-revelation. The divine self-revelation is inherently and (fundamentally) personal, and the response it calls for will similarly be personal. Contrast this with theological speculation and argument by analogy, both of which are possible even where there is little *personal* commitment to the divine. Being personal, the divine self-revelation will surpass human understanding. But the essential unknowability of the divine persons and the unfathomable, apophatic character of divine truth should not be taken as meaning that God wishes to hide himself from man. The very inaccessibility of the divine truth to the human *intellect* can serve to draw the human person away from speculation into direct personal knowledge of the divine—wherein alone he can find fulfillment.[67] Of Maximus's theological outlook and account of the Christian life, Lossky writes:

> We have here a vision of God which surpasses the intellect as well as the senses; *for this reason it is addressed to the whole man*; a communion of *personal* man with the *personal* God.[68]

There remains a further understanding of what it is to be human that warrants discussion. Its exposition is far from simple, but I believe it accounts for the facts better than any other. It is the view that the human person exists as an integrated psycho-somatic whole, having his unity in his spirit, his person.

---

65. Sophrony, *Saint Silouan*, 354, 357.

66. Sophrony, *Saint Silouan*, 353–60; and see 117–20 below.

67. Created persons too are mysterious and unknowable, the more so the more fully personal they are. Even human persons can only be known to one another through love—i.e., through relationship, not through intellectual endeavor or any other, less than personal, means.

68. Lossky, *Vision of God*, 110. Emphasis added. Lossky looks also to Simeon the New Theologian, for whom "the face to face vision [of God] is a communion, a kind of existential communion with Christ, where each person in this communion finds fulfillment, knowing God personally and being personally known by him."

8

An Holistic Understanding of Human Make-Up

THE UNDERSTANDING OF THE human person which considers him an integrated whole has a long history. Schwöbel suggests that among biblical exegetes "a far-ranging consensus" exists that the Christian Scriptures assume an holistic view of man, seeing him as "a unity of soul, body and mind"[1]—or more commonly perhaps as a unity of "body, soul and spirit," where "soul" designates his mental capacities both intellectual and emotional. Whichever division is adopted, the Scriptures also assume that human life has an intrinsic corporate, communal dimension.

Paul commonly works with a bipartite model of human make-up but sometimes adopts a tripartite variant. "May the God of peace himself sanctify you wholly; and may your spirit, soul, and body be kept sound and blameless" (1 Thess 5:23).[2] No fundamental conflict need exist between the bipartite and tripartite models.[3] It is notable that Paul's conceptual framework and language, though influenced by Hebrew tradition and Greek philosophy, are essentially non-technical.[4] He is happy to use various models, and nowhere sets out a systematic account of human make-up. One advantage of the tripartite model for this present study is that it makes it unlikely that the person will be identified with some single component in his make-up—his mind, emotions, body, etc. Again, it makes it less likely that any one

1. Schwöbel, *Persons Human and Divine*, 8. The classic account is Robinson, *Holy Spirit*. Ward (*Defence of the Soul*, 147f.) looks to the holistic view. Cooper (*Body, Soul and Life Everlasting*) argues that dualism is more a part of Scriptural tradition that is often recognized.

2. Here "soul" (*psychē*) can be identified with mind (thoughts) and emotions (feelings), while "spirit" (*pneuma*) equates to "person," cf. 1 Cor 2: 13–14, and see *TDNT* 9:663 (3b). On Paul's anthropology see *JBC* 79:120–12; *TDNT* 6:415ff., esp. 434–36; Stacey, *Pauline View of Man*. On the sophisticated (but variable) tripartite anthropology of Maximus see Thunberg, *Microcosm and Mediator*, 179–205.

3. "The difference between the partisans of trichotomy and of dichotomy is in effect simply one of terminology." Lossky, *Mystical Theology*, 127; Meyendorff, *Byzantine Theology*,141–42. See also Ware, "Soul in Greek Christianity," 54–56.

4. On Paul's (non-technical) synthesis of Greek and Hebrew thinking about human make-up see *TDNT* 9:648.

aspect will be excluded from the account—the body despised, for example. But the key point is that it opens the way for an ontology of *personhood*. Any identification of man with one or other aspect of his nature—body or soul—is precluded.[5]

If the Scriptural tradition assumes the human person to be an integrated whole, it also recognizes what might be termed a particular locus of personhood, namely the heart.[6] Baumgärtel summarizes the Old Testament view: the heart is not only literal and physical: it is the "innermost part of man" and "the seat of rational functions."[7] From the heart "comes planning and volition;" at the same time "moral and religious conduct are rooted in the heart."[8] Behm offers a summary of usage in Classical and Hellenistic Greek and the New Testament. Initially, *kardia* simply designated the physical organ, but came sometimes to be used figuratively to denote the seat of moral and intellectual life. Plato ascribes certain functions of the soul to *kardia*. This tendency was developed by the Stoics. Aristotle confined himself to a more biological view. In the LXX, *kardia* is primarily "the principle and organ of man's personal life," and hence, "the seat of his moral and religious life."[9] Behm's comments on New Testament usage are bold and unequivocal:

> [NT] use of [*kardia*] agrees with the OT use as distinct from the Greek. Even more strongly than the LXX it concentrates on the heart as the main organ of psychic and spiritual life, the place in man at which God bears witness to himself.[10]

Behm records the many ways in which the heart is considered "the centre of the inner life of man and the source or seat of all the forces and functions of soul and spirit." In the heart "dwell the feelings and emotions, desires and passions," such that the heart is the "seat of understanding, . . . source of thought and reflection . . . , seat of will, . . . source of resolves." In summary,

---

5. Cf. Zizioulas, "Human Capacity and Human Incapacity," 423f.

6. Also, *TDNT* 3:605–14, esp. 606–7 (on the OT); 609–11 (on LXX and Hellenic Judaism); 612–13 (on NT usage); also *TDNT* 9: 608–59 (on *psychē*, esp. vis-à-vis *kardia*); see esp.: 626–28 ("The Heart as the Centre of Life and the Epitome of the Person" in OT); 629–30 (the relationship between soul (*nephesh*) and *heart* (*leb*) in the Old Testament); 641–42 (on *kardia* vis-à-vis *psychē*). See also Wolff, *Anthropology*, 52–53; Nowell, "Purity of Heart in the Old Testament," 17–18.

7. *TDNT* 3:606.

8. *TDNT* 3:607.

9. *TDNT* 3:608–9.

10. *TDNT* 3:611–13, where he gives wide references, from all strands of New Testament tradition. Note the designation of God as *kardiognōtēs*, "the One who knows the heart" (Acts 1:24: 15:8), an idea common throughout both Old and New Testaments, even where this term does not occur. See *TDNT* 3:613.

the heart is "supremely the one centre in man to which God turns, in which life is rooted, which determines moral conduct."[11]

Eastern Christian ascetic tradition takes a similar view. The glossary to the recent English translation of the *Philokalia* describes the heart (*kardia*) as

> not simply the physical organ but the spiritual centre of man's being, man as made in the image of God, his deepest truest self, or the inner shrine, to be entered only through sacrifice and death, in which the mystery of union between the divine and the human is consummated.[12]

The term *heart* has "an all-embracing significance," and "prayer of the heart" means prayer "not just of the emotions and affections, but of the whole person, including the body."[13] John Climacus is quoted as taking the psalmist's statement, "I called with my whole heart" to mean "with body, soul, and spirit."[14]

Eastern ascetic and theological tradition sees the heart as closely related to the *mind* or *intellect* (*nous*). For Diadochus the intellect constitutes the heart's innermost aspect.[15] Almost universally, the intellect (*nous*) is contrasted with the discursive, rationalizing, and logical principle in man, commonly termed *reason* (*dianoia*). The intellect can grasp the inner principles both of created things and of divine truth. With the intellect man understands by "immediate experience" (what Isaac the Syrian terms

---

11. *TDNT* 3:611–12.

12. *Philokalia* 1:360. Cf. Ware, "Soul in Greek Christianity." Thunberg (*Microcosm and Mediator*, 119) writes of Maximus, a major representative of this tradition, that can express the "conviction that there is a personal aspect in man's life, which goes, as it were, beyond his nature and represents his inner unity, as well as his relationship to God." On patristic usage in general see Guillaumont, "noms du coeur dans l'antiquité," and *DS* 2, 2281–88. Ware ("Soul in Greek Christianity," 58–59) suggests similarities between *kardia* in the Greek Fathers and *memoria* in Augustine (e.g., *Confessions* Bk 10).

13. *Philokalia* 1:361. In the Scriptural and patristic traditions and in later Eastern ascetic writings the *physical* heart is itself presented as the locus of personhood—and as, for example, the place where prayer goes on. For the relationship of the physical heart to the "spiritual heart" and of the heart and the mind (*nous*) see Vlachos, *Orthodox Psychotherapy*, 156–72. Ware, "Paying with the body." Sophrony (*On Prayer*, 14) explains, "Though this love is sensed by the physical heart, by its nature it is spiritual, metaphysical." Cf. *Philokalia* 1: 361–62.

14. *Ladder*, Step 28 (see Moore, *John Climacus*, 257f.).

15. *Philokalia* 1:287 (§88). The intellect dwells in "the depths of the soul—that is to say, the intellect" (*to bathos tēs psychēs toutestin eis ton noun*), Diadochus, *Philokalia* 1:280 (§79).

"simple cognition"[16]), not through reflection or study. Sophrony says that God reveals himself to man, "mainly through the heart," explaining that through such *personal* revelation"—the divine persons addressing the heart of man—man can know for himself the truth and substance of the New Testament revelation.[17] He writes, "As love, the hypostasis requires other hypostases. . . . [W]hen the human *persona* stands before Him who names himself 'I AM THAT I AM' (Ex. 3:14) he will perceive, not only the divine glory, but also his own potential glory."[18] (We might add that he will also perceive the reality of his own createdness—both of his contingency and of his fallenness, his sin.)

The spiritual dimension in human life—which I am identifying with the heart-spirit—is not to be seen just as one aspect of the human person. Rather, the heart-spirit should be seen as the locus of the unity of the *whole* self. The terms *heart* and *person* designate both the unifying center of the person and the person as an integrated whole.

The heart is precisely that which makes the human person *personal.* Each person is, by divine gift, a unique someone. Lossky states: "Person-hood belongs to every human being by virtue of a singular and unique relationship to God who created him 'in his image.'"[19] Sophrony writes:

> In the Divine Being the Hypostasis constitutes the innermost esoteric principle of Being. Similarly, in the human being the hypostasis is the most intrinsic fundamental. *Persona* is "the hidden man of the heart . . ." (I Pe. 3:4)—the most precious kernel of man's whole being, manifested in his capacity for self-knowledge and self-determination; in his possession of creative energy; in his talent for cognition not only of the created world but also of the Divine world.[20]

I have mentioned the *personal* character of human activity: Graham sings—not Graham's voice, body or mind. Likewise, with the sacraments

---

16. *Philokalia* 1:362, 364 (glossary notes on intellect and mind). Cf. "[T]heology will never be abstract, working through concepts, but contemplative: raising the mind to those realities which pass all understanding." Lossky, *Mystical Theology*, 43.

17. Sophrony, *His Life is Mine*, 44. This revelation "makes the general revelation of the New Testament spiritually familiar.".

18. Sophrony, *His Life is Mine*, 45.

19. Lossky, *Image and Likeness*, 137. Note that elsewhere (*Mystical Theology*, 201) he writes; 'The spirit (*nous*) in human nature corresponds most nearly to the person.'

20. Sophrony, *His Life is Mine*, 44f. Sophrony insists both on the "absolute" value of the person and on the apophatic character of personhood. The person is "capable of containing the fullness of divine and human life" and can only be known personally, i.e., through relationship.

and the sacramental life: it is the *person* who is baptized; the *person* who offers worship; the *person* who receives communion. And it is the divine *persons* who are worshipped—not their abstracted nature.[21] Prayer is always a personal activity, not simply an emotional or intellectual one. Similarly, the Scriptures are directed to the *person*, rather than simply to the mind or emotions, and only insofar as they elicit a *personal* response do they accomplish their purpose.

In summary, the revelation of divine mysteries—whether in prayer, the sacraments, worship—is made primarily to the human person and calls for a personal response, a response from "the heart." Those of limited intellectual capacity (through congenital weakness, disability or illness) can respond *personally* to God, and can appropriately be baptized and take their place in the Christian community.

Questions will always remain about the status of those of (apparently) negligible brain function. The human person ordinarily lives and relates to others in and through his nature—he even relates to himself in and through his nature—and it may be that that nature can become so incapacitated as no longer able to function as an effective vehicle of personal presence and action. (That this might sometimes happen does not, however, make it easy to judge exactly when, if ever, it has actually occurred.)

Restoring the Image

The effects of the fall are many. Fallen man loses sight of his fundamental dependence upon God and cannot discern the depth and wonder of God's love for him. In his ignorance, he becomes fearful of God. The fall also damages the communion right and proper between all human persons. Each finds himself more or less at odds with everyone else—and inclined to be resentful of such dependence on others as he is aware of. Within each individual a multiplexity of competing desires unsettles him and undermines his integrity. His relationship to his own created nature suffers distortion. So does his relationship to creation at large. Crucially, he misunderstands or mis-perceives his own potential. He cannot fully understand (or accurately imagine) what it would be like to be in communion with God with other people or with the rest of creation. Ignorant of where his true beatitude lies, he chases after false hopes and worships false gods. Mistrustful of God's plans for him, he looks for comfort and security. Fearful of radical change, he is content to settle down in a world he is familiar with. He is content, in other words, to remain in his fallenness—and his brokenness.

---

21. See Augustine, *Confessions*, 10.

The primary relationship with God will always be spiritual-personal; but those who are drawn into close encounter with God are likely to find that this affects their whole psycho-somatic make-up—their emotions and intellect, and their body too. Insofar as anyone has attained purity of heart, such that his communion in Christ is well advanced, his psycho-somatic make-up will function as an integrated whole, the various elements working together in harmony.[22] The divine self-revelation (received spiritually) will be interpreted by the intellect; the emotions (linking mind and body) will stir action, and the body will do what is necessary. In total, the psycho-somatic whole (i.e., the *person*) will serve the divine purpose. But after the Fall and outside Christ the divinely intended hierarchy within human make-up is inverted.[23] Rather than the body serving the mind, with the mind taking its lead from the spirit (itself in communion with the divine), what happens is that the demands and passions of the flesh[24] (including the desire for self-expression and self-perpetuation) stir the emotions, whose entreaties the intellect then seeks to satisfy and quell—while the heart-spirit tags along behind, half forgotten and, as a consequence of its neglect, withering. Tragically, fallen man, disordered and dysfunctional, misunderstands and misinterprets the divine call. The call to love and self-loss, he perceives, not as an invitation to enter a path that will lead to fullness of life, but as threatening his annihilation.[25]

Here I want to add a few further comments. Zizioulas suggests, "empirical man is 'the raw material' for the conception or creation of the real man."[26] The life of this world allows God's creative work on man's behalf to go forward. It is the setting in which people can learn to appreciate and enter into God's promises. But if God entrusts to each person a share in the redemptive work of Christ—and I have suggested that unless God calls people to share this work then he is not calling them to fullness of Christlikeness—then it can be taken on trust that God will put each person in that place, that setting, where he can best make his contribution to Christ's work. Importantly, part of God's gift to each person may be the particular psychophysical make-up which God "entrusts" to him—with all its strengths and weaknesses. Perhaps such an idea has to be taken on faith; for much in each and everyone's make-up is probably burdensome to that person. But it may

22. Cf. Lossky, *Mystical Theology*, 239; Meyendorff, *Byzantine Theology*, 14; Gysi, *Hidden Treasure*, 18ff.

23. Cf. Maximus, *Cent.Var.* 3:21 (*Philokalia* 2, 214). Cf. Palamas, "After the fall our inner being naturally adapts itself to our outer form," *Triads* 1.2.8.

24. *Philokalia* 1:363; cf. Ware, "Soul in Greek Christianity," 59–62.

25. Cf. Armitage, "Knowing and Unknowing," 9–11.

26. Zizioulas, "Human Capacity and Human Incapacity," 402

be that from the perspective of the End everyone will see that his or her psycho-physical constitution and the details of his or her life history were always blessings—even if they came in heavy disguise.

I have spoken of the essential unity of the human person and the way that the body and mind can be vehicles of personal presence and action. Could it be that in the world to come each person's resurrection body will be determined by the quality of the life he lived in this world? The what of *what* he is will be determined by the *who* of who he has become in this life. Insofar as someone has allowed his natural capacities, passions, and desires to be redeemed and regenerated, those capacities will be returned to him in eternal and abiding form. Those who have not allowed their contingent created capacities to be renewed may in the future *lack those capacities altogether*. This does not mean that people will have capacities determined by what they *deserve*. Rather they will given those capacities they have shown themselves *to be able to cope with* (cf. the Parable of the Talents; Matt 25:14ff.).

Those who find themselves lacking some of these eternal capacities may not feel deprived. Although their lives may be less full than they might have been, they will be content with their lot. Indeed, even in this life, things that entice or enchant some, play no part in the lives of others. Some have no appetite for opera, or no taste for fine wines, but do not feel themselves deprived.[27]

Boojamra has spoken dismissively of those who take Christian discipleship to be, in his inelegant phrase, "a one shot deal."[28] Talk of the "saved" and the "lost"—common in some of the churches of the Reformation but without counterpart in the Scriptures—he sees as implying that a one-off "decision for Christ" is enough to secure a place in the Kingdom. But the clear implication of the ontology of personhood with which I have been working is that this life is one in which people are to *prepare themselves* for life in the Kingdom, something which can only happen gradually. "For Christian life . . . is a process of conversion into Christ."[29] Only insofar as someone makes progress in conversion and acquires the virtues proper to Christ will it be possible for him to share fully in the life of the world to come. "[T]he eschatological, definitive victory of Christ must be

---

27. See also Simeon the New Theologian, *Ethical Treatises* 10:508–16 (SC 129, 296).

28. Boojamra suggests that such an idea is totally alien to the thinking of the early Church and insists that Christian education must be seen as a lifelong process, involving "lifelong transformation," Boojamra, *Foundations*, 13; cf. Schmemann, *For the Life of the World*, 78.

29. Taft, *Liturgical Understanding*, 9; cf. Searle, "Journey of Conversion," 48–9; Searle, "Liturgy as Metaphor," 112ff.

repeated in each one of us."[30] Those failing to make progress in conversion of life might have some part in the life of the End, but rather less than they might have had.

If Christian formation is not presented as a process of continuous growth, then the opportunities which God provides for acquiring the virtues required for life in the Kingdom might be missed. The ascetic tradition is unanimous about the need for on-going (post-baptismal) conversion. Brock, for example, reviewing Syriac tradition,[31] quotes Philoxenus and his description of three "births"—natural birth; baptism (whereby the Christian becomes a child of God); and a birth "of [one's] own will" resulting from the ascetic process whereby the Christian becomes established (mature) in a "spiritual life."[32] Those who take it that one-off conversion to Christ suffices may become disillusioned, and even abandon their discipleship, once they become aware that, for all their one-time enthusiasm, sin and disorder persist within them. Christian spiritual tradition, especially monastic tradition, has much to say on the stages of on-going conversion to Christ. The wider Church has much to learn from the masters of Christian ascetic life.

Active and Passive in the Way of Christian Growth

Both Eastern and Western Christian traditions have described two key aspects or stages in Christian growth. Eastern monastic tradition speaks of the active (or ascetic) and the contemplative stages.[33] John of the Cross speaks of active and passive nights of both soul and spirit.[34] In the first stage of conversion, often termed the *active* stage, the Christian is called to take steps to reform his life. During the second stage, the *passive*, he is called to surrender himself into ever greater dependence upon God, waiting on him and trusting in him while he himself works in the Christian a process of purification and regeneration. In fact, even during the early stages of conversion, even if it seems to the Christian that he is the one doing all the work (e.g., attending church, offering worship, praying, striving to live a disciplined life) in reality God is always the more active. He inspires, directs, and enables the Christian's conversion. But only after the Christian has made some progress will he see this.

---

30. Taft, *Liturgical Understanding*, 9.

31. *TSS*, 199–215.

32. *Discourse 9*; cf. Letter to Patricius, 97.

33. Cf. Armitage, "Knowing and Unknowing in Orthodox Spirituality."

34. *Ascent* I.i.2–3; *Night* 1.8.1; cf. Dicken, *Crucible of Love*, esp. 227–30.

The "passivity'" of the second stage must not be misunderstood; it is, so to speak, an "active passivity." The Christian is called *actively* to *surrender* himself into the hands of God, and to endure in patient trust while God's re-creative work is going on within him—and within his own created humanity. Mother Maria talks of the Christian work as that of "carrying" evil, and of overcoming all the "re-action, re-sentment, re-venge" within, of overcoming all conditioning.[35] The Christian carries the burden, God works the necessary re-creation.

This recreative work which God accomplishes in the Christian is commonly seen as passing through three stages, traditionally termed the purgative, illuminative, and unitive.[36] The theological tradition (from Paul onwards) has always struggled to articulate its realization that the whole work of redemption and re-creation is essentially God's work, while yet the Christian is called personally (i.e., in some sense actively) to appropriate the redemption—and the new life—which Christ offers. In allowing God's purgative and illuminative work to go forward within him, the Christian disciple proceeds towards that inner integration and that capacity for fully personal relationships that is God's ultimate will for him. The mature disciple is both fully and distinctly himself—and, as it were, *wholly* himself—while yet he is able also to be fully in relationship to others.

Mankind's capacity for personal relationship makes it possible for him to exercise a priestly ministry on creation's behalf. Sophrony writes, "the Divine Spirit embraces all that exists. Man as hypostasis is a principle uniting the plurality of cosmic being; capable of containing the fullness of divine and human life."[37] Through the exercise of this priestly ministry the human person can help to bring all of creation into right relationship with God. Insofar as this has happened, impersonal creation, while yet remaining impersonal (i.e., it does not become a person or number of persons), becomes able to bear a personal presence. This is what has happened with such things as relics and icons and with the sacramental "signs" or tokens of divine presence: the eucharistic species, the water of baptism, and the oil of chrism. It can happen too with temporal "objects": events, occasions, anniversaries, and the temporal cycles of the day, week, and liturgical year—these can come to

---

35. Gysi, *Jesus Prayer*, 43–44. Elsewhere she writes "Within ourselves we carry a hideous cauldron of passivity . . . of Anti-Spirit, which . . . turns mills of accusation and rejection," i.e., re-actions and responses, often rooted in the unredeemed unconscious, which will be less than personal. See Gysi, *Orthodox Potential*; cf. *Hidden Treasure*, 23.

36. Cf. Harton, *Elements of the Spiritual Life*, 305–32; Bouyer, *Introduction to Spirituality*, 243ff.

37. Sophrony, *His Life is Mine*, 43; cf. Lossky, *Image and Likeness*, 185–87.

bear personal presence. There can for the Christian be no communion in the divine which is not communion with the divine persons.

The Divine Action in the Life of the Christian: A Transforming, Unifying, *Spiritual* Action

At certain stages in Christian development, epiphenomena may occur: visions, bodily sensations, and intellectual insights, and the like. The effects can sometimes be overwhelming—as for Paul on the road to Damascus. But the ascetic tradition of both East and West[38] warns against the misinterpretation of such phenomena. Mainstream tradition is emphatic: God's primary purpose in any encounter with man is always man's *spiritual* growth. Man's work is to cooperate with this spiritual purpose, not to give his attention to psycho-physical epiphenomena. But since such phenomena are akin to the mundane perceptual and mental phenomena of "ordinary life," people often find it easier to relate to them rather than to that more profound work of God which is going on at the level of the spirit.[39] As progress is made in the spiritual life, however, so the human person becomes more of an integrated whole: body, soul, and spirit begin to work in harmony. For those who have made sufficient progress, the physical senses, reintegrated with the spirit, become able to discern the essentially spiritual action of God. Notably, Gregory Palamas claimed that the divine glory is directly perceptible to human senses—a claim integral to his holistic anthropology.[40]

---

38. On Eastern tradition see, for example, Lossky, *Vision of God*, 115–23; Burgess, *Holy Spirit: Eastern Christian Tradition*. Burgess outlines (3–4) the argument between those who (like Cassian and East Syrian, ʿAbdīshoʿ Ḥāzzaya) held that physical perception of things essentially spiritual was possible and those (like Evagrius) taking the contrary view that true knowledge of God transcended the senses; here Burgess also mentions the synthesis of Maximus (see also 40–45). In due course Simeon the New Theologian would suggest that the ecstasies and ravishments commonly *identified* with mystical experience are appropriate only to beginners and novices, i.e., to those unaccustomed to the divine (see Sermon 45; Ed. of Mount Athos (Russian) II, 488–89 (cf. Lossky, *Vision of God*, 120). For the person who has become more mature in the spiritual life communion in the divine is not unsettling or overwhelming in this way. See Lossky, *Mystical Theology*, 208f.; Lossky, *Vision of God*, 120, also Burgess, *Holy Spirit: Eastern Christian Tradition*, 53–62.

For an account of the (degenerate) move in Western thought from a concern with the divine source of epiphenomena to the phenomena themselves see McIntosh, *Mystical Theology*, 65–69. For a review of the Western approach to mystical phenomena see Bouyer, *Introduction to Spirituality*, 298–300. For an account of the Scholastic psychological model employed by John of the Cross see Dicken, *Crucible of Love*, 404ff.

39. Cf. Lossky's comments on Isaac of Syria (*Mystical Theology*, 208f.).

40. See Meyendorff, *Gregory Palamas*, 142–45, 150–52.

John of the Cross suggests that, during the process of spiritual growth, God will sometimes impart grace directly into the human spirit, by-passing the soul (emotions, intellect, physical senses).

> [T]he sensual part of a man has no capacity for that which is spirit, and thus, when it is the spirit that receives pleasure the flesh is left without savour. . . . [T]he spirit which all the time is being fed, goes forward in strength, and with more alertness and solicitude than before. . . . God now begins to communicate Himself to [the soul], no longer through the sense . . . , but by pure spirit . . . he communicates Himself to it by an act of simple contemplation, to which neither the exterior nor the interior senses of the lower part of the soul can attain.[41]

To say that the divine revelation and the human response occur primarily at the level of the heart or spirit is only to say that the origin and end both of the revelation and of the response is *personal*. What God reveals to man is not, in essence, a set of abstract truths about himself or a system of moral principles; he reveals, rather, *himself*. And he requires from man a *personal* response—a response which ultimately, encompasses body, soul, and spirit, but which cannot be reduced to the merely physical, intellectual or emotional. It cannot be less than personal:

The world has value only insofar as we see and receive the revelations and energies of the *person* of God who, in his essence, cannot be described, but whose energies are already at work in all creation . . . leading it towards its resurrection.[42]

---

41. *Night*, Bk. 1: 9:4; 9:8; cf. Maximus, *Thal.* 60 (PG90.624a), and Isaac of Nineveh (*Treaties* 22, 37, etc. Discussed in Alfeyev, *Isaac the Syrian*, 217–68).

42. Staniloae, *Victory of the Cross*, 21.

9

Christian Education—
Context and Process

Growth towards Fullness of Personhood:
A *Shared* Vocation

THE GOAL OF CHRISTIAN life is participation in the perfect relationships that constitute the life of the Kingdom—personal relationships, that is, between God and man, and between human persons. But if man's goal is participation in personal relationships, then his way of growth into that goal will be through learning to live in relationship with others. The life of the Church can be seen as the primary context ordained by God for created persons to learn to appropriate the virtues proper to Christ thereby become able to share (or be "fitted for") the life of the End. Within created space and time Church witness to and, so to speak, bears within itself the life of the End. That is, it exists as the communion of the created in the divine. But the Church also exists as an *economic provision*—that is, as a context for human formation and growth. The Church is both a witness to the End and the way of entry into that End.

In order that the Church might function as an effective context for personal formation God has enabled (or inspired) the introduction of patterns of life which will facilitate the growth of its members. This is part of what Lossky terms "the economy of the Spirit."[1] It can be argued that all human corporate life, whether in the family or in some other social grouping, was always intended (or ordained) by God to provide a context (for everyone involved) for growth in personal relationships. The development within Judaism of those patterns of life which the Church would ultimately inherit enabled Jewish life to function as a context for personal growth. In a parallel way, the work of the prophetic figures in Israel's history was significant: they taught the people to discern God's hand in all the events of their lives, personal and corporate, seemingly calamitous or seemingly propitious.

---

1. See Lossky, *Mystical Theology*, 156.

Importantly, the same Spirit who was at work to enable Israel and the primitive Church to establish patterns of life is still at work today. He enables the Church to revive and reform those patterns and to renew its prophetic ministry. He also looks to renew within the Church its ministry of teaching. Importantly, the Christian teacher, whether evangelist, catechist, or educator, is called to have a concern not just for the intellectual formation of those in his or her care, but for their spiritual well-being too. That concern can find expression in teaching about the faith and in his words of advice, but the teacher's concern for the spiritual growth and wellbeing of those in his or her care must go further. The teacher is called not only to inform people about the will of God, but to help them respond to the divine initiative. This the teacher does through helping those in his or her care appropriate the freedom which God wishes for them. It is a spiritual work. The work of teaching and the work of spiritual direction and pastoral care go hand in hand. Many scriptural texts, even in the Old Testament, show that intercession was central to the ministry of the prophets.[2]

Anyone called to a ministry of teaching or spiritual leadership can be seen as being presented, first of all, with the challenge of their own repentance and the call to re-order their own lives. But such people are also called—as a second aspect of their vocation—to help establish such structures and patterns of life as will help the members of their communities to make their own response to the divine revelation. And, like the prophets of OT times, such people are called to called to intercede for those in their care. The pattern recurs throughout the history of God's people.

Importantly, the corporate life of the Christian community provides a framework for the growth for *every* member of that community, each ministering to the growth of the others. Boojamra writes: "[T]he entire Church is educator, . . . each member . . . is a learner."[3] Not only do the more mature teach, assist, and support those newer to the faith, but newcomers help their teachers make further growth. Good learners, through their willingness to respond to the divine initiative, invite (or challenge) their teachers to deepen their own discipleship and commitment. The union of all human persons at the level of the heart means that wherever one person is entering more

---

2. E.g., Gen 18:22–32; Exod 32:11–14, 30–32; Num 14:13–19; 21:7; Isa 53:12; Jer 15:1; 18:20. Further references in Barr, *Escaping from Fundamentalism*, 34–36.

3. Boojamra, "Family and Community in Religious Development," 7. Also, "Christian education is by its nature total education. It involves total persons throughout their lives, and it involves the total parish in every aspect of its life," Boojamra, "Family and Community in Religious Development," 8.

fully into the divinely-appointed destiny of all humankind, so he (whether "leader" or "learner") will be drawing others forward too.[4]

Growth through Participation in the Spiritual Conflict

Because of the disorder present in the world through sin, Christian growth inevitably involves participation in conflict. There is conflict between the divine will (which seeks to draw all things to unity) and everything which seeks to divide or to resist the divine will. Baptism incorporates the Christian into the *unifying* energy and action of Christ; but as it does this, it also brings the Christian into conflict with everything which resists being drawn into the unity of Christ. To share Christ's life necessarily involves, therefore, sharing in his reconciliatory work.

The sin and disorder which the Christian is called to overcome appear as (i) the sin and disorder within the Christian himself; (ii) the sin and the disorder within the Church at large and within the local Christian community; (iii) the sin and disorder in the wider world and in creation at large. Through his Baptism the Christian has been given a place on the *winning* side in the spiritual conflict. Christ has already won the definitive victory and his victory cannot be reversed.[5] But the Christian's place in the risen and glorified Christ, though a gift, has to be appropriated. It is appropriated through the acquisition of the Christian (or Christ-centered) virtues, chief among which is always a willingness to suffer for the well-being of others. Sharing Christ's life means sharing his work, and this means sharing in his willingness to suffer for the sake of the wellbeing of others.

4. Admittedly, there are some who have made great spiritual progress with little (apparent) support from others, and even in the face of much opposition: people like Anthony, Francis, Seraphim, and Silouan. Their ministry often helped to renew life of the Church at large, and they are accounted spiritual giants. But in large part, what confirms them as giants is precisely their capacity to make progress against the odds and with little human aid—though we cannot always be sure what aid, whether human or (even perhaps) angelic they had. The account of Jesus looking to his friends in Gethsemane can be read as indicating that he (as mortal man) looked for human support. It may be important to recognize that at his crucifixion his mother and her companions offered him just such support—and why should we not believe this genuinely helped him?

5. I believe this is how the division between the "saved" and the "lost" in the Book of Revelation is to be read (e.g., Rev 21:8). The life of the Kingdom is what it is. There is no place within it for sin or for anyone who, *persisting* in his sin, would seek to damage, destroy or "spoil" that life. Those whose names are in the Book of Life are those willing to be incorporated into the paschal love of the Kingdom. Those outside are the would-be spoilers.

Corporate Aspects of the Spiritual Conflict and the Work of Renewal

There is a corporate dimension to the spiritual conflict. All are caught up the sin of Adam. Each person's sin will have consequences for others. Social disorder, alienation, warfare—many would see these as consequences of sin. It is difficult (often impossible) to explain why any particular individual or social group suffers in the way they do—and it is especially difficult to see why the innocent suffer. But at the same time, it is easy to see that sin always adds to the disorder and suffering in the world. Importantly, there is no simple "karmic," cause and effect, relationship between sin and suffering or sin and sickness. There is disorder in the world and we are all caught up in it in different ways. (So the wise person does not ask, "What have I done to deserve this?" nor "who is to blame," but asks rather, "What am I going to do now that this has happened?")

Nevertheless, while the corporate character of human life makes each human person a victim of the world's disorder; it also means that each one of us is also potentially part of God's answer to the problem of this disorder. Insofar as anyone is willing to labor and suffer with Christ for the world's healing and renewal, so that person enters into deeper union with Christ and contributes to the transformation of what might be called the spiritual climate of the world. Sophrony writes:

> The ontological unity of humanity is such that every separate individual overcoming of evil . . . inflicts such a defeat on cosmic evil that its consequences have a beneficial effect on the world as a whole.[6]

He continues:

> [The] nature of cosmic evil is such that, vanquished in certain hypostases it suffers a defeat . . . quite disproportionate. . . . [A] saint is an extraordinary precious phenomenon for all mankind . . . .[7]

Those who repent do so on behalf of all humanity, opening the way for the renewal and regeneration of all.

Those involved in the leadership of the Christian community will be called to guide and direct the community's participation in this redemptive ministry of Christ. But they cannot do this simply by standing apart, giving

---

6. Sophrony, *Saint Silouan*, 222; cf. Sophrony, *His Life is Mine*, 68f.

7. Sophrony, *Saint Silouan*, 223.

advice from the sidelines. Like Christ, they are called to suffer the effects of the judgment falling upon the world. And like him, they must suffer that judgment in their own selves. That suffering, if it is to be redemptive (and "successful") must be personal. Whether felt in the body, the mind or the emotions, that suffering will only be redemptive, will only be "successful," if it is accepted freely and willingly. In other words, if it is accepted personally.

It cannot be over emphasized that it is the *acceptance* of suffering, not the suffering itself that is redemptive. With the willingness to accept suffering comes an openness to God which allows his redemptive love to enter the world—to enter both the sufferer and their situation.

Those who share Christ's healing and redemptive work do so *by not allowing suffering or the pressure of temptation to turn them from their purpose or drive them to resentment or despair.* Thereby they rob sin of its power. Standing thus in the cross, they stand where the re-creative divine mercy flows into the world. This work can only be accomplished through participation in Christ, more specifically, through participation in Christ as he now is, in his eschatological glory. To the eschatological Christ belong all the virtues and graces which he acquired through the course of his life (see 168 below). Therefore to stand in Christ is to stand in all the virtues proper to the passion, the resurrection, and Pentecost. To share in Christ's work is to stand where the re-creative grace of the Spirit is flowing into the world; in other words, it is to stand in the cross.

Creative Suffering:
The Work That Sees Curse Become Blessing [8]

> At the end of *Paradise Lost* Adam is astonished "that all this good of evil shall produce" (xii, 470). This is the exact reverse of the programme Satan had envisaged in Book I.[9]

Sophrony maintains that everyone must go by the way of suffering.[10] Some choose to embrace suffering; others endure it only because they cannot find any way of escape.

8. See also Mother Maria's account of the "work of love" (Thekla, *Mother Maria,* 85–99), where she talks of the "dis-evil-ing of evil" and of "the integration of evil," i.e., "the carrying and redirection [of evil] into the one transcendent aim," Thekla, *Mother Maria,* 87, 85.

9. Lewis, Preface to *Paradise Lost,* 67; cf. *Paradise Lost,* vii, 613.

10. Sophrony, *His Life is Mine,* 74–75, also 37–40, 51, 59, etc. Zizioulas explores the place of suffering in Dostoevsky's vision of human formation and growth. Zizioulas, "Human Capacity and Human Incapacity," 430. Also "[T]he action of the enemy is permitted by God's will to the extent that it is necessary for us . . . . [H]umility needs to

Since the fall, there have been two kinds of suffering. There is a "healthy," "natural," morally neutral suffering grounded in the challenge of growth. It can be physical, mental or emotional. It is akin to the healthy ache of muscles after a hard day's labor, or the mental exhaustion after a tough game of cards. The second type of suffering derives from sin. It always has about it an air of evil, an element of disorder. It results from cruelty, violence, and torture; it results from oppression and mistreatment. This second kind of suffering has its ultimate root in the rebellion of those created persons (angelic and human) who have sought to secure their own well-being, in wilful disregard of God's purposes. Failing to trust in the divine beneficence they become preoccupied with self-preservation. They see others as rivals, or as objects to be used. There is no need to see this second kind of suffering as part of God's original plan. But God has made it possible for even this kind of suffering to be used creatively, so that good can come from it.

There is nothing inherently good or glorious about this second type of suffering; there is only glory in its creative use. Schmemann writes:

> [I]n Christ suffering is not "removed"; it is transformed into victory. . . . Through [Christ's] suffering . . . all suffering acquired a meaning [and] has been given the power to become itself the sign, the sacrament, the proclamation, the "coming" of that victory; the defeat of man, his very *dying* becomes a victory.[11]

As for learning to suffer creatively, William Law, recalling St Paul's injunction, "give thanks whatever happens" (1 Thess 5:17; cf. Eph 5:20), counsels:

> If anyone would tell you the shortest, surest way to all happiness and . . . perfection, he must tell you to make it a rule . . . to thank and praise God for everything that happens to you. For it is certain that whatever seeming calamity happens . . . , if you thank and praise God for it, you turn it into a blessing. . . . [A] thankful spirit turns all that it touches into happiness.[12]

Regarding the outcome of suffering, Abbé Huvelin (1838–1910) puts the matter plainly:

> Christ, in making the heart greater and more capable of great things, has at the same time made it more capable of feeling suffering . . . . He has made the heart capable of suffering. He has transformed suffering. . . . To suffer with Christ is to be more

---

be tested," Bacovcin, *Way of a Pilgrim*, 20.

11. Schmemann, *For the Life of the World*, 103–4.

12. Law, *Serious Call*, 197 (ch. 15); cf. Rom 8:28, 38.

extended in charity; it is to feel more the sufferings of others and
to press them to the heart. . . . Suffering makes us greater than
we would ever wish to be.[13]

Suffering can unite people; and unite them *in Christ*—in him as *End*, as
(personalized) *Kingdom*—as *fullness of love*.

The Son worked the redemption of the world. He did so by remaining
open to the Father even in the midst of suffering. Why was he willing to
suffer as he did? I would suggest that he do so because *only thus could the
world come to know the Father's love*. Love is revealed in a willingness to put
others first, and that will often mean to suffer (or to risk loss) for the sake of
their wellbeing. In other words, personhood is only realized in and through
a willingness to put others first and if needs be to suffer for them.[14]

All humankind is called to knowledge of and participation in the divine love. But that love is not "natural" to fallen humanity. It comes to man
only as gift. God desires that people should know and share in this love; but
they cannot do so in the abstract. That love must be exercised. It must be
practised. And there is no greater or more perfect way of doing this than
through bearing suffering and sin. The measure or anyone's willingness to
suffer is the measure of his love. As John of the Cross has it, by "putting love
in where love is not"[15] sin is overcome and its effects reversed. More love can
be "put in" where sin and suffering are at their greatest.

I have said that the spiritual conflict is encountered at various levels,
personal and corporate. Although it affects the whole world, the spiritual
conflict rages particularly fiercely wherever evil seeks to exploit goodness
or to destroy freedom—for example, in labor and concentration camps.[16] It
rages where the *person* is under threat. In a concentration camp, freedom
is destroyed or denied. (Inadvertently, those perpetrating cruelty surrender
their own freedom, binding themselves to their fallenness and putting their
personhood at risk.[17]) The monastery can be seen as standing as counterpart to the concentration camp. The monk aspires to shed the false, delusive
freedom beloved of a fallen world, and to appropriate the freedom of Christ.
And yet because freedom is a critical issue throughout the modern world,

13. Quoted in Louth, *Wilderness of God*, 18f. On Huvelin see Lefebvre, *Abbé Huvelin*.

14. Cf. Schroeder's phrase "suffering towards personhood," Schroeder, "Suffering
Towards Personhood" (esp. 261–62).

15. John of the Cross, *Letters* 12.

16. Solzhenitsyn, *Gulag Arcipelago* 2, 579–654; Clément, *Spirit of Solzhenitsyn*, 10,
191–94, 216. An important recent addition to the literature is Bouteneff, *Father Arseny*.

17. Clément, *Spirit of Solzhenitsyn*, 42–45; Fackenheim, *To Mend the World*, 273
("On Philosophy after the Holocaust").

the spiritual conflict rages across contemporary secularized society. Contemporary consumer society offers a false, illusory freedom ("have whatever you want"), while it fails to understand the freedom of Christ: the freedom not to have to try to secure one's own well-being.

The Spiritual Conflict and Church Renewal

The early centuries of the Church saw rapid (often violent) political and social change. From apostolic times onwards, many of those credited with establishing the Church's theological tradition endured times of persecution and episodes of hostility. The patterns of life they helped to develop sustained nascent Christian communities during turbulent times. And the theological tradition which developed emerged in parallel with liturgical, sacramental, hagiographic, iconographic, and ascetic traditions, and alongside a tradition of social (pastoral) concern. All the various aspects of the tradition of the Church were interdependent. All derived from a common experience of life in Christ, and all were directed towards the same end. "[T]he creed and the life of the church are so interwoven that no one can understand either without the other."[18]

The Church is called to proclaim to each historical era the unchanging gospel of God's redemptive, re-creative love. But only insofar as the Christian community is assimilated to Christ and participates in his work will it be able to do this. Indeed, if the Church is not participating in Christ's redemptive work has it any gospel to proclaim? Insofar, however, as the Church does share in Christ's re-creative ministry, so it can help renew the world's hope in God. The world will see that the divine love meets its most pressing needs and heals its most distressing wounds.

The Gospel accounts of Christ's sufferings, death, and resurrection reveal Christ's own response to the spiritual conflict. They show him *accepting* what was happening to him. These accounts reveal what might be termed an "active passivity." During his trial and at his death the Son did not fight back against his persecutors or seek to escape the trials that befell him. But he was not a passive victim. Rather, he committed himself to the active work of trusting in the Father's love and of resisting the temptation to turn from his purpose. He was passive in that he did not seek to secure his own future, his own survival, his own beatitude. He was *active* in his trust of the Father's goodness. (These same Gospel accounts, by the way,

18. Cf., Bebawi, "Eastern Orthodox Worship," 117. Earlier in the work (113) he makes much the same point when he explains, "Generations of Orthodox authors transformed what we may consider dry theology into poetry and prayer and put it all in the form of praise."

reveal the passivity of the Son's persecutors; they are shown as victims of their own inner turmoil, driven by blind passion and ill-founded hopes and fears. They seek to secure their own future, to make the world as they would have it be. Even the majority of Christ's disciples are shown to be victims of unresolved hopes and fears.)

The Gospels present a vision of God and of his kingdom. They also issue a challenge and pose a question: "Do I die with and in Christ, or do I seek to kill him and escape the challenge he presents?"[19] On the answer we give hangs our eternal destiny. The challenge Christ presents is the challenge of *who* he is and of *who* he calls us to be. "Can you love as I love?" We are not challenged to conform ourselves to some moral ideal. We are called to be conformed, each of us in our own unique and irreplaceable way, to Christ. This being so, the work of the Christian educator is to help everyone entrusted to his or her care to *learn* to give the right answer and make the right response to Christ's challenge. There are at least two stages to this process. The educator is called to build people's confidence in God's promises. The educator is also called to support the disciple's response to those promises. There are various aspects to this work, but ultimately it cannot but be a spiritual work, a work of prayerful, *personal*, spiritual support.

Through participation in the spiritual conflict, the Christian can come to stand within Christ. And standing in the Son, the Christian comes to direct, first-hand knowledge of God, and stands, so to speak, within the life and relationships of the Trinity. The Holy Spirit enables this. By enabling the Christian's participation in the life of the Son, he enables the Christian to know the great truths of life, as it were, from the inside.[20] And those who have come to such knowledge, become part of the living tradition of the Church.[21] They become *living evidence* of God's existence and love.[22]

The Patterns and Structures of Church Life

Schmemann sees the liturgical life of the Church as the principal context for "the eternal self-revelation of the Church" and "the fulfillment of the Church

19. Cf. Schmeman, *Holy Week*, 21–25; also Schmemann, *Eucharist*, 206.

20. Because of the ontological unity in Christ of all people, such a person also comes to know other people from, so to speak, the inside. He or she comes to know them as God himself knows them.

21. See, e.g., Sophrony, *His Life is Mine*, 44f.

22. Lionel Blue explains that while seeking to answer the question "What's the evidence [for God]?" he came to realize that "you have to become your own evidence," something which can only come "by letting the God you worship refashion you," Blue, *Bedside Manna*, 21.

in her divine human-plenitude"[23]—i.e., for receiving a vision of new life in Christ and beginning to appropriate that life. Vital though Schmemann's insight is, it needs qualification. For while worship can be accounted the preeminent context for encounter with God, Christ is present to humankind in many other ways. Boojamra, for example, acknowledges that participation in the liturgical life of the Church is essential to Christian formation but insists that more is needed. "Christian life has other aspects—prayer, ministry, etc., and Church membership concerns also ethical and intellectual matters."[24] Historically, "integration into the community was accomplished primarily through the liturgy, but never liturgy in isolation from the rest of the Church's life, witness, and service."[25] He warns:

> A liturgical thrust is at the heart of this socialization paradigm, and inasmuch as it represents true community action (*leitourgia*), it may in fact be the leading element. Too often, however, an exclusively liturgical model has been offered as the Orthodox paradigm par excellence.[26]

Within the Eucharist the Church realizes the very essence of its life and being. Schmemann writes:

> The Eucharist is *the* Sacrament of the Church, i.e. her eternal actualization as the Body of Christ, united in Christ by the Holy Spirit. Therefore the Eucharist is not only the "most important" of all the offices, it is also the source and goal of the entire liturgical life of the Church.[27]

But the Eucharist is not a single concern, isolated from the rest of Christian life. It is that which gives shape and structure, meaning and content to everything that belongs to the life of the Church. Christian study, worship, celebration of the sacraments and daily Offices, fellowship, growing into the inter-personal relationships proper to the community, and so

---

23. Schmemann, *Liturgical Theology*, 12. In the same place Schmemann presents worship as, "the public act which eternally actualizes the nature of the Church . . ., an act, moreover, that is not partial, having reference to only one function of the Church . . ., or expressing only one of her aspects, but which embraces, expresses, inspires, and defines the whole Church, her whole essential nature, her whole life."

24. Boojamra, *Foundations*, 30.

25. Boojamra, *Foundations*, 31. Boojamra also speaks of the "multidimensional integration into the actual community of faith," Boojamra, *Foundations*, 31. He also states: "[T]he Church's life in all its aspects is the matrix for the education ministry," Boojamra, *Foundations*, 7.

26. Boojamra, *Foundations*, 34. cf. 8.

27. Schmemann, *Liturgical Theology*, 20.

on—all these both flow from the celebration of the Eucharist and lead back towards it. The Church is called to celebrate the Eucharist and then to allow its whole life to take on a eucharistic shape. And this will be a *paschal* shape. The Church is called to find the cross—and the resurrection—in all things.[28] Weeping with those who weep and rejoicing with those who rejoice, the Church is called to find Christ in all circumstances and everyone's life. Christ has united himself with all humankind, and as creator and redeemer, origin and goal, he is everywhere present. It is the work of the Church not just to proclaim this, but to realize it and manifest it.

Christian Asceticism

Because of the unitive character of human make-up, spiritual growth can be initiated, supported, and fostered through events at any level of human life, intellectual, emotional, physical, aesthetic, etc.

The goal of Christian asceticism is to set the Christian free from all that would hold him or her back from responding to God and from all that might restrict the flow of divine love. The quest is to be free from all that binds the Christian to his fallen nature—to *mere* nature, to the past. Christian asceticism is directed towards the redemption and re-ordering of what ascetic theology terms the appetites or "passions," whether physical, intellectual or emotional.[29] Central to this process is an asceticism of the mind. The Christian is called to lay aside or leave behind that spirit of cynicism, complaint, and doubt which is rooted in a pessimistic, fallen worldview.[30] He is called to embrace the spirit of joy and gratitude proper to Christ himself—that *thanksgiving* of which we saw William Law speak (108 above). Thus, while fasting plays a part in Christian asceticism, so too can the right use of food. As the *Didaché* has it: "You gave men food and drink that they might *give you thanks (hina soi eucharistēsōsin)*" (10:3). Fallen man has to *learn* how and when to give thanks. A pattern of Church life including worship, prayer, feasting (as well as fasting), ministry to the needy, and

28. Staniloae, *Victory of the Cross, passim*, esp. 5, 21.

29. See *Philokalia* 1, 385; cf. *appetites* and *desires* in John of the Cross; e.g., Dicken, *Crucible of Love*, 56–57, 334–41.

30. This process involves, not the suppression or denial of thoughts or desires which at odds with God's purposes. It involves, rather, allowing such thoughts, urges, and desires to be present while *not allowing* them to govern us. The concern here is not with controlling our thoughts but rather with not letting our thoughts or urges control us. This is akin to Christ's own work in his passion and on the cross: he did not seek to escape the suffering (or even to suppress the desire to escape it), but he did not allow the turmoil around him (or even such turmoil as there was within) to divert him from his course.

celebration with the jubilant—this can help to promote the regeneration of the human mind and the recovery of a spirit of gratitude. Fallen man has to learn how to be grateful and joyful.

Central to the work of Christian asceticism is what can be termed the "healing of the memory." To have the freedom to be incorporated into Christ the Christian must allow the Spirit to release him from past conditioning and from the "wounds" that life has inflicted. Thereby he can become "incorporated" into Christ's own past and into *his* understanding of the world—what might be termed his memory. As a consequence of having grown up in a fallen world, unredeemed man has a distorted or disordered memory. This false memory—this misreading of life—inclines man to perpetuate his fallenness. It is an ascetic work to deny these false memories and to appropriate that new "memory" which belongs to Christ.

Providence and the Unfolding Divine Purpose

In seeing its whole life as the context for growth in relationship to God, the Church embraces and advances the vocation once laid upon the Israelites. Fundamental to Jewish self-understanding was the *experience* of *being formed as God's people*. The patterns of religious practice and belief which emerged in Judaism can only be understood in this context. These patterns arose and developed from the experience of being chosen and formed by God and they provided a framework for response to his initiative. The same experience of being chosen and formed should also be fundamental to the life of the Church in each generation. Unless the Church is in living relationship to God and knows itself to be in the process of being renewed—i.e., of being renewed by God—what has it to offer the world?

Personhood, Personal Experience, and the Theological Tradition

IF THE HUMAN PERSON is a unified whole constituted of many inter-relating elements (body, soul, intellect, emotions, etc.), then growth towards maturity can proceed along many lines and by many means. God's action in the Eucharist, for example, encompasses all that belongs to the worship and the worshippers. Christian liturgy incorporates poetic as well as propositional texts, and it involves the worshippers' senses and their physicality—through incense, music, icons, through eating and drinking at the table of the Eucharistic, through participation in liturgical movement and action: the sign of the cross, prostrations, bows, processions. The mind does not have priority. As Gregory Dix famously recognized, at the Last Supper Jesus directed his disciples, "*Do* this in remembrance of me," but did not instruct them to understand, interpret or explain what they had been called to do.[1]

Schmemann, arguing that the *experience* of divine things will often precede understanding, looks to the psalm verse: "Taste and see that the Lord is good" (Ps 34:8).

> What then should Christian education be, if not . . . introduction into [the] life of the Church, an unfolding of its meaning, its contents and purpose? And how can it introduce anyone into this life, if not by *participation* in the liturgical services on the one hand, and their explanation on the other hand? "O taste and see how good is the Lord": taste first, then see—i.e., understand. The method of liturgical catechesis is the truly Orthodox method of education because it proceeds from the Church and because the Church is its goal. In the past the catechumens were first brought into the church gathering, and only then the meaning, the joy, and the purpose of this gathering was explained to them. And what would we communicate in our Christian community today, if *explanation* is not preceded by *experience*, by

---

1. Dix, *Shape of the Liturgy*, 12–15.

all that we unconsciously inhale and assimilate even before we begin to understand?[2]

Where the Church stresses the importance of the intellect, the initial stages of evangelization and formation are likely to focus on explanation of "the things concerning Jesus" (cf. Acts 18:25), and subsequent education be largely concerned with further analysis and exposition. In those traditions which value highly the emotions—whether evangelical, charismatic, or one deriving from that late mediaeval Catholicism which focused concern on the affections[3]—evangelization and formation tends to be concerned with inculcating and fostering a vigorous emotional response to God. But neither an intellectualist nor an emotionalist approach is adequate to the gospel. Significantly, many of the young Russian intellectuals who converted to Christianity during the 1980s claimed that argument and intellectual insight played little part in their conversion. Often the turning point was the perception of the truth of the gospel or the reality of the risen Christ at some non-intellectual level—often as an intuition of God's personal presence.[4] Christian discipleship will stall where the focus of attention is not the person of God but rather on the disciple and his or her thoughts about God or feelings towards him. After the pattern of Dionysian and Maximian mysticism, the disciple's *experience* of God is to be transcended (and not allowed to become an end in itself) so that the *communion* with God can deepen.[5]

It remains true that whatever is disclosed to the human spirit requires interpretation and articulation; otherwise the Christian is unable to communicate his perceptions to others or even articulate it for himself. But all observation and interpretation is theory-laden. What is perceived is affected by what is thought likely or possible. It belongs to theologians to establish interpretational frameworks which will enable people to make sense of their experience, frameworks which must themselves be grounded in the Church's experience and not in speculation (cf. Matt 16:17)—and such frameworks must not be allowed to become ends in themselves. The hermeneutic circle can be broken, as I have suggested above, by the in-breaking of the divine life (74 above). Mother Maria writes: "Truth is the Mystery of the person of

---

2. Schmemann, *Liturgy and Life*, 13f. Cf. Meyendorff, *Byzantine Theology*, 6f., 191–210; Boojamra, *Foundations*, 14. See also Cyril of Jerusalem, *Cat. Or.* (NPNF 7, 144).

3. McIntosh, *Mystical Theology*, 69–75.

4. Cf. Goricheva, *Talking about God*, 17f., 50–52; Bourdeaux, *Risen Indeed*, esp. 24–37, 36f.

5. See McIntosh, *Mystical Theology*, 44–62.

Christ; and, because it is a person, the Mystery is inseparably linked with the event: the event of encounter."[6]

Personal Experience and the Theological Tradition

Meyendorff examines the idea that the experience of life in Christ provides the foundation for the Christian theological tradition. He accepts that Christian theology "may and should be based on Scripture, on the doctrinal decisions of the Church's magisterium, [and] on the witness of the saints," but insists that "to be a true theology"—

> it must reach beyond the letter of Scripture, beyond the formulae used in definitions, beyond the language employed by the saints to communicate their experience. For only then will it be able to discern the unity of Revelation, a unity which is not simply an intellectual coherence and constancy, but a living reality experienced in the continuity of the one Church throughout the ages.[7]

At the dawn of the twentieth century, Pavel Florensky expressed this forcefully: "living religious experience [is] the sole legitimate way to gain knowledge of dogmas."[8]

Conversely, theological tradition can help people towards direct knowledge of the realities of which they speak. Lossky writes:

> Christian theology is always . . . a means: a unity of knowledge subserving an end, which transcends all knowledge. This ultimate end is union with God or deification . . . . All the development of the dogmatic battles which the Church has waged down the centuries appear to us . . . as dominated by the constant preoccupation which the Church has had to safeguard, at each moment of her history, for all Christians, the possibility of attaining to the fullness of mystical union.[9]

6. Gysi, *Orthodox Potential*, 142.

7. Meyendorff, *Byzantine Theology*, 13. He continues, "[T]he Holy Spirit is the only guarantor and guardian of the continuity; no external criterion which would be required for a man's created perception or intellection would be sufficient." Also, "The true theologian was one who saw and experienced the content of his theology," Meyendorff, *Byzantine Theology*, 9; cf. Sophrony, *His Life is Mine*, 44f.

8. Florensky, *Pillar and Ground of the Truth*, 5; cf., Losky, *Mystical Theology*, 238f.

9. Lossky, *Mystical Theology*, 9f. Cf. "[M]an's true knowledge of God is the fruit of his deification effected by God," Mantzaridis, *Deification of Man*, 115. For a modern account of the relationship between spirituality (or mysticism) and theology see McIntosh, *Mystical Theology*, esp. chs 1–2.

The Christian theological tradition attempts to elucidate an *experience* of God's action in the world, of encounter with God himself. It also seeks to promote direct, first-hand encounter with God.[10] A prima-facie case emerges for arguing that God himself desires that the theological tradition should serve this end. The first Christian theologians had a pastoral concern. Paul's ministry, for example, is grounded in a conviction about what God has done in Christ. "[I]n Christ God was reconciling the world to himself" (2 Cor 5:19, cf. 5:18, Rom 5:10f., Col 1:21f.), and Paul himself looked, not only to live within that reconciliation himself, but to help others do the same. "We entreat you . . . be reconciled to God" (2 Cor 5:20, cf. Col 1:28–29). From the Jerusalem Council (Acts 15) onwards the Church's discussion of doctrinal issues was principally intended, not to solve the theoretical questions, but to correct misapprehensions or misrepresentations which might endanger the life and witness of the Church.[11] The interplay of doctrine and praxis is evidenced in the records of Church Councils where decisions on pastoral matters intermingle with rulings on doctrine. The majority of the acknowledged Church Fathers were much involved with the pastoral care of their communities, and although many of them were philosophically sophisticated they made little attempt to formulate any positive theological system.[12] Even momentous patristic and conciliar decisions (such as the *ousia-hypostasis* distinction) were not intended to be *philosophically* satisfying.[13] The intention was to rebut anything deemed alien to the gospel and to affirm what was essential, but there was little con-

10. Cf. Lossky's statement (*Mystical Theology*, 9): "There is . . . no Christian mysticism without theology; but, above all, there is no theology without mysticism." See Balthasar ("Theology and Holiness," 190) on this theme in Augustine and the Cappadocians.

11. "In the Byzantine period, as in the patristic, neither the councils nor the theologians show particular interest in positive theological systems. With a few exceptions . . . the conciliar statements assume a negative form; they condemn distortions of Christian Truth, rather than elaborate its positive content—which is taken for granted as the living Tradition and as a wholesome Truth standing beyond and above doctrinal formulae," Meyendorff, *Byzantine Theology*, 4; cf. 10f.

12. Meyendorff, *Byzantine Theology*, 4. Nellas speaks enthusiastically of the patristic injunction: "Fear a system as you would a lion," Nellas, *Deification in Christ*, 16 (he gives no patristic reference). Some, e.g., Origen and Dydimus the Blind, were more speculative, but even they were also entrusted with pastoral concerns.

13. Meyendorff, *Byzantine Theology*, 4f. Bebawi writes: "It is a mistake to think of the doctrine of the Trinity as an *explanation* of the nature of the Godhead," Bebawi, "Eastern Orthodox Worship," 119. Meyendorff suggests that the Cappadocians remained loyal to the *ousia/hypostasis* terminology, regardless of criticisms, "because they saw no other means of preserving the Biblical experience of salvation in the fully identifiable and distinct persons of Christ and the Spirit, an experience which could never enter the categories of philosophical essentialism," Meyendorff, *Byzantine Theology*, 181f; cf. Rahner, *Trinity*, 110f.

cern with philosophical coherence.[14] Only after a theological tradition and a body of doctrine were well established did philosophical and theological speculation increase, such that eventually, and especially in the West, the organic link between theology and praxis was broken and theology became predominantly an intellectual exercise, something which would have been inconceivable in earlier generations.[15]

In other words, the early Christian tradition sees theology as both grounded in and turned towards the mystery of God. The term often used to describe this theology is "mystical theology."[16] This term *mystical theology* is a difficult one. Since the emergence of the notion of the individual, and especially in a post-Cartesian era, the ideas both of *mystery* and of *experience* are liable to be misunderstood. The mystery with which the Church's theological tradition is concerned is not some corpus of esoteric knowledge, the preserve of the privileged few. It is the mystery of who God is and of what he calls man to be; and this is not a mystery that God hides away or keeps secret. It is a mystery God seeks to disclose; indeed God has created each human person with no other intention than that he or she should come to live within this mystery. Moreover, this mystery will be experienced, not as private, inner experience—after the fashion in which mystical experience came to be conceived in the mediaeval West[17]—but as participation in a new and different order of relationships. It means, first of all, entry into a new relationship with God, but also entry into new relationship with others, and indeed with the whole of creation. *For those who participate in this mystery the whole character of life, its very foundation is changed.* As Zizioulas explains, initiation into Christ brings "the emergence of a new identity through a new set of relationships, those provided by the Church as the communion of the Spirit."[18] These new relationships can only be engaged in *personally*. They have implications for the whole of human make-up; each Christian is involved in them body, soul, and spirit. The Christian is not simply introduced into intellectual knowledge of God, nor into "spiri-

14. For example, Gregory of Nyssa, *Not Three Gods* (PG45:115–36), repeatedly insists that three hypostases does not mean three gods but he does not seek to explain philosophically how this might be so. Cf. Gregory Nazianzen (*Or. 23.8*): "They are One distinctly and distinct conjointly, somewhat paradoxical as that formula may be." See also Basil, *HS* 18.

15. On this split see Morris, *Discovery of the Individual*, 165f.; McIntosh, *Mystical Theology*, 62–89; Balthasar, "Theology and Holiness"; Louth, *Theology and Spirituality*.

16. The term itself dates back only to Pseudo-Dionysius, but the idea or understanding behind it is more primitive. See McIntosh, *Mystical Theology*, 30–34, 44–61.

17. McIntosh, *Mystical Theology*, 7–8.

18. SCMCS I, 28.

tual" awareness of him (as if spiritual experience were a private experience, separable from the other aspects of human make-up or attainable by the isolated individual, separated from his brother and sisters). As the Christian progresses he or she is brought to personal knowledge of God and of all that belongs to him. This direct, "mystical knowledge" of God, far from being esoteric and exclusivist, is all-inclusive. It does not render the affairs and concerns of space and time insignificant or meaningless. And it is not an escape from them. It brings them into perspective and gives them meaning and value. The entire created realm belongs to God. And the same God in whom creation has its origin also gives to creation its ultimate value. Creation has no ultimate value separate from God's intention for it.

The whole of the Church's life—its liturgy, teaching, pastoral ministry, etc.—is ultimately concerned with this mystery. Everything inter-relates, inter-connects. Renewal of pastoral and liturgical practice can be expected to lead to renewed experience of who God is—and therefore to theological renewal. In turn, theological renewal can be expected to promote further developments in liturgical and pastoral praxis and a better understanding of the Church's relationship to the prevailing culture—which in turn might help clarify the agenda for Christian education. For although the essential mysteries at the heart of the gospel are unchanging, as history goes forward and cultures evolve so the Church must equip its members to cope with the particular challenges (and opportunities) that these new conditions bring. I return to this theme later in this section and in my final chapter.

The Paradox in Theology: Speaking of the Mystery

Apophatic Theology and the Response of Faith

The Christian theological tradition contains much apparent paradox. This is found not least in the doctrines of the Trinity and the incarnation, and in the Church's teaching on freedom and obedience (which amounts to its teaching on the Holy Spirit). Lossky explains:

> [W]e must live the dogma expressing a revealed truth, which appears to us as an unfathomable mystery, in such fashion that instead of assimilating the mystery to our mode of understanding, we should, on the contrary, look for a profound change, an inner transformation of the spirit, enabling us to experience it mystically.[19]

19. Lossky, *Mystical Theology*, 8.

The theological tradition *challenges* the believer.[20] The "inner trans-formation of the spirit" called for here is not solely the adoption of a new set of ideas, but a re-orientation of the whole person, "a spiritual rebirth."[21] This means not a simple modification or adaptation of the old life to new circumstances, but a new beginning (cf. 2 Cor 5:17). Life is moved onto the new ground of the Son's redeemed and perfected humanity and the new dynamic of his perfect relationship, by the Spirit, to the Father, and to all creation.[22]

Considering the paradoxes in Christian doctrine (sometimes termed "antinomies"[23]), Lossky explains:

> It is not a question of suppressing the antinomy by adapting dogma to our understanding, but of a change of heart and mind enabling us to attain to the contemplation of the reality, which reveals itself to us as it raises us to God, and unites us, according to our several capacities, with him.[24]

This apophaticism acknowledges that divine truth transcends human understanding: the human mind cannot grasp it, human language is inadequate to express it. But this apophaticism is not just a philosophical pseudo-sophistication in which every affirmation is neatly balanced with a corresponding denial. It is an apophaticism which looks neither to idolize the mind, nor to deny it a place in spiritual life. It looks, rather, to giving the mind no more (and no less) than its due.

Lossky writes,

> A movement of apophasis . . . accompanies the Trinitarian theology of the Cappadocians and, in the last analysis, decon-ceptualizes the concepts which are ascribed to the mystery of a personal God in His transcendent nature.[25]

Radically, for example, it is claimed that although God exists, he does so in a manner so unlike that of any creature that he could also be said not to

---

20. Lossky, *Mystical Theology*, 40–43.

21. Cf. Lossky, *Mystical Theology*, 238f.

22. "[Apophaticism] is an existential attitude which involves the whole man: there is no theology apart from experience; it is necessary to change, to become a new man," Lossky, *Mystical Theology*, 39. Cf. Palamas, PG 34:188c. Cf. Musther, "Exploration into God," 63–65.

23. See Meyendorff, *Byzantine Theology*, 5, 224–27.

24. Lossky, *Mystical Theology*, 43.

25. Lossky, *Image and Likeness*, 24.

exist.[26] Apophaticism represents, then, not just a philosophical stance, but a disposition of the heart: a disposition of faith, of trust, one involving the "obedience of faith" (cf. Rom 1:5). For faith, as praxis, as trust, concerns the *person*, not just the intellect. At its purest and most extravagant, faith is realized in the openness to the unknown of the paschal mystery: in that dying into the hands of love where there is no *objective* guarantee of safety but only the *personal* guarantee of God's goodness. Christian apophaticism is faith leading to personal knowledge. It issues in what Meyendorff calls "a contemplation greater than knowledge."[27] Lossky considers that Christian theology "will never be abstract, working through concepts, but contemplative: raising the mind to those realities which pass all understanding"[28]—to *personal* knowledge of God, to union with him and participation in his life.

A tension, an antinomy, lies at the heart of the theological enterprise. This is clearly recognized in Byzantine tradition, where there is the belief—described by Meyendorff as "optimistic"—that although the human mind cannot *fully* comprehend the divine revelation nor human language express it, nevertheless salvific truth *can* be expressed in ways that are accessible (and valuable) to the human mind.[29]

The essential content of Christian revelation is the *person* of the Son. And although human language cannot fully express that revelation, the Son is the eternal divine *Logos*, and therefore human language, thought, and reason can be part of the divine economy—Lossky's "economy of the Spirit."[30] The Spirit can enable human language to speak *effectively* of ultimate realities, to bear the content and even the "energy" of the divine life—of the divine revelation and the call to repentance and discipleship.

But the Spirit guides the Church not only into the effective use of language, but into the development of effective patterns of life—liturgical, pastoral, catechetical, etc. These will be patterns which help to reveal divine truth and mediate divine grace. Such patterns function "inspirationally." They mediate the life of the End. But like the words of Scripture and the Creeds, these patterns and practices do not work automatically or by magic. Nothing

---

26. Cf. Dionysisus, *Myst*, 5 (PG3:1045d–1048b); cf. Palamas, PG 150:937a, 1176b.; Krivocheine, "Gregory Palamas," 138.

27. Meyendorff, *Byzantine Theology*, 13 (quoting Palamas *Triads* 2:3:67). Cf. Bebawi, "Eastern Orthodox Worship," 120; Lossky, *Mystical Theology*, 37. Florensky takes for the epigraph of his book a phrase from Gregory of Nyssa: "Knowledge becomes love," *Soul*, PG46:96c; cf. Florensky, *Pillar and Ground*, 65, 462, n.115.

28. Lossky, *Mystical Theology*, 43.

29. Meyendorff, *Byzantine Theology*, 5. For a Western account of some of the issues involved here see Mascall, *Words and Images*.

30. Lossky, *Mystical Theology*, 156ff.

in the theological tradition or in any other aspect of Christian tradition functions effectively except that it functions through the personal response of the Christian to what was always a personal initiative of God.

The Fundamental Challenge in Education

Plato may have been the first to consider the question: can wisdom, truth or knowledge of ultimate mysteries be taught? (cf. Letter 7: 340b–341e[31]). Mother Maria Gysi saw this question as central to her own vocation.[32] She came to the conclusion, "No, it is not possible. . . . We have no direct means of infusing and transferring the love of our souls into others."[33] She believed that Plato had reached this same conclusion—and that St Benedict had too. But she also claimed that both Plato and Benedict held that in the right circumstances truth will "seize upon" the disciple.[34] The work of the educator is to prepare the way for this to happen.

Explaining his work as a teacher of literature C. S. Lewis said, "Oddly as it may sound, I conceive that it is the chief duty of the interpreter to begin analyses and *to leave them unfinished*."[35] In fostering a student's engagement with a text, the teacher looks for a result which he himself is unable to produce, and where any attempt by him to do so would be counter-productive. Likewise, the Christian educator must strive to prepare the disciple for an encounter with Christ, but then stand back and leave room for that to happen. Just as Lewis as a teacher of literature allowed room for the text to speak, so the Christian educator must allow room for God to speak—and to act.[36]

The Church possesses no clear-cut, unambiguous story, easily taught and learnt, or automatically commanding allegiance. What the Church does

31. Whether or not Plato is the author of this particular letter, this passage can be seen as expressing "the question which challenged [Plato] all his life." See Gysi, *Hidden Treasure*, 13ff.

32. Gysi, *Hidden Treasure, passim*; also Gysi, *Realism*, 45–46. Cf. Schmemann (*Journals*, 8, 41): "It is a common mistake to think that education is on the level of ideas. No! It is always a transmission of experience. . . . The most important question is how does objective truth become subjective."

33. Gysi, *Hidden Treasure*, 13.

34. Parmenides 130e.

35. Lewis, *Allegory of Love*, 345, emphasis added. Lewis is writing of the interpretation of poetry, specifically here of images in Spencer's *Faerie Queen*. But the idea is of more general application.

36. Is it important for theologians to recognize that God will not be interested in hypothetical questions and cannot be expected to answer them?

provide is a way of *approaching* Christ, of moving into ever deepening relationship with him.

It is the legitimate aim of a school or college course in religious studies to explore ideas about God and to give information about the history of the Church and the Christian tradition. But the educational and formational ministry of the Christian community must have a different concern. Within the Church, teaching about Christ is effective and worthwhile only where it nurtures in the disciple those dispositions which will place him of her where he or she can receive the grace to live according to Christ, i.e., the grace to be *indwelt* by Christ and to live *in* Christ, as a member of his body. (An assumption that classroom-type learning is the foundation of discipleship is perhaps a legacy of the Reformation, where divided Catholics and Protestants wanted the informed allegiance of their respective supporters and particularly of their children.[37])

This classroom approach, with its emphasis on explanation and book learning, challenges the learner intellectually, but otherwise does little to shape him or her. Faith becomes a matter of adherence to a system of beliefs, not of active trust in God (cf. the contrast between the Latin terms

---

37. See Boojamra, *Foundations*, 33, 41, 70. Many Christian educationalists have contributed to a clearer understanding of the Church's educational ministry (e.g., Astley, *Christian Religious Education*; and the papers in Francis, *Christian Perspectives for Education*). Often, however, this work is undermined by a less than adequate vision of the gospel. Astley's *Philosophy of Christian Religious Education* represents a good example. Astley himself says, "Christians may argue about what constitutes Christian religious education because they do not agree as to what constitutes Christianity. In my experience most . . . disagreements about Christian religious education are of this kind" (10). He proposes working with a "broad" conception of Christian education (9), insisting that Christian religious education cannot be reduced to academic study, but is "a confessional, churchly activity of evangelism, instruction and nurture" (cf. 77). Evangelization and catechesis belong to the same life-long work (12). He acknowledges the importance of the communal dimension in Christian life (82, 90–92, 274) and is adamant that Christian education has a practical concern (114f.), suggesting all of life provides opportunities for learning and growth (see esp. ch. 6). But he confronts what he calls "that powerful theological lobby that distinguishes the gospel of God's act and revelation from that most human, fallible and mundane of phenomena—religion" (111). He refers specifically to Barth, *Church Dogmatics*, vol. I, Part 2, esp. 303, 314, 325–61). He comments: "Theology may focus solely on hidden states such as God-relatedness . . . . But it will . . . [have] little to say that is of much practical use. . . . [E]ducational practice needs a definition of being Christian that is of some use to it. Epistemology takes precedence over ontology in education, and the useful version of epistemology is a version of empiricism" (115). But Astley finds that his only option involves identifying "being Christian" with "doing things Christianly" (115), which surely, by anyone's reckoning, is a very weak definition. My own belief is that unless all things claiming to be Christian are grounded in ontological concerns, then they are of little value at all: ontological issues have always lain at the heart of the gospel: *ei tis en Christō, kainē ktisis*, 2 Cor 5:17; cf. John 1:12, etc.

fides and *fiducia*).[38] And although moral instruction and exhortation may feature in a classroom approach to Christian education, in and of themselves they cannot bring about deep or lasting change. Boojamra writes, "Correct doctrine is valuable not as an academic exercise, but as a model which arises from faith and which allows faith to happen,"[39] and it is possible to describe the Church's moral concern in similar terms. "Jesus Christ as the ideal man, the man who is with God, and finally is God . . . This is the foundational morality of the Gospel, not the do's and don'ts . . . but the *very person* of Jesus."[40] In patristic tradition, as Boojamra explains, the concern of morality "was not behaviour; it was being (ontology), having as its ultimate goal assimilation of the person to God . . . through the humanity of Christ."[41] Where it is not identified with intellectual formation, Christian education is often interpreted as ethical formation. But Christian morality should not be seen as a human work leading to communion with Christ, but as a *consequence*, an *outworking*, of the Christian's communion in or with him. "I tell you, her sins, which were many, have been forgiven; hence she has shown great love" (Luke 7:47).

Moral exhortation and study of doctrine are useful only insofar as they function personally and assist the Christian deepen his relationship with Christ. Within the life of the Christian community, Christ can be encountered and faith in him can be learnt (or appropriated). Here the mini-church of the Christian family is significant.[42] As in classical Judaism three things—the family, the person, and the community of faith—stand "dynamically interrelated and interacting."[43] The faith proper to the community is learnt (or appropriated) through shared ritual and practice. Learning the shared beliefs of the community is only one element in this process; for some, including children and those of limited intellectual accomplishment, it will be a minor element.[44] To quote St Basil, the Christian community is called to create and live within that "disposition" (*diathesis*) or culture where faith can happen.[45]

38. Cf. Thatcher, *Truly a Person*, 135.

39. Boojamra, *Foundations*, 73; cf. 69: "You cannot teach children faith, but . . . can teach them *about* religion. . . . Faith comes as a gift of God to a person willing/able to receive it . . . ." Cf. Westerhoff, *Will Our Children Have Faith?* 22.

40. Boojamra, *Foundations*, 124.

41. Boojamra, *Foundations*, 121.

42. Cf. Boojamra, *Foundations*, 60–106, esp. 69–70, also 52f.; see also Boojamra, "Christian Integration"; "Family and Community in Religious Development."

43. Boojamra, *Foundations*, 164. See Marrou, *Education in Antiquity*, 314.

44. See Boojamra, *Foundations*, 89f.

45. *Moral Rules* 80:22.

The Classroom Model of Christian Education

In Boojamra's terms, the pattern of Christian education is *"formational, not informational."*[46] The Christian neophyte/disciple has not embarked on a course of academic study and the classroom paradigm is an inadequate model for the educational/formational ministry of the Church.[47] The neophyte's practical training in Christian life is more akin to an apprenticeship than a studentship.[48] Perhaps even apprenticeship is not an entirely fully adequate model. The training undertaken by the neophyte should affect *every* aspect of his or her life and lead to the re-ordering of all his or her relationships and his or her whole conceptual framework.[49]

I spoke above of theology and Christian life as being concerned with knowledge of and participation in the mystery of who God is. The process of Christian formation might be described as *mystagogic*. Mystagogy is the ancient term for the process whereby neophytes are introduced into religious mysteries—classically the Eleusinian mysteries or something similar. In Christian tradition the term mystagogy has been used (by Dionysius, Maximus and others) to speak of the process whereby the Christian disciple is introduced into a more complete knowledge of the mysteries proper to the Church. But as I have said, these are not the mysteries of a body of esoteric knowledge, but the *relationships* that are at the heart of the gospel—relationships with Christ, and (in him, by the Spirit) with the Father, with the other members of the eschatological community, and indeed with creation—all of which relationships are inherently mysterious, unfathomable.

Perhaps there is no better model for Christian education/formation than the monastic novitiate. Monastic formation involves the study of doctrine and Church history, but also the acquisition of practical skills, and an appropriate *askēsis*—of body and mind. It is directed towards the regeneration of the disciple in his entirety—in his personhood.[50] Moreover, monastic life is inherently communal or corporate: the novice is called to become integrated into the shared life of the community—its worship, prayer, stewardship of creation, and any ministry it might have to

---

46. Boojamra, *Foundations*, 10.

47. Boojamra, *Foundations*, 8, 10, 16, 33; cf. Westerhoff, *Will Our Children Have Faith?* 3:5.

48. In the New Testament *mathētēs* generally bears the meaning "trainee," "learner," not "pupil" or "scholar." Cf. *manthanō* in LS.

49. Boojamra, *Foundations*, 36–37.

50. See. Also Boojamra (*Foundations*, 112): "There is an . . . integrating aspect to *askesis* . . . ."

the wider world. In short, the novice is called to appropriate the faith and experience of his community.[51]

The monastic novitiate represents a "socialization model" of Christian formation. Boojamra, looking at formation within parish communities, looks to just such a model. As he sees it, the Christian neophyte must take an active and responsible part in the whole life of the Christian community.[52] "[P]eople, both children and adults, become Christians not by learning *about* Christianity but by being integrated into an existing Church," and they do this "through experiencing the rites, symbols, and stories of the community."[53] Meeks borrows a term from Stanley Hauerwas and describes the first Christian communities as "communities of character."[54] Such communities look to re-shaping behavior through a dialectic between community and self. "Character takes shape," Meeks explains, "within a social process."[55] But the "character" with which the Church is concerned is not moral rectitude, however defined. It is holiness, as defined by the paschal mystery. Thus the "social process" within which that character is formed must be defined in relation to the eucharistic life of the Church, a life all-encompassing and thorough-goingly paschal. It reflects the life of the heavenly Jerusalem. It is in relation to the eschatological community of the heavenly Jerusalem that the Church discovers, defines, and realizes itself. If, then, a socialization model of Christian formation is adopted, it must be recognized that the "society" into which the Christian learns to become incorporated is not simply the life of the Christian community here on earth, but of the eschatological community of the heavenly Jerusalem (cf. Eph 2:19; Phil 3:20).

Schmemann writes:

> I emphasize: [the aim of religious education] is not merely the communication of "religious knowledge," not training a human being to become a "good person," but the "edification"—the "building up"—of a member of the body of Christ, a member of that new "chosen race" and "holy nation" (1 Pe. 2:9) whose mysterious life began at Pentecost . . . . Religious education is nothing else but the disclosing of that which happened to man

51. Meyendorff, *Marriage*, 59–60; Boojamra, *Foundations*, 50, 168f.

52. Boojamra, *Foundations*, 29–59, and *passim*. See also Marthaler, "Socialization," Abraham, *Logic of Evangelism*, 13, 38f., 98f.

53. Boojamra, *Foundations*, 30–31.

54. Hauerwas, *Community of Character*. Cf. Gustafson, "Church," 83–95; cf. Verhey, *Ethics and the New Testament*.

55. Meeks, *Moral World of the First Christians*, 12.

when he was born again through water and the Spirit, and was made a *member of the Church*.[56]

Membership of the Church is not an end in itself, but serves as a prelude and preparation for participation in the life of the world to come—with theosis, total conformity to Christ through personal participation in his life, as the ultimate goal.[57]

Moral and Ethical Formation and the Paschal Mystery

Boojamra considers personhood, being in the "divine image," and moral development as "intimately tied together."[58] He discusses the contribution to the understanding of moral development and personal growth made by such developmental psychologists as Erickson, Piaget, Kohlberg.[59] Here I shall not explore their views but I would suggest that in all discussion of human development it will be necessary to clarify both the ultimate ground for moral behavior and its ultimate goal. At one time, the Church could invoke various authorities: the Scriptures, the Magisterium, the established tradition of the Church. But in a post-Enlightenment, post-Nietzschian era, such appeals have little power. There remains, however, one authority which is transcendent and absolute. It is the *personal* authority of the crucified and risen Christ—and by extension, the authority of those united to him in his dying and rising to new life.

Of course, the paschal, personal love of the Trinity and of the saints is inherently self-sacrificial and non-coercive. Personal maturity looks for the freedom and maturity of others. Anyone exercising (or claiming) authority in Christ's name—as bishop, pastor, superior of a religious community, spiritual guide, etc.—must look to enable the freedom of others (and to inspire their free choice of God's will for them).

Only on this inherently personal, self-sacrificial, non-coercive authority, and on this alone, a secure and worthwhile morality can be built. It will be a personal morality, a morality of virtue.[60]

---

56. Schmemann, *Liturgy and Life*, 11.

57. Boojamra, *Foundations*, 31.

58. Boojamra, *Foundations*, 119.

59. Boojamra, *Foundations*, ch. 4, esp. 124–62; also 40–45.

60. For recent philosophical interest in virtue see MacIntyre, *After Virtue*; MacIntyre, *Whose Justice?*; MacIntyre, *Three Rival Versions*. On Virtue Ethics see *OCCT*, 742b; Crisp and Slote, *Virtue Ethics*; Statman, *Virtue Ethics*, 1–41; Trianosky, "What is Virtue Ethics," 42–55. For an attempt to establish a non-theistic ethics of virtue see, e.g.,

In summary, it appears the process of personal growth should not be identified with intellectual formation, social refinement or cultural sophistication. The scriptural tradition of the 'anawim (i.e., "the poor and despised of the Lord") suggests that cultural sophistication is not central to God's will for humankind.[61] Similarly, the biblical tradition honouring the "wisdom of the simple" views intellectual sophistication with caution (cf. Matt 11:25ff; 1 Cor 1:26–31). The tradition of the "holy fool," best known in Russian Orthodoxy, but not unique to that tradition, indicates that spiritual maturity should not be identified with the psychological integration or "wholeness" promoted by present-day psychotherapies.[62] Intellectual and aesthetic formation *may* facilitate human maturity, and therapy can help heal the effects of sin on human make-up, but they bear only indirectly on the life's ultimate goal. The gospels show Jesus frequently warning, after the manner of the OT prophets, that success in worldly matters can cause complacency and indifference to the things of God.

Freedom and Discipleship

At the heart of the Church's educational ministry is the challenge to help the disciple make a free response to God's initiative. I have already touched on this theme, and I suggested that there are two sides or parts to this work: the work of setting the individual free both from false conceptions of God and himself and also the work of setting the disciple from the fear that these induce. In other words, the disciple is to be set free from his past, his conditioning, his *fallen nature*. But even someone free from all these is not necessarily living in conformity to the divine will. He is simply in that place where he can *choose* to respond to the divine will. But that choice still has to be made. Knowing the divine will and choosing to do it are different things. The familiar claim "I would have no trouble doing the divine will if only I really *knew* what it was!" is naïve. The prophet Jonah was not in doubt about the divine will. He simply didn't want to do it. Ignorance is only part of the problem that Christian education has to address.

And this is where the second part of the work of Christian formation comes in. The Christian educator and the Christian community are charged with encouraging and supporting disciples while they make their free response to God—and with inspiring them to make their response to him.

Heller, *Ethics of Personality*.

61. See Bouyer, *Christian Spirituality*, vol 1, 43f.; Cf. Causse, *Les pauvres d'Israël*.

62. Ware, "Great Fast," *passim* (see bibliog. at 26.n5); Saward, *Perfect Fools*. Yannaras, *Freedom of Morality*, 65–75.

Since that response must indeed be *free* and *personal* there can be no place in the Church's educational ministry for bullying, bribery, intimidation or any other form of coercion, however (supposedly) well intentioned. In other words, the educator and the Christian community have to offer inspiring *personal* support, something only possible because of that deep communion existing between persons at the level of the heart.

Section Summary

I have sought to show that Christian education and Christian discipleship must be concerned primarily with growth towards personal maturity. I have explored the nature of personhood and the relationship between personhood and the various "aspects" of human make-up. I have also explored the link between personal maturity and the paschal mystery. I have spoken of the way in which a prerequisite for personal maturity is that disposition of gratitude which opens the way for creative use of the suffering and disorder that are so much a part of life in a sin-stricken world.

I have also explored the idea that the primary context for personal growth is the life of the Christian community. That life provides a context in which people can be supported while they are freed from all that binds them to their fallenness and they acquire the courage (or faith) to make their free response to God, and so become able to relate *personally* to the Trinity, to other human persons and even to non-human creation. This is a process which I believe can best be described as mystagogic: through baptism the Christian is introduced into the mystery of communion in Christ and into the relationships of the Kingdom; the work of Christian formation is to help people learn to live within those mysteries—mysteries which are concerned, not with esoteric knowledge, but with the mystery of what it is to be a person and to live in fully personal (loving) relationship with God and with others.

In my next section I shall explore the idea that the right use of various temporal cycles—in particular the seven-day week—can help the life of the Church function effectively as a context for personal growth.

Part II

Towards a Theology of Liturgical Time

Eschatology and the Liturgy of Time

ACCORDING TO A CELEBRATED phrase of Pius XI, "Spiritually we are all Semites."[1] The significance of the Jewish background to Christianity has been increasingly recognized in recent times.[2] Among the things which the primitive Church inherited from Judaism were an appreciation of God's involvement in history and an approach to the use of time. These helped to shape the hopes and practices of the first Christians and can be seen as fundamental to the gospel.[3]

An Inherent Dualism

The emergence of a Christian liturgy of time and the part played by a liturgy of time in Christian life figure prominently in Schmemann's work. He insists both on an important continuity between Judaism and the Church and on the revolutionary newness of all things Christian.[4] He identifies in early Christian worship what he terms a "liturgical dualism." Regular daily, weekly, and yearly cycles were fundamental; but so too was a strong eschatological sense, one deriving from the conviction that in Christ all the promises of God and all the hopes of his people had been fulfilled.[5]

What, then, is the relationship between the cyclical and the "once-for-all' in the Christian cult? What place has a liturgy of time in an eschatological cult? The key lies, so Schmemann suggests, in the Hebrew worldview.

---

1. See Bouyer, *Christian Spirituality*, vol 1, 3.

2. See, e.g., Wernle, *Beginnings of Christinaity* I, 33. Talley, looking back to a series of lectures given by Gregory Dix in 1949 recalls: "I can still remember verbatim . . . his opening sentence: 'Our understanding of our forms of worship underwent a radical transformation some forty years ago when it finally occurred to someone that Jesus was a Jew.'" Talley, "Eucharistic Prayer of the Ancient Church," 138.

3. On first-century Jewish eschatology see Wright, *People of God*, chs. 9–10, esp. 247–48, 268–272, also 459–64.

4. Schmemann, *Liturgical Theology*, 40.

5. Cf. Schmemann, *Liturgical Theology*, 47. Cf., Wright, *People of God*, 459.

Here—

> eschatology does not signify a renunciation of time as some-
> thing corrupt, nor a victory over time, nor an exit out of it. On
> the contrary, within this conception time itself can be described
> as eschatological, in the sense that in it those events develop
> and happen by means of which time is given its meaning, which
> makes it a process or history, and which direct it toward an *es-
> chaton* and not just towards an ending or precipice . . . .[6]

Schmemann continues, "[the] *eschaton* is . . . not simply an ending,
but the fulfillment of that which has developed in time, that to which time is
subordinated as means is to end, that which fills it with meaning."[7] He goes
on to say something of the utmost importance:

> The cycles of time (of "natural" time) are not self-sufficient for
> the Jew, since they are always wholly subordinated to Yahweh,
> to a personal God. *Time in this sense is defined by its movement
> towards the fulfillment of God's plan or design for the world,
> which will come about in and through time, by its movement in
> the direction of the Lord's day.* The "liturgy of time" in Judaism
> is the expression of this biblical and in fact "eschatological"
> theology of time.[8]

In other words, the recurrent cycles of a liturgy of time (the day, week, and
year, etc.) minister to the fulfillment of the single, eschatological goal towards
which history was always moving. This is essential. The realms of time and
eternity, of historical process and ultimate goal, are in communion with one
another. This realization, according to Schmemann, gives special value to the
Hebrew conception of time. It also gives value and meaning to the Hebrew
use of various temporal cycles. Schmemann considers the same conception
as central to Christian tradition: "[The] worship of the Church . . . was from
the very beginning and still is our entrance into, our communion with, the

6. Schmemann, *Liturgical Theology*, 55f. It is worth noting that Schmemann does
not enter here into the debate about the exact character of the Jewish conception of
time, and specifically not to Cullmann and his claim that a pagan cyclical notion of
time should be contrasted with a Jewish linear conception. See Cullmann, *Christ and
Time*. For criticism of Cullmann see McIntyre, *Christian Doctrine of History*, 42f.; Barr,
Biblical Words for Time (note that Barr does not commit himself to any judgment of
Cullmann's *conclusions*). For the view that other Near Eastern cultures also developed
or held a linear understanding of history see, Albrektson, *History and the Gods*; Seters,
In Search of History; Saggs, *Encounter with the Divine*, ch. 3. The insights of such critics
usefully qualify Cullmann's hypothesis, but do not require its wholesale rejection.

7. Schmemann, *Liturgical Theology*, 55.

8. Schmemann, *Liturgical Theology*, 56. Emphasis added.

new life of the Kingdom.[9] This worship is concerned "wholly and exclusively with the fact of the coming of the Messiah and the events of his messianic ministry: his preaching, death, and resurrection."[10] But because Christ has accomplished his work and attained to glory *while yet choosing to remain present to the world,* the temporal historical process now incorporates the end towards which it is directed.

For there was one thing the Jewish cult, for all its value, could not do. It could prepare the way for the coming of Christ. It could "reveal and proclaim a doctrine of God, the world, and man which in a way provided all the 'conditions' of the messianic faith." But it could never claim that "what had been announced in the past had now become a fact."[11] This is crucial. Something was *accomplished* in and through the work of Christ, something unique and defining. It is this that Christian worship proclaims and celebrates.

It follows, therefore, that in Christian worship there is a dualism, a tension between established order and newness. From his earliest works, Schmemann sought to explore the basic structure, order or shape of Christian worship, what he terms the "Ordo."[12] But if the pattern and structures of Christian worship derive from the old cult of Jewish tradition—such that baptism and Eucharist, the daily, weekly, and annual prayer cycles all have Jewish antecedents[13]—nevertheless, the *content* of this cult was essentially new. "The [first] disciples understood this cult as the *parousia,* the presence of Christ."[14] This Christ is both the historical Christ and the risen and glorified Christ.[15] And he is always present to the Church *as person,* not as mere exemplar or abstract ideal. Precisely because he is person he remains essentially unpredictable, always "new," always alive.

The liturgical cycles adopted and employed by the Church are not, then, closed in on themselves or self-sufficient. They do not function either mechanically or by magic. They have their origin in God's personal engagement

9. Schmemann, *Great Lent,* 13.

10. Schmemann, *Liturgical Theology,* 48.

11. Schmemann, *Liturgical Theology,* 49. Christian worship is not concerned with proclaiming ideals, ideals, for instance, about how human life might be. Its concern is with realized historical fact.

12. Schmemann, *Liturgical Theology,* 37f. On the definition of the Ordo see Schmemann, *Liturgical Theology,* 28f.

13. Beckwith, "Jewish Background," 44–45; 47–50; Taft, *Liturgy of the Hours,* 3–11; Guiver, *Company of Voices,* 49–53, 219; Bradshaw, *Daily Prayer,* chs. 1–2; Cobb, "History of the Christian Year," 407, 411, 414.

14. Schmemann, *Liturgical Theology,* 50.

15. Cf. Schmemann, *Liturgical Theology,* 34.

with the world and they minister to an end which is personal. In all Christian liturgy and prayer Christ himself holds open the possibility of a direct encounter between the Christian and himself. In all Christian prayer and worship the Son is more "present" and more "active" than is the Christian (though the worshipper will be able to discern the presence of Christ only insofar as he himself is personally present in the worship).

It might be said that the communion between time and eternity, between the once-for-all (historical) and the cyclical (temporal) exists in the person of Christ himself. The Son bears within himself both the meaning of time and history, and the content, the substance, of the End. He is both the End and the way into that End. And he is these as person.

What, then, is the status and value of the Church's "liturgy of time"? Against those who argue that the early Church knew nothing of such a liturgy,[16] Schmemann insists it was present from the very beginning. He calls on many authorities in support of his basic conviction that "[the] structure of Christian worship originates in the worship of Judaism, primarily in its synagogue variation."[17] And synagogue worship was intrinsically linked with liturgy of time. So too was another deeply significant Jewish influence on the emerging Christian liturgy: the Jewish domestic liturgies, most notably mealtime prayers and graces, especially those connected with the Passover and Sabbath and other recurrent festivals. These exerted considerable influence, not least on development of the eucharistic prayers.[18] It is inconceivable that the first Christians, all of them Jews, would have abandoned the temporal cycles and patterns long familiar to them from synagogue and home. Dugmore traced the observance of the liturgical day, week, and year to the apostolic period, seeing them all as integral to the nascent Church's *lex orandi*.[19]

I have spoken of the way Schmemann sees the Eucharist as the defining sacrament of the Church (31 above). Here it can be added that for Schmemann one of the characteristics of the Eucharist is that it provides the possibility of transcending time.

16. E.g., Dix, *Shape of the Liturgy*, 326, cf. 319f., 325.

17. Schmemann, *Liturgical Theology*, 42. He notes that English liturgiologist P. Freeman defended this thesis in the late nineteenth century (cf. Freeman, *Divine Office*, I). He looks for support to Oesterley, *Jewish Background*; Gavin, *Jewish Antecedents*; Dugmore, *Influence of the Synagogue*. Cf. Schmemann, *Liturgical Theology*, 44, and notes p. 70.

18. Bouyer, *Life and Liturgy*, 115–28; Bouyer, *Eucharist*, chs. 2–5 (15–113). Cf. Talley, "Eucharistic Prayer of the Ancient Church"; Ligier, "Last Supper to the Eucharist," 1973.

19. Dugmore, *Influence of the Synagogue*, 57; cf. Schmemann, *Liturgical Theology*, 42.

> The worship of the Church has at its real centre the constant renewal and repetition in time of the . . . the Eucharist. . . . [This] is the actualization of one, single, unrepeatable event, and the essence of the Sacrament consists first of all in the possibility of the conquest of time, i.e. the manifestation and realization (within this Sacrament) of a past event in all its supra-temporal, eternal reality and effectiveness.[20]

The Eucharist—often repeated, ever new—reaches back to the events of Christ's life and reaches forward to the trans-temporal fulfillment of all things that belongs to him as eschatological Lord.

The Paschal Mystery

Everything turns on the paschal mystery. In and through the paschal mystery the Son completed his work and established communion between the temporal and the eternal. By his death Christ redeemed death and gave it new meaning. "[B]y his . . . death Christ changed the very nature of death, made it a *passage*—a 'passover,' a 'Pascha'—into the Kingdom of God."[21] Through participation in the paschal mystery human life can transcend itself and overcome the constraints and limitations of Adamic human nature. In the paschal mystery time can be transcended, such that it becomes the setting in which created human persons enter into communion with the eternal.

The paschal mystery is celebrated constantly by the Church, most obviously every Paschal triduum.[22]

> [I]n the centre of [the Church's] liturgical life, as its heart and climax, as the sun whose rays penetrate everywhere, stands *Pascha*. . . . The entire worship of the Church is organized around Easter, and therefore the liturgical year, i.e., the sequence of seasons and feasts, becomes a journey, a pilgrimage towards

20. Schmemann, *Liturgical Theology*, 34f.

21. Schmemann, *Great Lent*, 12. Schmemann explains, "Easter is our return every year to our own Baptism, whereas Lent is our preparation for that return—the slow and sustained effort to perform, at the end, our own 'passage' or 'pascha' into the new life of Christ. . . . Each year Lent and Easter are . . . the rediscovery by us of what we were made through our own baptismal death and resurrection." Schmemann, *Great Lent*, 14. Bouyer (*Paschal Mysery*, xiv) writes: "Christ died for us, not in order to dispense us from dying, but rather to make us capable of dying efficaciously, of dying to the old man, in order to live again as the new man who will die no more." See also Evdokimov, "St Seraphim of Sarov," 12.

22. On these "micro-chronic" cycles and remembrance of the trans-temporal End see Mantzaridis, *Time and Man*, 98–106.

Pascha, the *End*, which is at the same time the *Beginning*: the end of all that is "old"; the beginning of the new life, a constant "passage" from "this world" into the Kingdom already revealed in Christ.[23]

Schmemann continues: "[At] Easter we celebrate Christ's resurrection as something that happened and still happens *to us*. For each one of us received that new life and the power to accept it and live by it," and again, "The new life which almost two thousand years ago shone forth from the grave, has been given to us."[24] But the same resurrection, the same gift of new life, is celebrated in every act of Christian worship, most notably in every Eucharist.

Baptism is the sacrament of entrance into new life, and the Church, when it shares in the Eucharist, is invited to enter into the fulfillment of all God's promises. But no one can appropriate that new life all at once. He or she needs to grow into it; and to that end the church needs to offer a programme of growth, a way of formation, of discipleship. Here the regular liturgical cycles can play a part. All of them have the paschal mystery at their heart and in all of them Christ crucified and glorified is encountered. He is encountered *as fullness of personhood*; and he also invites people to make to him a personal response, or indeed, a *personalizing* response to his presence, one in and through which the disciple can move towards realizing fullness of personhood.

Probably the majority of Christians only rarely perceive the personal divine presence during worship.[25] As I mentioned above, only insofar as someone has realized his own personhood is he able directly to perceive the personhood of others. But through their participation in the structures and patterns of Church life the members of the Church can be learning to relate to God and to one another in a more personal way, even before they fully appreciate what they are doing.

I would suggest that even if the Jewish understanding of time and history are fulfilled in Christ, the Church still has much to learn from Jewish tradition, and not just from ancient, bygone Jewish tradition, but from Jewish life and tradition as they exists today. Perhaps some truths and insights first revealed to the Jews have yet to be fully appropriated by the Church. By divine providence Jewish tradition may hold in trust for the Church insights which are intended for the whole world. Central

---

23. Schmemann, *Great Lent*, 13. Cf. Bouyer, *Paschal Mysery*, xiii.

24. Schmemann, *Great Lent*, 11f.

25. But such perception is possible. See, for example, the testimony regarding Seraphim (below, p. 238, n. 36) and the Curé d'Ars (see Trochu, *Curé d'Ars*, 527–30).

here might be, perhaps, a sense of the sacramentality of "ordinary" daily life, as exemplified in Jewish concern with the family and with local community life—and in particular, as revealed in the Jewish tradition of quasi-liturgical meals, celebrated in the home or by the gathered community. Also important might be the Jewish understanding of God's involvement in history. And it may be that the Church has much to learn from the Jewish understanding of and approach to time and—so I believe—most especially from their use of the seven-day week.

12

The Jewish Week and the Jewish Concern with Time

JEWISH PHILOSOPHER AND THEOLOGIAN, Abraham J. Heschel (1907–72) opens his prayerful and scholarly study of the Sabbath with the claim that, while "[t]echnical civilisation is man's conquest of space," this triumph is "frequently achieved [only] by sacrificing an essential ingredient of existence, namely, time."[1] The remainder of Heschel's book explains how the Bible and traditional Judaism take a different approach.

> The Bible is more concerned with time than with space. It pays more attention to generations, to events, than to countries, to things; it is more concerned with history than with geography. To understand the teaching of the Bible, one must accept its premise that time has a meaning for life which is at least equal to that of space; that time has a significance and sovereignty of its own. . . . Judaism is a *religion of time* aiming at the *sanctification of time*.[2]

In striving to counteract what he considers a pernicious preoccupation with the spacial and the material, Heschel perhaps understates the Bible's concern with space (e.g., geography and topography). He makes little, for example, of such central Jewish concerns as the land, the temple, the city of Jerusalem, and the notion of exile. A more rounded view would look to the sanctification both of time and of space and material objects, seeing no ultimate divide between the two.[3] The aim of this "religion of time" is not

---

1. Heschel, *Sabbath*, 6.

2. Heschel, *Sabbath*, 6 & 8.

3. Heschel himself more or less acknowledges as much; see Heschel, *The Sabbath*, 3. Sacks suggests that Jews from the most diverse cultural backgrounds are drawn together by "only two things . . . the land of Israel and the Shabbat, one a place, the other a time," Sacks, *Faith in the Future*, 135. See also Engel, *Hebrew Concept of Time*. Margaret Barker has argued that temple worship and temple tradition were much more significant in the development of early Church tradition than the generality of other scholars have recognized. She more or less presents them as the key elements in the formation

merely the sanctification of time, but (as Heschel would surely agree) the sanctification of the person and the community. Despite these reservations, there is much in what Heschel says.

Heschel's work is grounded in the traditional Jewish view that the most important thing about time is that it *belongs to God*. Implicit in this is the belief that God is constantly *active* in time, that time has direction and is purposeful. Thus, week by week, the Sabbath takes its character not from the choice of Jews to observe that day in particular ways, but from God choosing to give the day a particular character and purpose. Time and history together constitute a setting in which created life and divine life meet, and where, by divine grace, transient human life can enter into communion with the eternal divine life. This meeting between the created and the divine always comes about at God's initiative, and he it is who determines the meeting's purpose and outcome. His ways are mysterious. They transcend human comprehension and will always take fallen man somewhat by surprise. The temporal patterns and cycles of Jewish life—the liturgical day, week, month, and year; the holy days; festal and penitential seasons—these have their origin and primary significance in God. They are not products of human ingenuity, or simply an expedient means to some practical (this-worldly) end. The human contribution to the development of this observation of special days is undeniable, but is always secondary.

Without the acknowledgment that the Jews understand their festal seasons and holy days along the lines outlined above, mainstream Jewish spiritual tradition becomes meaningless.[4] Fundamental to Jewish tradition is the belief that God is personally active within the community's life and worship. The same understanding belongs also to the mainstream Christian tradition. And while this understanding does not sit comfortably with the rationalistic, reductionist worldviews popular today, it explains much in Christian tradition which otherwise will appear superstitious or nonsensical.

Is this view justified? As I have suggested, the Jewish concern with time goes hand-in-hand with an interest in history. It is often argued that whereas other Mediterranean and Near Eastern cultures tended to think cyclically—developing, for example, myths to celebrate the cycles evident in

---

of primitive Christian tradition. See, for example, *Great High Priest*; *Temple Theology*; *Temple Mysticism*. I am not persuaded by her arguments.

4. Some have argued, e.g., Green (*SCMJS* I, xvi–xx), that it is a mistake to think in terms of a single monolithic or even "main-stream" Jewish spirituality, and that, on the contrary, there is a whole variety of spiritualities within Judaism. Nevertheless, it can hardly be argued that the understanding of time outlined here has not been widely held in Judaism from biblical times to the present. Green himself implies as much (xiii).

the natural year—the OT shows the Israelites using a linear conception of time: both time and history lead somewhere.[5] Over the centuries the Jews' expectations about this "somewhere" were revised and refined. But the destination was never simply "anywhere." The goal was always seen as having been chosen and appointed by God—his Kingdom. The goal was not mere survival; neither was it restoration to a primordial paradise.

Belief in God's past action and confidence in his continuing concern led the Jews to commemorate a series of saving events. Convinced of God's ceaseless and all-pervading concern, they also saw the cycles and rhythms of nature as further demonstrations of his providential care.

Here it is worth noting that even today thinkers from mainstream Jewish tradition have been little concerned with abstract questions about the nature of time or the relation of time to eternity (after the manner, for example, of the classical Greek philosophers, the later neo-Platonists, even Hindu or Buddhist thinkers.[6] The Jewish concern has always been practical. Heschel writes: "While Jewish tradition offers us no definition of the concept of eternity, it tells us how to experience the taste of eternity or eternal life within time."[7]

Communion in the Holy

Heschel explains that many cultures tend to see particular material objects and geographical locations as holy and as offering potential contact with the divine: holy sites, cities, relics, etc. The Jews, by contrast, always expected to make contact with God in and through "holy times"—holy days and seasons.[8] These holy times, moreover, are not identical or interchangeable. "Unlike space-minded man to whom time is unvaried, iterative, homoge-

5. Classically in Cullmann, *Christ and Time*, 51–61, etc. And see above, 134, n. 6.

6. Cf. Sorabji (*Time, Creation and the Continuum*) reviews a vast amount of historical material from the period 500 BCE to 500 CE and also includes some material from later Christian and Islamic sources. See also the collection of essays gathered in the Unesco document *Cultures and Time* (1976) which includes a general introduction by Paul Ricoeur and papers on the concepts of time and history in a range of world cultures, old and new.

7. Heschel, *Sabbath*, 74.

8. Heschel points out (*Sabbath*, 9) that the first mention in the Bible of holiness (Gen 2:3) is when the sabbath is so described (or defined) Only after the rebellion at Sinai is the erection of a Tabernacle commanded. "Holiness of time would have been sufficient to the world. Holiness of space was a necessary compromise with the nature of man," Heschel *Sabbath*, 104; he quotes *Midrash Aggada* 27:1, and Ginzberg, *Legends of the Jews* 3, 148f. In the Decalogue the word "holy" occurs only in relation to the Sabbath.

neous, to whom all hours are alike, qualitiless, empty shells, the Bible senses the diversified character of time. There are no two hours alike."[9] To particular times belong particular graces.

Here Heschel introduces a powerful image. He speaks of an "architecture of time," arguing that in response to God's initiative the Jews established ordered rhythms and patterns of life within which they could make their home and *meet with him*.[10] This is crucial. For if time is the primary setting for meeting with God, he can be met even by those in exile or those living in prison camps.[11]

> Jewish ritual may be characterised as the art of significant forms in time . . . . Most of its observances—the Sabbath, the New Moon, the festivals, the Sabbatical and the Jubilee year—depend on a certain hour of the day or season of the year. It is, for example, the evening, the morning, or afternoon that brings with it the call to prayer. The main themes of faith lie within the realm of time. We remember the day of the exodus from Egypt, the day when Israel stood at Sinai; and our Messianic hope is the expectation of a day, of the end of days.[12]

Aspects of the Jewish feasts, holy days, and holy seasons indicate origins in primitive agricultural or pastoral celebrations. Passover, for example, combines elements from the celebration of a nomadic pastoral community (the sacrificial lamb), with elements from the celebration of a settled community engaged in arable farming (the unleavened bread and so on).[13] But eventually each major Jewish festival came to focus on some aspect of the saving work of God—either the process by which that work went forward, or its goal. Pentecost, for instance, was once a harvest festival—relating to the wheat harvest, in contrast with the barley harvest celebrated seven weeks earlier at Passover—but it became a celebration of the gift of the Torah, and of the establishment of the covenant on Mount Sinai. Even the Day of Atone-

9. Heschel, *Sabbath*, 8.

10. Millrgram (*Sabbath*, 229) describes the Sabbath as a "City of Refuge" where the Jew "did not merely recover from the ordeals of the week, but gathered . . . strength . . . to face . . . the coming week." Cf. the idea of rest not as a reward for labors done but as preparation for wok to come. This is sometimes described as "resting forward." Rest was the *first* activity of activity of Adam in Gen 1–2. Cf. "The place of rest . . . the launchpad for a life of active service," Horsfall, *Place of Rest*, 123.

11. Cf. Gillet, *Communion in the Messiah*, 241–42; Sacks, *Faith in the Future*, 136.

12. Heschel, *Sabbath*, 8. "The Sabbath is a sanctuary we build, *a sanctuary in time*," Heschel, *Man Is Not Alone*, 29. The metaphor of the Sabbath as a "palace" is also used, Heschel, *Sabbath*, 12.

13. *Jerusalem Bible Commentary*, 76:124–65, esp. 137–39, 147–48, 162.

ment which might be seen as different in that it does not commemorate a saving event, nevertheless, it provides an opportunity for community and each individual within it to return to right relationship with God and so enter into a knowledge of things eschatological. Generally, each feast celebrates God's past saving work and looks towards future fulfillment. And this is especially so for the two principal feasts: Passover and Sabbath.

Here it will be worth exploring the idea that the Church might have much to learn from the contemporary Jewish quest for the renewal of Sabbath observance and from the way in which the Sabbath is believed to give a *taste* of the life of the End.

13

The Sabbath in Jewish Thought and Life

THE SABBATH HAS LONG been considered one of the most important Jewish institutions. The claim has been made that during those times of crisis which threatened the very existence of Judaism—during the Babylonian Exile, for example, and the many centuries following the destruction of Jerusalem in 135 CE—observance of the Sabbath held Jewish life together. Millgram opens his popular anthology *Sabbath: Day of Delight* with a quotation from Hebrew essayist Ahad Ha-'Am (1856–1927): "More than Israel has kept the Sabbath, it is the Sabbath that has kept Israel."[1] Millgram suggests that Ahad Ha-'Am is not alone in his belief. "He reflects the universal regard for the Sabbath as it revealed itself in the life and literature of the Jews up to the nineteenth century."[2] Like Heschel, Millgram has a practical aim: he seeks to restore the Sabbath to its central place in Jewish life. This is also the declared purpose of Kaplan's *Sabbath: Day of Eternity*.[3] After an opening discussion of the reasons for Sabbath observance, Kaplan writes: "All this highlights one point: *The Sabbath is the most important institution in Judaism*. It is the primary ritual, the very touchstone of our faith."[4] Blu Greenberg, in a work looking to foster traditional Jewish practice in the modern Jewish family, devotes her first seventy pages to Sabbath beliefs and practices.[5]

If contemporary Judaism considers the Sabbath one of the crowning glories of Jewish cultural and religious tradition and a vast literature looks to the renewal of Sabbath practice, opinions vary about the reason why Sabbath observance is so important. Liberals have emphasized the utilitarian value of the Sabbath: it guarantees regular rest, provides opportunities for social engagement, fosters health and well-being, and contributes to

---

1. Millgram, *Sabbath*, 1; cf. 253 (quotation from Ha-'Am, *Al Parashat Derachim*, 3:79).

2. Heschel, *Sabbath*, 14.

3. Kaplan, *Sabbath*.

4. Kaplan, *Sabbath*, 7.

5. Greenberg, *How to Run a Traditional Jewish Household*, 25–95. Buber looked to a "renewed understanding of God's Name and a renewed sacramental meal"—and to a renewal of the Sabbath. See Buber, *Moses*, 82–83; Vermes, *Buber*, 82.

week-day, work-time efficiency. But traditionalists like Heschel, Millgram, Greenberg, and Kaplan reject a merely utilitarian view.[6] Heschel presents what he claims is the biblical perspective: "The Sabbath is not for the sake of the weekdays; the weekdays are for the sake of the Sabbath. [It] is not an interlude but the climax of living."[7]

The Sabbath is *the* holy day in Judaism—the type and model of all holy days.[8] Participation in the Sabbath gives a foretaste of the life of the world to come.

> Six days a week we live under the tyranny of things of space; on the Sabbath we try to become attuned to *holiness in time*. It is the day on which we are called upon to share in what is eternal in time . . . .[9]

The Sabbath is vehicle to the transforming divine presence.

> [The Sabbath] is not a different state of consciousness but a different climate; it is as if the appearance of all things [is] somehow changed. The primary awareness is one of being *within* the Sabbath, rather than of the Sabbath being within us. We may not know whether our sentiments are noble, but the air of the day surrounds us like spring, which spreads over the land without our aid or notice.[10]

The Sabbath is "not a date but an atmosphere."[11]

---

6. Cf. Heschel, *Man Is Not Alone*, 13f. Heschel refers to Philo, *De Speciablibus Legibus*, II, 60 (Loeb Classics, Philo, VII); and cf. Aristotle *Nichomachean Ethics*, X, 6. Kaplan in arguing against the utilitarian view notes that the call is to rest "whether we are tired or not," Kaplan, *Sabbath*, 9. Wittgenstein suggested, "The Sabbath is not primarily a time for rest, for relaxation. We ought to contemplate our labours from without, not just from within," Wittgenstein, *Culture and Value*, 80.

7. Heschel, *Sabbath*, 14. Cf. Zohar, I, 75.

8. "The Sabbath is queen and mother of all the holidays [=holy days]. . . . Each of the holidays is some aspect of the Sabbath." Braun, *Jewish Holy Days*, xv.

9. Heschel, *Sabbath*, 10. The very title of Kaplan's work *Sabbath: Day of Eternity* suggests the same understanding. Kaplan states: "The Sabbath is a rehearsal for revolution. On every Sabbath we partake of the Future world—of the peace and harmony of the Messianic Age. . . . The Sabbath keeps us aware of our final goal in life." Kaplan, *Sabbath*, 24. Cf. *Sefer HaChinuch* 32; *Ephodi* on *Moreh Nevuchim* 2:31; *Derech HaShem* 4:7:2. By contrast, Sacks, while insisting that Sabbath observance is essential to Jewish identity and culture, takes a more prosaic, non-mystical view. He concentrates wholly on what the community does on the Sabbath, without suggesting that anything might be happening *ab extra*, from God's side. Sacks, *Faith in the Future*, 132–37.

10. Heschel, *Sabbath*, 21.

11. Heschel, *Sabbath*, 21.

The difference between the Sabbath and all other days is not to be noticed in the physical structure of things, in their spacial dimension. Things do not change on that day. There is only a difference in the dimension of time, in the relation of the universe to God. The Sabbath preceded creation and the Sabbath completed creation, it is all of the spirit that the world can bear.[12]

How wonderful that final phrase! This notion of the special "atmosphere" or "climate" of the Sabbath is most important.

Heschel insists that the Sabbath does more than stand in majesty at the end of time, as the goal of life. God himself is *active* on every Sabbath, imparting to the day its special character.

The Sabbath is the most precious present man has received from the treasure-house of God. All week we think: The spirit is too far away. . . . On the Sabbath the spirit stands and pleads: Accept all excellence from me. . . . Yet what the spirit offers is too august for our trivial minds. We accept the ease and relief and miss the inspirations of the day, where it comes from and what it stands for. This is why we pray for understanding: "May Thy children realize and understand that their rest comes from Thee, and that to rest means to sanctify Thy name."[13]

If it is possible to err by accepting "ease and relief and [missing] the inspirations of the day," then the opposite error, much criticized in the Gospels,[14] sees the Sabbath become a burden. Rabbinic tradition addressed this issue, and, looking to expressions in Isa 58:13, argued that the Sabbath is rightly a delight, a joy.

To sanctify the seventh day does not mean: thou shalt mortify thyself, but, on the contrary: Thou shalt sanctify it with all thy heart, with all thy soul and with all thy senses. "Sanctify the Sabbath by choice meals, by beautiful garments; delight your soul with pleasure and I will reward you for this very pleasure."[15]

12. Heschel, *Sabbath*, 21. "'Last in creation, first in intention," the Sabbath is "the end of the creation of heaven and earth'", Heschel, *Man Is Not Alone*, 14. The quotations are from *Lechah Dodi*, composed by Rabbi Solomon Alkabetz and sung at the Evening Service for the Sabbath (see Singer, *Authorized Daily Prayer Book*, 146). See also Jacobson, *The Sabbath Service*.

13. Heschel, *Sabbath*, 18. The quotation is from the Sabbath afternoon service (cf. Singer, *Authorized Daily Prayer*, 238). The Sabbath is personified in a whole variety of ways: Queen, Bride, God's only daughter; cf. Heschel, *Sabbath*, 53f, 105, n.13. These metaphors indicate the personalist character of Jewish spirituality.

14. "The sabbath was made for man, not man for the sabbath." Mark 2:27, etc.

15. Heschel, *Sabbath*, 19. The quotation is from *Deuteronomy rabba*, 3,1; Heschel

Heschel speaks lyrically of love for the Sabbath: "The Sabbath is endowed with a felicity which enraptures the soul, which glides into our thoughts with a healing sympathy. . . . It is a day that can soothe all sadness away."[16] He explains,

> The Sabbath is a reminder of two worlds—this world and the world to come; it is an example of both worlds. For the Sabbath is joy, holiness, and rest; joy is part of this world; holiness and rest are something of the world to come.[17]

In observing the Sabbath the Jews look to pass beyond mere submission to a divine command. Each Sabbath commemorates the creation of the world and celebrates the wonder of holiness in time. The Sabbath is, "a day of rest, a day of freedom," a day which is like "a lord and king of all other days," a "lord and king in the commonwealth of time."[18]

Heschel tells the story of a rabbi imprisoned in a cave. Although there was no light and he could not distinguish day from night, he regularly felt different on the Sabbath because his habitual desire for tobacco would leave him.[19] The supposition is that something *happens* on the Sabbath. The Sabbath is not observed in order to make the day holy but in recognition of the holiness that God gives it. Man's response to God's goodness—i.e., grateful celebration, not miserable self-denial—looks to enable God's action to penetrate the human heart. As Heschel puts it, each Sabbath eve, "a beautifying surplus of soul visits our mortal bones and lingers on."[20]

Jewish tradition speculates little on *how* time can vary in this way. It simply insists that it does. Stories evoking the atmosphere of the Sabbath abound, often of the utmost charm.[21]

---

refers the reader to *Midrash Tehillim*, ch. 90. Cf. *Mekilta on Exodus*, 31, 13: "The Sabbath was committed unto you not you unto the Sabbath."

16. Heschel, *Sabbath*, 20; cf. p. 15.

17. Heschel, *Sabbath*, 19; the quotation seems to come from Al Nakawa (d. 1391), *Menorat he-Maor*, ed. Enelow, II: 182.

18. Shibbloe ha-Leqet, ch. 126. (Cf. Ode 8 of the *Great (Paschal) Canon of St John Damascene*.)

19. Cf. Heschel, *Sabbath*, 29.

20. Heschel, *Sabbath*, 68.

21. For a selection see Millgram, *Sabbath*, ch.14 (and p. 483); Jaffe, *Tales*; also Newman, *Talmudic Anthology*, 395–405, Newman, *Hasidic Anthology*, 404–12; Gillet, *Communion in the Messiah*, 241–42. Millgram explains that the stories collected for reading to children on the Sabbath are intended "not necessarily to teach religion of morals [but] to provide . . . an 'Oneg Shabbat*, a delightful Sabbath experience." Millgram, *Sabbath*, 99. Further examples and bibliography, Millgram, *Sabbath*, 99–148; 487–88.

Legend relates that Rabbi Loew of Prague (died 1609) was called "the Tall Rabbi Loew," because on the Sabbath he looked as if he were a head taller than during the six days of the week.[22] Whoever looked on the Sabbath at Rabbi Hayim of Teshernovitz (died 1813), the story goes, could see a rose on his cheek. The same Rabbi Hayim writes: "We have seen with our own eyes the tremendous change that the holiness of the Sabbath brings about in the life of a saint. The light of holiness blazes in his heart like tongues of fire, and he is overcome with rapture and yearning to serve God . . . all night and all day." . . . As soon as his preparations in honour of the Sabbath are completed "an effulgence of Sabbath-holiness illumines his face. So resplendent is his countenance that one almost hesitates to come close to him."[23]

As for contemporary Judaism, Greenberg witnesses:

> On Shabbat, I can almost feel the difference in the air I breath, in the way the incandescent lamps give off light in my living room, in the way the children's skins glow, or in the way the trees sway. Immediately after I light my candles, it is as if I flicked a switch that turned Shabbat on in the world . . . . Remarkable as this experience is, even more remarkable is that it happens every seventh day of my life.[24]

For Greenberg the Sabbath has both immediate practical value and a transcendent dimension. Her introductory paragraphs on the Sabbath close with a moving confession:

> No system that engages a variety of human beings can be absolutely perfect. But, to the average Orthodox Jew, Shabbat comes very close to perfection. It is a day of release and of reenergizing; a day of family and community; of spirit and of physical well-being. It is a day of prayer and study; of synagogue and home; a day of rest and self-indulgence; of compassion and self-esteem. It is ancient, yet contemporary; a day for all seasons. A gift and a responsibility. Without it I could not live.[25]

22. Heschel, *Sabbath*, 88. Heschel notes "a similar legend is told about Rabbi Joshua Horowitz, see *Nezir ha-Shem*" (Lemberg, 1869, preface).

23. Heschel, *Sabbath*, 88f. (notes p. 117). (The story is from *Sidduro shel Shabbat*, Warsaw 1872: 8f.)

24. Greenberg, *Traditional Jewish Household*, 25f. Here she refers also to the experience of family members and friends.

25. Greenberg, *Traditional Jewish Household*, 29. More prosaically, she recalls the encouraging fridge-sticker in a friend's kitchen: "Hang in there, Shabbos is coming,"

Heschel describes the mysterious, almost magical quality of the Sabbath:

> The world to come is characterized by the kind of holiness possessed by the Sabbath in this world. . . . According to the Talmud, the Sabbath is *me'en 'olam ha-ba*, which means: "somewhat like" eternity or the world to come.[26]

He quotes a legend mentioned in *Mekilta to Exodus* 31:17.

> At the time God was giving the Torah to Israel, he said to them: My children, if you accept the Torah and observe my mitzot [commands], I will give you for all eternity a thing most precious that I have in my possession.
>
> —And what, asked Israel . . . , is that?
>
> —The world to come.
>
> —Show us in this world an example of the world to come.
>
> —The Sabbath is an example of the world to come.[27]

If sharing the Sabbath gives a foretaste of the experience of eternity, then eternity can be imagined as one continuous Sabbath. Rabbi Akiba claimed that in the temple the Levites sang songs proper to each day of the week, and the Sabbath psalm was "a song for the time to come, for the day that shall be all Sabbath and all rest, in the life eternal."[28] This description of the "all Sabbath" echoes New Testament descriptions of the Kingdom: "There is neither eating nor drinking nor worldly transactions, but the righteous sit enthroned, their crowns on their heads, and they enjoy the lustre of the Shechinah."[29]

Communion with the divine gives existence as a whole its meaning. That communion is established in and through time. Time provides

---

Greenberg, *Traditional Jewish Household*, 27.

26. Cf. Heschel, *Sabbath*, 74 where several passages are quoted (without detailed references). Heschel suggests that this the idea that Sabbath and eternity are one—or of the same essence—is ancient. He quotes *Vita Adae and Evae* (41.1), "The Seventh day is the sign of the resurrection and the world to come." In Charles, *Apocrypha and Pseudoepigraphia*, 151.

27. Quoted Heschel, *Sabbath*, 73. Alphabet of Rabbi Akiba, *otzar Midrashim*, 407; see also 403 and the Midrash quoted in *Kad ha-Qemah, Shabbat*.

28. *Mishna Tamid*, end. Cf. *Rosh Hashanah* 31a, where this Mishna is specifically attributed to Rabbi Akiba

29. Heschel gives as refs: *Abot de-Natan*, ch. 1, where the final passage is found. The description of the world to come is also transmitted in the name of Rab. *Berachot* 17a. See also *Midrash Tehillim*, ch. 92, ed. Buber: 201a; Cf. Matt 19:28; Rev 3:21, 20:4.

opportunities for learning to appropriate the eternal. It also serves as a vehicle by which the eternal is made present. Heschel writes: "the secret of being is the eternal within time."[30]

The final paragraphs of Heschel's work summarize his view of the Sabbath:

> This is the task of man: to conquer space and sanctify time. . . .
> We must conquer space in order to sanctify time. All week long
> we are called upon to sanctify life through employing the things
> of space. On the Sabbath it is given to us to share in the holiness
> that is in the heart of time.[31]

Time belongs to God. He is active in time and uses it both to make himself known and to draw people to himself. In Jewish tradition the Sabbath has a *practical* significance; it provides a taste of the goal towards which life is directed and the opportunity to learn to appreciate that taste:

> Unless one learns how to relish the taste of the Sabbath while
> still in this world . . . one will be unable to enjoy the taste of
> eternity in the world to come.[32]

Has the Sabbath—i.e., Saturday, in distinction from Sunday—a value and significance neglected by the Church? There is evidence of renewed Christian interest in the Sabbath, as in Moltmann's study of the Christian doctrine of creation: "The sabbath is the true hallmark of every biblical—every Jewish and also every Christian—doctrine of creation."[33] But it will not suffice simply to develop a doctrine of the Sabbath. Jewish tradition has not been nourished by a *doctrine* of the Sabbath, but by Sabbath *observance*. It is the observance of the Sabbath, not the theology of the Sabbath, that gives a taste of the Kingdom.

Before developing the argument further, the history of the seven-day week should be examined—a history full of surprises.

---

30. Heschel, *Sabbath*, 101.
31. Heschel, *Sabbath*, 101.
32. Heschel, *Sabbath*, 74. Here "unable" takes the sense "unfitted," not "forbidden."
33. Moltmann, *God in Creation*, 6. Cf. Lash, "Friday, Saturday, Sunday".

14

Historical Considerations 1

The Emergence and Development of the Seven-Day Week

The Origin of the Sabbath and the Seven Day Week[1]

IF WE ARE ASKED to attend a meeting on a given *date*, the first thing we are likely to ask is which *day* of the week that date will fall on. And if someone asks us, "What's the *date* today?" no one is surprised if we need to check a calendar or the front page of a newspaper before we can be sure. On the other hand, if someone asks us, "What *day* is it today?" they would be very surprised if we have to check the front of a paper before replying. It is indicative of how much the weekly cycle is part of our lives that few calendar reforms have ever sought to challenge it or change it (see 153 below).

For example, the Gregorian reforms promulgated in 1582 (after centuries of debate) moved the *date*, but left the seven-day cycle unchanged. So it was that for the first adopters of the new system *Thursday*, 4 October 1582 (on the Julian calendar) was followed by *Friday*, 15 October 1582 (on

---

1. For the early history of the seven-day week see Colson, *Week*; Zerubavel, *Seven Day Circle*, 5–26; also Rordorf, *Sunday*, 9–42; Sarna, *Understanding Genesis*, 18–21; Sarna, *Exploring Exodus*, 145–48; Sarna, *Exodus: Shemot*, 111–12; *Genesis: Be-Reshit*, 14–15, 343. For further history of the Christian week see Hessey, *Sunday*, esp. 23–96, 161–225; Rordorf, *Sunday, passim*. Webster, *Rest Days*, 215ff., 224ff., 227ff., 253ff.; Sharf, "Eighth Day of the Week." Webster discusses also the many other weekly patterns (from three-day to ten-day) that have been used elsewhere in the world (see his index, 325). See also Zerubavel, *Seven Day Circle*, 44–59. A standard work (though one I have not been able to consult) is Roscher, *Fristen und Wochen*. On an Egyptian ten-day week, a possible influence on the Jews before the exodus, see Parker, "Calendars and Chronology," 17.

On the Jewish week and Sabbath see Dressler, "Sabbath in the Old Testament"; Colson, *Week*, 11–17 (also 121–22); Zerubavel, *Seven Day Circle*, 6–11; Rordorf, *Sunday*, 10–24; Andreasen, "Old Testament Sabbath," 94–121; Lohse *TWNT* 7:1–35; Greenberg, *EJ* 14:557–62; Hasel *ABD* 5:849–56; also Mishna tractate "Shabbath" in Danby, *Mishnah*, 100–121, and Neusner, *Mishna*, 179–208.

the Gregorian calendar). These reforms were adopted almost immediately in the Catholic countries of Western and Central Europe, but were only gradually adopted elsewhere: by the Scandinavian nations in 1700; by England (and its colonies) in 1752; by the Soviet Union in 1918 and by Turkey in 1928.[2] This made life (and especially business life) complicated. The fact that different countries assigned different *dates* to the same *day* complicated international affairs, but how much more complicated things would have been had not the seven-day week rolled on unchallenged and unchanged.[3] Today some of the Eastern Churches still use the Julian calendar.[4] This complicates ecumenical (even inter-Orthodox) relations. But if the days of the week were out-of-step, how much worse it would be, with Easter Sunday in the Western calendar falling for the Orthodox, not (as it often does now) on a Sunday in Lent, but rather, on a weekday.

Various revisions of the seven-day week have been proposed, but only two have ever been implemented with state sanction.[5] Following the Revolution of 1787, the French sought to decimalize their calendar and clock. A ten-day week was also initially proposed for post-Revolutionary Russia; and eventually in 1929 a five-day week was introduced. Both the French and Russian revisions were inspired in part by anti-Christian ideology. But both were unpopular and soon abandoned.[6] Any subsequent proposal for the reform of the week—many are listed on the internet—has encountered resistance from traditional Christians and Muslims, and above all from the Jewish community. For whatever anyone else might do, the Jews will persist in observing their Sabbath every seventh day.[7] They have observed their seven-day unbroken for perhaps 3,000 years. They have no intention of abandoning it now. Richards suggests that the seven-day week "may well be among the oldest surviving human institutions," a convention observed "without interruption" throughout "most of recorded time."[8]

2. For the reform see Richards, *Mapping Time*, 238–56, 352–53. For the dates of the adoption of the reform see Richards, *Mapping Time*, Table 19.1 (p.248f.). In 1912 the Russian Olympic team arrived in London twelve days late for the games. For a listing of the various adoption dates see: "Conversion between Julian and Gregorian calendars," last modified on 11 July 2015. The article quotes the Nautical Almanac Offices of the United Kingdom and United States (1961) and carries a jpeg of the relevant table. https://en.wikipedia.org/wiki/Conversion_between_Julian_and_Gregorian_calendars.

3. Richards, *Mapping Time*, 247–52, 352–53; Duncan, *Calendar*, 288–320.

4. See Ware, *Festal Menaion*, 563–64.

5. See Richards, *Mapping Time*, 110–22.

6. See Richards, *Mapping Time*, 256–64 (398–9); 276–79.

7. See Millgram, *Sabbath*, 349–59; Richards, *Mapping Time*, 279.

8. Richards, *Mapping Time*, 265. The only recorded interruptions were occasioned by the demands of the International Date Line. In 1867 the Alaskan Aleuts had to

Despite the continuity of the seven-day pattern its origins remain surprisingly uncertain. It is commonly assumed that the seven-day week (like the day, the month, and the year) corresponds to some natural phenomenon, the phases of the moon, for example. But as Rordorf says, the seven-day week "runs contrary to every natural arrangement of time."[9] Neither the solar year (approximately 365¼ days) nor the lunar month (approximately 29½ days[10]) is divisible by seven—so that month by month the new moon occurs on a different day.[11] Long familiarity with the first Genesis creation-account (Gen 1–2:3) has perhaps led many to assume that the seven-day week has been observed since the dawn of time, but this cannot be so. The week, unlike the day, month, and year, is a human institution, not a natural phenomenon.

Weekly Patterns in the Ancient World

It comes as a surprise to many that the classical world knew nothing of a regular week and that the seven-day week was adopted in the Greco-Roman world only around the time that the Church was coming into being. The month was a basic unit in ancient calendars but was not generally divided into any smaller unit or any recurring cycle that ran on unceasingly and invariably. In many places a regular pattern of recurrent market-days was

observe a one-off eight-day week to bring them into step with the rest of America, and in 1884 a one-off six-day week was observed in the Philippines, again to bring them into step with other communities on their latitude (see Richards, *loc. cit.*).

9. Rordorf, *Sunday*, 18. Medical science has been unable to find any biological basis for the week, seven-day or otherwise. Many physiological functions follow a circadian (approx. twenty-four-hour) rhythm, others a monthly (approx. twenty-eight-day) pattern. But despite the best efforts of such researchers as Claus Hoffmann, no internal clock working to an intermediate pattern has been found (*pace* Aveni, *Empires of Time*, 100f.).

10. Precise times are given in Richards, *Mapping Time*, 387–90. See Colson, *Week*, 1–3.

11. It would be foolish to dismiss the idea that a concern with the regularly recurrent lunar cycle might have exerted some influence on the origin of the seven-day week. Webster (*Rest Days*, esp. ch. 6) demonstrates that in almost every human society the belief has arisen that the moon exerts an influence (most often malevolent) on both natural events and human life. But nowhere in the Hebrew Scriptures is the origin of the seven-day week *explained* in terms of the lunar phases, and the observance of a seven-day cycle soon came to be completely divorced from any concern with the lunar cycles. See Rordorf, *Sunday*, 19–20. Throughout recorded history the week and the month have run on independently of one another.

On the Jewish New Moon festival see also Berrin, *New Moon*, esp. xxxi–xxxv (contributed by Blu Greenberg); 3–12 (Arlene Agus); 260–266 (from the editor). On the moon in timekeeping and spirituality see also Cain, *Luna*; Brueton, *Many Moons*.

observed, including the eight-day week ("nundinae") of the Romans.[12] But none of these shaped or structured life as the Jewish week did. Still less did any market day cycle shape and direct the hopes and aspirations of a community in the way the Sabbath did for the Jews.

Apart from the Jewish week, only one seven-day cycle is known from the ancient world. This is the so-called planetary or astrological week. It probably came into use in the Roman world during the Hellenic period, probably in the first century CE.[13] Grounded in esoteric astrological beliefs, this seven-day cycle exerted little influence on Roman public life. In a sense it was not a "public" week at all, but something only of private concern and observation—rather as astrology is a private matter today with no place in the public calendar.[14] The astrological week left its principal long-term legacy in its system of names for the days of the week, which, having been adopted in most of Western Europe towards the end of the Roman period, are still in widespread use today.[15] It is somewhat bizarre, however, that the Church finds itself observing the Ascension on "Thor's day" and that Christmas will fall perhaps on "Woden's day."

12. Webster (*Rest Days*, 101–23) records the observance of market weeks in various parts of the world, with a period of anything from three to ten days. See also 'Nundinae' in *DA*. Cf. W. Kroll, 'Nundinae', PW 17.2, 1467–72; Webster, *Rest days*, 120–23 (esp. 120, n.2); Michels, *Calendar of the Roman Republic*, 26–30, 84–89, 103–6, 164–67, 191–206; Richards, *Mapping Time*, 210–11. Rordorf accounts as modest the influence of this eight-day week on the week that we now observe (Rordorf, *Sunday*, 10, esp. n.1). Webster (*Rest Days*, 122) sees it as more significant (Webster, *Rest Days*, n. 2).

13. See Rordorf, *Sunday*, 26–33.

14. See Colson, *Week*, 20–35; Rordorf, *Sunday*, 24–38; Zerubavel, *Seven Day Circle*, 12–20, Richards, *Rest Days*, 268–73. Despite the Babylonian interest in astrology, there is no evidence for the Babylonians observing a planetary week. Note that the determining factor in the "astrological" week seems to have been the planetary hour; i.e., the continuous seven-fold successive influence of the seven then-known "planets" (including sun and moon) on the hours of the day, such that each of the successive days is "governed" by a different planet, according to a constantly repeating seven-fold cycle (7×24=168, which is the total number of hours in a week, but note that each 24th hour will fall under a different "governor" or "regent" according to a seven-fold cycle). The sequence of planetary influence is the reverse of their apparent distances from the earth, as suggested by the period of their passage across the heavens. Saturn as slowest is taken to be most distant, and is taken to govern the first hour of the astrological week and therefore gives its name to the first day, Saturday. See Richards, *Mapping Time*, 269–71 (note Table 21.1). An interest in astrological hours long continued; see, e.g., Chaucer, *Knight's Tale*, lines 2217, 2273, 2367. A parallel concern with planetary influence on time and the unfolding historical scheme perhaps lies behind Shakespeare's seven ages of man (*As You Like It*, Prologue); it would seem to derive from Ptolemy (see Aveni, *Empires of Time*, 104–5).

15. For various traditions for naming the days, including the planetary names see Richards, *Mapping Time*, 279–83; 391–97.

In spite of this particular legacy, it seems that the Jewish custom of a seven-day week was the principal factor leading to the eventual adoption by the Roman Empire of a seven day week. Rordorf speaks of the "veritable triumphal procession" of the Jewish week.[16] No doubt, however, Colson is right to suggest that familiarity with the astrological week would have prepared the gentile world for the acceptance of what was basically a Jewish seven-day pattern.[17]

The Jewish week took its meaning from the Sabbath (Heb. *šabbât*, Gk. *sabbaton* or *sabbata*; *hebdoma* is also used[18]), and the other six days were named according to their relation to it.[19] Although the origin of Sabbath observance remains uncertain, the presence of the Sabbath commandment in each stratum of the Pentateuch attests to its antiquity.[20] Scholars generally agree that the Sabbath (and the seven-day week) were current not later than the eighth century BCE—well before the time of the exile and the time these biblical texts took shape.[21]

Equally, however, scholars cannot be sure why Sabbath observance was first adopted.[22] Rordorf writes:

> The background to the [Jewish] seven-day week . . . still remain[s] a mystery. It is nothing more than conjecture to assert that it goes back to the phases of the moon, or that it has developed from the numinousness of the number seven, or that it is connected with the economic necessity of holding markets, let alone that it may be traced back to one of the non-weekly models which we have mentioned.[23]

---

16. Rordorf, *Sunday*, 10.

17. Colson, *Week*, 106–7; Richards, *Mapping Time*, 268.

18. The etymology and original meaning of the word *šabbât* has been much debated. See Dressler "Sabbath in the Old Testament," 23f. and 37, nn.25–30. Dressler points out (37, n.30) that whatever the derivation and primitive meaning of the word "Sabbath" there is no reason to doubt that for the Jews the word soon took the meaning 'to rest from work'.

19. None of them except the sixth day (Friday, in Heb. *'ereb šabbât* or *ma'alêy*, "eve of the Sabbath"; Gk. *paraskeué*, "day of preparation," or *prosabbaton*, "day before the Sabbath") was given any special significance or designation. The others were simply *numbered* consecutively: first day (= Sunday), second day (= Monday), etc.

20. See Cannon, "Weekly Sabbath," 325–27.

21. Cf. 2 Kgs 4:23; 11:44; 16:18; Isa 1:13; Hos 2:13; Amos 8:5.

22. For a brief discussion of possible extra-biblical origins of the Sabbath and an extensive bibliography see Dressler, "Sabbath in the Old Testament," 21–41. See Colson, *Week*, 11–17; Rordorf, *Sunday*, 10–24; Robinson, *Old Testament Sabbath*.

23. Rordorf, *Sunday*, 24. Cf. Moore, *Judaism*, ii 22.

His last phrases refer to theories about intercalary days and possible links between the Hebrew word *sabbath* and the Babylonian word *shapath* ("full moon"). He continues, "No certain proof can be adduced for any of these conjectures: in fact, all they do is complicate our understanding of the Israelite week."[24]

He then makes a crucial point:

> The Old Testament sources themselves give us clear informa-
> tion about the original *meaning* of the seven-day week and the
> weekly day of rest in Israel, but they do nothing to explain the
> *provenance* of the seven-day structure of this week.[25]

Dressler agrees that "the evidence is unequivocal: the Sabbath originated in Israel as God's special institution for his people."[26] Likewise Andreasen, after acknowledging the complexity of underlying influences, finds himself compelled to concede that of far greater concern for the Jews than the *origin* of the Sabbath was its *meaning*.

> ... Israel not only kept the sabbath, she also contemplated it, and
> strangely enough it is the record of her contemplation rather
> than of her observation which predominates in the Old Testa-
> ment . . . .[27]

For the Jews, the key factor was that the Sabbath's origin lay with *God*, illustrated by the first Old Testament creation account of God "resting" (*shabath*) on the seventh day. Since this passage is to be attributed to the

24. Rordorf, *Sunday*, 24.

25. Rordorf, *Sunday*, 24.

26. Dressler, "Sabbath in the Old Testament," 23f. (cf. 36f. and 37, n.31). Dressler lists among those who have doubted that such a momentous phenomena as the Sabbath and seven-day week could have had a Jewish origin, Noth, von Rad, Ringren, Buber (Dressler, "Sabbath in the Old Testament," 36–37). Alfred Jeremias makes the point plainly: "The institution of a weekly cycle was a great intellectual accomplishment. From whom the Israelites got it cannot be determined. *They could not have invented it*; there is no trace left that the Israelites, who were decidedly dependent in cultural matters, occupied themselves with such things" (*Das Alte Testament,* 182, emphasis added). Dressler sees no place for such skepticism; in support he looks to Vriezen, *Religion of Anciet Israel*, 150; Zimmerli, *Mose*, 117. That having been said, others hold that the Jews are responsible for several of the most significant innovations in human history, not least ethical monotheism. See Sacks, *Faith in the Future*, 44, 47. Boorstin (*Discoverers*, 12) sees the adoption of a regular week as an affirmation of humanity's independence from natural forces—astronomical events, the seasons, etc. (Commitment to a planetary week, conversely, suggests independence only from *visible* natural phenomena; cf. Boorstin, *Discoverers*, 24.)

27. Andreasen, "Old Testament Sabbath," 14f. Andreasen ("Old Testament Sabbath," 15) identifies evidence for this "contemplation" even in the earliest sabbath texts.

priestly editors, it was not written to *establish* a weekly rhythm or a weekly day of rest; rather it explains a practice already long familiar.[28]

The Origins and Development of the Jewish Week[29]

The Old Testament Sabbath texts and their interrelationships are complex.[30] Sabbath observance is decreed in both versions of the Decalogue (Exod 20 and Deut 5:6–21) and in each is preceded only by commandments concerned with the most fundamental aspects of man's relationship to God. The Sabbath texts have been much re-worked, and contain ambiguous phrases and expressions. For this present work, the differences between the versions—long debated in Judaism[31]—are less significant than the fact that each version is so complex that it must be the result of much reflection and re-working, something which indicates the importance of the Sabbath in the Jewish worldview. Both read more like poetry than legislation, even than the kind of legislation in primitive documents such as the Codes of Lipit-Ishtar, Eshnunna, Hammurabi, and the Hittite Codes—still less the kind of legislation found in early Roman documents. Each passage is profoundly theological, speaking overtly of the *mystery* of who God is, of what he is like. The authors and editors of the Sabbath texts appear not so much to be framing a command as articulating a vision. The aim of the Sabbath commandment appears to be not so much the control of human behavior as the bringing of human life into the sphere of the divine action. The Torah has meaning only in the broader context of the *vision* of God and the vision of his purpose for humankind.[32]

---

28. Robinson (*Old Testament Sabbath*, 22) criticizes Andreasen. He argues: "The question of the origin of the sabbath is indispensable for understanding its basic meaning and, therefore, the search for the origin and development of the sabbath cannot be abandoned so lightly." Robinson's reductionism is unacceptable. He implies that the "real meaning" of an institution is to be discovered through study of its earliest form. The implied principle is: "To find the real meaning look back, look to how it began."

29. In addition to texts already mentioned (152, n. 1) see Moore, *Judaism*, ii 21–39.

30. For a close and detailed discussion of the texts see Robinson, *Old Testament Sabbath*. For the interplay between the various different factors influencing the development of the Sabbath see von Rad, "There Remains Still a Rest," 94–102, esp. 97ff., also Rordorf, *Sunday*, 16f. and 48ff. See Dressler, "Sabbath in the Old Testament," 24ff.

31. E.g., Maimonides, *Guide*, 219; Albo *Principles*, 246–8; Millgram, *Sabbath*, 338.

32. Moore defines "Torah" as "the comprehensive name for the divine revelation, written and oral, in which the Jews possessed the sole standard and norm of their religion," Moore, *Judaism*, i.263. The word *Torah* is often translated "law" (or "Law") but in Jewish tradition it carries rather the sense "teaching" or "instruction." Nevertheless

It could be argued that throughout the Bible, instructions are issued and commands given only after some *vision* has been given which has revealed something of the ultimate outcome of the way of life being commanded. This vision makes commitment to the divine injunction attractive and worthwhile. God's call to Abraham to leave his homeland, for instance, came hand in glove with the promise of rich future blessings (Gen 12:2; cf. 13:14; 15:1–6). It is through the experience of delight, rather than of fear or anguished guilt, that the way of redemption is opened. Promise and hope, these come first. "Taste and see."

Old Testament Meditation on the Significance of the Sabbath

Injunctions and exhortations to Sabbath observance occur throughout the OT, but little is said about how the day was observed.[33] The exilic period seems to have seen an intensification of Sabbath observance and an increasing concern with the meaning and significance of the institution. Cut off from the land, and knowing that the temple had been destroyed, the exiles sought as best they could to re-affirm their commitment to the covenant. Renewal of Sabbath observance was central to the process whereby concern for the Torah grew and the nation came to identify itself primarily in relation to the Torah, rather than to the land or the temple.[34] This is the era of the Pentateuchal texts. Gradually the Sabbath became increasingly significant. The scale of the change was great: the Pentateuch contains a mere handful of texts on the Sabbath, the *Mishna* (completed around 200 CE) contains a vast quantity of relevant material, estimated to include some thirty-nine articles and 1,521 passages.[35]

The first Genesis creation account, while not using the word *Sabbath*, presents the seventh day as the goal and completion of God's work. "[A]ll the creative activities of God flow into a universal period of rest."[36]

---

it is important to recognize that its earlier meaning is "revelation" (which is also the meaning of its etymological root). Both Exodus and Deuteronomy set the giving of the commandments in the context of the vision of the divine glory (cf. Exod 19:16–25; Deut 5:23–25). The title "Torah" came eventually to be applied both to the whole of the Hebrew Scriptures and to the oral tradition—their common theme being the revelation of God. Cf. Russell, *Between the Testaments*, 42.

33. See Dressler, "Sabbath in the Old Testament," 32–34; Elliger *Leviticus*, 313; Lincoln, "From Sabbath to Lord's Day," 352.

34. Russell, *Between the Testaments*, 48ff.

35. Banks, *Jesus and the Law*, 102–3; Moore, *Judaism*, ii 28–33.

36. Dressler, "Sabbath in the Old Testament," 29. This seventh day is open-ended,

The on-going significance of the Sabbath for Jewish life was its relationship to God and to the End towards which he had destined humankind. Implicitly, however, the first creation account gives universal significance to the whole weekly cycle. The seven-day week is the timetable of God's once-for-all work in creation, and the framework within which the world now orders its response to God. H. B. Porter comments:

> Here is every day, every week, every year, and the life-span of every man. But our story as we have it is most concerned over one specific time, the week. In the age when our text was completed, the week was clearly considered by the sacred writers as an institution of the utmost sanctity, the observance of which draws the life of man towards the life of God.[37]

The priestly tradition sets the Sabbath in a framework that both reaches back to the day of creation and reaches forwards to the future, even to the End. The Sabbath commemorates God's creative work, looks to his future blessings, and is a sign of his enduring commitment to his people. The Sabbath becomes a day of promise. For although the Sabbath texts in the Pentateuch contain no explicit promises, later texts make much of the reward which will follow on Sabbath observance: the blessings of joy, peace, and well-being. The scope of those promises is vast: *all* will benefit, even those on the very fringes of society, such as the alien and the eunuch (see Isa 56:2, 4–5, 6–7; 58:13–14).

Sabbath Observance from the Exile to the Time of Jesus [38]

By the first century BCE the Diaspora community was probably as large as the community living in Palestine. "By the time of Christ, Judaism was the single most vital religious movement in the Greco-Roman world."[39] Both

---

and the formula "evening came and morning came," which used for each of the first six days, is not used for the seventh. The importance of the *seventh* day is brought out by way in which the final verses of the Hebrew text comprises three seven-word sentences, each of which ends with the term "seventh day."

37. Porter, *Sunday*, 2. On the Genesis seven-day pattern see Lincoln, "From Sabbath to Lord's Day," 349, 398, and for the significance of this pattern Carson, *From Sabbath to Lord's Day*, 45; 54, n.3.

38. See Rowland, "Sabbath Observance in Judaism," 43–55.

39. Frend (*Rise of Christianity*, 42): "By the time of Jesus ministry, Judaism was becoming the melting pot of conflicting ideas all claiming to be the true interpretation of Torah. Everywhere there was vigour, growth, and expectation." To a whole spectrum of Jewish traditions, from the grandeur of worship at the temple (the focus of national

in the Diaspora and in Palestine, Jewish practice was diverse.[40] Between various groups there probably existed measures both of antagonism and of common concern.[41] Common to all, and allowing each particular group to see itself as Jewish, was a commitment to the Torah and to the Sabbath,[42] even though there was considerable disagreement about how the Torah was to be read and perhaps, also, about how the Sabbath should be observed.[43] Perhaps the majority of Jews were little concerned with the minutiae of Sabbath practice.[44] Everywhere, even in Palestine where the temple had been re-built and communal life re-established, Judaism struggled with intrusive secular influences.[45]

It was largely in the face of on-going oppression and trials that Jewish messianic hopes grew.[46] The Sabbath had a place in these hopes. Increasingly the belief grew that, week by week, the Sabbath gave a foretaste of the Kingdom. Beyond that, the conviction grew that God's promised deliverance from all tribulation would be hastened by faithful Sabbath observance (Isa 56:1–8; 58:13; cf. Jer 17:24–26; also *Melkhita Ex.* 16.25ff). If Israel could keep just two Sabbaths properly, then the day of deliverance would dawn (*Shab.* 118b).[47]

---

identity), to zealots, Pharisees, Platonizing philosophers, desert ascetics—to all of this the Christians were to some extent heirs. Cf. Rordorf, *Sunday,* 31.

40. See Ferguson, *Backgrounds,* 480–99. Allegorical interpretations of the Sabbath offered by Philo (first cent. CE) and before him Aristobulus (second cent. BCE) are of little significance for this present work (see Hengel, *Judaism and Hellenism,* 166–69 in the main text, and also pp. 108–9 in his notes).

41. Russell, *Early Judaism to Early Church,* 1–22.

42. Hellenism itself took many forms. See Russell, *Between the Testaments,* 22, 50; 85ff.; Rordorf *Sunday,* 47ff.

43. Cf. Goodman, "Legal Puzzels," 227.

44. Goldenberg, "Jewish Sabbath in the Roman World," *passim.*

45. Russell, *Between the Testaments,* 13–40. For Jewish influence on surrounding culture see Schürer, II.ii–iii. For the extent of the dispersion see Rordorf, *Sunday,* 31–33. On Babylonian diaspora see Neusner, *History of the Jews.* For the Jews in Asia Minor see, Kraabel, "Paganism and Judaism," 13–34; in Rome, Leon, *Jews of Ancient Rome,* and Smallwood, *Jews under Roman Rule.* On Gentile attitudes to Sabbath observance see Lohse, *sabbaton,* TDNT 7:17, nn.134–35; Stein, *Jews and Judaism,* and Goldenberg, "Jewish Sabbath in the Roman World," 414–47, esp. 430ff. Primary sources for Greek and Roman comment on the Jews are in Feldman, *Jewish Life and Thought.* (For the Sabbath, see especially 366–73.)

46. See Russell, *Between the Testaments,* 119ff.

47. Cf. Levi in *Jer. Ta'anit* 64a—where *one* well-kept sabbath would suffice (see Moore, *Judaism,* ii 26, n.1). Lohse has collected the Sabbath regulations and reviewed their development; *TDNT* VII, 6–18; cf *Mishna* Shab. (Neusner ed. 179–208).

The Function of the Sabbath in Later Pre-Christian Judaism

Sabbath observance served three important functions in the Old Testament era: it helped to build and maintain the self-identity of the Jewish nation; it kept the nation mindful of God's involvement in the world (his work in the past, his promise of future fulfillment); and it gave the life of the Jewish community a sense of direction and purpose, helping the community to see the whole of its life in relationship with God. These three worked together to help the community grow in its relationship to God. Importantly, however, Sabbath observance meant more than simply accepting a belief. The Sabbath had to be *practised* and *lived*. Their commitment to the Sabbath involved the Jews in doing something—even if, somewhat paradoxically, that something was resting.[48]

So too today, such significance as the Sabbath may have for the Church will lie, not in the theology of the Sabbath, but in the Sabbath *as an event*. The Sabbath encompasses matters of universal concern, not least because it looks to that *blessing of peace* for which all humanity longs (where "peace" equates to "fullness of life" and a willingness to work for the wellbeing of others, even of former enemies—not merely "absence of conflict"[49]). But for the Church of today, as for the Jews of all times, the crucial thing is to *observe* the Sabbath. The Sabbath exists as something to be experienced, not as something to be thought about—just as Christ himself, the fulfillment of the Sabbath, exists as someone to be *encountered*, and not as an ideal to be pondered.

Providentialist Readings of History

It would be foolish to argue that because historical research has failed to discover the origins of Jewish observance of the Sabbath it can be assumed that the Sabbath came to the Jews directly from the hand of God through Moses on Mount Sinai. But even if the origins of the Sabbath and seven-day week are unknown, historical research does make it clear that the Jews came to believe that the seven-day week had divine warrant and that they saw the Sabbath, not just as a social institution, but as something fundamental to their relationship to God. Today providentialist interpretations of history are far from fashionable. But all historiography has its theoretical underpinnings. As Wright puts it: "All historians have theological presuppositions.

48. Note also that the call to the Jews was not just to obey the Law but to teach and to *study* it, to be students of God's Law. Cf. Sacks, *Faith in the Future*, 48.

49. There is an *energy* to the divine peace. See above, 19.

Atheism and agnosticism count as much as faith."[50] Bebbington is among those who have argued that a providentialist reading of history can be as coherent and respectful of the findings of scholarly research as any other. He sees the Christian historian as uniquely privileged: he or she can draw on what is best in other historiographical traditions, while yet adding something new and otherwise beyond reach.[51]

Can it be argued, then, that the development of the week among the Jews and the subsequent worldwide spread of their seven-day pattern perhaps occurred providentially, under divine guidance? Could it be further argued that the divine purpose in this was to provide a vehicle for the proclamation of the paschal mystery (of suffering turned to joy and of death leading to life) and a setting for growth into that mystery? If it is only in and through the paschal mystery that man can attain to maturity, then we might assume that if God wishes him to reach maturity then he would have established patterns that would help facilitate growth into that mystery.

50. Wright, in Wright and Borg, *Meaning of Jesus*, 16.

51. Bebbington, *Patterns in History*, 169–71. Butterfield (*Christianity and History*) offered a robust defence of historical providentialism. Recall Daniélou's criticism of the "intolerable flatness" of biographies of Jesus or histories of the Church that seek to ignore or remove the divine dimension; Daniélou, *Christian Centuries*, 4. For a review of recent contributions to the debate about the status of Christian historical thought see Bebbington, *Patterns in History*, ch. 8. There is perhaps a growing realization amongst historians that objectivity is not be identified with indifference or lack of passion. See Haskell, "Objectivity is not Neutrality," 129–157; Evans, *Defence of History*, 194f., 251f. Jervell wonders whether, "Theology of history has deserted the field and handed it over to *Geschichtsphilosophie*, philosophy of history," and asks, "Is the reason that such an undertaking is not possible anymore? If so, why not?" Jervell, *Theology of Acts*, 135f.

15

Jesus and the Emergence of the Christian Week

> Christ yesterday and today,
> > the beginning and the end,
> > > Alpha and Omega;
> > > all times belong to him and all the ages;
> > > > to him be the power and the glory for ever and ever.
> > > > Amen.[1]

IN THIS CHAPTER I shall look at two things. My main concern shall be with Jesus' use of time during the incarnation, and particularly his use of the seven-day cycle. But because I see his life and work as having transformed the very nature of time I also want to introduce some theological issues. I shall delay a full and more complete discussion of these theological matters until after I have recounted something, not only of Jesus' use of the seven-day week, but of the entire history of the Christian use of that cycle. But I need to say something now about the revolutionary effect which Jesus had upon time; otherwise there will be much in that history that will make little sense.

It is notoriously difficult to determine how either Jesus himself or the evangelists viewed the Sabbath.[2] The Gospels present Jesus habitually attending Sabbath synagogue worship (Mark 1:21 par.; 1:39 par.; 6:2 par.; John 18:20; cf. Luke 4:16); but they also show him wilfully infringing Sabbath regulations; sometimes it appears that he healed on the Sabbath *in order* to stir up his opponents.[3]

1. Prayer at the blessing of the Paschal candle in the Easter Vigil of the Roman Rite, *Sunday Missal* (1975) 209.

2. See Carson, "Jesus and the Sabbath"; Lohse looks at Jesus' words about the Sabbath *TDNT* 7:20–31.

3. See Carson, "Jesus and the Sabbath"; cf. Linclon, "From Sabbath to Lord's Day," 360. Significantly, violation of the Sabbath was not among the charges brought against Jesus at his trial. There is no evidence of the infant Church suffering any persecution specifically because of its failure or refusal to observe the Sabbath (Rordorf, *Sunday*, 119).

Perhaps it is not possible to appreciate the NT authors' understanding of the Sabbath unless it is recognized that the first Christians believed that Jesus had fulfilled all the successive covenants God had established with his people, including the covenant made with Moses and of which, crucially, the Sabbath was the sign.[4] The first Christians came to believe that the righteousness and sanctification they had sought through the Torah was now theirs *in Christ*. He was their peace—the "peace which passes all understanding" (Phil 4:7).[5] No NT text states it precisely, but many imply that Christ is the fulfillment of the Mosaic Sabbath. And indeed they go further.

The first generation of Christians came to believe that in and through the resurrection of Jesus God had inaugurated a new creation. Jesus is presented in the NT as Son and Word of God; as Alpha and Omega; as Beginning and End. In seeking to explain the work of Christ the NT authors frequently recall that God is Creator and that the world exists in relation to him. Yet they also present Christ himself as the ground and goal of creation (cf. John 1; Heb 1; Col 1:15–20). From the beginning *all* things have had their meaning in him. "All things were made through him and for him" (Col 1:16). Explicit in these staggering claims is the idea that all material creation has its origin, continued existence, and ultimate end in relation to Christ, and that all humankind does so too. But implicit here is also the idea that *all of time* and *history* finds its meaning in him. The material world, human life and all of history are in the Son's hands, but so too are the temporal cycles by which life is organized—the day, the week, the year etc. Here we see again that tension which the early Church recognized and which I mentioned above: although the second creation is definitive, the first creation still has value.

If there is continuity between the Jewish and Christian understandings of time, the latter also includes something radically new. Judaism sees time as belonging to God and as leading somewhere: he is working out his purposes and despite life's ups and downs, time is full of promise. For the Church, however, history is, in one sense already complete: in Christ, God has completed his purpose. With the resurrection, writes Bouyer, "the history of humanity is entirely written."[6] For the Church, the uncertain (if

---

4. Allison (*New Moses*) explores the idea that Matthew's gospel presents Jesus as the new Moses; but strangely, Allison does not mention the theme of the Sabbath or mosaic covenant sign. Salardini (*Matthew's Christian-Jewish Community*, 126; cf. 268–72) outlines first-century Jewish Sabbath practice and suggests that such also was early Christian practice. Although he says "echoes from Moses and the Exodus are constant" (182) he makes no mention of the Mosaic covenant or its sign.

5. Cf. Banks, *Jesus and the Law*, 122f.; Lincoln, "From Sabbath to Lord's Day," 362ff.

6. Bouyer, *Paschal Mysery*, 292. Here Bouyer also says: "The first creation . . .

glorious) end which Judaism anticipates already exists. Bouyer again, "The generations yet to come will only receive the plenitude to which all the others before them were gradually leading."[7]

The realization that in Christ God completed his work is as old as the gospel itself and is present throughout the NT. John of the Cross would later interpret a phrase from the opening of the Letter to the Hebrews as implying that, having "spoken through his Son" (cf. Heb 1:1), God, "now has nothing more to say."[8] This same claim might be restated: "God has *acted* through his Son and now has nothing more to do—except, that is, to gather the world into what has been accomplished."[9]

Schmemann writes:

> The difference between Christianity and Judaism is not in their . . . theology of time, but in their conception of the events by which this time is spiritually measured. For Judaism time is eschatological in the sense that it is still directed towards the coming of the Messiah and the messianic Kingdom. In Christian time the Messiah has already come, is already revealed.

He continues:

> The new element [is] the fact that the event which . . . in the old Judaistic conception constituted the "centre" of time . . . has already begun. And this event, in turn, is eschatological, since in it is revealed and defined the ultimate meaning of all things— creation, history, salvation.[10]

Making the same point Zizioulas refers to the work of Joachim Jeremias.

> [T]he phrase "Kingdom of heaven" is very often translated as "heavenly Kingdom" i.e., in spacial and often Platonic contrast with whatever exists or is done on earth. . . . In the NT, as . . . Jeremias observes "the Kingdom is always and everywhere understood in eschatological terms. It signifies the time of salvation, the consummation of the world, the restoration of broken communion between God and man."[11]

---

marked the beginning of time; the other [the resurrection] . . . the end of time."

7. Bouyer, *Paschal Mysery*, 292; cf. 19ff.

8. *Ascent*, II.xxii (cf. Heb 1:1); Staniloae, *Experience of God*, 1, 37–38; also Staniloae, *Experience of God*, 2, 40–41; cf. Maximus, *Thal.* 22; PG90:317d.

9. Cf. Heb 7:27, 10:10.

10. Schmemann, *Liturgical Theology*, 56f.

11. Zizioulas, "Eucharist and the Kingdom," part 1, 3 n.4, quoting Jeremias (apparently, *Euchaistic Words of Jesus*, 226).

These are profound matters. Essential to the Church's understanding of time is this: that the End *already exists* in Christ, and it exists *as Christ*. This is the view of Orthodox theologians in general,[12] but is shared by many non-Orthodox biblical scholars, including Wright[13] and Koenig.[14] Regan explains: "[T]he eschaton [End] is really not a thing (*eschaton*) but a person (*eschatos*). It is the Lord himself—the last man, the spiritual man—the one in whom God and man have met in the Spirit."[15] Such a view provides a foundation for a fully sacramental understanding of creation and must be the basis for any eschatologically oriented theory of Christian discipleship. For in the Christ who is the End exists a new set of relationships; he invites man to live within these relationships and to make them his own: relationship with God, relationships between human persons, and relationships between them and creation. I shall return to discuss this sacramental understanding of creation later. First it will be useful to explore the process whereby Christ accomplished his work and inaugurated the new creation of the eschatological Kingdom.

The Son's Growth into Fullness of Human Maturity

Various key elements in the process by which the divine persons brought human nature to the completion they had always intended can now be explored. In particular it will be useful to examine the sequence of events through which the incarnate Son *grew* to fullness of human maturity, thereby enabling his humanity—the created humanity he took from Mary and held in common with all created human persons[16]—to share fully in the relationship with the Father that he had always known in his uncreated

---

12. In addition to the authors already mentioned, see, e.g., Gysi, *Orthodox Potential*, 142. From (non-Chalcedonian) Indian Orthodox tradition see Philip, "Anaphora of St James," 38ff.

13. See, e.g., Wright, *People of God*, 459–64.

14. See Koenig, *Christ in Eschatology*. See also Taft, *Liturgical Understanding*, 1–3, esp. 8: "[The Gospels] introduce us to a new mode of his [Christ's] presence, a presence . . . real and experienced, yet quite different from the former presence . . . Jesus is with us, but not as he was before."

15. Regan, "Aspects of Liturgical Celebration," 346–47.

16. See Weinandy, *Likeness of Sinful Flesh*, esp. 21–70, also Colin in Weinandy, *Likeness of Sinful Flesh*, x–xi. Meyendorff, *Byzantine Theology*, 157: "[T]the Byzantine theologians are authentically concerned about recognizing in Christ *our fallen humanity*, but their minds are less clear about the moment when, in Jesus, this humanity became the transfigured, perfect and 'natural' humanity of the New Man."

divinity; for only thus was human nature redeemed and only thus could a *new humanity*, a *new human nature* come into being.

There was nothing arbitrary about the content and character of the stages through which Christ grew. Each contributed to the final result, and, as it were, remains a factor within the life of the glorified Son. Rather as (say) those who want to play water polo must first learn to swim—for moment by moment during the course of that game they will have to be swimming—so the demands the Father makes of the incarnate Son—the stages in his growth, the "skills," dispositions or virtues he had to acquire—these represent *necessary* conditions for the participation of his human nature in the relationships of the Kingdom. They were not stages through which he passed and left behind, as a train passes through a succession of railway stations, leaving each behind before travelling on to the next. Rather, the process of growth was accumulative: progressively grace added to grace. And in this process no early stage was ever superseded, abandoned, or left behind. The early stages of has grown are integral to his maturity.

It is a poor analogy, but we can think of it like this: the simple arithmetical skills learnt in junior school are integral to the expertise of the professional mathematician. Likewise, the sacrificial obedience of Christ's earlier years was the foundation for the sacrificial obedience of his maturity. Similarly, for the Christian, he or she must grow by grace, step by step, progressively building towards maturity of loving response and sacrificial self-giving.

The call to love can be paraphrased thus: "Those who do not love cannot share the life of the Kingdom." And it can be understood like this: God is not saying to the Christian, "If you will not love, you will find that I will not allow you to share the life of heaven"; he is explaining, "If you will not love you will find that you are not *equipped* to share the heavenly life."[17]

The well-known claim of Irenaeus is significant here: man was created immature, as a child, with a vocation to growth.[18] At his origin man's nature was not defective or disordered, but was incomplete. As Nellas puts it, "Even before the fall, [man] was in need of 'salvation.'"[19]

> The Lord redeemed man from slavery to sin, death and the devil, but he also put into effect the work that had not been

17. Cf. Macdonald, "Child in the Midst," and Lewis, *Great Divorce*.

18. See *AP*. 12; *AH*. 4:37:4, 7; 4:38:23; and the discussion in, for example, Minns, *Irenaeus*, 56–82, esp. 66–76. Note the important idea that Christ had to recapitulate the life of Adam (see e.g. *AH*. 3:16:6; 5:20:2—21:2; 3:21:10), and within this, the belief that Christ passed through all the stages of human life, living into his fifties (*AH*. 2:22:4).

19. See Nellas, *Deification in Christ*, 38. (Basil speaks of the day of Christ's birth as the "birthday of mankind." *Nativity* 6, PG31:1473a.)

effected by Adam. He united him with God, granting him true "being" in God and raising him to a new creation. . . . [Christ's] relationship with man is not only that of healer. The salvation of man is something much wider than redemption; it coincides with deification.[20]

This deification is, more precisely, Christification.[21] The work which Christ accomplished bore fruit; in the first place that fruit was *his own life*, a human life in fullness of relationship with the divine life. By the divine goodness, that life is held open to human participation. Maximus says, "God the divine Logos wishes to effect the mystery of his incarnation always and in all things."[22] The incarnation can be recapitulated in all who are willing to allow it; but the (personal) divine initiative requires a (personal) human response, a willingness to live in faith, hope and love.

"Decisive Moments": Steps Along the Way

Fr Sophrony suggests that in the divine economy:

> there are certain "moments" which the Church regards as of special importance, and which she calls to mind every year by feast-days. . . . Each one of these "moments" of God's self-revelation to man is organically and indissolubly linked with all the others; but the Day of Pentecost, when we celebrate the Descent of the Holy Spirit, marks the completion of the Revelation of the Almighty . . . .[23]

It will be useful to explore some of these key "moments" and to suggest something of what might be involved in the Christian's recapitulation of Christ's way of growth.

The Annunciation and Birth (Luke 1:26—2:21; Matt 1–2)

God's work on behalf of mankind did not begin with the incarnation. It began at the moment of creation. The created order, unimaginably vast and complex as it is, was to constitute the setting in which man could both come into being and learn to respond to the divine initiative. At the Annunciation, when the Son began to take flesh in Mary's womb, a new stage

---

20. Nellas, Deification in Christ, 39.
21. For the seeds of this idea in Irenaeus see, e.g., *AH*. 3:18:1.
22. *Am.*, PG91:1084d
23. Sophrony, "Unity of the Church," 2.

of the divine work began. God had ever been committed to humankind; but God's active involvement in human history was limited by the human capacity to recognize and respond to him. The incarnation could not take place until long preparation had brought into being a person (Mary) and a community (the devout first-century Jews) with the maturity of faith to make an adequate response.

Few nowadays read the accounts of the birth as simple reportage. Certainly, Jesus was born. But the circumstances are something of a mystery. Crucially—but perhaps surprisingly—for the interpretation of Christ's life which I preset in this study, the birth is not especially important. It is less significant than the annunciation. The Church sees the birth of the Son as a turning point in human history, and that is right: the Savior appears, God among men. But it is the annunciation rather than the birth that tells us most about God's commitment to humankind and humankind's redemption. The annunciation both marks a new beginning in God's relationship to mankind and also tells us about the response for which God looks. Mary's "*Fiat*" (Luke 1:38) gives expression to the open-hearted faith that God's looks for in humanity, and without which God's purposes cannot be accomplished.

As for Jesus' early life, the Gospels and early Church tradition tell us little about this. Luke's statement "he grew in stature and wisdom and God's favor was with him" (Luke 2:40) assumes that he did indeed need to grow—an important point. And though it is perhaps pointless to pry into Jesus' psychology, there is no need to believe that he would not have progressed through the same stages of growth as paediatricians and educational psychologists now tell us all other people do: acquiring a capacity for focusing the eyes, balancing on two feet, recognizing others, then building vocabulary, number skills, and so on.

The Baptism (Matt 3:1–17; Mark 1:9f., Luke 3:1–22)

Crucial in the story of Jesus are the accounts of his baptism, the prelude to his active ministry. Significantly, liturgical celebration of the baptism/ Epiphany (6th January) is generally taken to antedate the introduction into the calendar of a separate celebration of the nativity.[24]

The Son's decision to become incarnate was not made in his *humanity*, for, of course, that humanity only begun to exist at the annunciation. His baptism, however, can be seen as the moment when he committed himself

24. See *ODCC* "Christmas" and "Epiphany." For the celebration of the baptism/ epiphany as the beginning of the liturgical year see the discussion in Talley, *Origins of the Liturgical Year*, 134–35.

in his adopted humanity, by an act of his human will, to the work which he had taken on through a choice made in his *divinity* at the annunciation. At his baptism the Son recapitulated the decision he had previously made in his divinity to be united with fallen man and to share fallen mankind's lot. Significantly, Jesus made this choice when a mature adult—"about thirty years old" (Luke 3:23). The wonder of the baptism lies in the Son's free (human) decision to be wholly one with suffering, sin-stricken humanity. He says in effect: "I will share your sufferings, that you may know the Father's love." This human choice led him to the experience human sufferings of both the types I mentioned above: "healthy" and "caused by sin" (108; cf. Heb 2:17). He experienced these sufferings in and through his adopted humanity. He had to endure them as a *person*. His baptism represents his personal (human and divine) consent to future suffering.

For the Christian, Christ's baptism has its analogue in the decision that the Christian is called to make to share the sufferings of others that they may come to know the Father's love. The Christian is called not merely to abstract devotion to God, but to loving service of others, after the image of the love which the divine persons have for the world (cf. John 14:12; cf. p. 6 above). The decision to accept this vocation can be made by the adult Christian at his baptism, but not, of course, by the infant. Confirmation—sometimes described as a sacrament looking for a meaning—might have value here.[25] The Gospel accounts present the baptism as a trinitarian event: the Spirit descends on the Son and the Father bears him witness. This "resting upon" the Son of the Spirit can be seen as confirming the Son in his vocation, and as bringing the call to self-sacrificial ministry and the grace to fulfill that ministry. For the Christian, Confirmation can be seen both as bringing a call to take a mature, active, responsible part in the worship and ministry of the Church and also as conferring the authority and grace to do so.[26] The baptized and confirmed Christian is called to appropriate the life he or she has been given in Christ; this he or she does by cooperating with the grace that the Spirit imparts. Thereby the Christian becomes united with Christ, gradually becoming, as the process moves towards completion, all that the Father would have the Christian be.

25. For a review of practice and interpretation, with extensive bibliography see *ODCC* "Confirmation."

26. See Schmemann, *Liturgy and Life*, 13.

THE YEARS OF CHRIST'S MINISTRY

The Gospels do not set out to give a complete biography of Jesus. They show him engaged in a ministry of teaching and healing, and they show him proclaiming the coming of God's Kingdom. But they give little indication of the time, date, or location of many of the events. What they do make clear, however, is that many in Israel came to believe that God was powerfully at work in Jesus. He is presented as teaching with unique authority, as performing miraculous signs and healings, as issuing rebukes and warnings in God's name, as subduing evil spirits, as offering forgiveness—all of which betokened God's presence and intimated that a new age was dawning. For the Church today, the significance of this is that Christians are called not only to believe in the Son but to "do the same works that he did" (cf. John 5:20) and, more still, to accomplish "greater works" (John 14:12).

Significantly, the Gospels present the ministry of Jesus as being accomplished only in the face of hostility. Large sections of the religious and political establishment were violently opposed to him. Moreover, he had also to overcome a certain resistance which he found *within himself*. He knew human frailty, and his created humanity sometimes struggled with the demands made upon it, most notably in Gethsemane (Mark 14:32–42, par.). I shall say more of that in a moment; but here it is worth acknowledging that, just as Christ went by the way of suffering, so too for all Christians the way of growth will include suffering. Not that there is anything good about suffering *per se*, but rather, because it is only through the created use of suffering that the Christian can be fully united with Christ, fully like him. This is the blessing concealed within suffering.[27]

The years of Christ's ministry have this further significance for those who would now follow him. His years of teaching and healing revealed his compassion for all. Yet central to his work was also a ministry of *judgment*. Like John Baptist and the OT prophets, Jesus challenged those he encountered. To a fallen world the gospel comes as a challenge. But this challenge is not about morality or religious duty. It is the challenge to live in a particular kind of relationship with God and with other people. This challenge can be summarized as: "Love as I love." The two commandment which the Gospels present as cardinal, namely, "Love the Lord God with all your heart and soul and mind and strength, and love your neighbor as yourself"[28] both concern *relationship*—they amount to a call to be fully open (heart and soul and mind and strength) to God and to other people. Sin, as I have said before,

---

27. See 101 ff. above; also Gal 5:16–19; Col 1:24.

28. Mark 12:30–31 and par. These commandments look back to Deut 6:4,5 and Lev 19:18.

is always to do with failure in relationships. At its root, sin is not a matter of breaking rules or regulations—not even the commandments; it is always concerned with breaking relationships, indeed with breaking hearts.

Implicit in this call to be Christ-like is a willingness to work for the sake of others, for the sake, that is of the restoration of one's human brothers and sisters to right relationships. The goal is right relationship with God and right relationships within the human community. (Cf. the comments above on peace; p. 162.)

This Christian call will often (perhaps always) involve a call to suffer for the sake of the well-being of others, just as Christ does, and yet more, even to die for their sakes, just as he does. For although Jesus confronted the world as judge, he did so in compassion. He willingly labored and suffered for the world's healing and redemption. If the Church is to become fully Christ-like it must also share his ministry of judgment (cf. Matt 19:28, par.); but it can only do so insofar as it will stand within his compassion. Before the Church can remove the speck in the world's eye, it must remove the plank from its own; and that plank I take to be lovelessness, judgmentalism (Matt 7:1–6). Of Jesus' encounter with the rich young man it is said, "Jesus, looking at him, *loved* him and said . . . sell what you own . . .; then come follow me" (Mark 10:17–22).[29] No one in the Church, whether archbishop or layperson, can stand within Christ's prophetic judgment of the world except insofar as he or she loves as Christ does. But practical ministry to the sick, needy, lonely, and lost, etc.—these provide opportunities for Christians to *acquire* and *realize* that compassion. They provide opportunities to learn to see others as Christ himself sees them.

The Transfiguration (Mark 9:2–8, and par.)

The Feast of the Transfiguration entered the Eastern liturgical year in the middle of the first millennium. Although not inscribed in the Roman calendar until 1457, it was probably widely celebrated in the West from the mid-ninth century.[30] But the transfiguration represents an event unlike the majority of those commemorated in the liturgical year. The patristic and liturgical traditions contain nothing to suggest that anything was *accomplished* within the humanity of the incarnate Word at the transfiguration, only that on the mountain the disciples were allowed to perceive the glory

29. For this "two-phase" ministry of judgment grounded in mercy see, e.g., Luke 6:27–38; 6:39–42.

30. For the history of the feast see McGuckin, *Transfiguration*; Martimort, *Liturgy and Time*, 97–8; Mercenier, *Prière des Eglisse*, 259ff.

which, though previously concealed from human view, had always belonged to him as eternal Son.

> The light seen by Christ's three disciples on Mount Tabor existed within Christ both before and after the transfiguration, as the natural brightness of his divinity. When he was transfigured . . . Christ did not put on or introduce a new aspect that he did not previously possess, but revealed . . . a part of the radiance that was his from the beginning.[31]

Lossky writes, "The transfiguration was not a phenomenon circumscribed in space and time; Christ underwent no change at that moment, even in his human nature . . . ."[32]

It is probably because nothing was accomplished in Christ's humanity at the transfiguration that it is not recalled in the eucharistic canons. What happened on the Mount was not part of the *work* of the incarnation, even though the overall purpose of the incarnation was to enable human persons to know and live by the divine energy manifested to human view on Tabor.[33]

Holy Week[34]

The Son's work was completed in the final week of his life, during which he brought his human nature into fullness of conformity with his eternal divinity. Entering into Jerusalem on Palm Sunday he reaffirms his commitment to his mission, a commitment to which he would remain faithful, despite the growing pressure during the following days to turn from his task. Decisive were the passion and cross, but no less significant (and in its own way equally decisive) was the inauguration of the Eucharist. Schmemann sees the Eucharist, not simply as pre-figuring or anticipating the passion, but as precipitating it.[35]

31. Manzaridis, *Deification*, 100; cf. Manzaridis, *Orthodox Spiritual Life*, 152f. Also Gregory Palamas, *Agioreitikos Tomos*, PG150:1232c; Homily 34, PG151:433ab. See also John Damascene, *Transfig.* 12, PG 96:564c.

32. Lossky, *Mystical Theology*, 223.

33. For a discussion of (i) the relationship of the uncreated light to the divine *nature* and (ii) the potential relationship of the uncreated divine light to (created) human nature (body and soul) see, e.g., Mantzaridis, *Deification*, 99–104.

34. For discussion of the events of this week as recorded in the early Church as later interpreted in the liturgical traditions of East and West see Schmemann, *Holy Week*; Bouyer, *Paschal Mysery*. For a theologically profound account of Holy Week and paschal mystery but one with an express pastoral concern see Bishop, *Passion Drama*, Bishop, *Easter Drama*.

35. Cf. Schmemann, *Eucharist*, 204–6: "[Judas] saw, he heard, he felt the kingdom

Maundy Thursday

"It was night" (John 13: 30). According to Jewish reckoning, by the time of the Last Supper, the sixth day would already have begun—another indication that the Eucharist marked the beginning of Christ's re-creative work, for the Genesis account places the creation of Adam on the sixth day. In the Eucharist the incarnate Son (both God and man) gives himself into the hands of his disciples so they might share, in their created humanity, in the divine life. As such the Eucharist is the counterpart of the crucifixion; for on the cross the Son (both God and man) gives himself into the hands of the Father so that his humanity might come into fullness of right relationship to the Father. Whether the Last Supper was a Passover meal or not (and the debate continues) the prayers that Jesus offered at the meal would have had much the same basic form and content, centering on thanksgiving for God's work in creation, God's provision of opportunities for growth, and his redemptive work on man's behalf.[36] In offering these prayers the Son expresses gratitude for the Father's gift to him of a created (human) life, for the Father's on-going work in history, and for the opportunity he provides to accomplish the work of redeeming and perfecting the world (cf. John 17). In and through these prayers, the Son also implicitly gives thanks for his share in human history—and therefore (such is his humility) also gives thanks for his human brothers and sisters.

Schmemann presents the Last Supper as "the manifestation of the goal, . . . the manifestation of the *end*. . . . With the Last Supper Christ's earthly ministry was completed."[37] Schmemann suggests that everything that either Christ himself or the Church accomplished after the Last Supper was a consequence of the "decisive and saving victory" which the Eucharist represents.[38] On such an understanding, the cross was the consequence of the Last Supper. How could this be? All hostility to Christ and to his kingdom can be seen as reactions to the challenge of Christ's love. The accounts of the Last Supper and of the days leading up to it differ in many details, but each suggests that the Son's openness to the Father confronted the disciples with a challenge beyond their worst imaginings. He left them in no doubt

---

of God . . . and . . . he *did not want* this kingdom" (206).

36. Bouyer, *Eucharist*, 97–100; Cabié, *Church at Prayer, Eucharist*, 21, n.1; Brown, *Death of the Messiah*, 555–56, 576–79; cf. Jeremias, *Eucharistic Words of Jesus*, esp. 41–84. Also Klawans, "Was Jesus' Last Supper a Seder?" and Klawans further discussion at: http://www.biblicalarchaeology.org/daily/people-cultures-in-the-bible/jesus-historical-jesus/jesus-last-supper-passover-seder-meal/ (biblicalarchaeology.org 2.12.2016)

37. Schmemann, *Eucharist*, 204 (cf. John 13:31; 17:4).

38. Schmemann, *Eucharist*, 204.

that they were being called to follow where he led. Hope of a comfortable, easy or "successful" life drained from their hearts. Thrown into confusion, none of the disciples responded well. No one knew how. But all except Judas held sufficiently to his trust in God that his faith could be deepened. Judas alone felt himself compelled to strike out and destroy the challenge that seemed intent on destroying him.[39]

To share in the Eucharist is to share in Christ's life: his prayer and self-offering, his reconciliatory ministry on behalf of the world, his divine-human maturity. Insofar as the eucharistic community enters into their celebration, they are being reconciled to God and to one another. In the process they help to gather the wider world into its destiny. And through sharing in the Eucharist, they become better equipped to share in Christ's ministry beyond the eucharistic celebration in humdrum daily life—in what some have termed "the liturgy after the liturgy."[40]

The Passion and Cross

I have suggested that even in an unfallen world some pain and suffering would have existed, but I have also said that this suffering would not have been identical with the suffering consequent upon sin. In an unfallen world there might even have been death, but only a death in itself wholesome. This death would represent a natural movement or progression, one leading to increased communion with God. It would not have been a death threatening annihilation.[41] In an unfallen world there could have been no cross, if for no other reason than that no one would have been willing to carry out a crucifixion.

In a fallen world the work of reconciliation was accomplished through the cross. The powers of evil sought to turn the Son from his purpose or induce him to despair—ultimately to destroy him. But even when the assaults of evil were at their worst and death loomed, the Son was not diverted from his course. He remained open to the Father. In doing so he was implicitly consenting to being raised to new life: open to give his life to the Father, he was open to receive from him new life.

While Mark and Matthew have the dying Christ uttering a "great cry" (Matt 27:50; Mark 15:37), John has him proclaiming victory: "*Tetelestai*: It is [or *has been*] finished, completed, accomplished" (19:30). Jesus announces the completion of his work; he does not say "*I* am finished," but

---

39. Cf. Schmemann, *Eucharist*, 206 (cf. 138–40).
40. See Bria, *Liturgy after the Liturgy*.
41. Cf. Lewis, *Out of the Silent Planet*, esp. ch. 19 and postscript.

"*It* is finished." Here is human life brought into fullness of conformity to the divine life. Here the Son realizes in his human nature (by the decisions of his human will) the *humility* always proper to his divinity. Here is the overcoming and reversal of fallen man's pride.[42]

Having attained to this humility, the Son is no longer vulnerable to the threats of the devil. Importantly, this openness was no temporary state. He did not pass *through* the cross to a better life, one beyond the reach of evil, where Satan could not reach him. The devil cannot harm the glorified Son, not because the Son is shielded from him, but because although Satan is always doing his very worst, the Son has become *indifferent* to his actions. He has, so to speak, made his home in the cross. He is *always* dying into the hands of the Father. Just as the paschal mystery belongs *eternally* to the life of the Trinity, so it has become the abiding (eternal) disposition of the divine-human Son. Luke's final words of the crucified Christ, "Father, into your hands I commend my spirit" express what is now the Son's *constant* or on-going state of self-offering.

John presents Jesus as saying before his arrest, "the ruler of this world . . . has no power over me" (14:30: *ho tou kosmou archōv . . . en emoi ouk echei ouden*). Fear of suffering and death have lost their power; and sin—i.e., all that derives from the urge to secure one's own existence and well-being, in disregard of God's will and the good of others—has lost its allure. The Son is not conditioned by the hopes and fears that are the legacy of the fall. And now, living as he does in the fullness of the Father's love, such hopes and fears can never impact on him or take hold of him.

Satan's assaults, threats, and temptations offered the Son opportunities for service. Through them he deepened his love for God and for his neighbor. Christian growth will now come, not through excluding evil, but through learning to make creative use of evil. Evil never *becomes* good, but it can be used *for* good. Each act of faith or obedience weakens Satan, who has little or no power of his own but lives parasitically, preying upon the power and energy of others.[43] Obedience holds open those channels through which love flows from God to mankind.

Common to the NT and Church Fathers is the conviction that Christ saved the world by his death, and not in any other way.[44] Now Christ makes it possible even for death to be used creatively. Schmemann writes:

> In *this* world there shall be tribulation[;] . . . suffering remains
> . . . awfully "normal." And yet Christ says, "be of good cheer, I

42. Cf. Schmemann, *Holy Week*, 38–40.

43. Gysi, *Orthodox Potential*, 132.

44. Cf. Bouyer, *Christian Spirituality* I, 230–34.

have overcome the world" (Jn 16:33). Through his own suffering, not only has all suffering acquired new meaning but it has been given the power to become itself the sign, the sacrament, the proclamation, the "coming" of that victory; the defeat of man, his very *dying* has become a way of Life.[45]

He continues, "The beginning of this victory is Christ's death"—adding, "The whole life of the Church is in a way the sacrament of our death, because all of it is the proclamation of the Lord's death, the confession of his resurrection."[46] Participation in Christ's death opens the Church and the Christian to new life.[47]

Boros developed a theology that viewed the whole of life as a preparation for death. "The final decision [made at death] is in part determined by the preparatory decisions taken during the course of a lifetime."[48] Boros sees such a death as also a birth, claiming that by embracing death we can attain to fullness of freedom.

> Only in death can volition achieve full union in act with itself, by freely accepting (or rejecting) everything for which it has been striving. . . . [H]uman volition before death is never more than embryonic. Death is birth. In its "prenatal" mode of existence, the will learns the movements that will be indispensable to it on the day of its birth. In the course of its earthly development, it is in training for the decisive and final act of the will. Death is thus the act of will *simpliciter*.[49]

In Christ's death, his obedience is perfected: "Christ is man and as *viator* was not able to give full human expression to his redemptive obedience until he did so in death. His death effects our salvation because in it is summed up all the fullness of the human expression of Christ's obedience."[50]

The liturgical commemoration of the passion and its prayerful recollection open the way for the grace required to live by self-sacrificial love to

---

45. Schmemann, *For the Life*, 103f.

46. Schmemann, *For the Life*, 104. On good death and creative suffering, see Sittser, *Grace Disguised*, ch. 3.

47. Cf. Gysi, *Life in Letters*, 118–25; also Lewis, *George Macdonald*, 34 and the notion of "good death" which Lewis discovered in the writings of George MacDonald. In *Lilith*, ch. 3, MacDonald also writes: "You will be dead so long as you refuse to die" (see Lewis, *George Macdonald*, 176).

48. Boros, *Moment of Truth*, 97. Cf. "In death . . . the decisions of a lifetime are gathered together, and in the individual decisions of a lifetime . . . death is being rehearsed," Boros, *Moment of Truth*, 194.

49. Boros, *Moment of Truth*, 30.

50. Boros, *Moment of Truth*, 144.

flow into the world. Paradoxically, participation in the passion is possible because the Church already participates in the grace of the resurrection. Christ (in the fullness of his crucified and risen humanity) and the Christian mutually indwell one another. The Church is not called to *copy* or imitate Christ but to participate in him, i.e., to be transparent to his presence and open to the action of the Spirit.

The resurrection did not follow immediately upon Christ's death—although we can imagine that it might (cf. Matt 27:52). The body of Jesus spent a day in the tomb. What is the significance of this?

SATURDAY IN THE TOMB[51]

Schmemann suggests that for the majority of Christians Holy Saturday is simply an interval between Friday's tragedy and the reversal of Easter Sunday.[52] He insists, however, that Holy Saturday (in Eastern tradition called "Great Sabbath") is more than this. Schmemann's understanding of Holy Saturday and more generally of the place of the Sabbath in the divine economy is the basis of what follows.

Schmemann believes the key to understanding Holy Saturday is the realization that Christ *rests* in the tomb, rests *in the goodness of the Father*— rather as he had rested in the Father's goodness on every Sabbath of his earthly life.

But what of the prohibitions and proscriptions which were always part of Sabbath observance in the first century? What place might they have in the divine economy; for Jesus himself seems often to have ridden over them rough-shod? There is an important ascetic dimension to the Sabbath. We are called, even on the Sabbath, to deny certain urges and impulses. The prohibition of laborious work means that we have time for rest. But in setting a limit to man's industry and activity the Sabbath prohibitions and proscriptions also offer an opportunity to *learn* to trust in God and to *practise* resting in the divine goodness. And this is necessary, because *fallen man finds it hard to resist the temptation to try to secure his own future.*

In the Jewish household, Friday is given over to making provisions for the day of rest, particularly for Sabbath meals; but such work must end as dusk draws on. Even if the preparations are incomplete, work must stop. And what then is left but trust in the divine goodness? This is important.

---

51. Cf. Schmemann, *Holy Week* 35–47; also *Holy Week*, 67–73; Bouyer, *Paschal Mysery*, 249–57. Cf. Gillet, *Year of Grace*, 158ff., which begins, "There is no day with a more complex character than Holy Saturday."

52. Cf. Schmemann, *Holy Week*, 35–36.

For when life itself eventually draws to a close, who will be ready? Who will have accomplished all that he or she intended? Friday evening is an opportunity to turn in humble confidence to God. "I'm not ready. I'm sorry. But I look to your goodness." This looking towards God represents, not an irresponsible passivity, but an "active-passivity," a reorientation of the person towards (active) dependence upon God. Such resting is difficult. It involves a certain "dying," a certain self-loss. The Sabbath prohibitions challenge fallen humanity to abandon the urge to secure its own future, its own beatitude. These prohibitions can, therefore, encourage or facilitate growth in faith and trust.

The total trust realized and expressed in such rest can be seen as representing the final, most mature stage in Christian faith.[53] It gives expression to the belief that salvation comes as a gift. This active-passivity defines the final, most mature level of Christian prayer. It expresses the realization, "Ultimately I can do nothing for myself. But there again, I *need* do nothing for myself: for God is good." All Christian life must be seen as being oriented towards the acquisition of such faith. For only those who have abandoned hope in their capacity (or their need) to secure their own well-being are able to live fully in the flow and re-flow of divine love.

Christ in the tomb is to be seen as resting in the divine goodness. He kept Sabbath. The Christian community can observe Sabbath rest both as an opportunity to experience something of divine goodness and as an opportunity to *practise* trusting in God.

I should mention here, if only briefly, an alternative understanding of Holy Saturday, one developed by Balthasar and grounded in the mystical experience of his friend Adrienne von Speyr.[54] For many years Speyr experienced a sense of desolation after the Good Friday liturgy. She took this to indicate that Christ's time in the tomb and his descent into hell represented the final stage of his work and the limit of his separation from the Father.[55] I would take the view that the redemptive work of the Son is completed on the cross, and that it was here that he knew utter desolation and separation from God. This is the view of Eastern Orthodoxy but also of many Western

---

53. Cf. Origen, *Joh.*, Frag. 80; *TSS*, 117, etc.

54. For studies see Saward, Mysteries of March, 108–33; Mareschi, *La histiologia di Hans Urs von Balthasar*, 151ff; Maas, *Gott und die Hölle*, 245ff.; Löser, *Im Geiste des Origenes*, 237–46.

55. See Balthasar, *Mysterium Paschale*, 49–83, 148–88; also Saward, *Mysteries of March*, 108, 128. Certain mediaeval texts, notably passages from Nicholas of Cusa, can be read as suggesting that the Son's descent, rather than simply his death, marks the fullest extent of his abasement; see Balthasar, *Mysterium Paschale*, 170–72.

theologians and mystics too, John of the Cross among them.[56] Indeed, Balthasar acknowledges the eccentricity of his own view.[57] Von Speyr takes issue with John of the Cross, arguing that he has misinterpreted his experiences.[58] But might one suggest—without calling into question her sanctity—that she has misinterpreted hers? May her experience of desolation be seen as a side-effect of the Spirit's attempts to gather into light whatever remained dark in her own heart? Balthasar says, "theologically Purgatory cannot take its rise elsewhere than in the events of Holy Saturday."[59] But the Eastern tradition is adamant that the descent into hell is a *victorious* descent. It is hell that is harrowed, not Christ. Florovsky writes:

> The Descent of Christ into Hell is the manifestation of Life amid the hopelessness of death: it is victory . . . . By no means is it the "taking upon" Himself by Christ of the "hellish torments of God-forsakenness." The Lord descends as Victor . . . in his glory, not in humiliation . . . .[60]

Florovsky's words express that traditional Orthodox view, as represented in its iconographic tradition.[61] Contrast this with Saward's com-

56. See Ware, *Lenten Triodion*, 62–63; *Ascent* II:22.

57. Balthasar, *Mysterium Paschale*, 179–80; cf. Sayward, *Mysteries of March*, 113–14, 118–23.

58. See Saward, *Mysteries of March*, 128.

59. Balthasar, *Mysterium Paschale*, 178.

60. Florovsky, *Creation and Redemption*, 142; cf. Ouspensky, *Meaing of Icons*, 189f. Florovsky expressly takes issue (*Creation and Redemption*, 304 n.121) with Calvin and those who adopted the "new and unheard-of heresy," grounded in a penal conception of the Atonement, that Christ took upon himself the "hellish torments of God-forsakenness." See also Meyendorff, "Holy Saturday".

61. See Ouspensky, *Meaning of Icons*, 185–88; Balthasar and Speyr (*Kreuz and Hölle*, 203, 337) question this view (see Saward, *Mysteries of March*, 113–14). Cf. Schmemann, *Holy Week*, 40–46, esp. 43–4. Note that although Ouspensky talks of the descent as "the last step made by Christ on the way of his abasement" (*Meaning of Icons*, 188) he need not be read as taking the same view as Balthasar. For, unlike Balthasar, he makes no attempt to develop a theology (or a history) of Christ's time in the tomb, and there is other evidence which indicates that Ouspensky follows the standard Orthodox line and sees in the cross the completion of the Son's work. See, e.g., Ouspensky, *Meaning of Icons*, 180 where the cross is spoken of as "the limit" of Christ's "voluntary abasement." (This passage is by Ouspensky's collaborator, Vladimir Lossky, but there is no reason to believe Ouspensky does not share this view). See also Evdokimov, *Art of the Icon*, 313–27. Evdokimov follows Eastern tradition in insisting on the brute *reality* of Christ's death but refrains from attempting to explain what happened to the Son after his death, except, that is, to look to liturgical texts which insist on his *resting* in the tomb and on his *glorious* and *life-giving* appearance to those trapped in Hades (322–24). Wisely, however, he also insists that Christ's time in the tomb is "a mystery surrounded by silence" (325).

ment (looking to Balthasar and Speyr), "Jesus does not descend as Risen but as Dead."[62]

For my part, I share Florovsky's view: it is the *risen* Christ who descends and who makes himself known to the departed. The matter is somewhat hypothetical, but I would place the descent on Holy Saturday, but *in the evening*. In other words, and using Jewish time divisions, the descent takes place *after* the Saturday (of rest) is already giving way to the Sunday of the resurrection. There is a parallel perhaps between, on the one hand, the events of the evening of Maundy Thursday and of Good Friday, and on the other, the events of Saturday evening and Easter Morning. Just as the Last Supper is a "private" anticipation of the events of Good Friday, so the descent is a hidden or "private" anticipation of the resurrection—but one that takes place in the grace of the resurrection, just as the Eucharist takes place in the grace of the utter self-loss of the crucifixion.[63]

RESURRECTION AND GLORIFICATION[64]

The resurrection of Christ's humanity is to be seen as the natural fruit of his passion. Having opened himself to the Father in his dying, he is open to receive the resurrection life. But Christ being who he is, the resurrection inaugurates a new life, not just for him, but for all creation, It is, "the coming of the new creation and the breakthrough of the life from above."[65] It is *within* the resurrection that the Church lives and has its being. And it is only because it stands within the resurrection, i.e., within the eschatological Christ, that the Church is able to take up the cross, share in Christ's passion and participate in his ministry of reconciliation.[66]

Importantly, the new life, being Christ's life, is beyond threat of death or destruction. It cannot be spoiled or go astray. That harm that was done

62. Saward, *Mysteries of March*, 113.

63. I must note that in a troparion at the *start* of Orthodox Matins for Holy Saturday there occurs the phrase, "Going down to death, O Life immortal, Thou hast slain hell with the light of thy divinity," Ware, *Lenten Triodion*, 623. Resurrection is a theme of the liturgy (but mainly later in the service; cf. Schmemann, *Holy Week*, 41–46); other themes are death and rest.

64. For the celebration of Easter see Tally, *Liturgical Year*, 1–57; Jounel in Martimort, *Liturgy and Time*, 4 33–76; Greenarcre and Haselock, *Sacrament of Easter*, esp. 148–69. For Sunday, more generally, very valuable is Porter, *Sunday*; cf. Jungmann, *Meaning of Sunday*.

65. Gregory Naz., *De nov. Dom.* 5; PG36:612.

66. See figure 1 (270 below). Here the Last Day is represented as a Sabbath, one which can be seen as the fulfillment of what is initiated in the resurrection. (A full-color version of the image is available on the website accompanying this book.)

by sin, leading to the impairment in human knowledge of God and of communion with him, the breaking of the unity binding all humankind into one, and also the virtual destruction of the inner coherence of each person—the new life stands beyond all that. It cannot suffer harm or loss, but will ever endure as *one* life (Christ's life), lived in communion by many persons, each of whom is an integrated whole. What is possible, however, is that the Christian, having been baptized into this new life, chooses not to live by it—and rejects its demands. It almost goes without saying that the Christian will struggle fully to live the new life given at baptism. It is a life which, though given once-and-for-all, must be appropriated by the Christian step by step, a little at a time. The journey towards maturity will involve many setbacks, many disappointments, many failures. But at heart, the new life given at baptism cannot be damaged or lost. Repentance and renewal are always possible. Indeed, by grace, the Christian can turn to good anything and everything that would seek to inflict harm; and even sin itself, though never desirable, has built into it this one grace, this one benefit, this one blessing: it is humbling.[67] By his openness to God even in the midst of trials and torments, failures and disappointments, the Christian can learn to participate in Christ's humility. Thereby whatever can be redeemed is redeemed. All is gift: the Christian is called, not to accomplish his own salvation, but to be united with Christ and to allow Christ to live and work deep within.

Whenever the Church celebrates the resurrection (be it Easter, any Sunday, or whenever) it opens itself to the inflowing of new life. That life comes as a gift, but as a gift that has to be received, appropriated. The members of the Church will be able to appropriate that life only insofar as they are willing to be gathered into the self-forgetful and self-sacrificial ministry and prayer of Christ himself. Only insofar as they are willing to leave behind their old ways, old ways of thinking and acting, fallen ways of viewing and judging others—will they be able to live the new life.

---

67. Or it *can* be humbling. Confronted by an awareness of our sin, our wilfulness, our waywardness we *can* allow this awareness to humble us; but we have always this other option: we can choose to harden ourselves against God and against his entreaties, either falling into despair or railing against God and (what we see as) the injustices of life.

THE ASCENSION AND PENTECOST[68]

The resurrection and the ascension are inseparable aspects of the glorification of Christ.[69] The Ascension was not celebrated as a separate feast until the fourth century. The Gospels and other NT writings are inconsistent in their treatment of the ascension (rather as they are in their accounts of the resurrection). But they are consistent in affirming that the man who ate with his disciples in the upper room on Thursday, and died on Friday, later rose from the dead, to be glorified and to reign with the Father. They are consistent too in their affirmation that the Son's death and subsequent glorification are the ground of his present (and continuing) activity in the Church and the world.

Commonly the ascension is presented as the fulfillment of the incarnation: "with the ascension of Christ . . . the work of God's economy and of man's deification was made complete."[70] Rahner sees the ascension not as Christ's entry into a ready-made heaven, but as his creation of heaven, understood as a nexus of personal relationships.[71] This is an important idea, and I would not disagree with the suggestion that Christ, by his ascension, *created* heaven. But I would also suggest that something more can be said. Indeed, I would suggest that Pentecost represents the fulfillment of the Son's vocation.

Neither the ascension nor Pentecost should be separated from the resurrection.[72] But the Son's gift of the Spirit to his disciples can be seen as both realizing and manifesting the fullness of divine-human maturity. Within the Trinity the Father wishes the Son to be all that he himself is. (The Father is not like those human fathers who do not really want their children not to grow up and therefore look to keep them subservient.) Imaging the Father's love, the Son prays before his passion that his fol-

68. Ascension: Talley, *Liturgical Year*, 66–70; Martimort, *Liturgy and Time*, 58–64; Leclerq *DACL* 14:259–74; Bobrinskoy, "Ascension of Christ." Pentecost: Gunstone, *Pentecost*, esp. 48–56; For the celebration of the *day*, rather than the fifty-day season, of Pentecost see Martimort, *Liturgy and Time*, 59–61; also Talley, *Liturgical Year*, 57–66 (esp. 66).

69. "All but two of the New Testament texts . . . treat of Christ's being in heaven as the immediate consequence of his resurrection," Boros, *Moment of Truth*, 158.

70. Mantzaridis, *Orthodox Spiritual Life*, 153. I see no particular connection between the Ascension as "theological event" and the day of the week on which it has come to be observed, Thursday.

71. See Pahn, *Eternity in Time*, 167. Note however that the creation of Hell (if not Hades) can also be seen as the consequence of the Son's glorification. See, e.g., Saward, *Mysteries of March*, 118–20; Balthasar, *Mysterium Paschale*, 246.

72. Boros, *Moment of Truth*, 198.

lowers may attain to his own knowledge of the Father (John 17). True to his word, having brought a new humanity into being through his passion and resurrection, the Son then shares his risen life with his followers, and thus *he realizes fullness of likeness to the Father*. In this way, Pentecost can be seen as a *necessary* aspect of the Son's maturity, his perfection. It is only in *sharing* his risen life (rather than in keeping it for himself) that the incarnate Son become fully conformed to the Father.

In summary: the Son, open to give—to be *wholly given*—at the Last Super and on the Cross, was thereby also open to receive, to receive the fullness of resurrection life. But it did not end there: open to receive resurrection life, the Son was also open to share, to share that life with his human brothers and sisters. At Pentecost, he shared with them that fullness of relationship to the Father (by the Spirit) which was, so to speak, his birthright as Son eternal and which was also his accomplishment as divine-human incarnate Son.[73]

I do not recall finding this idea, expressed in this way, in other authors. It may be original to me. Its significance for the Church and the Christian vocation is this: the Son's willingness to open his risen life to the participation of others is proof of the maturity of his love, so too all human perfection involves a willingness to share, to give unstintingly—and indeed to do so even to those who do not deserve it. Spiritual growth must find fulfillment in spiritual paternity/maternity. Integral to spiritual paternity and challenging all who have leadership is the question: Will you share your status or would you prefer to stand alone and have others submissive? Equally fundamental is the question addressed to everyone looking for spiritual growth: Are you in this only for yourself or for the good of others too?

73. Of course, that life, though gift, still has to be appropriated by those to whom it is made available, something the Son, by his Spirit, is ever himself at work to make possible.

16

Historical Considerations 2

The Week in Early Christian Tradition

Now IT WILL BE useful to outline something of the Church's use of the seven-day week. My aim here is strictly limited. I hope to show that nothing in Church tradition undermines or invalidates the proposals I shall make about the use of the week. Beyond this, I hope to show that at one time or another the Church has adopted practices that suggest an understanding of liturgical time akin to the one in which I still ground my suggestions. I shall not attempt to recount the entire history of the Christian week. We can look to others for that.[1] I shall focus on three key issues. First, the question of the relationship between the Sabbath and Sunday; secondly, the place and status of Saturday in the Christian dispensation; and thirdly, the important but difficult question of the motives and the conceptual frameworks that shaped the development of the week, and which have subsequently influenced the way in which the history of the week has been read.

Much of the confusion and disagreement about the Saturday/Sunday issue has its origin, so I shall argue, not in a mistaken reading of primary texts but in a theological error. It is notable, for example, that few recent commentators have considered the possibility that Saturday and Sunday might each have its own distinct character; such that, week by week, each might be observed in its own way, with the two days working together to help to make the life of the community a more effective context for disciple-ship and mission. It is this complementarity which I shall seek to explore and exploit in the pattern of the week.

1. See, e.g., Rordorf, "Sunday: The Fulness of Christian Liturgical Time"; Rordorf, *Sunday*, esp. 38–42, 80–153, 177–293; *TDNT* 7:20–35; Colson, *Week*, 82–107; Mc-Casland, "Origin of the Lord's Day"; Beckwith, *This is the Day*; Ferguson, "Sabbath or Sunday?"; Bauckham, "Sabbath and Sunday Rest in the Post-Apostolic Church"; Ri-esenfeld, "Sabbat et jour du Seigneur"; Daniélou, *Christian Centuries*, vol. 1, 222–86; Regan, *Dies dominica*; Bacchiocchi, *Sabbath to Sunday*; Jounel, "Sunday and the Week." For the subsequent development of the Christian week, see Hessey, *Sunday*, 213–302; Hodgkins, *Sunday*; Bauckham, "Sabbath and Sunday Rest in the Medieval Church"; Parker, *English Sabbath*; Wigley, *Victorian Sunday*.

The Christian Week in Recent Scholarship[2]

Rordorf's work on the history of the Christian Sunday is invaluable.[3] He argues that Sunday emerged as the principal day of Christian worship from the beginning,[4] and that only with the Peace of Constantine did it come to be designated a day of rest, and furthermore, that not until the sixth century was the fourth commandment used to justify Sunday observance.[5] Before Constantine, worship, and in particular the Eucharist, more or less defined Sunday: "No Lord's Day without the Lord's Supper."[6] In the nascent Church, Jewish Christians continued to observe Saturday as the Sabbath; but throughout this period Sunday and Saturday were always kept distinct; each had its own character.[7] Sunday was the Lord's Day; Saturday the Sabbath. Rordorf's own work looks principally towards re-establishing Sunday as a eucharistic day.[8] He is willing, however, to allow a place for the observance of Saturday as a Sabbath (a practice I shall term the "Saturday-Sabbath"), but in so doing would see Saturday, not as an alternative to Sunday, but as its complement. It would have a distinct character of its own.[9]

Not all scholars share Rordorf's reading of early Church practice. First Francke, and then Beckwith and Stott, argue for early emergence of Sunday-Sabbatarianism.[10] Jewett and Lee advocate variations on this Sabbatarianism.[11] Meanwhile, the Seventh-day Adventist Bacchiocchi argues that Saturday-Sabbath observance was the Christian norm until the second destruction of Jerusalem in 135 CE. He contends that Sunday observance arose in Rome during Hadrian's rule (117–35 CE) when repression of the Jews prompted the Church to adopt practices that would mark it out from other religions. Sunday was singled out as an appropriate day for Christian worship, because this would allow incorporation of the symbolism belonging to pagan Sun cults.[12] (Do we see in these authors'

---

2. Carson (*Sabbath to Lord's Day*, 13–16) reviews recent scholarship, but neglects the Orthodox.

3. See esp. Rordorf, *Sunday*, and "Sunday: The Fulness of Christian Liturgical Time."

4. Rordorf, *Sunday*, 154.

5. Rordorf, *Sunday*, 169–71.

6. Cf. Rordorf, *Sunday*, 173, 301–7.

7. Rordorf, *Sunday*, 151.

8. Rordorf, *Sunday*, 301–7.

9. Rordorf, *Sunday*, 153, n.1.

10. Fancke, *Van Sabbath naar Zondag*; Beckwith, *This Is the Day*.

11. Lee, *Covenental Sabbath*; Jewett, *Lord's Day*.

12. Bacchiochi, *Sabbath to Sunday*, ch. 8 (esp. 268–69).

attempts to defend the traditions to which their respective communities were already deeply committed?)

In 1982, under the editorship of Carson, a group of Cambridge post-graduates published their reflections on the Sabbath/Sunday problem.[13] They were not persuaded that the Sabbath is presented in the Old Testament as "creation ordinance," binding for all time. Neither were they convinced that the distinctions on which the Sabbatarians built their transference theories were valid; nor (*contra* Bacchiocchi) that Sunday observance was a second-century innovation.[14] They were confident, however, that "although Sunday observance arose in NT times, it was not conceived as a Christian *Sabbath*."[15]

The scholarship of the Carson group is meticulous and wide-ranging, but their conclusions are rather disappointing. They see nothing more behind the Sabbath ordinance than a divine recognition of man's needs for rest and refreshment. Their claims for Sunday and the modern Church are modest: they acknowledge an enduring need for a regular day of rest, but see "no compelling reason why [this] has to be Sunday."[16] And although they acknowledge that worship is central to the Lord's Day,[17] unlike Rordorf, they do not seek to give priority to eucharistic worship. Their objective for Sunday worship is very limited: the "joyful celebration of the rest which Christ provides" should enable the community to "enter into and live out that rest," with the result that through the working week "there will be an inner liberation, a genuine leisure in the way in which they go about both . . . work and . . . play."[18] The implicit spirituality is non-sacramental and apparently without ontological implications. Human involvement in worship seems to take place only at the level of the human mind, memory, and emotions. And although Sunday worship is seen to imply "mutual exhortation to enter into and live out [the] rest" won by Christ, there is no suggestion that the Church is called to share in what is ontologically "one life."[19]

The scholarship of Rordorf and the Cambridge group is impressive. They have identified some of the distortions which have entered into Sunday observance and the theology of Sunday. But it is only with

---

13. Carson, *Sabbath to Lord's Day*.

14. See Carson, *Sabbath to Lord's Day*, 15–16; Linclon, "Sabbath to Lord's Day: A Biblical Perspective."

15. Carson, *Sabbath to Lord's Day*, 16.

16. Lincoln, "Sabbath to Lord's Day: A Biblical Perspective," 404.

17. Lincoln, "Sabbath to Lord's Day: A Biblical Perspective," 405.

18. Lincoln, "Sabbath to Lord's Day: A Biblical Perspective," 405.

19. Lincoln, "Sabbath to Lord's Day: A Biblical Perspective," 405.

Schmemann and the Orthodox that a more complete and positive understanding comes into view.[20]

Schmemann sets out a profound and helpful understanding of the relationship between Saturday and Sunday. He sees the whole of Christian life as rooted in Sunday (and its annual counterpart Easter).[21] Sunday is properly a festal day: a day of thanksgiving for the gift of new life in Christ, a day of Eucharist. But Schmemann sees Saturday also as "a day not of *fast* but of *feast*."[22] God himself "instituted it as a feast" (cf. Gen 2:3) and "no one can abolish that which God has ordered."[23] Saturday is not a fast day even during Lent.[24] Schmemann specifically rejects the view that the Sabbath has been transferred to Sunday: "Nothing in the Scriptures or tradition can substantiate this belief."[25] The Sabbath remains a sign that creation is good, and the Sabbath commandment can be seen as directing the world to the recognition of this.

> To keep the sabbath as was meant from the beginning means therefore that life can be meaningful, happy, creative; it can be that which God made it to be. And the sabbath, the day of rest on which we *enjoy* the fruits of our work and activities remains forever the blessing which God bestowed on the world and its life.[26]

However, Schmemann also insists that there is a certain *discontinuity* between the Jewish and Christian understandings of the Sabbath. "For in Christ nothing remains the same but everything is fulfilled, transcended, and given new meaning."[27]

> If the sabbath in its ultimate spiritual reality is the presence of the divine "very good" in the very texture of this world, it is "this world" that in Christ is revealed in a new light and is also made something new by him. . . . And here is the supreme "break" which for a Christian makes "all things new." The goodness of

---

20. Hessey to some extent anticipates it. See Hessey, *Sunday*, esp. 171–214.

21. Schmemann, *Great Lent*, 11–15; *Eucharist*, 50–52, 55–59, etc.

22. Schmemann, *Great Lent*, 67.

23. Schmemann, *Great Lent*, 67.

24. Strictly, the ascetic fast continues on Lenten Saturdays, so that the diet is restricted, just as it is on Lenten Sundays. But celebration of the Eucharist is both permissible and desirable on Lenten Saturdays. Therefore, no more than Lenten Sundays can Lenten Saturdays be days of total fast.

25. Schmemann, *Great Lent*, 67.

26. Schmemann, *Great Lent*, 67f.

27. Schmemann, *Great Lent*, 68.

the world and of all things in it are now referred to their final consummation in God . . . .[28]

This consummation will only be revealed in its fullness after this world has come to an end. Insofar as "this world" has rejected Christ it has enslaved itself to a falsehood, which is why "the way of salvation" cannot be "through evolution, improvement or 'progress'" but only "through the Cross, Death, and Resurrection."[29] But Schmemann is adamant that this world and this life are not to be rejected, for it is in the midst of this life that the in-breaking of the new life must be discovered. It will be discovered in and through eucharist, thanksgiving, celebration, joy. The Sabbath has its part to play here. "Christ's Death restores the seventh day, making it a day of re-creation, of the overcoming and destruction of that which made this world a triumph of death."[30]

As a day both for celebrating the goodness of creation, and as time of vigil and expectation, Saturday has a double character. It stands at the end of time, as fulfillment; yet it also stands *between* this world and the next, as the day *before* the Lord's Day. Schmemann speaks of it as, paradoxically, a day both of *feast* and of *death*.

> It is a *feast* because it is in this world and in its time Christ overcame death and inaugurated his Kingdom, because His Incarnation, Death, and Resurrection are the fulfillment of Creation in which God rejoiced at the beginning. It is a day of *death* because in Christ's Death the world died, and its salvation, fulfillment and transfiguration are beyond the grave, in the "age to come."[31]

Death, in this sense, is not cause for ultimate despair, but is that *which turns human thoughts and hopes to God*. Saturday gives a taste of ultimate joy—"taste and see'"—but within this world that joy will never be complete, never fully satisfying. Saturday can serve, therefore, to turn the human heart to God. Those who taste of its goodness can, on the one hand, be drawn into ever-deeper relationship with the One in whom fullness of eternal joy abides, while on the other, the very fact that Saturday will always be somewhat unsatisfying makes it difficult for anyone to believe that life in this world is mankind's ultimate goal.

As for the week as a whole, Schmemann sees this as "a movement from [the heights of] Tabor into the world." And he sees each day as "a *step* in this

---

28. Schmemann, *Great Lent*, 68.
29. Schmemann, *Great Lent*, 68.
30. Schmemann, *Great Lent*, 72f.
31. Schmemann, *Great Lent*, 69.

movement," one which offers "a moment of decision."[32] Each step—though Schmemann does not say so in as many words—invites the Church to *exercise* the grace given afresh each Sunday, thereby to appropriate the gift of new life in a fully personal way. Day by day the Church *journeys* towards its ultimate Sabbath rest; and in this journeying its members are offered successive opportunities to grow towards fullness of personal maturity.

Factors Significant in the Emergence and Development of the Christian Week [33]

There can be little doubt that the first Christians took the seven-day week for granted. It had long been natural to Jewish social and religious culture. And the surrounding Greco-Roman world, through long familiarity with the Jews, would have known of this seven-day cycle and would not have been surprised to see a new Jewish religious movement (such as the Church was taken to be) living within this pattern.[34] Pagan converts in Palestine would have adopted the seven-day week as something intrinsic to the culture they were entering; outside of Palestine pagan converts would also have familiar enough with Jewish practice—the diaspora was widely influential—that they too might happily have fallen in with the seven-day cycle. Familiarity with the astrological week might also have played a part.

Early Christian use of the week would largely have been shaped by the same two factors that shaped so much else in Christian thought and practice: the need, on the one hand, to affirm that all had been fulfilled in Christ, so that a new era had been initiated; and the need, on the other hand, to acknowledge that even in this new era the spatio-temporal world was essential to the divine economy, so that there would be a place (even a need) for a new "law"—that is, for an ordered, regular, disciplined life. The Church looked, then, to establish (or maintain) patterns of life that could provide a framework for discipleship. A seven-day cycle could have been seen as part of this, not least because Jesus had brought his work to completion within this pattern and rose to new life on the first day of the week, the day traditionally associated in Judaism with new beginnings.[35]

32. Schmemann, *Eucharist*, 52.

33. For bibliography see 152, n. 1 above. Rordorf, in *Sabbat et Dimanche*, gives the majority of texts relevant to the early history of the week both in their original languages and in French translation.

34. See 161, n. 45 above.

35. Below, 193, n. 41–42.

But two errors were possible. The Church might succumb to a "spiritualizing" tendency, locating Christ in a "spiritual realm" above and beyond everyday, this-worldly life. Associating itself (and its salvation) with a "spiritualized" Christ, and despising the created world of space and time, the Church would fail to make use of the opportunities for growth which the material and temporal realms offer. But if, as I have argued, the created world exists for no other purpose than to offer the possibility of growth, then space and time and all that belongs to them are indispensable if growth is to be made.

The alternative error possible to the early Church was that it might, not spiritualize Christ, but rather *historicize* him, locating him, as it were, in the past, and failing to recognize the reality of his *present, ongoing* action in the world day by day and moment by moment. Where the Church adopts this understanding it will be inclined to perpetuate those patterns of life which had been appropriate in the old dispensation but which now, since Christ's resurrection, were in need of radical reinterpretation. The challenge is to affirm that the new creation begun in the resurrection represents something radically new while yet insisting that the Jewish legacy still has value. It was through living within the created realm and through participation in the Jewish life of his time—and through redemption of them—that Christ brought the new creation into being. And these two between them—i.e., the created realm and the redeemed and renewed Jewish tradition—constitute the context within which men and women can learn to share the resurrection life.

The NT shows the Church struggling with these issues. Paul, for example, sometimes challenges the tendency to undervalue this world (see 2 Thess 3:6–12) and elsewhere looks to counter retrogressive Judaizing (e.g., Gal 4:8–11; 3:10; 5:3). Was it this need to counter a retrogressive Judaizing tendency that led many of the first Christians to distance themselves from the bulk of Jewish tradition, including Sabbath observance?

The Days of the Week in the Christian Dispensation: Sunday

The development of Sunday as *the* Christian day is the most obvious innovation in the Christian week. Bacciocchi's contention that this is a late (and non-Palestinian) development has generally been rejected.[36] Widely

36. Bacchiocchi, *Sabbath to Sunday*, esp. ch.5; cf. Carson, *Sabbath to Lord's Day*, 15–6, 19; Bauckham, "The Lord's Day," 237–38; Bauckham, "Sabbath and Sunday Rest in the Post-Apostolic Church," 270–73; Lincoln, "From Sabbath to Lord's Day: A Biblical Perspective," 400–440.

accepted is Rordorf's view that, although it may be impossible "to discover for certain the origin of the observance of Sunday," nevertheless

> several arguments can be cogently advanced for the opinion that the Christian observance of Sunday is a genuinely Christian creation, which reaches back into the oldest period of the primitive community and even to the intention of the risen Lord himself.[37]

No word of Jesus in the gospels directs his followers to Sunday worship, and no NT text enjoins worship on the first day of the week, but various texts (1 Cor 16:1ff; Acts 20:7; Rev 1:10[38]) indicate that the infant Church adopted Sunday worship, and more general considerations point to a Palestinian origin. But perhaps nothing indicates more effectively the importance of Sunday for the early Church than the simple insistence of all four evangelists—who at this point show no textual dependency—that Jesus rose to new life on the "first day of the week" (*mia tōn sabbatōn*).[39] This linking of the resurrection with the day on which the original creation is commemorated—not to mention other "new beginnings" in the Jewish people's relationship to God; e.g., the inauguration of sacrificial worship in the tabernacle[40]—strongly suggests that the evangelists were keen to indicate the radical innovation brought about by the resurrection.[41] The fact that the evangelists record the *day* of the resurrection but make no mention of the year or the exact date[42] suggests that they see the resurrection as primarily not as an event in history (though it was that) but as an event in the divine economy. Had they been viewing it principally as an event in history, the year and date would have been important (cf. Luke 2:1-2); but as an event in the divine economy, the day is important, for that economy is celebrated in the weekly cycle, with the litur-

37. Rordorf, *Sunday*, 237, cf. 215-37. See Jounel, "Sunday and the Week," 12f.; Bauckham, "Sabbath and Sunday Rest in the Post-Apostolic Church," 236-38.

38. See Rordorf, *Sunday*, 231. Pliny writing to Trajan (112 CE) states that Christians gather early on a fixed day (*stato die*—generally taken to be Sunday) and then after a morning service go on their way before gathering again for a meal (10.96 [97].7) Pliny is drawing on witnesses whose testimony describes a state of affairs that would have existed some time before the date of his letter.

39. Mark 16:2; Matt 28:1; Luke 24:1; John 20:1 The Gospels also locate the resurrection on the "third day," and in Jewish tradition the "third day" represents the day of a definitive divine action (cf. Hos 6:2; Jon 1:17; 2:10).

40. See SB I, 1054. (Ps-Eusebius of Alexandria (fifth century) makes such links explicitly. See Jounel, "Sunday and the Week," 18.)

41. The Bible opens and closes on Sunday. See Gen 1:1-5; Rev 1:10 (Porter, *Sunday*, 1, 30).

42. Porter, *Sunday*, 31; cf. Rordorf, *Sunday*, 212.

gical seasons playing only a supporting role. The Sabbath took precedence over all the feasts, including Passover.[43]

Rather, as Sabbath observance had come virtually to define Jewish identity in the first century, so Sunday observance soon came more or less to define the Christian community. Sabbath worship in home and synagogue had served to keep the Jews mindful of God's past actions, his ongoing work, and future promises, and had also helped to strengthen relationships within the Jewish community. Sunday worship, celebrated by small committed communities, did much the same for the Church. The similarities extend further. Both the Jewish and the Christian communities saw themselves not as social groups meeting at their own initiative, but as communities called into being by God and having their life (and future) in his hands. They recognized that in their worship something of the eternal, eschatological divine life was disclosed and they recognized also that through participation in this worship the community could learn to participate in that life. In its worship, the Christian community not only learnt about the resurrection, but encountered it. Indeed, it encountered the risen Christ, who was himself both the hope and goal of the community's life and the one who made it possible for the community to enter into that goal. In their use of the week, both the Jewish and the Christian communities looked, not just to recall God's past action, but to keep themselves in the place where his action continued. Within their commemoration of his past action, God was again at work on their behalf. Both traditions were convinced that their weekly practice had a spiritual dimension: God himself took an interest and was actively involved. Both believed, so we might say, that God in his own way was observing the day too.

But while Sunday soon became *the* special day for Christians, other days in the weekly cycle also had significance. It can hardly be an accident that all four gospels locate the crucifixion on Friday, Preparation Day, the sixth day of the week, the day on which, according to Genesis, man was originally created.[44] (Note again that, because the Last Supper began after dusk it

43. The very structure of the Gospels indicates something of the ongoing significance of the seven-day cycle for the early Church. In John's Gospel many of the key episodes are unfolded over a seven day period. See Saxby, "Time-Scheme in the Gospel of John"; Brown, *Gospel according to John (I-XII)*, cxlii, 106, 429–30, 525, 597, 858. Something similar applies in other New Testament writings. See Davies, *Gospel according to Saint Matthew*, 161–88, esp. 162 §4 (but see 87 note c); cf. Austin Farrer on the Book of Revelation, "John's book is a 'week' of weeks," (Farrer, *Rebirth of Images*, 91, and *passim*, esp. chs. 2–3).

44. They are less clear about the relation between the crucifixion and Passover. On the variation between the synoptics and the John's Gospel in the dating of that year's Passover see Brown, *Death of the Messiah*, 555–56, 576–79; Talley, *Liturgical Year*,

too, according to Jewish reckoning, belonged to Friday.) And again, nothing in the Gospels says more either about Jesus' relationship to the Sabbath or about the continuing significance of Saturday for the Church than the insistence of the Gospels that Jesus spent the Sabbath between his crucifixion and his resurrection in the tomb—with the clear implication that he was resting there (Luke 23:56 has the disciples resting "as the Law required"). The sequence Friday-Saturday-Sunday sees Christ (i) completing his work, (ii) resting after that work, and (iii) beginning a new life—a life with implications for the whole world and everyone in it. I would suggest that it is possible to see something "given" in this pattern. The Jewish week would have been rendered meaningless if, for example, Jesus had risen on the Sabbath. His rising on the *first* day of the week was, however, wholly appropriate; it both fulfilled the Jewish tradition of the week and moved it forward.[45]

There is, nonetheless, an important difference between what was accomplished on the first day of the original creation and what was accomplished in the resurrection. As I have said, the Son's rising to new life on the morning of the first day not only inaugurated a new creation, but produced the first-fruits of that new creation—namely his own risen life. The *goal* of the resurrection life is already present on resurrection day, for Christ himself if not for others. In Luke 24:50–51 and John 20:17, the ascension is presented as having taken place on that first day. John goes further. Luke has the disciples "waiting in the city" for Jesus' fulfillment of the Father's promise (24:49). But in what is generally taken to be his version of Pentecost, John locates the gift of the Spirit on the day of the resurrection (20:22). It is significant that Pentecost, the "Feast of Weeks," was originally a feast of first-fruits (Lev 23:15; Exod 34:22; Deut 16:9–10).[46] (If, as may have been the case, Pentecost was commemorated on Sunday in the year of Christ's resurrection, such an occurrence would have made these themes all the more obvious to the first Christians.) According to John, the greeting offered by the risen Christ to his disciples on the evening of the resurrection (20:21; cf.

28–29 (cf. 232) accepts the revisionist framework of Jaubert, *La date de la cène*; but see the compelling criticisms of Jeremias, *Euchaistic Words*, 24–26.

Apparently it was in commemoration of the creation of Adam that Friday was chosen as the weekly holy day in Islam. See McCasland, "The Origin of the Lord's Day," 82; "Sabbath" in *ERE* 10:894.

45. The location of this cycle in the paschal season is important too. It too indicates that Christ has indeed "passed over" from one kind of life to another.

46. Cf. Porter, *Sunday*, 29, where he shows how this idea was taken up in the post-apostolic era. (Did Pentecost occur on a Sunday in the year of the resurrection? See Lincoln, "From Sabbath to Lord's Day: A Biblical Perspective," 383; Porter, *Sunday*, 37; Rordorf, *Sunday*, 187ff., esp. 187, n.1; SB II, 598–600. See also Talley, *Liturgical Year*, 57–59. On the origin of fast days and feast days see Goudoever, *Biblical Calendars*.

20:27) was the traditional Jewish greeting: "*Shalom*." In the context of the resurrection this greeting perhaps bears a special meaning: "All is fulfilled." Coming from the mouth of the risen Lord, this greeting not only looks to the End, but declares it present—even renders it present.

The Adoption of a Weekly Celebration

One question that has not attracted much attention is why the Church came to celebrate a *weekly* memorial of the resurrection. The death and resurrection were closely linked with the *annual* feast of Passover, so why weren't the resurrection and the Eucharist celebrated just once a year? And why on *Sunday*—for the first Eucharist had been on a Thursday?[47]

The priority given to the weekly cycle over the annual might indicate that in early Christian thought the notion of *new creation* was more prominent than that of new *Passover*. Certainly the week and not the year became the basic Christian cycle. Talley in his study of the development of the liturgical year is unequivocal:

> Sunday was the primary celebration of the resurrection, the day
> on which—week by week—the church gathered in the Spirit to
> be with him who makes himself known in the breaking of bread,
> and to enjoy the foretaste of his Kingdom.[48]

He goes on to explain that it would be "useless" to describe the primitive Sunday as a "little Easter," for up to the third century it was Sunday and not Easter that was "the fundamental celebration and liturgical experience of the resurrection."[49] Vogel suggested that the astonishing thing about the Christian year is not that it developed so slowly, but that it developed at all.[50]

Sabbath Observance in the Apostolic Church[51]

The attitude of the earliest Christians to the Sabbath was not simple. Jesus himself had not explicitly abrogated the Sabbath commandment,[52] and

---

47. Rordorf, *Sunday*, 233.

48. Talley, *Liturgical Calendar*, 76.

49. Talley, *Liturgical Calendar*, 76.

50. Vogel, *Sources de l'histoire du culte chrétien*, 264, n.77.

51. Lincoln, "Sabbath, Rest, and Eschatology"; Bauckham, "The Lord's Day"; Kraft, *Sabbath Observance in Early Christianity*; Rordorf, *Sunday*, 80–153; Cotton, *Sabbath to Sunday*.

52. See Lincoln, "From Sabbath to Lord's Day: A Biblical Perspective," 401; *TDNT*

although the evidence is scanty and inconclusive, it is widely agreed that the first Hebrew Christians continued to keep Sabbath.[53] There would have been considerable pressure to do so: convictions about the abiding validity of Torah, lack of explicit dominical teaching to the contrary, habit and religious conservativism, social pressure, apprehension about unnecessarily provoking the Jewish authorities to violent opposition, the quest to find opportunities for evangelization—all would have played a part.[54] Even so, Lincoln's judgment seems sound: "In the NT church there were as many attitudes to the observance of the Sabbath as there were to the keeping of the Mosaic Law."[55] The Jerusalem Council (c. 48–49) did not demand Sabbath observance of gentile converts (Acts 15:20; cf. 21:25).[56]

Most of the evidence about Sabbath observance in the early Church comes from Paul. That evidence is indirect and somewhat equivocal. Paul was keen to defend the new faith from those who would impose on it an obsolete understanding of the relationship between God and man, but this does not mean that he was opposed to Sabbath observance *per se*. De Lacey suggests that Paul "refuses to dogmatize" about Sabbath observance. [57]

A passage in Colossians has often been seen as giving the key to the question of primitive Christian understanding of the use of time.[58]

> Let no one pass judgement on you in questions of food or drink or with regard to a festival or a new moon or Sabbath. These are only a shadow (*skia*) of what is to come; but their substance (*sōma*) belongs to Christ. (Col 2:16f.)

7:28–32; Carson, "Jesus and the Sabbath."

53. See Turner, "Sabbath, Sunday and the Law in the Pauline Epistles," 124ff.; Lincoln, "From Sabbath to Lord's Day: A Biblical Perspective," 365; Bacchiocchi, *Sabbath to Sunday*, 151. Rordorf (*Sunday*, 149f.) rejects the idea that the first gentile Christians observed any Sabbath, but can offer no adequate explanation for the re-entry of Sabbath observance in a Church no longer predominantly Jewish.

54. Cf. Turner, "Sabbath, Sunday and the Law in the Pauline Epistles," 124–26; Lincoln, "From Sabbath to Lord's Day: A Biblical Perspective," 366.

55. Lincoln, "From Sabbath to Lord's Day: A Biblical Perspective," 364f. Also Rordorf, *Sunday*, 118.

56. Circumcision was not demanded of *gentile* converts, suggesting that Jewish Christians continued the practice. Can the same be said of the Sabbath? Was Sabbath observance not required of converts because Sunday had already taken the place of the Sabbath in Christian life? Possibly. But see Turner, "Sabbath, Sunday and the Law in the Pauline Epistles," 135ff.

57. De Lacey, "The Sabbath/Sunday Question in the Pauline Corpus," 183f. (cf. 180–84).

58. See, e.g., the discussion in Rordorf, *Sunday*, 101; also *TDNT* 7:30.

An obvious implication is that there is no place for special "days and times and seasons" in the Christian dispensation. But it is likely that this letter was addressed to a largely non-Jewish community and that the aim of this passage was to counter, not a regressive Judaizing, but a pagan-Christian syncretism with Jewish elements (cf. 2:8, 20).[59] If this is so, then Sabbath observance is not being prohibited: the passage is only seeking to ensure that such observance is kept in right relationship to the full message of the gospel. The argument is not, then, about the observance of "times, days, seasons"; it is about the misuse of the things of this world—and ultimately their idolization (3:18–23).

As we have seen, the idea that pre-Christian culture foreshadowed the truth that was to be made manifest in Christ was taken up by later theologians. It is prominent in the Letter to the Hebrews, where another important question occurs. Here, as in Colossians, much is made of the Platonist notion that elements in this world foreshadow the ultimate truth. "[T]he Sabbath and the other festivals of Israelite and Jewish origin were like silhouettes cast by that which was to come: now, however, the reality has come, the 'substance' which cast these shadows."[60] *Fulfillment* is one of the principal themes of Hebrews, and the Sabbath (like priesthood and sacrifice) is one of the elements of the old tradition that has found fulfillment in Christ (Heb 3:7—4:11; cf. 8:5).[61] The train of thought is as follows: the final work of creation is that rest into which God entered on the seventh day; humankind was to benefit from this rest, was, indeed, to participate in it; but since the Jews failed to enter this rest (cf. Ps 95:11), God has established a new order, a new dispensation, and in this new dispensation he offers another chance to enter his rest; in fact, the new day has dawned: the eschatological rest is a present reality for the Church in and through Christ. This is the "sabbath rest" which "still remains for the people of God."[62]

What does this say about Sabbath observance in the NT era? The author of Hebrews is a visionary, relatively little concerned with everyday practicalities (but see 10:32–39; 12:12—13:17). He seeks to *explain* what

59. See Turner, "Sabbath, Sunday and the Law in the Pauline Epistles," 367f.; and for a different view see de Lacy, "The Sabbath/Sunday Question in the Pauline Corpus," 182f.

60. Rordorf, *Sunday*, 101. On later use of the contrast between *skia* and *sōma* see, for example, Syriac, *Didascalia* 26; Epiphanius, *Haer.* 8.6.8; cf. 30.32.7-9; 66.23; Gregory the Great, *Ep.* 13.1. See Rordorf, *Sunday*, 113.

61. See Filson, "*Yesterday.*"

62. See Rordorf, *Sunday*, 89. Hebrews 3 contains the only New Testament use of *sabbatismos*. The term occurs again from Origen onwards. For further refs to Heb 3:7ff. see Rordorf, *Sunday*, 111 n.4; von Rad ("There Remains Still a Rest," 101f.) sees Heb 3:7—4:11 as not concerned solely with future rest.

God has accomplished in Christ. He looks to keep the Church orientated towards the End and can be seen as seeking to ensure that neither Sabbath observance nor any other activity should be undertaken except in relation to the Christ who is himself the fulfillment of God's promises and Israel's hopes. But there is no need to read him as repudiating Sabbath observance. The themes of new day and new opportunity recur throughout the letter; and nothing precludes the possibility that Sabbath observance, renewed and re-interpreted, might play a part in enabling people to enter into the new life now opened up. Indeed, no NT text, either explicitly or implicitly, presents Sabbath observance as redundant. Later in the Church's history, as we shall see, Sabbath observance became widespread.

Sunday in the Second Century

The *Didaché* (c. 80–120 CE) calls for a gathering on the "Lord's own day" (*kata kuriakēn de kuriou*) for the celebration of what is clearly the Eucharist (14).[63] Ignatius (c. 107 CE) distinguishes the new dispensation from the old: "no longer keeping Sabbath *(mēketi sabbatizonte)* but living for the Lord's day (*alla kata kuriakēn zōntes*)," and he links the weekly observation of Sunday directly with the resurrection: on this day "our life sprang up through him [Christ] and his death" (*Magn.* 9.1).

The *Epistle of Barnabas* (usually dated 132–35 CE[64]) interprets Sunday in relation to the resurrection and the new creation: ". . . we joyfully celebrate the eighth day—the same day on which Jesus rose from the dead, and having been manifested, ascended into heaven" (15). Relentlessly hostile to all things Jewish, the author believes that the Jews had always completely misunderstood their tradition. None of the OT ordinances—circumcision, the Sabbath, or the dietary laws—should ever have been observed literally. Their real meaning was always spiritual and mystical. Because of its tendency to esoteric spiritualization, *Barnabas* is of little value for this present work. It is significant, however, that even in *Barnabas* the theme of new creation is fundamental to Sunday. Note too the absence of any suggestion that Sunday should be seen as a Christian Sabbath. Indeed the term "eighth day" radically differentiates Sunday from the Sabbath.

Justin gives the first full account of Sunday worship. Significant is the emphasis he gives to the creative work of God and to the resurrection.

63. Jurgens (*Faith of the Early Fathers*, vol. 1., 5, n.30) suggests that the redundancy in *kuriakēn de kuriou* indicates that the term *Lord's Day* had become "common usage" for Sunday, so that "it is now used as a distinct term apart from its root meaning."

64. *EEC* 168; some prefer an earlier date and are open to a possible link with Paul; cf. Tugwell, *Apostolic Fathers*, 30, 44.

> Sunday (*he hēmera tou hēliou*) is the day on which we all gather
> in our common assembly, because it is the first day, the day on
> which God, changing darkness and matter, created the world;
> it is also the day on which Jesus Christ our savior rose from the
> dead. (*First Apology*, 67.3–7; cf. *Dial.* 138.1)[65]

Justin has previously described baptism as taking place on Sunday (*First Apology* 61)—another rite of new life, of re-birth, re-creation.

The fact that the evidence for Sunday worship is from such varied sources—with, for example, the *Didaché* originating in Palestine or Syria, Ignatius having been based in Antioch, Justin teaching in Rome (but with a Palestinian background), and *Barnabas* written (most probably) in Alexandria—suggests that Sunday observance was both widespread and highly valued from the Church's earliest days. The fact that passages from Ignatius, "Barnabas" and Justin use different names for Sunday: "the Lord's day," "the eighth day," and "Sunday," respectively—each of which represents an alternative to the "first day of the week" of the Gospels[66]—this too suggests widespread early observance of Sunday.

Nowhere in the early Church, however, is there any evidence of Sunday observance being explained in terms of the Sabbath commandment. Almost all scholars accept that the first Christians did not conceive of Sunday as a day of rest, and that the tendency to pattern Sunday after the Sabbath only arose much later.[67] Rordorf's summary is useful—the Jewish Sabbath was primarily a day of rest, with worship coming to play a part; the Christian Sunday was primarily a day of worship, with rest being added later.[68]

Other Early Developments

Here a number of other early developments in the Christian week might be noted. The *Didaché* (8:1) reports and encourages the practice of fasting

65. Cf. Rordorf. *Sunday*, 107, 202ff, 251ff; 253–62.

66. On the names for Sunday, see Botte, "Les dénominations du dimanche," 7–28; Rordorf, *Sunday*, 274–93; Bauckham, "The Lord's Day," 221–50; Lincoln, "From Sabbath to Lord's Day: A Biblical Perspective," 383, 384f. On "eighth day"—used from Barnabas and Justin onwards, through to the Cappadocians and Augustine, but never used in colloquial speech—see Dumaine, *DACL* IV, col. 882ff.; Rordorf, *Sunday*, 276, n.2; 284f. Only later (see Rordorf, *Sunday*, 214) does the title "resurrection day" (*anastasimos ēmera*) appear.

67. Exceptions are Beckwith (Beckwith and Stott, *This is the Day*, 27–29, 43–47) and Stott (in Beckwith and Stott, *This is the Day*, 140–41). Cf. Beckwith and Stott, "The Day, its Divisions and its Limits."

68. Rordorf, *Sunday*, 154.

twice-weekly, but on Wednesday and Friday, and not on Monday and Thurs-day when the "hypocrites" (i.e., the Jews) are fasting.[69] Whether or not these arose out of a desire to commemorate the arrest and passion of Jesus, they came to be understood in relation to these;[70] Tertullian, for example, indicated that both Wednesday and Friday were devoted to the sorrowful commemoration of the passion of Christ.[71] Innocent I (402–17) would later establish the Roman custom of regular Saturday fasting, relating this to the passion: since the apostles mourned and hid themselves on both Friday and Saturday, it is fitting to fast on both days.[72]

It is further evidence that newness and resurrection were the themes of the Christian Sunday that although on weekdays (especially Wednesday and Friday) kneeling was the posture for prayer, this position was expressly forbidden on Sunday when standing was appropriate—as through the fifty days of Easter (Tertullian *Bapt.* 20; *De oratione*, 23; cf. *De corona* 3. Cf. 1 Tim 2:8). Many later writers bear witness to this practice, and various councils insisted on it. The prohibition of kneeling came to parallel the prohibition of Sunday fasting.[73]

Saturday and Sabbath before Constantine

If there is good evidence that the early Jewish Christians kept Sabbath,[74] it is clear too that the practice soon declined, possibly as a result of the early

69. Moore, *Judaism*, 260. See Rordorf, *Sunday*, 184ff., esp. 184, n.4. Some of Origen's commentaries were for non-eucharistic Wednesday and Friday assemblies (Socrates, *EH* 5.22 PG67:636–37). In the East, voluntary fasting on Wednesday and Friday increasingly became customary; cf. Clement Alex. *Str.* 7:12:75.

70. Epiphanius, *De fid.*, ed. K. Holl (GCS 37), 522; see Jaubert, *La date de la cène*, 88.

71. Tertullian, *Fasting* 10 (CSEL 20, 287). Wednesday and Friday were the most commonly designated week-day fasts throughout the Middle Ages. Schreiber, *Gemein-schaften des Mittelalters*, 286; Jungmann, *Missarum Sollemnia* I, 512–14.

72. Jungmann, *Pastoral Liturgy*, 252ff. Innocent I, *Ep.* 25, *ad Decentium Eugubinum*, PL 20:555.

73. Ps.-Justin, *Quaest. et resp. ad orthod.* 115 (PG 7:2:1233) speaks of this as an apostolic custom and refers to the *De pascha*, a lost treatise of Irenaeus. See also *Acta Pauli* (*New Testament Apoc.* II, 370); Tertullian, *Cor.* 3; *Prayer* 23; Epiphanius, *De fid.*, 22.8f.; Athanasius, *Syntagma* 2; Basil, *HS* 27.64; *Const. Apost.* II.59.4 [or *Const. Apost.* VIII.45.1]; Council of Nicea, *Can.* 20; *Testamentum domini nostri Jesu Christi* II.12. Augustine *Ep.* 55:28.

74. In addition to the references above (196ff.) see Eusebius, *HE* III.27; Epiphanius, *Haer.* 30.2.2; cf. 29.7.5; Irenaeus, *AH* 1.26.2. Cf. Justin, *Dial.* 47.2; cf. Rordorf, *Sunday*, 136.

Rordorf (*Sunday*, 136, n.5) notes that the Ethiopian Church keeps Sabbath, and even seems to hypostasize Sabbath as a female angel. There is very likely some link between

Church's felt need to distance itself from Judaism.[75] There is little evidence for Saturday-Sabbath observance in the second century.[76] But Rordorf suggests that by the third century, and particularly in the fourth, "the Sabbath . . . begins to be held in high esteem, and this development was widespread, particularly in the east, but also in the west of the Roman Empire."[77]

It was possibly in North Africa that Saturday was first given special importance. Tertullian states that some Christians refrained from kneeling at prayer on Saturday as well as on Sunday (*De oratione* 23).[78] Later, in his Montanist period, Tertullian himself comes out against fasting on Saturday. The passage says much about the weekly pattern as he knew it, and something about the annual cycle too:

> If there is a new creation (*conditio*) in Christ, our solemnities too will be bound to be new: else, if the apostle has erased all devotion absolutely of seasons, and days, and months and years, why do we celebrate the passover as an annual rotation . . . ? Why in the ensuing fifty days do we spend our time in all exultation? Why do we devote to stations the fourth and six days of the week, and to fasts the preparation day? . . . You sometimes continue your station even over the Sabbath, a day never to be kept as a fast except at the passover season . . . (*De jejunio* 14; cf. his earlier rejection of Saturday fasting, *De oratione* 23).

Here we see the first signs of a tradition that came to be generally observed throughout the whole Church: the practice of fasting on Holy Saturday. To explain why Holy Saturday should be observed as a fast day Tertullian looks to Mark 2:20 ("When the bridegroom is taken away . . . on that day they will fast") (*De jejunio* 2, cf. 14:3).[79] But later in the same work (15:2) he insists that during the 40 days leading up to Easter fasting was not only to be excepted

---

this Christian practice and practice of the Ethiopian Jews, the Falashas (see Leslau, *Falascha Anthology*).

75. Rordorff discusses possible reasons for this decline, *EECh*, "Sabbath" (748).

76. But see Irenaeus PG8:1012; Origen PG12:749. "Origen's picture of the Sabbath is strangely reminiscent of the of the best rabbinic teaching on the subject," Dugmore, *Influence of the Synagogue*, 31.

77. Rordorf, *Sunday*, 142. Cf. Rordorf, *Sabbat et Dimanche*, ix–ix.

78. See Rordorf, *Sunday*, 142; cf. 267f. For the development of Saturday-Sabbath observance see Cotton, *Sabbath to Sunday*.

79. Though he also notes, with regret and alarm, that the distinction between Holy Saturday and other Saturdays is beginning to break down (*De jejunio* 14). Evidence from Irenaeus (via Eusebius) suggests that during this period the whole Western church adopted the practice of fasting on Holy Saturday (*HE* V.24.12). For the regulations on Lenten fasting see Ware, "Meaning of the Great Fast," 35–37.

on Sundays but on Saturdays too. Elsewhere he is adamant: "[Jesus] would have put an end to the Sabbath, even to the creator himself, if he had commanded his disciples to fast on the Sabbath day" (*Adv. Marc.* IV.12).[80]

The East continued the primitive usage, and outlawed Saturday fasting (excepting Holy Saturday). But Saturday fasting came to be widely practised in the West.[81] There it perhaps developed in parallel with the development of the idea of each Sunday as Easter in miniature; or may have been added to Friday fasting by *superpositio*.[82] Other factors may also have played a part. Marcion fasted on Saturdays to demonstrate his hatred for the God of the Jews (cf. Epiphanius, *Haer.* 42.3.3; cf. Tertullian, *Adv. Marc.* IV.12). Some pagans fasted on Saturdays "out of dread of the planet Saturn."[83] Perhaps all these factors contributed to the growth of Saturday fasting in the West.[84]

Opposition to Saturday fasting was, however, both fierce and widespread. "[S]ome are . . . putting credence in vain illusions and diabolical teachings by often ordering a fast on the Sabbath and on the Lord's day, and this certainly has not been ordained by Christ" (Hippolytus, *Comm. in Dan.* IV.20.3); "If a cleric is found fasting on Sunday or on the Sabbath, with the exception of that one alone [Holy Saturday], he shall be cursed; if a lay person is found, he shall be excommunicated" (*Apostolic Canons* 66); "If anyone fasts on the Lord's day or on the Sabbath, with the one exception of the paschal Sabbath, he is a murderer of Christ" (Ps.-Ignatius: *Philad.* 13). *Canon* 51 of the Council of Laodicaea (Mansi II.571) fixes memorial days of martyrs on Saturdays and Sundays during the Lenten fast.[85]

80. On Saturday fasting see Rordorf, *Sunday*, 143, and the references given there, esp. n.3.

81. Rome observed a weekly Saturday fast: Augustine *Ep.* 36; Cassian, *Inst.* III.10; Innocent I, *Ep.* 25.4.7 (PL 20.555). For the practice in North Africa see Augustine *Ep.* 36. For the tradition in Spain see *Canon* 26 of the Council of Elvira (Mansi II.10). But Saturday fasting was not observed in Milan (see Augustine *Ep.* 36).

82. Baptism candidates fasted on the Saturday before their baptism; cf. Victorinus, *De fabrica mundi* (CSEL) 5; but note the Council of Elvira (*Canon* 26; Mansi II.10) seems to oppose this (Rordorf, *Sunday*, 144; cf. 265, n.4). Rordorf (*Sunday*, 126) asks whether the sadness of the Saturday before the first Easter influenced the attitude of Jesus' disciples to the Sabbath. He notes (*Sunday*, 126, n.1) that in the (relatively late) Gospel of Peter (26, 58–60) and Gospel of Hebrews (in Jerome, *Vir. ill.* 2), and in *Epist. Apost.* 9–11 the paralyzing grief to which the disciples then succumbed after the crucifixion is more strongly emphasized than in any canonical text, and is linked with the practice of fasting.

83. Rordorf, *Sunday*, 32 n.3, 136 n.2.

84. On later Western developments see Jounel, "Sunday and the Week," 27. Ember weeks, which include a Saturday fast, are a Western tradition. See Bruyne, "des rogations," 14–18.

85. In calculating the forty days of Lent both Saturday and Sunday, as *non*-fast

The Eastern rejection of Saturday fasting was part of a gradual move towards a more positive approach to the day. Was this because the threat of a backward-looking Judaizing had waned? In the third and fourth centuries, Saturday became a eucharistic day. "[B]y the fourth century [Saturday] has acquired a eucharistic celebration everywhere except Rome and Alexandria."[86] The particular theme of Saturday became, as Bauckham explains, the commemoration of creation: the first creation is acknowledged to be of God and as still having value.[87] Eucharistic worship on Saturday is clearly the topic in the third-century Ethiopic version of the so-called *Egyptian Church Order* (22): "On the Sabbath and on the first day of the week the bishop . . . [or] the presbyters shall break the bread."[88] Epiphanius knows of worship in several churches (*De fide* 24.7).[89] Socrates speaks of "almost all the churches throughout the world" celebrating the sacred mysteries on the Sabbath every week.[90] Around Alexandria and in the Thebaïd there is Eucharistic worship on the evening of the Sabbath—presumably Saturday evening (but possibly Friday evening) (*HE* V.22). Cassian tells of communion at 3 p.m. on both Saturday and Sunday (*Inst. coenob.* III.2). Rordorf, referring to T. Zahn, comments:

> The placing of the Sabbath virtually on the same level as Sunday, especially with regard to the celebration of the Eucharist, is attested by abundant evidence so far as the churches of Constantinople, Cappadocia and Pontus, Antioch and Egypt are concerned.[91]

Saturday and Sunday worship are linked in the *Apostolic Constitutions*: "Especially on the Sabbath day and on the day when the Lord has risen

---

days, were excluded from the calculation. See also Athanasius, *Epist. heortast.* 6.13 (PG 26:1389); *Syntagma* 2 (PG 28:840); *Pilrgimage of Egeria*, 27.

86. Taft, *Liturgical Understanding*, 62. Cf. Rordorf, *Sunday*, 142–53.

87. Even so, as Bauckham ("Sabbath and Sunday Rest in the Post-Apostolic Church," 282) notes, an anti-Judaizing element endured: "writers who encourage this observance specifically prohibit idleness."

88. Rordorf, looking to Dugmore refutes various suggestions to the contrary. Rordorf, *Sunday*, 146, nn.3–4; see Dugmore, *Influence of the Synagogue*, 34.

89. Cf. *Testamentum Domini Jesu Christi* I.22f.

90. The exceptions, as Taft noted, are the churches of Alexandria and Rome (n. 86 above).

91. Rordorf, *Sunday*, 147, n.3. Rordorf (*Sunday*, 149) warns against thinking that the sabbath observance that flourished in the fourth century was the blossoming of a tradition that had continued uninterupted from the beginnings of the gentile Church— as in Dugmore, *Influence of the Synagogue*, 146, n.3; Kraft, *Sabbath Observance in Early Christianity*, 18–33. The evidence is inconclusive.

hasten to church eager . . . to devote praise to God who has made the universe through Jesus . . . and who has awakened him from the dead" (II.59.3; cf. II.36.1; 36.2; VIII.33.2). The complementarity of the two creations is made clear in an earlier section of the same work: "Celebrate the Sabbath and the Lord's day as festival days, for the former is a memorial of creation, the latter a memorial of the resurrection" (VII.23.3).

Sozomen records that it was the practice of some Desert Fathers to gather—was it for the Eucharist?—on both the first and *last* days of the week (EH 3:14 PG67:1072c; 6.31 PG67:1388b).[92] Regnault discusses this practice, demonstrating that it was widespread.[93] Conversation and shared-meals characterized the weekend as much as corporate worship, spiritual discourse and common prayer, including, perhaps, a Saturday afternoon *agapé*—which possibly included wine[94]—which *preceded* an evening Eucharist and was enjoyed by anchorites "dressed in their finest tunics".[95] Regnault half jokes that the desert fathers invented the weekend.[96] One account speaks of seven brothers gathering on Saturday afternoon to spend twenty-four hours in Scripture recitation, prayer, and shared meals (but with no mention of a Eucharist—or wine!).[97] This practice of hermits gathering for Saturday and Sunday fellowship long continued. It is recorded that Gregory Palamas (fourteenth century) when living an eremitic life would spend five days in isolation, but that then "on Saturday and Sunday he came out of isolation to celebrate the Eucharist, and talk with the brothers in the hermitage: that was the type of life most strongly recommended by hesicast tradition from the beginning."[98] It is similarly recorded that early Celtic Christian communities commonly observed both Saturday and Sunday.[99]

92. Cf. Socrates *EH* 5:22, PG67:636b; Sozomen *EH* 6:36.

93. Regnault, *Day to Day Life of the Desert Fathers*, 162–73: "The Community Weekend." Cf. Veilleux, *Life of Saint Pachomius*, 232, 237; Ward, *Sayings of the Desert Fathers*, 171, 213; Cassian, *Inst.* 3:2; 5:26; *Conf.* 3:1; Palladius *HL* 7:5; Russel, *Lives of the Desert Fathers*.

94. Regnault, *Day to Day Life of the Desert Fathers*, 169.

95. Regnault, *Day to Day Life of the Desert Fathers*, 165, 169–71; cf. Ward, *Sayings of the Desert Fathers*, 240.

96. Regnault, *Day to Day Life of the Desert Fathers*, 162. The term "weekend" (originating in the mid-seventeenth century) is, of course, a misnomer.

97. See Regnault, *Day to Day Life of the Desert Fathers*, 171.

98. Meyendorff, *Gregory Palamas*, 38f. See Philotheus *Encomion*, PG151:574cd. Cf. John Moscus, *Patum spiritale*, 4–5, PG87:2856bc.

99. Hardinge, *Celtic Church in Britain*, 75–90.

In the East, fasting on all Saturdays except Holy Saturday remains forbidden.[100] And the difference between Eastern and Western in Saturday observance was a key issue at the time of the Great Schism (1054).[101]

Rordorf asks whether a direct line led from the Sabbath observance in the churches of Asia Minor to Sabbath observance in the Church at large during the third and fourth centuries.[102] He thinks not, but goes on to point out that the "joyous celebration" of the Sabbath in the third and fourth centuries was of a distinctly Christian character.

> [T]he sabbath became the day on which the *first* creation was commemorated, while Sunday represented the second creation. This memorial of creation was Christocentric. Through him, the pre-existent Son, the world had been created in the beginning: through him, incarnate and risen, the second creation (that of redemption) had been called into being. . . . Saturday and Sunday were memorials of these divine acts: Saturday was the day on which the first creation was brought to completion, and on Sunday the second creation was inaugurated. Elements of both salvation and christological interest did, therefore, play a part in the sabbath observance of Christians at that time.[103]

In a Sunday sermon Gregory Nyssa complains, "With what kind of eyes do you wish to behold the Lord's day, if you do not hold the Sabbath in honor? Do you not know that the two days are sisters [*adelphai*] and that if you behave disrespectfully towards the one, you hurt [*proskpoueis*] the other?" (*De castigatione*, PG46:309). Chrysostom knew of Christians who attended the synagogue and kept Jewish festivals (*Adv. Jud.* 1.1; 8.8) and Gregory I, in criticizing such a practice (*Ep.* 13.1) makes it clear that some had adopted it. Generally there is little evidence for a five-day working-week

---

100. Meyendorff, *Byzantine Theology*, 121; Schmemann, *Great Lent*, 49–52; 67–73.

101. Schmemann says that despite later concern with such dogmatic differences as the *filioque* and papal supremacy, at the time of the rift the "subjects of the dispute" were "the ritual divergences . . . such as fasting on Saturday." Schmemann, *Historical Road of Eastern Orthodoxy*, 248.

102. Rordorf, *Sunday*, 150; cf. Simon, *Versus Israel*, 383.

103. Rordorf, *Sunday*, 151ff. Rordorf (*Sunday*, 148) warns against two recurrent errors in interpreting or explaining the Christian development of Saturday. First, regard for the Sabbath is not simply a post-Constantinian development. Hippolytus both speaks out against fasting on the Sabbath (*Dan.* IV.20) and gives evidence of worship on the Sabbath (*AT* 22) The Ethiopic text of *Apostolic Tradition* even places the consecration of a bishop on the Sabbath. We have seen Tertullian presupposing Sabbath worship. Rordorf (*Sunday*, 149, n.1) argues against the idea of Zahn that mention of the sabbath in the *Apostolic Constitutions* are interpolations.

in the ancient world,[104] but in the *Apostolic Constitutions* we have, "I, Paul, and I, Peter, have decreed: slaves should work on five days; on Saturday and the Lord's day, however, they should not have any work, on account of the religious instruction in the Church" (VIII.33.1–2).[105]

The fourth century sees, so it seems, both Sunday and Saturday widely observed in the Church, but each in a distinct way. Things were to change.

104. Rordorf, *Sabbat et Dimanche*, 93, n.1.

105. A similar command to rest on both "Sabbaths" occurs in the *Apostolic Canons*. See *Can.* 66 (Horner, *Statutes of the Apostles*, 210ff.) This passage is possibly an interpolation, see Rordorf, *Sunday*, 146, n.2.

17

Historical Considerations 3
Degeneration and Deformation

Sunday as a Day of Rest and the Rise of Sabbatarianism

> "Until well into the second century we do not find the slightest indication . . . that Christians marked Sunday by any kind of abstention from work."[1]

ELSEWHERE RORDORF EXPLAINS THAT in the apostolic and post-apostolic periods, "whenever we come across the use of the Decalogue within the Christian Church, the Sabbath commandment is always missing"— "probably we should see reflected in this silence a certain amount of uncertainty how the Sabbath commandment was to be interpreted."[2]

All this was to change with the peace of Constantine.

Imperial Sunday Legislation

Promulgated under Constantine in March 321, the *Codex Justinianus* III.12:2 (*de feriis*)[3] decreed a total public rest from work on Sunday, though work in private was not restricted and farmers were exempted.[4] Constantine's motives have been much debated.[5] Elsewhere he seems to sanction

---

1. Rordorf, *Sunday*, 154ff.

2. Rordorf, *Sunday*, 107. Of course it is discussed in *Barnabas*, but only to show that the command had always been misunderstood.

3. Text in Rordorf, *Sabbat et Dimanche*, 162f.; see also *Codex Theodosianus* II 8:1 [July 321] (Rordorf, loc cit.).

4. Contrast this with Jewish Law, where agricultural work was expressly proscribed and regulations about domestic activity on the Sabbath had proliferated. Rordorf, *Sunday*, 163.

5. Rordorf, *Sunday*, 164–66; Stern, *Le calendrier de 354*.

or encourage worship of the sun (*Vita Const.* 4.19)[6] and it has to be asked whether he was hoping to unite the Empire under sun worship. According to *Vita Const.* 4.18 he wished to distinguish Friday as well as Sunday.[7] Was he seeking to honor Christ on Friday and the Sun-god on Sunday?[8]

Whatever Constantine's motives, the consequences of his actions were enormous. Rordorf writes:

> Right down to the fourth century, the idea of rest played abso-lutely no part in the Christian Sunday. Christians like everyone else worked on that day. It would not have occurred to them to do otherwise. It was only when . . . Constantine the Great elevated Sunday to be the statutory day of rest in the Roman Empire that Christians tried to give a theological basis to the rest from work on Sunday which was now demanded by the State; to this end they fell back on the sabbath commandment.[9]

The process was not quick. Indirectly Augustine played an important part. Nowhere does he argue that Christian observance of Sunday should be based on the Sabbath commandment;[10] nevertheless, he frequently interprets the Sabbath commandment in a spiritualized way: the true Sabbath is the end of all restlessness and "Our Sabbath is in the heart."[11] Augustine's spiritual Sabbath dominated Western theological writing through to the rise of Scholasticism. But it was not until the sixth century that the Sabbath commandment became an important part of the justification of

6. Rordorf, *Sunday*, 181f. argues against the suggestion that a sun-cult might have had any influence on the Christian Sunday.

7. "[He promulgated a law for all citizens . . .] to hold in honour the day before the Sabbath, in memory of all that the saviour of the world is reported to have done on that day"; see Rordorf, *Sunday*, 164. Cf. Sozomen, *EH* I.8.12.

8. On the Church's attempts to show that worship of the sun was fulfilled in Christ, the Son, see Rordorf, *Sunday*, 285ff.

On Eusebius and the transfer of Sabbath regulations to Sunday see Bauckahm, "Sabbath and Sunday Rest in the Post-Apostolic Church," 282 (cf. p. 284, on *skia* and *eikōn*.)

From 386 onwards performances in the circus and theatre were prohibited on Sundays: *Cod. Theod.* XV.5.2. This legislation had frequently to be re-enacted. Sunday Sports became a problem—*Cod. Theod.* XV.5.5; II.8.20, 23; cf. *Cod. Justin.* III.12.9 (11).

9. Rordorf, *Sunday*, 296f.

10. *Contra* the arguments of Stott (Beckwith, "Jewish Background to Christian Worship," 136–38). As Bauckham ("Sabbath and Sunday Rest in the Medieval Church," 307) says, had Augustine wanted to make some direct link between Sunday and the fourth commandment he would have done so much more clearly.

11. *Enarr. in Ps.* 91:2 (*CCL* 39:1280). See Rordorf, *Sunday*, 103–5; Bauckahm, "Sabbath and Sunday Rest in the Medieval Church," 300–302. Cf. Maximus who has a field-day with the idea: *Cent. vars:* 5:24 (*Philokalia* 2:272); he even presents a spiritualized triduum: *Cent.Theo.* 1:37–64 (*Philokalia* 2:122–25).

Sunday rest from work.[12] At this time, the spurious "Epistle from Heaven" made its appearance. Reputed to have come directly from the hand of the glorified Christ, it refers to the commandment he had "previously given" in which he demanded that Sunday be hallowed through abstinence from work. Although the letter was soon dismissed as counterfeit it exerted considerable influence.[13]

Gradually, OT commandments and injunctions came to be interpreted analogically, rather than allegorically. The whole of Western religious culture was affected and although it was never quite forgotten that Mosaic law had (as such) been abrogated, this interpretative principle was pushed very far. Christendom was envisaged as a theocracy, after the model of OT Israel, with the king ruling by divine sanction. The clergy were seen as a sacrificing priesthood, comparable to the Levitical priesthood. Little by little Church discipline took on a more juridical character and a Christian casuistry emerged.[14] The OT Sabbath regulations were applied to the Christian Sunday, and the day came to be couched about with restrictive regulations.[15]

Sabbatarianism did not, however, go unchallenged. In the monastic world, on the grounds that "the Devil makes work for idle hands," there was resistance to the idea of Sunday *rest*.[16] This, together with Gregory the Great's attempts to counter Sunday rest (*Ep.* 13:3), indicates that Sunday work was not proscribed by ecclesiastical law.[17] Rordorf quotes Huber: "It is striking that no council of the Church in this period refers to the imperial legislation about Sunday or thinks of incorporating this law of the State into ecclesiastical legislation."[18] "Equally remarkable," suggests Rordorf, "is the fact that in their writings the fathers of the Church in the post-Constantinian era never treated the State's legislation about Sunday as a basis for their own position."[19]

---

12. Rordorf, *Sunday*, 171. Ephrem of Syria gives the first extant evidence of the Sabbath commandment being related directly to Sunday, though here his thought is that, free from work on Sunday, the Christian has more opportunity for sin. *Sermo ad nocturnum dominicae resurrectionis* 4 (text in Rordorf, *Sabbat et Dimanche*, 116).

13. Rordorf, *Sunday*, 171; Parker, *English Sabbath*, 9–10, 18, 23.

14. Bauckham, "Sabbath and Sunday Rest in the Medieval Church," 303. Cf. Huber, *Geist und Buchstabe der Sonntagsruhe*, 173.

15. Cf. Parker, *English Sabbath*, 17.

16. Benedict *Rule*, ch. 48, *PL* 66.704; Palladius, *HL* 138, PG 34:1236; cf. Council of Laodicea, *Canon* 29 (text Rordorf, *Sunday*, 150, n.3).

17. "Some wait for Sunday just to be idle" (PG86:1:417, a sermon of uncertain provenance. See Rordorf, *Sunday*, 168, n.2).

18. Rordorf, Sunday, 167, quoting Huber, *Geist und Buchstabe der Sonntagsruhe*, 81f.

19. Rordorf, *Sunday*, 167.

Bauckham insists, "In spite of the Constantinian legislation it is clear that true Sabbatarianism was a medieval, not a patristic development."[20] In a later work, Bauckham explains that there was little theological interest in the topic.

> Medieval Sabbatarianism was not properly a theological development at all. It grew from below, from popular sentiment, and was imposed from above, by legislation. It was a long time before theologians provided more than a means of accommodating it.[21]

Nevertheless it is clear that the Constantinian legislation eventually produced widespread confusion about the Saturday-Sunday relationship and widespread decline in Saturday-Sabbath observance. Rordorf suggests, "After the fifth century sabbath worship . . . disappeared from the . . . Church."[22] But this is not altogether true. Rordorf himself acknowledges, "The Abyssinian Church does indeed, provide an exception; there worship on the sabbath has been preserved"—something, so he suggests, "made possible by the Church's isolation from other churches."[23] But in the Eastern Church more generally—both the Eastern Orthodox and Oriental Orthodox churches—a Saturday-Sabbath tradition of some kind has remained. Most importantly, as we have seen, Saturday remains a eucharistic day, with fasting prohibited.

With the Scholastics a theological justification for Sabbatarianism emerged. Distinguishing "moral" and "ceremonial" (or "ritual") aspects of the Decalogue (a distinction made nowhere in the NT), they counted the former as universally binding and the latter as culturally conditioned, and so only of limited, temporary application. Of the fourth commandment, it was held that the directive to weekly rest belongs to moral law and so is of enduring authority and application; meanwhile the designation of *Saturday* as the day for the observance of this rest was seen as mere convention—and so was susceptible to change. The way was open, therefore, for the Church to observe the fourth commandment "literally" while yet observing it on Sunday, not Saturday.[24]

---

20. Bauckham, *Sunday*, 287.

21. Bauckham, "Sabbath and Sunday Rest in the Medieval Church," 302.

22. Rordorf, *Sunday*, 153.

23. Rordorf, *Sunday*, 153, n.2.

24. Bauckham ("Sabbath and Sunday Rest in the Medieval Church," 304f.) suggests that only with Peter Comestor (d. 1179) was the Sabbath commandment applied "literally" to Christian observance of the first day. *Historia scholastica: liber Exodi* cap. 39 (PL198:1165). The same idea is found in Albertus Magnus (d. 1280) (cf. W. Thomas

A Changing World: The Later Middle Ages, the Reformation and After

Many have written of the changes that took place in liturgical life and spiritual tradition in post-Constantinian era. Jungmann, discerns "shifts of accent and changes of viewpoint" which have "left their mark . . . down to our own day." He attributes to the period between Gregory the Great and St Bernard "as great a revolution in Western religious life as in any other period."[25] Whereas the liturgy of the early Church had been "dominated by the Easter motif [which] had its reflection in the weekly cycle," so later, as the liturgical year developed, a "rivalry" arose between the various feasts.[26] The original Sunday theme of Easter and the resurrection became overlaid with themes culled from Christmas and Epiphany. Not only the resurrection and the descent of the Spirit, but also the incarnation has to be assigned to Sunday.[27] Thus, Sunday becomes a day dedicated to the glorification of the Trinity. A further consequence was that the weekly cycle is re-cast: Sunday becomes the first day of a week whose basic trinitarian motif is to be continued throughout the subsequent days in the votive Masses *de Sapientia* and *de Spiritu Sancto*.[28]

At the same time that Sunday "lost its Easter character," so Friday came to be a day on which the redemption was celebrated: the cross becomes the key redemptive event—in relative isolation from (and to the neglect of) the resurrection.[29] Jungmann sees this as symptomatic of a more general loss of direction. The worship of the early Church had been corporate, public, and strongly eschatological, but the mediaeval "revolution in religious culture"[30] saw many changes: the people were distanced from the priest and

---

ECL 3:2278). Thomas (*ELC* 3:2090) dates the Christian application of the Sabbath commandment to Sunday as early as c. 800. But if Thomas is right, then, as Bauckham says, his sources are not typical.

25. Jungmann, *Pastoral Liturgy*, 1.

26. Jungmann, *Pastoral Liturgy*, 2; cf. 253, where he describes the liturgical week in the early Church as "a faint copy of Holy Week."

27. Jungmann, *Pastoral Liturgy*, 3 (cf. 254, 266, 272, 276). Jungmann refers (3 n.2) to John's (=pseudo-John's) *liber et dormitione Mariae* (ed. Tischendorff, *Apocalypses apocryphae*, Leipzig 1866, 106ff.); *Bobbio Missal* ed. Loew (HBS 58) 150. Cf. H. Dumaine: DACL IV:986ff.

28. Jungmann, *Pastoral Liturgy*, 256. He refers to Franz, Die Messe im deutchen Mittelalter, 136–149 and Klaus, Ursprung und Verbreitung der Driefaltigkeitmesse. See Table 1.

29. Jungmann, *Pastoral Liturgy*, 256.

30. The phrase is the subtitle of Part 1 of Jungmann's work: "The Defeat of Tutonic Arianism and the Revolution in Religious Culture in the Early Middle Ages."

the altar, and reception of communion became infrequent; many of the priest's prayers came to be said silently (translation of the liturgy into the vernacular had not only failed to happen, but had been formally prohibited). Distancing people from the liturgical action in this way meant that soon they were only able to relate to the liturgy as something symbolic. "[I]n the early period mystery predominates—the world of grace, what is objective and corporate: in the Middle Ages, the emphasis is laid more upon what is subjective and individual."[31] Christian hope is moved toward *future* redemption. Significantly, the same period saw a gradual loss of awareness of the personal presence and action of the Spirit.[32]

The observance of the week during the later medieval period is of little interest for this present study. Such innovations as there were—for example, the weekly cycle of mass themes introduced by Alcuin and given wide use under the patronage of Charlemagne (see Table 2, 281 below)—have little to say to the modern Church.[33]

Parker has reviewed fourteenth- and fifteenth-century English Sabbatarianism and argued that Elizabethan Sabbatarianism cannot be isolated from its medieval origins.[34] Pre-Reformation England saw both Church and State seeking to impose Sabbatarian observance, much as they would in the post-Reformation era.[35] Sabbatarianism took hold in the popular imagination.[36]

The attempts of the Reformers to confront the degeneracy they detected in the Church were vitiated by their inadequate understanding of the Christian ascetic tradition and of the early tradition of corporate worship. (Loss of contact with Christian East played its part here.) Both Luther and Calvin found interpretation of the fourth commandment a problem.[37]

31. Jungmann, *Pastoral Liturgy*, 5ff.; Cf. Herwegen, *Kirche und Selle*, 4, 15f.; 23f. Herwegen, *Antike, Germanentum und Christentum*, 41ff., 238.

32. Burgess, Holy Spirit: Medieval Roman Catholic and Reformation Traditions, 1–6.

33. Jungmann, *Pastoral Liturgy*, 251–77. Also Ellard (*Alcuin Liturgist*, 226): "The place of week-days as a fixed sequence was first acknowledged by Alcuin. It was with Alcuin's assistance that Charlemagne finally spread the Roman liturgy throughout his realms and so created a uniform liturgical order; but it was Alcuin likewise who composed a whole set of Mass rituals over and above the Roman liturgy and with notable deviation from its spirit. From that time onward seven of these frequently recur as Masses for week-days."

34. Parker, *English Sabbath*, 5. See pp. 9–16 for a summary of mediaeval sabbatarianism through to the fourteenth and fifteenth centuries.

35. Parker, *English Sabbath*, 14, n.22.

36. See, for example, the tradition of "St. Sunday." Parker, *English Sabbath*, 12, n.15.

37. Rordorf, *Sunday*, 173. The Reformers expressly disavowed the Sunday-Sabbath

(Significantly, while both saw it as principally concerned with "resting from sin," neither seems to suggest any link between Sabbath rest and the doctrine of salvation by grace.) In the post-Reformation world two contrasting understandings of what constitutes a well-kept Sunday acquired adherents. Protestant tradition took the defining characteristic of the Christian Sunday to be "abstinence," principally, of course, from sin, but—just to be on the safe side—from anything pleasurable. Scottish Presbyterianism and Welsh Calvinism are extreme versions of this approach. Catholic tradition, on the other hand, took it for granted that Sunday is for celebration, first and foremost, of course, for worship, but also for the enjoyment of sports, games, and other innocent pleasures—as with the "Book of Sports" of James I (1617, 1633).[38]

One consequence of the desire to be faithful to the Scriptures and the fourth commandment was the emergence during the seventeenth and early eighteenth centuries of the so-called "seventh-day men," mostly Baptists, who "observed Saturday as the divinely appointed day of rest and Christian worship."[39] The movement came to exert considerable influence especially in America, helping to lay the foundation for Seventh-day Adventism.[40]

Modern Times: The Contemporary Secular Week

Western culture has changed dramatically during the last century and a half, and with it understanding of and attitudes to the seven-day week have changed too. Sunday religious observance has declined, work patterns have changed, trading laws have been re-written, and the possibilities for leisure-time activities have increased hugely. For many, Sunday is the busiest day of the week—taken up with sport, shopping, entertainments, excursions.

But with these changes, other yet more fundamental changes (and challenges) have come too. Life has become more vastly complex, so that everyone (in the prosperous West at least) is confronted with endless choices: how to spend their money and time, how to order their lives, what to value, what to pursue. And in this consumerist culture, one of the choices facing people is something almost unimaginable in earlier

---

link. See also Bauckham, "The Lord's Day," 24–26.

38. See Parker, *English Sabbath*. "Book of Sports" in MC, 565–68; cf. Davies, *Caroline Captivity*, 172–204.

39. Ball, *Seventh-Day Men*, 1; Katz, *Sabbath and Sectarianism*. See Parker, *English Sabbath*, 24.

40. Spalding, *Origin and History of the Seventh-day Adventists*.

periods: what to believe. Religious belief and religious practice have become optional—and privatized.

But if, as I suggested in Section 1, man's nature and destiny are "given," then only action directed towards the attainment of that destiny will be truly satisfying. But it can never be enough for the Church to encourage people to assent to Christian belief. The Church is called to encourage and enable people to use the circumstances and happenings of their lives in ways that will equip them to become apt or "fitted" for sharing the life of heaven. The Church must function mystagogically, where the mystery into which is leading people is not some "inward" (privatized) bliss, but participation in the shared relationships of the End. Insofar as the life of the Church reveals the desirability of the life of the End, insofar, that is, as it functions sacramentally and epiphanically—it will inspire people to prepare themselves for that life. The renewal of Sunday worship, and more generally the renewal of the Church's weekly pattern of life, might play a part in this. It might both help reveal the goal, the End, and provide a context a setting for response to that End.

The Changing Authority Underlying Sunday Observance

Jewish observance of the Sabbath and seven-day week was grounded in the belief that God had enjoined this upon their nation, their people. The early Christians observed Sunday and their weekly pattern in the conviction that by so doing they kept themselves in that "place" where they might meet with Christ and grow in the new life he was offering. During the period when everyone who belonged to the Church did so from choice, there was no need to impose or enjoin Sunday observance, and no need to punish or threaten the lax—except by pointing out that in cutting themselves off from the life of the Church they were cutting themselves off themselves from Christ.[41] (Though we may wonder about the children of early disciples: were they as recalcitrant and refractory as children today? I expect so—and rather hope so!)

After Constantine, Sunday observance became a social norm, buttressed by legislation. Eventually the Fourth Commandment was summoned to reinforce Sunday observance. Where Church authority was held in high regard, decrees and directives about Sunday observance carried weight. As

---

41. Cf. *Can.* 11 of the Council of Sardica (*c.* 343) (Mansi III, 20): "if a layman has not taken part for three weeks in the Sunday worship of the community in which he lives, he is to be excluded from the communion of the Church"; also *Const. Apost.* II.61.

respect for the Church has declined, so this has changed. Today, all values and customs are in question and there is widespread suspicion of all claims to authority. At the same times fundamentalisms have arisen—moral, theological, religious (or whatever); but no fundamentalism will be acceptable to more than a minority. And importantly, insofar as fundamentalisms look to produce conditioned and controlled patterns of belief and behaviour (which they do), they cannot bring people to personal maturity.

Today, now that so many of the structures and patterns which once supported Christian discipleship have been stripped way, is there any authority to which the Church can look to encourage Sunday observance? Perhaps the only authority that can now carry conviction will be the authority "natural" to mature personhood. This is an authority grounded in the divine authority and in the divine love. It is shared in by everyone who, through self-denial and growth in compassion, is becoming conformed to the divine image. This authority, grounded as it is in the ultimate ontological category of personhood, is in one sense absolute. But by its very nature this authority will be non-coercive. The mature person respects the personhood and freedom of others while yet being eager to foster and support their growth. He or she holds open the way for people to make their free response to God. As so often in this study, personhood and freedom emerge as interdependent key concepts.

18

Towards Renewal of the Christian Week

THE NINETEENTH CENTURY SAW the beginnings of a recovery of a more rounded understanding of the week. Among Anglicans, Hessey's work was important. Massively learned, Hessey sought to clarify the distinction between Sunday and the Sabbath and to trace the history of the confusion of the two. His concern was essentially pastoral.

> I believe that great confusion of thought exists on this deeply important subject [Sunday], and that the institution in question, though sufficiently venerable in itself, has been regarded as identical with, instead of at the most analogous to, one of greater antiquity indeed, but of more limited application, the Sabbath of the Fourth Commandment. I believe that from this confusion have arisen not merely misapprehensions of a speculative nature, but errors affecting practice, and productive of misunderstanding among brethren.[1]

He continues:

> But I see, further that this [circumstance] was not always so; that there was a time when *Kuriaké* and *Sabbaton* respectively had their meanings accurately and sharply defined.[2]

Such misunderstanding remains widespread, though some progress has been made towards rediscovering this distinction.[3]

A recovery in Sunday practice has gone hand in hand with a renewed appreciation of the centrality of the place of Easter and the Paschal mystery

---

1. Hessey, *Sunday*, 3f.

2. Hessey, *Sunday*, 4

3. Such works as Dawn (*Keeping the Sabbath*) commonly offer valuable suggestions about keeping a day of rest, but treat Sunday as the Sabbath. Rordorf suggests, "Even the most significant modern attempt to devise a theology for holidays and festivals, that of Karl Barth (*Church Dogmatics* III.4, ET 1961, 47–72) is not quite exempt from this [confusion]," Rordorf, *Sunday*, 298f.

in Christian life, and a renewed concern for Eucharistic worship.[4] In contemporary Roman practice, for example, only the most important feasts can now displace Sunday.[5]

Nevertheless, much remains to be done. For example, the Apostolic Letter *Dies Domini* (1998) insists on the importance of Sunday observance and seeks "to recover [its] deep doctrinal foundations."[6] It insists that the Eucharist is central to Sunday (cf. §35ff.), but (disappointingly) it also more or less equates Sunday with the Sabbath and sees rest as a primary element in Sunday observance—while ignoring the question of how the Sabbath commandment came to be applied to Sunday.[7] It also evades the question of why a day of new life should also be a day for resting.

As I have said, Rordorf's study of Sunday looks to the renewal of eucharistic celebration. "If we do not celebrate any Lord's Supper on Sunday, we have basically no right to call Sunday the 'Lord's day.'"[8] Many Orthodox, especially in the Western diaspora, have looked to Schmemann for guidance about liturgical (and especially eucharistic) renewal.[9] Among the Orthodox, as in the Western Catholic traditions, the laity has been urged to more frequent Sunday communion.[10]

Some liturgists and theologians have looked not only for a renewal of Sunday observance but also a renewal of the Christian Saturday. Orthodox liturgical conservatism has meant the perpetuation of something of the primitive understanding of the Saturday-Sunday relationship survives in liturgical texts and customs—even though this relationship seems so little understood that *practice* is often somewhat confused.[11] Schmemann, however, whose understanding is acute, implicitly looks to the renewal of

---

4. White, *Catholic Worship*, 93–106; For a more general history of the Triduum, though one with a particular concern for Anglican practice, see Greenacre and Haselock, *Sacrament of Easter*, esp. 159–68.

5. White, *Catholic Worship*, 127–28. See also O'Brian, *Documents on the Liturgy*, 1156. For post-war Roman liturgical renewal see also Bugnini, *Reform of the Liturgy*. For the unfolding story see White, *Catholic Worship*, 16–19, 36–38, 84–85, 106–7, 129–33.

6. *Dies Domini*, §6.

7. *Dies Domini*, §§13, 8, 23, etc.

8. Rordorf, *Sunday*, 305f.

9. cf. Fisch, in Schmemann, *Liturgy and Tradition*, 1–10, esp. 7–9.

10. See, e.g., Schmemann, "Holy Things for the Holy."

11. Coniaris demonstrates that confusion can linger even where we might least expect it. Within the same chapter he sometimes distinguishes Saturday (=Sabbath) and Sunday, and at other times treats Sunday as the Sabbath (Coniaris, *Sacred Symbols II*, 21–58, esp., 21–23, 28–30).

the Christina Saturday observance.[12] Rordorf, having suggested, "Rest (i.e., rest from work) is, theologically speaking, an extremely important idea, but we may not equate it with Sunday rest,"[13] continues, "One might consider whether, in the age of a five-day week, a fresh justification could be given to a Christian sabbath observance . . . . It would certainly be interpreted as a mark of our solidarity with the Jews."[14]

> We could find our inspiration in the sabbath observance (which bore no trace of Judaism) of the Gentile Christian Church of the third to fifth centuries. At that time Christians remembered on the sabbath the first creation, and old covenant, just as they celebrated on Sunday the second creation, the new life in the Holy Spirit. The weekly progression from Saturday to Sunday was for them a real experience of the "progress" of salvation history.[15]

Gordon Mursell, in the epilogue to a recently published account of Christian spirituality, one which he edited, writes:

> If we were to single out just one of the innumerable resources offered to us by the Bible and the Christian spiritual tradition as we face the new millennium, it might be the sabbath. For this is at once the crown and conundrum of the divine creation. The day on which God paused for breath is an enduring reminder . . . that we are made for more than work. We are made for worship, for play, for childlike wonder, for a constant experience of renewal and re-creation . . . .[16]

There is nothing to indicate whether Mursell is thinking here of Saturday or Sunday as the sabbath; but what says applies all the more where both Saturday and Sunday are being celebrated, each in its own way.

The Renewal of the Christian Week

The widespread liturgical renewal witnessed in the twentieth century saw, in places, the development of *weekly* patterns of life. Commonly, such patterns have sought to give the week a paschal theme or shape. The community

12. Cf. Schmemann, *For the Life of the World*, 50.

13. Rordorf, *Sunday*, 300.

14. Rordorf, *Sunday*, 153, n. Cf. Gillet, *Communion in the Messiah*, 129–30; Doze, *Joseph*.

15. Rordorf, *Sunday*, 301. Compare the comments of Moltmann, above p. 151.

16. Mursell, *Story of Spirituality*, 367. Here Mursell also speaks of "the eternal Sabbath for which we wee made."

at Taizé, for example, gives its week a paschal character through its use of Friday vigil before the cross and Saturday evening vigil of watching and waiting. (For this and the other communities mentioned in this paragraph see Table 3.) At St Gervaise in Paris, the Community of Jerusalem—founded in 1975 and committed to bringing contemplative prayer to the heart of the city—keeps a weekly pattern with a fairly well developed paschal theme.[17] In North America, the Orthodox monastic community at New Skete (Cambridge, NY), observe a developed weekly pattern of life and worship.[18] In England, the Society of St Francis, an Anglican Franciscan community, revised its Office in the 1980s and chose to give each day of the week a theme. Quite deliberately, these daily themes correspond to themes in the liturgical year. Sunday: Easter; Monday: Pentecost; Tuesday: Advent; etc. The intention is that throughout each of the major liturgical seasons the material for the appropriate day (e.g., Tuesday in Advent) will be used *every* day, with only psalmody and Scripture readings changing daily. This pattern was taken up in *Celebrating Common Prayer (CCP)*.[19]

Interesting though such developments are, most of them have been introduced without much consideration of their theological foundation or theological implications. This means perhaps that the full potential of the weekly pattern has yet to be recognized or exploited. In my final chapters I shall present a theology of liturgical time which I believe validates the development of the liturgical week and which might also provide a basis for further development. First, however, I shall outline developments in the use of the week in two communities with which I have been involved.

17. Peers, "Schools of Prayer 30; Pingault, *Renouveau de L'Eglise*, 134–41, esp. 138–39, where the weekly pattern is explained. The founder told me that in its early days of the community the weekly pattern was more pronounced and Saturday was kept in quiet prayer and vigil. Within a year of its foundation, however, Monday became the day of prayer, and Saturdays was observed as an ordinary week-day, save for an hour of corporate vigil during the evening.

18. Peers, "Schools of Prayer," 35.

19. Ingenious though the pattern is, it was not adopted for the revision of the Church of England's Alternative Service Book, *Common Worship: Daily Prayer*, 2002f.). Experience with *CCP* showed that use of the same day's office throughout a whole liturgical season soon became tiresome.

St Patrick's Hove, CSWG, and the Emergence of the Pattern of the Week

I outlined something of the history of CSWG and of St Patrick's Hove in my Prologue. Here I want to discuss further the weekly pattern of life that has come into use in these communities.

At the very time that CSWG founded its monastery in Hove (June 1985) the Community began to develop its weekly pattern of life and worship. For several years it had been using forms of Office featuring daily themes, but these themes had had little effect on the day-to-day life of the Community outside of chapel. It was suggested in the spring of 1985, however—I myself made the suggestion—that the liturgical themes could be given expression in the ordering of the daily life of the Community.[20]

My aim was to bring out the paschal character of the week. I suggested moving the Sunday Eucharist from its customary early morning slot (7.15am) to mid-morning (11am). I also proposed that the Community's rest day be moved from Monday to Saturday. The aim was to make Saturday a day of rest and reflection at the end of the working week—a Sabbath, but one leading into a vigil and so looking to Sunday.

These suggestions were adopted. Subsequently the Thursday Eucharist was moved to the evening (7pm) immediately following Vespers. The celebration would be preceded by a "semi-festal" meal, beginning with candle-lighting and an extended blessing over bread and wine (or, more usually, unfermented grape juice). The hope was that this pattern, a simplified version of the meal in the Upper Room, might help the Community prepare itself for the celebration of the Eucharist.

In due course the Friday worship was also revised. Ferial Fridays had long been observed as fast days. During the 1970s, in recognition of the fact that the celebration of the Eucharist is inappropriate on fast-days,[21] a form of Pre-Sanctified Rite was introduced: communion was received from elements consecrated the previous day. This Pre-Sanctified Rite was celebrated early in the morning (7am). In 1986, however, I proposed that the celebration be moved to early evening, so that the day-long period of fasting could end with Communion.[22] At the same time, the form of the rite was also revised. (I had no part in this revision.) The new form owed much to

20. The patterns pre- and post-1985 are compared in Table 4 (283–84 below).

21. See Schmemann, *Great Lent*, 45–6. On the history and theology of the Presanctifed Rite see Uspensky, *Evening Worship of the Orthodox Church*, 111–190.

22. When the Presanctified Rite was celebrated in the morning it was followed by a simple breakfast. Thus the period of fasting, before it had hardly begun, was interrupted both by Communion and by a meal.

Uspensky's *Evening Worship*.[23] It should to be noted that even after the revision the rite remained essentially a *fast-day* rite, rather than a *Friday* rite. It is as appropriate for any other penitential day as for a Friday—a Lenten Wednesday, for example.[24]

In 1989 the Community began a major revision of its daily Offices.[25] It was decided at this time to review and make more extensive use of the daily liturgical themes. (See Table 4; cf. Table 3.) The theme for Sunday was the resurrection and, by extension, other new beginnings. From Thursday to Sunday the paschal mystery is unfolded—Eucharist, passion, the day in the tomb, resurrection. The early days in the week were also given themes: Monday, the angelic orders; Tuesday, John the Baptist; Wednesday, the Mother of God; and Thursday, the apostles. There is no obvious rationale to the Monday-Thursday pattern, but the themes can be seen as representing successive stages in the divine dispensation, and the movement from heavenly life, through incarnation to mission.

The Pattern of the Week in St Patrick's

First, it is worth noting that when CSWG arrived in Hove the weekly liturgical pattern already observed by the parish was apt for development. The Eucharist was celebrated each Thursday evening and this celebration was followed by a time of teaching and prayer. There was a mid-day Eucharist each Saturday. It had also long been the custom at St Patrick's only to have one Eucharist on Sunday.

The pattern that developed is outlined in Table 4. This gives the weekly time-table for worship and an indication of the numbers attending. A set of leaflets which I produced for the parish explains something of the theory underlying the pattern of the week and offers guidance on how parishioners might best make use of this pattern, both by joining with the community in the parish church and in their own homes.[26]

In the development of the Eucharist and of the Offices it was intended that the forms of worship should be introduced that would both invite and

23. Uspensky, *Evening Worship of the Orthodox Church.*

24. This is in marked contrast with the form of Pre-Sanctified which came into use at St Patrick's, which is specifically a Friday liturgy and includes a reading of the passion and intercessions based on the seven words from the cross. See below, 224f.

25. It was also decided to introduce a (two-and-a-half-hour) Vigil on Saturday evenings and the eve of major feasts.

26. See website: LivingInThe8thDay.co.uk.

enable the prayer and worship of the *whole* community.[27] At the Eucharist the deacon plays an active part. He or she serves not so much as an "assistant to the priest" (as is common in Western tradition), but rather as someone who links the *laity* to the action at the altar.[28] He or she explains the liturgical action to the gathered congregation, calling them to be involved—"Let us pray . . . , " "Let us pay attention . . . ," "Let us gather . . . ." (Ideally there would be a *team* of deacons, each sharing, in the work of facilitating the active involvement of the community in the worship, according to his or her gifts and experience—in music, as youth leader, lector, etc.—) The laity are involved in the offertory, baking the bread and providing the wine, and also in gathering and offering intercessions, and collecting gifts of food for the homeless.[29] The whole congregation gathers around the altar for the Eucharistic prayer.

Incense is used at every Office and every Eucharist. There is no choir, organ or instrumental accompaniment, but cantors lead the singing, and thereby help to facilitate the singing of the rest of the community. All the worship is sung, even if only a handful are present (and even when the singing is not at all expert).

Shared meals in the parish rooms became important. A simple parish breakfast follows the Sunday Eucharist. At Easter, Christmas, and Pentecost a more formal meal is organized. Weekly, a simple shared meal follows the Saturday (mid-day) Eucharist. People are also encouraged to host shared meals in their homes—and not to invite only their friends.

Worship is linked with mission, most especially at the Sunday evening worship, called "Come and See." (Table 4) The basic structure of this is the same as for evening worship through the week—with lamp-lighting, offering of incense, liturgy of the word and short homily or address (a "thought for the day and the coming week"), intercession, and final prayers and blessing. But on Sundays the tone is lighter: the chants are simpler, the lamp-lighting more dramatic (everyone in the congregation holds a hand-candle lit from the central candle). There is an opportunity for the congregation to discuss the homily. Half-way through the evening, a simple buffet meal is held in

---

27. Children are welcome at the Sunday Eucharist—though some provision is made for them to have their own teaching session during the time that the homily is delivered in Church. Cf. Schmemann, *Liturgy and Life*, 8: "Sunday Schools surely are an outcome of a Protestant philosophy of education."

28. On this "go-between ministry of the diaconate" see, e.g., Osborne, "Living in the Future," 30–34 .

29. An instruction pamphlet for the baking of the bread is produced. See LivingIn-The8thDay.co.uk.

the church-rooms, after which the congregation returns to the worship-area for silent prayer, the offering of intercessions, and a final blessing.

The Daily Pattern through the Week

Through the week morning and evening Offices are celebrated daily. By the mid 1990s there were often between fifteen and twenty-five people present at each Office. The focus of Morning Praise is a daily proclamation of the gospel. The four Gospels are read through in course, the daily portion being around a dozen verses. A brief homily follows—or sometimes a discussion of the Gospel reading. After a canticle (usually the Benedictus), the congregation gathers before the altar to offer intercessions and the Our Father, and for the final blessing.

Through the week, Evening Prayer begins with the church in almost total darkness. After invocation of the Holy Spirit, Christ is proclaimed as "light of the world" and a lighted candle brought in procession into the middle of the worship area. This is the focal point (the chief *epiphanic* event) in the worship, equivalent to the Gospel proclamation at Morning Praise. After other lights have been lit (including lights before the icons), the Liturgy of the Word follows. It ends with the Magnificat. Then intercessions and the Our Father are offered. On Monday, Wednesday, and Thursdays, the Eucharist follows Evening Prayer. Otherwise, the Office ends with a blessing.

Throughout the week the parish is engaged in ministry to the local homeless—a "liturgy beyond the Liturgy."[30] Overnight accommodation is provided, as well as meals and a series of social events. The pattern of the week provides a framework for this ministry. It gives the week rhythm, shape, and direction.

Fridays in ordinary time are observed with fasting and prayer. There is silent vigil before Morning Praise. Throughout the day a large icon of the Cross stands in the center of the worship area. People are encouraged to visit for times of private prayer. The climax of the day is the celebration of a Pre-Sanctified Rite in the early evening. (See website: LivingInThe8thDay.co.uk) This celebration draws from the traditional RC and Anglo-Catholic Good Friday worship. It includes a reading of the Passion, Veneration of the Cross, and Communion from the Reserved Sacrament. Communion is the natural conclusion to Christian fasting. "Every fast has to end in Holy Communion."[31] Once the community has received communion it has, therefore, concluded its fast. The liturgy can

---

30. Ware, "Time for the Lord to Act," 20.
31. Matthew, *Communion of Love*, 122.

appropriately be followed, therefore, by a simple meal, usually of hot chocolate and spice-bread. People then return home, with the idea that Friday evening be given over to rest and relaxation, after the pattern of the Jewish Sabbath-Eve. Some families will host a Friday evening meal, inviting others from the congregation and outsiders too. It is the custom that all conversation at these meals should be bright and cheerful: since Christ has done all that needs to be done there is nothing to complain about. Grumbling is prohibited, and so is talk of politics, business, or anything potentially contentious. The challenge is to enter into the peace which Christ has established and to recognize that by his cross all things have been rendered "very good" (cf. Gen 1:31).

Saturday is observed as a rest day. Morning Prayer begins later and is often followed by a shared breakfast and Bible study. The mid-day Eucharist is followed by a simple shared meal, during which the community is invited to reflect on the week that had ended. The expectation is God himself is giving his own "atmosphere" to these occasions, one which people can enter into and "absorb"—if only they are wiling to lay aside the cynicism and pessimism they have picked up from the dominant secular culture. (Those who have to work on Saturday are encouraged to set aside some time, perhaps an hour, for complete ease and rest.[32]) Saturday evening is given over to vigil—or at least includes a period of vigil. In the monastery the vigil lasts two-and-a-half hours; it includes a series of six readings separated by psalms and canticles. In St Patrick's Evening Prayer includes a period of silence (fifteen or twenty minutes) before the final blessing.

My own experience of trying to observe Friday-evenings and Saturdays as times of rest and fellowship—and for many years I have been hosting Friday evening meals and Saturday morning breakfast-cum-Bible-studies[33]—has led me to the belief that, provided people are open to the possibility of their lives being changed, then sharing in these events can indeed be transformational. Through them people can enter into a new vision and a new understanding of the divine goodness. People may enjoy the fellowship of the Friday evening or might learn new things about the Scriptural tradition in the Saturday morning Bible-studies, but *something else is going on too*. Something is happening at a deeper level than the intellect or emotions. People can come to taste something of the divine goodness. These occasions serve not only as occasions of human

---

32. Cf. Millgram, *Sabbath*, 14.

33. Some of those who attend will have a long history of mental health problems or social marginalization.

fellowship, but as vehicles of divine presence, and so can serve to facilitate personal renewal and growth.

Pastoral Considerations

The pattern of the week as lived at St Patrick's makes considerable demands on the community. Only very committed members (people with few other commitments and an obliging family) can attend all the worship and associated events. Not everyone is either willing or able to make such a commitment. But that does not invalidate the use of the pattern. The pattern gives a framework for the community's life. Within that framework certain times and events stand out as particularly important: the Sunday Eucharist, Thursday evenings, etc. People will attend what they can—and what they want to. The value of the pattern is that it holds all events within the basic framework of the paschal mystery and that it allows room for growth; people can take on more when they are ready. And if the pattern lived to the full is very demanding—well, the gospel has always been demanding. (It is worth pointing out that the demands of the pattern are no greater than those required of committed adherents of any mainstream religion, or even of an ambitious athlete or musician.) At the same time, the pattern also offers uncommon support for discipleship .

I might add that newcomers to St Patrick's seem to adapt to the pattern quite naturally. Those with little experience of Christian life assume that all parishes observe it. I have heard it described as "logical" and "obvious." Much the same view is often taken by those well-grounded in Christian tradition. They too see the pattern of the week as giving "natural" expression to some of the central truths of the gospel—even if they sometimes balk at its demands.[34]

CSWG and St Patrick's: Comparisons

The monastic and parish communities live out their lives in very different circumstances and conditions, and therefore the two communities can appropriately observe the pattern of the week in somewhat different ways. A parish community lives its life in the hurly-burly of the secular world. The pace of monastic life is generally more measured. This being so, the worship

---

34. I might add that a number of other parishes, informally linked with St Patrick's have also adopted the pattern of the week, in more or less complete form. That pattern has also run "in the background" throughout a number of summer camps that various parishes have run.

of monastic and parish communities can appropriately be different in style. Monastic life is a marathon, and is best run at a steady pace, and to equip its members to live this life the community's worship can appropriately be steady and gentle. Parish worship, on the other hand, while it will include times for quiet and for silent reflection can also have a more pronounced rhythm or dynamic, one that will help to equip the worshippers for the busyness of the every-day world. The "natural energies" both of the monk and of the Christian living in secular world need to be redeemed, converted, and redirected, but people living in the secular world perhaps need to be "energized" in a somewhat different way from those living in monasteries if they are to cope with the demands with which the secular world confronts them.

It is worth noting that there has never been any attempt in St Patrick's to give themes to the first three days of the working week, Monday to Wednesday. Any such themes could only be selected more or less arbitrarily, and would tend distract from the significance of the paschal theme of the final days of the week. (I feel that the Monday to Wednesday themes in the CSWG Offices have palled in a way that the paschal themes have not.)

Update, the Year 2000

Late in 2000 the monastic community in Hove, recognizing that its membership was aging and that it was attracting few new vocations, began to consider withdrawing from the St Patrick's project. At the time I wrote the original text of this book (early 2002) the Community still occupied its property in Hove but was deliberating a move elsewhere. It no longer attended any of the worship in the parish church. The pattern of the week, however, is still observed by the parish, and in the two CSWG monasteries.

A Final Point

The pattern of the week is not a "programme for renewal." No more than any other aspect of liturgical renewal or any pattern of catachetics will it work automatically, as if by magic. Its ultimate goal and purpose is personal renewal, personal maturity, and it will only be effective and bear fruit if people engage personally with the grace it offers. What I believe it can do, however, is hold open a door for grace to flow into the life of the community. How that can be so is the theme of my final chapters.

19

Liturgical and Sacramental Encounter with Christ

In the Christian dispensation, time is neither discredited nor made redundant; it becomes an environment, a context for learning to make an ever-deepening response to the divine initiative and the divine presence. Jesuit Robert Taft writes:

> [T]he NT adds . . . the startling message that "God's time" has been fulfilled in Christ. . . . NT time is not some distinctive theory of time, but the fullness of time. What . . . is inaugurated is not some new philosophy of time but a new quality of life. The eschaton is not so much a new age as a new existence. . . . Since our *pleroma* is in God, what we are confronted with is not the *past* made present, or even the *future* present, but the *end* present, not in the sense of *finish* but of *completion*: God himself present to us.[1]

Such is, or at least should have been, the age-long experience of the Church. Time and history can be experienced as "Christified," as "full of Christ." They bear and mediate the divine presence. They incorporate the "End of history": the person of Christ.[2] Here in this chapter I want to explore the idea that in its liturgical remembrance of Christ the Church is looking, not to the past where once he acted, but to the End where he now reigns and from where he is active now—even today.

---

1. Taft, *Problems*, 3. Taft (pp. 4ff.) presents a wealth of NT references in support of his claims. (Here Taft also insists on the necessity of not being "distracted . . . by lofty disquisitions on kinds of time.")

2. Cf. Yannaras, *Freedom of Morality*, 105.

Eschatology and the Liturgy of Time: The Dualism Revisited

Wainwright argues that in creation and incarnation God "committed himself to time."[3] Christ's incarnation and death constitute the final and most profound expressions of a movement that began at creation.

> God's decision, by an irreducible act of will, to create a temporarily structured universe means that he must . . . "relate himself to it in a mode appropriate to its temporality." . . . In submitting himself to time, the servant Lord becomes time's redeemer: His sovereignty is exercised for the benefit of creatures whose drift is towards decay if they will not let themselves be included in his irreducible purpose of love.[4]

But if time originally came into being as one of God's *good* creatures, as a context for "passing over" from the "first life" (i.e., life as man is initially given it), into a new kind of life (that life which God always set before him as his ultimate destiny), then since the fall time has been ambiguous. It provides opportunities for progress and growth, yet also bears within itself the inevitability of death and decay.[5] Such is the status of "natural time." Re-created time, time reborn of the resurrection, is time *restored to its original purpose*—as vehicle of a creative "passover," a *transitus* into the life of the Kingdom. It is also time in which everything, including suffering and death, can be used creatively. It is time that has been rendered paschal, eucharistic. *This can happen only because God holds time in living relationship to the End.* Ultimately he has guided the Church to establish patterns and structures of the life that can minister to this *transitus*, something they can only do because of the communion he has established between time and the End.

The Eucharistic Transformation of Time

The Eucharist is the primary context in which the life of this world is gathered into fullness of right relationship with the life of the End. The Holy Gifts of bread and wine are taken up and transformed; so is the worshipping community; and so is everything else involved in the celebration—including

3. Wainwright, "Sacramental Time," 137.

4. Wainwright, "Sacramental Time," 138 (quoting Hebblethwaite, "Time and Eternity").

5. Wainwright, "Sacramental Time," 139.

time. In the Eucharist time does not *become* eternity; but the time of the liturgy becomes a locus for *communion* between this world and the End. Just as the bread of the Eucharist remains (transient) bread, while yet coming to bear and communicate a new life, eternal and unfading, so the eucharistic transformation of time renders time a bearer of the life of the resurrection—while yet time remains an element of (or a dimension in) this present world. Time which has been redeemed and re-created can produce (or lead to) that positive outcome that God always intended time to have. Zizioulas has said, "The Resurrection brought forth that time which can be the vehicle of our redemption. . . . Liturgical time is creative because of its openness to newness and to the inflowing of the *aeon*."[6] This encounter will always be personal. Yannaras writes:

> In the eucharist time is not measured objectively as an ordered succession from "before" to "after," nor as a rhythm of progressive and inexorable decay; instead time measures man's personal relationship with the world and with God, the dynamics of man's free response to the call of God's love. . . . The eucharist is a first experience of the [new] continuous time of personal immediacy . . . , transforming the individual desire for existential survival into . . . the immediacy of personal Presence.[7]

Wainwright has suggested that for Christians of *all traditions* (other than Zwinglians) the presence of Christ to his Church bears "more ontological substance than a psychological event in the mind of the individual."[8] Even for Calvin and the Wesleys, he suggests, Christ's presence is recognized as a pneumatological reality—realized by the Holy Spirit and recognized by those open to his action. Christ's personal presence by the Spirit in the hearts and lives of his followers is a witness to the resurrection, a life beyond the reach of death (cf. Rom 6:9).[9] It is a fulfillment of Christ's words that where two or three gather in his name he is in their midst (Matt

---

6. I believe these are direct quotations from a paper Zizioulas read at King's (cf. Zizioulas, "On Being a Person"). As I recall and as my notes have it, he went on to suggest that liturgical time is to be understood as being an *icon* of the End. In other words, it is a "signifying image of the reality in which the image participates or which it foreshadows." The important thing is that the image *participates* in the *reality* to which it relates.

7. Yannaras, *Freedom of Morality*, 104–5.

8. Wainwright, "Sacramental Time," 135. Cf. Zizioulas, "Eucharist and the Kingdom of God, II," quoted below, 237.

9. Wainwright, "Sacramental Time," 135.

18:20[10]), and of the dominical promise which closes that Gospel: "I am with you always, even to the end of time" (Matt 28:20).

But if all mainstream Christian traditions agree that God's action in human life is not merely a projection of subjective human experience but has substantial reality, then it also has to be acknowledged that different traditions have responded differently to the questions, "Where can Christ be met?" and "Where and when is God most powerfully active?" In liturgy? In pastoral ministry? In the mission field? When the believer opens his Bible? When Christians gather together to study the Bible? When the Christian struggles with temptation? There is no need to doubt that God is active in a whole range of circumstances. Worship, pastoral ministry, prayer, study of the Scriptures and Christian tradition—all of these represent, what we might term, "covenanted occasions of encounter," occasions when God has *promised* to be present. Perhaps it is best simply to say that God will be most fully present and active wherever the paschal mystery is being realized, which is why martyrdom will bear especially compelling witness to God. Though, from what I said in chapter 7 about the way the person is perceptible to us insofar as we have become persons, it follows that people will recognize God's presence at events like martyrdom—or in any other "covenanted occasion"—only insofar as they themselves are willing to be conformed to the paschal mystery.

The Problem of Historicism

Before continuing, I want to mention a common (and dangerous) misinterpretation of liturgical commemoration. We have seen that in recalling the events of Christ's life, the Church is involved in more than mere psychological remembrance of them; on the other hand, it should not be supposed that in commemorating such events the Church is in any way seeking to *re-enact* them. Such an error (often termed historicism) arises where the church is overly concerned with the temporal, historical aspects of Christ's life, to the neglect of the challenge to enter into living relationship with him *as he now is*. For example, the Church has lost sight of its purpose if it allows a desire (say) to determine the date and place of the crucifixion—or to possess a fragment of the "true cross"—to displace the desire to participate, here and now, in Christ's passion and in his redemptive, re-creative work.

Taft proposes, "The basic question on every level—historical, theological, pastoral—is the problem of *meaning*: just what are we doing when

10. Wainwright points out that the phraseology of Matt 18:20 is adopted in several Syrian anaphoras. Wainwright, "Sacramental Time," 135.

we celebrate a Christian feast?" He acknowledges that "the problem of any feast rooted not in myth but in sacred history is the problem of time and event, that is, the relationship between past unrepeatable event and present celebration."[11]

As he sees it,

> The salvation manifested [I would prefer *realized*] in the past lives on now as an active force in our lives if we encounter it anew and respond to it in faith, and we cannot do that unless we remember it. In the Old Testament, cultic memorial is one of the ways in which Israel *remembered*, making present the past saving events as a means of encountering in every generation the saving work of God.[12]

He reiterates a point repeated often in this chapter:

> That *present* encounter is the point of it all. In memorial we do not take a mythic trip into the past, nor do we drag the past into the present by repeating the primordial event in mythic drama. For the events we are dealing with are not myth but history. As such they are *ephapax*, once and for all. . . . [We] can neither repeat them nor return to them. But that is not to say they are dead, static, over and done with. . . . The events that began and first signalled this divine wooing of humankind may be past, *but the reality is ever present . . .* (Gen 13:15).[13]

But he remains clear about this most important point:

> [I]n memorializing the past we do not return to it or recreate it in the present. The past event is the efficacious sign of God's eternal saving activity, and as past it is contingent. *The reality it initiates and signifies, however, is neither past nor contingent but ever present in God*, and through faith to us, at every moment of our lives. . . . [The] ritual memorial is the present efficacious sign

---

11. Taft, *Problems*, 1.

12. Taft, *Problems*, 2; emphasis added. Note that, following Barr, Taft rejects the idea that some special Semitic philosophy of time underlies the Jewish/Christian tradition (cf. Barr, *Biblical Words for Time*). Taft writes: "What is true, however . . . , is (i) that the Bible presents an historical teleology, a strong sense of historical events as purposeful movement towards a goal, (ii) that it uses this sequence as a medium for presenting the story of an encounter with God, (iii) that it presents later cultic memorial celebrations of this encounter as a means of overcoming the separation in time and space from the actual saving event," Taft, *Problems*, 2 (cf. Barr, *Biblical Words for Time*, 144).

13. Taft, *Problems*, 2; emphasis added. Cf. Childs, *Memory and Tradition*, 81ff.

of the same eternal reality. The ritual moment, then, is a synthesis of past, present and future, as is always true in "God's time."[14]

Taft thus insists (as the Orthodox commonly insist) that for the Church the *Sitz in Leben* of Christ's saving acts will always be the *liturgy*—this is the primary context in which God's saving act in Christ is to be understood and appropriated. So it has been from the times of the NT, which "applied [Christ] and what he was and is to the present. . . . [T]he *Sitz in Leben* of the Gospels is the historical setting not of the original event, but of its telling during the early years of the primitive Church."[15] So it remains.[16]

Taft explains, "It is this, I think, that gives the lie to the notion that the celebration of any feast . . . is "historicism." For if feasts "historicize," then so do the Gospels. Do not both New Testament and liturgy tell us this holy history again and again as a perpetual anamnesis?"[17] For "In the Gospels . . . in liturgy, the focus is not on the past but on the power of God unto salvation—'and right now for you and me.'"[18]

Taft re-examines historicism in a later work. Following Talley, he rejects the idea (popularized by Dix[19]) that, with the fourth-century Peace of Constantine the Church largely lost its eschatological drive and perspective, substituting a backward-looking historicizing cult[20] (together with a historicizing "commemorative" tendency). Taft identifies a concern with history present from the beginning of the Church, but this concern he sees as always being held in relationship to eschatology and other concerns. In the Church, as Taft puts it (rather quaintly), "historicism is only one string in a full plate of spaghetti . . . and it is forced to compete with other tendencies of a decidedly dehistoricizing bent."[21] During the Middle Ages, with so-called "Franciscan piety," there arose that historicism "against which people rail today"'—"baby Jesus" in the Christmas crib, donkeys on Palm Sunday, etc.[22]

---

14. Taft, *Problems*, 2f.; emphasis added.

15. Taft, *Problems*, 6. (Cf. Tafts comments on Brown, *Birth of the Messiah*, and *Adult Christ at Christmas*—the infancy narratives.)

16. Taft, *Problems*, 7. Cf. 1 John 1:1–4.

17. Taft, *Problems*, 6. Cf. 2 Pet 1:12–16.

18. Taft, *Problems*, 7.

19. Cf. Dix, *Shape of the Liturgy*, 347–60.

20. Taft, "Historicism Revisited," 97–10; cf. Talley. *Reforming Tradition*, 75–86.

21. Taft, *Problems*, 16. Cf. Taft,"Historicism Revisited," 108: "[I]t is demonstrably clear that the meaning of every feast, Sunday included, is a synthesis"—in other words that several factors were at work: eschatology, historicism, pastoral needs, etc.

22. Taft,"Historicism Revisited," 106. See also Jungmann, *Place of Christ in Liturgical Prayer*, chs. 11–14. Cf. Leclercq, "La dévotion médiévale envers le crucifié," 119–132; Vandenbroucke, "La dévotion au crucifié à la fin du moyen âge," 133–43. The challenge

The risk with such piety is that it makes it easy for the focus of the worship to drift from God and his on-going action to the worshipper and the power of his imagination.

Zizioulas makes the point neatly: "In worship nothing leads us to the past, except to refer us through the past to the future."[23] He adds, "Only the rediscovery of iconic ontology will save us from both the paganism and the rationalism that lurk in our midst."[24]

> The veneration of icons, the recognition of supernatural proper-
> ties in holy relics, sacred vessels and objects, and so forth can
> become forms of paganism, if these objects are regarded as pos-
> sessing these properties *in their nature* and not in the personal
> presence of the saint with whom they are connected.[25]

This is a key point. The temporal cycles do not work by magic—or by "na-ture." But they can serve as vehicles of personal presence—and for personal response to a transcendent divine initiative. The tension between the ten-dency to historicism and eschatology is between past events and the tran-scendent God. It is resolved in the *person* of Christ, who unites them in himself, holding them in communion.

---

is addressed in such works as Brown, *Adult Christ at Christmas*. Schmemann discusses the early history of this trend; see, e.g., Schmemann, *Introduction to Liturgical Theology*, 86–101, 130–46, 154–56.

23. Zizioulas, "Symbolism and Realism in Orthodox Worship," 8. Zizioulas later dis-cusses the degeneration that came to occur when the focus moved from the Liturgy as the realization in the present of the eschatological Kingdom, and greater weight came to be given "to the imaging of the events in Christ's earthly life, and thus the eschatological orientation of liturgical symbolism [was] gradually attenuated." Zizioulas, "Symbolism and Realism in Orthodox Worship," 13; cf. Schultz *Byzantine Liturgy*, esp. 184ff.

24. Zizioulas, Symbolism and Realism in Orthodox Worship," 17.

25. Zizioulas, "Symbolism and Realism in Orthodox Worship," 11. From a quite dif-ferent tradition, Tillich (*Systematic Theology*, vol. 3, 122) makes much the same point: "It is important to draw the boundary . . . between the impact of a sacrament on the conscious through the unconscious self . . . and the magical techniques which influence the unconscious without the consent of the will . . . [If] it is exercised as a particular intentional act—bypassing the personal—it is a demonic distortion, and every sacra-ment is in danger of becoming demonic."

20

Past Event and Eternal Reality

Without some notion of a divine intention and purpose for creation, and particularly for humanity, . . . we have no real chance
of making theological sense of time. Time is a condition for the
realization of intention, for the achievement of a purpose.[1]

The Purpose of Time, the Use of Time

WAINWRIGHT, HAVING STATED THIS, quotes Olivier Clément: "Time is the
God-given opportunity to learn to love." Wainwright then continues:

> transformation into the moral and spiritual likeness of God
> takes place wherever and whenever humans freely requite his
> love. . . . [T]he period between the crucifixion and the parousia
> is time-for, time for the Church to preach the gospel of God's
> self-giving love in Christ and so facilitate a sharper response
> to the divine offer. [Conversely] where the love of Christ does
> not find an answer . . . , deliberate refusal is a self-inflicted
> judgement. . . . [I]ssues of ultimate destiny are being played
> out in time.[2]

This has obvious implications for Christian education, Christian formation.

At this point, another theme must be introduced. There is but one
divine mystery, one life of Christ, one life of God; yet that life is multifaceted. To share the life of Christ, is to share both his dying and his rising to
life; his fasting and his feasting; his activity and his rest; his receiving of
the Father's love and his returning of love to the Father. These all belong
to the *one* Christ, constituting one mystery. But it lies within the divine
sovereignty, nonetheless, to offer the Church *particular* opportunities to
appropriate *particular* aspects of the multifaceted mystery that is Christ.
The different days and seasons of the Church's liturgical cycles can bear

---

1. Wainwright, "Sacramental Time," 138.
2. Wainwright, "Sacramental Time," 138.

the grace of different aspects of that one life of Christ—bear it and make it accessible to the Church.

Here it must be stressed that the *whole grace* of the resurrection life, of the paschal mystery, of Christ and his Kingdom is *always* present to the Church at *every moment*. As Gillet has said, "In God, there is but one moment, in which everything is included."[3] It is emphatically not the case, for example, that the Church can only learn about the cross on Friday, or the resurrection on Sundays and during Eastertide. The whole paschal mystery, from beginning to end, is perpetually present to the Church. Nonetheless, Fridays can provide an especially effective time for learning about the passion, and Sundays and Eastertide for learning about the resurrection. This can only be explained by saying that God himself *chooses* to use particular times and seasons to open up particular aspects of the divine mystery to human participation, accommodating his revelation to suit human createdness.

Past Event and Eternal Reality. Anamnesis: Remembrance

The Eucharist, says Schmemann, commemorates a life which was realized once and for all within the conditions of the created world, and now exists eternally.

> The event which is "actualized" in the Eucharist is an event of the past when viewed within the categories of time, but by virtue of its eschatological, determining, completing significance it is also an event which is *taking place eternally*. The coming of the Messiah is a single event of the past, but in his coming, in his life, death and resurrection, his Kingdom has entered into the world, becoming the new life in the Spirit given by him as life within himself.[4]

In other words, by the action of the Holy Spirit, the life of Christ remains *continuously accessible* to the world—and participation in that life a real possibility.

3. Gillet, *Year of Grace*, 245f.

4. Schmemann, *Liturgical Theology*, 57. Emphasis added. Cf. Schmemann, *Eucharist*, 35: "[The] 'age which is to come' . . . is already 'in our midst.'" More generally on the biblical doctrine of remembrance see Thurian, *Eucharistic Memorial*, Part I, esp. 16ff., Thurian, *Eucharistic Memorial*, Part II, esp. 5ff. and 34ff., also Schmemann, *Eucharist*, 124–31; Childs *Memory and Tradition in Israel*. For a contrary view of remembrance see Beckwith, *TSS*, 49, etc.

The Scriptures and liturgical traditions of Judaism and Christianity constantly reiterate the call to the *remembrance* of God and his love. Conversely, humanity's sin is often represented as *forgetfulness* of God and inability (or unwillingness) to recognize his goodness. Israel was called to the remembrance of God; the Church to the remembrance of Christ. The call to be watchful is a key theme in the gospels and spiritual watchfulness (*nēpsis*) became a central theme in ascetic literature (cf. 1 Pet 5:8). The work of remembrance is grounded in the constant reading of the Scriptures and in the eucharistic memorial of the entire sweep of divine work. But essentially, the call is not to remembrance of a past event, but to remembrance of the End—of the divine *persons* in their intercommunion.

Christian remembrance can be seen to differ from (or transcend) the ordinary understanding of remembrance in three ways: it is eschatological; its content is the *person* of Christ (not just his acts); and thirdly, in and through the active involvement of the Spirit in this remembrance it can have a transforming, *ontological* effect.

Zizioulas writes:

> In psychology, remembrance means recalling the past. The basis for this meaning is Platonic, and in general ancient Greek. . . . This understanding is also based in common sense. None of us can comprehend what it means to "remember the future." This is because time, in our experience since the Fall, is *fragmentary*, and is inevitably divided into past, present and future, in a sequence which cannot naturally be reversed because of death. . . . Thus the future naturally comes after the past and present, making it meaningless to "remember" it.[5]

He continues:

> But what happens in a time which is freed from this fragmentation because death has been abolished? In such a case, the future is not separated from the past and the present. If indeed the future is that which gives meaning both to the past and to the present, it is then transformed into a source from which both equally draw their substance. . . . The future acquires "substance" (Heb 11:1), and can be "anticipated" so as to become part of our memory. Thus it is possible to talk about remembrance of the future.[6]

---

5. Zizioulas, "Eucharist and Kingdom, II," 29f.
6. Zizioulas, "Eucharist and Kingdom, II," 30.

Zizioulas notes that the liturgies of St Basil and of John Chrysostom include "a stumbling block" for common sense—the phrase, "remembering . . . the Cross, the tomb, the Resurrection on the third day, the Ascension into heaven, the sitting at the right hand *and the glorious second coming again* . . . ."[7]

He explains,

> In [the] Kingdom, everything is not turned into "present"—that would be a typically Platonic deliverance from death—but into the "future age which will not grow old," as St Basil calls the Kingdom, which being the state which ultimately prevails, the "truth" in the words of St Maximus the Confessor, is logically prior, since it is this that gives "substance" and meaning to both past and present. The "end" constitutes the "reason" for which both the past and the present "subsist" according to St Maximus (PG 90:621).

He continues:

> [The] "future age which does not end" becomes . . . not an effect, as happens in time as we know it after the Fall, but the *cause* of all past and present events. Consequently, remembrance of this "endless" future is not only possible, but is also ontologically definitive in the realm of the Eucharist as icon of the Kingdom. This is attested both in the Gospel descriptions of the Last Supper and in the liturgical practice of the Church..[8]

This recalls the way in which the eschatological Christ is and ever was the model for man (cf. ch.5 above). Zizioulas continues by emphasizing the importance of the ontological dimension in liturgical remembrance:

> At the Eucharist . . . we place the events and persons of the past and present within the context of the Kingdom . . . not simply . . . through . . . our imagination . . . but *ontologically*, i.e., with the purpose of giving these events and persons substance, so that they are not destroyed (by time and death). . . . This eternal survival of events and beings *cannot be secured by placing them in human memory* . . . since human memory, being created,

---

7. Zizioulas, "Eucharist and Kingdom, II," 30. Cf. Philip, "Theology of the Anaphora of St James," 39.

8. Zizioulas, "Eucharist and Kingdom, II," 30. Zizioulas notes at this point "The answer given by St Irenaeus remains the basis for Maximus' thinking: a future event (the coming of Christ) can annul an event in the past (e.g., the sacrifices of the Old Testament), not because the latter was evil and had to disappear, but because it existed solely for the sake of the future event, which gives it meaning and substance."

passes away. We mean that this person lives on *in the memory of God*. Only what exists in the thought of God really exists.[9]

Zizioulas concludes:

> We are truly alive only to the degree that God will remember us and . . . give us "substance" (hypostasis) in the Kingdom of his Son. The Eucharist, transferring us to this Kingdom, offers us the sacrifice of Christ "unto remission of sins" and also "unto eternal life," in other words as "eternal being and well being" (Maximus), our hypostatic-personal being in the "age which does not end or grow old" (Basil). . . . It is this *ontological* dimension in Christian remembrance that is so important and so alien to the popular understanding of remembrance.[10]

Zizioulas suggests that at the Last Supper Jesus was not interested in perpetuating his memory in the minds of his disciples. He wanted instead to link himself and his disciples with the eternal remembrance which the Father has of all things. Yet God's will, the purpose of his remembrance, is to gather those whom he "remembers" into the divine love—into the paschal mystery.

It is by the Holy Spirit that the life of Christ, the life of the End exists as something present and accessible, and not as some far-off ideal. The Spirit is active wherever the paschal mystery is being realized, notably in its liturgical commemoration, where Christ comes to take his people to himself and into his new life—while yet they live on earth.[11] This was the Church's understanding from earliest times. Schmemann writes:

> The Eucharist is . . . the manifestation of the Church as the new aeon; it is participation in the Kingdom as the *parousia*, . . . It is not the "repetition" of his advent or coming into the world, but the lifting up of the Church into his *parousia*, the Church's participation in his heavenly glory. . . . It would be wrong to ascribe . . . a [developed] theological interpretation . . . to Judeo-Christianity and the early Church. But there can be no doubt that even at that time . . . all the elements of this

9. Zizioulas, "Eucharist and Kingdom, II," 32.

10. Zizioulas, "Eucharist and Kingdom, II," 37.

11. Meyendorff (*Byzantine Theology*, 191) quotes Cabasilas: "It is possible for the saints in this present world, not only to be disposed and prepared for [eternal] life [in Christ], but also even now to live and act according to it" (*Life*, PG 150:496d). Meyendorff continues: "The Kingdom . . . is already accessible in the Body of Christ: this possibility of 'being in Christ' of 'participating' in the divine life—the 'natural state of humanity'—is . . . essentially manifested in the sacraments . . . of the Church."

future theological development were alive in the faith and experience of the Church.[12]

Here are themes already familiar from texts quoted in the chapters on
Christian education.

> In Christ the Kingdom has entered this world and exists in
> the Church. From the perspective of this world it is something
> in the future; in God it is eternal and actual, as well as future.
> Christians live wholly by the life of this world, they are flesh of
> its flesh, bone of its bone, yet at the same time their life as new
> is "hid with Christ in God" and will be manifested in glory in
> the second coming of Christ . . . , when the dualism of these
> two aeons is concluded and "this world" comes to an end. The
> Eucharist . . . is also the actualization of this new aeon within the
> old, the presence and manifestation in this age of the Kingdom
> . . . . The Eucharist is the parousia, the presence and manifesta-
> tion of Christ . . . .[13]

We can go further: the whole life of the Church is an exercise in "remembrance of God in Christ." This remembrance has ontological significance, bringing the Christian (or the Christian community) into the sphere
of *God's* remembrance—the realm of his salvific, life-imparting action.[14]

God's remembrance of human persons is, essentially, the remembrance of them *as* persons. He remembers them as they are in the deepest
reality of their being. Similarly, human remembrance of God should tend
towards remembrance of the divine *persons*—anything else is to treat the
divine persons as less than personal and to turn them into idols of human
imagining. Human remembrance of God and divine remembrance of man
cannot be separated from remembrance of the paschal mystery. Only within
the paschal mystery can human persons find true (substantial) existence.
Through remembrance of the paschal mystery they can come to recognize
the character and value of the gift which God offers, can see the essentially
paschal character of the divine life and of their own life too, and begin to
discern the infinite blessing concealed within paschal love.

---

12. Schmemann, *Liturgical Theology*, 57.

13. Schmemann, *Liturgical Theology*, 58.

14. For the same ideas in Western tradition see, e.g., Crichton, "A Theology of
Worship," 27; Macquarrie, *Mary for all Christians*, 95.

21

Towards an Iconographic Theology of Time

ZIZIOULAS HAS CLAIMED THAT the Orthodox Liturgy constitutes, "an image [icon] of the Kingdom of God, an image of the last times."[1] And we have seen him claim that only an "iconic ontology" can save the world from paganism or rationalism.[2] The Church is called to allow its whole life to become iconic, sacramental or Spirit-bearing, a vehicle of the *personal* presence of the Trinity. The notions of icon and sacrament are profound. From his earliest published writings, Schmemann sought to correct a misunderstanding of sacrament and icon which, though common in the West and widely adopted in the East, he saw as totally at odds with traditional Christian belief, indeed with the gospel itself.[3]

> [The] difference . . . between our contemporary understanding of the symbol and the original one consists in the fact that while today we understand the symbol as the representation of an *absent* reality, something that is not really in the sign itself (just as there is no real water in the chemical symbol H2O) in the original understanding it is the manifestation and presence of the *other* reality—but precisely as *other*, which, under given circumstances, cannot be manifested and made present in any other way than as symbol.[4]

Schmemann explains "sacrament" or "symbol" as follows:

> [T]he empirical (or "visible") and the spiritual (or "invisible") are united not *logically* (this "stands for" that) nor *analogically* (this "illustrates" that), nor yet by *cause and effect* (this is the "means" or "generator" of that), but *epiphanically*. One reality manifests (*epiphainō*) and *communicates* the other, but—and

1. Zizioulas, "Eucharist and Kingdom, I," 1; also Zizioulas "Eucharist and Kingdom, II"; "Eucharist and Kingdom, I"; "Symbolism and Realism."

2. Zizioulas, "Symbolism and Realism," 17.

3. Schmemann, *Liturgical Theology*, 16–25; cf. *Eucharist*, 13–14, 27–40; also *Eucharist*, 135–51; cf. Meyendorff, *Byzantine Theology*, 201–6.

4. Schmemann, *Eucharist*, 38.

this is immensely important—only to the degree to which the symbol itself is a participant in the spiritual reality and is able to or called upon to embody it.[5]

He goes on to claim, "Christian worship is symbolic [first] because . . . the world itself, as God's own creation, is symbolic, is *sacramental*"— i.e., is inherently a manifestation of God and of his Kingdom. Second, it is symbolic because it is the "Church's nature" and her task in this world "to fulfil this symbol, to realize it as the 'most real of realities.'"[6] And adds that Christian worship and the life of the Church should work together to reveal "the world, mankind and all creation as the 'matter' of a single all-embracing sacrament."[7]

Schmemann does not limit the notion of sacrament to the "seven sacraments."[8] He sees the very being of the Church, its whole life as sacramental: "the Church is herself a sacrament."[9] A sacrament links this world and the next, but does so by bringing the two into communion, so making possible the transformation of the former into the latter. "A sacrament is both cosmic and eschatological. It refers at the same time to God's world as he created it and to its fulfillment in the Kingdom."[10] Schmemann boldly states: "through the 'liturgy of time'—all time, all cosmos— . . . time, matter, life" is related to God "as a sacramental icon of Christ who is to 'fill all things with himself.'"[11]

The Church itself is a sacrament in both these senses:

[In] the cosmic sense because she manifests in "this world" the genuine world of God. . . . [In] the eschatological dimension because the original world of God's creation . . . has already been saved by Christ. And in liturgical experience and the life of

5. Schmemann, *Eucharist*, 39.

6. Schmemann, *Eucharist*, 40.

7. Schmemann, *Eucharist*, 40.

8. Cf. Schmemann, *Eucharist*, 117–51. Cf. Meyendorff, *ByzantineTheology*, 191: "Byzantine theology . . . never committed itself to any strict limitation on the number of sacraments. In the patristic period there was no technical term to designate 'sacraments' as a specific category of Church acts: the term *mysterion* was used primarily in the wider and general sense of 'mystery of salvation' and only in a subsidiary manner to designate the particular *actions* which bestow salvation." Meyendorff refers to Chrysostom, *Baptismal Catechesis*, SC 50:II:17:143.

9. Schmemann, *Eucharist*, 35. Cf. Crichton, "A Theology of Worship," 28: "Itself the sacrament of Christ, making him present by word and sacrament, the Church perpetually recalls the saving mystery."

10. Schmemann, *Eucharist*, 34.

11. See Fisch, *Liturgy and Tradition*, 56.

prayer it is never severed from that *end* for the sake of which it was created and saved . . . .[12]

Likewise Christian faith is sacramental: for it "is [and] manifests [and] grants that to which it is directed," namely, the approaching Kingdom.[13] As Schmemann explains "in her early tradition the Church was . . . the living experience of . . . new life."[14] Moreover,

> This experience—in which we find also the *institutional* struc-ture of the Church, her hierarchy, canons, liturgy, etc.—was *sacramental, symbolical* in its very nature, for the Church exists in order to be always changing into that same reality that she manifests, the fulfillment of the invisible in the visible, the heav-enly in the earthly, the spiritual in the material.[15]

"By its very nature the symbol unites disparate realities."[16] It is in this context that, as Zizioulas says, Maximus presents the concept of the Eucha-rist as *image* and *symbol* in relation to the concept of *causality*. "What takes place in the Divine Liturgy is an 'image' and 'symbol' of what is 'true.'" This might be read in a straightforwardly Platonist way wherein the

> perceptible and visible world is an image of a stable and eter-nal world that, being noetic and spiritual, is the truth, the true world. In consequence, one would say that what is accomplished in the Divine Liturgy is an image and reflection of the heavenly liturgy which is accomplished eternally, and which is the "arche-type" of the earthly Eucharist.[17]

But Maximus, Zizioulas says, "has a surprise in store."

> The Divine Eucharist is for him an image of the true Eucharist, which is nothing other than "the state of things to come." The truth of what is now accomplished in the synaxis is to be found not in a Platonic type of ideal reality but in a "reality of the fu-ture," in the Kingdom that is to come.[18]

---

12. Schmemann, *Eucharist*, 35.

13. Schmemann, *Eucharist*, 35.

14. Schmemann, *Eucharist*, 35.

15. Schmemann, *Eucharist*, 35.

16. Schmemann, *Eucharist*, 39.

17. Zizioulas, "Eucharist and Kingdom, I," 6.

18. Zizioulas, "Eucharist and Kingdom, I," 6. Note Schmemann is hesitant about the "symbolic" understanding of the Eucharist adopted by Maximus, and deriving from Pseudo-Dionysius. See Schmemann, *Eucharist*, 37–47 .

From this understanding, which Zizioulas sees as biblical, Maximus introduces the crucial element: time is one of the categories of existence and one of God's *good* creatures: time is useful; time is necessary.[19]

Zizioulas goes on to suggest that here Maximus challenges the Greek notion of causality—and turns it on its head.

> In ancient Greek and Western thought, as in common sense, a cause is logically but also chronologically prior to its effect. In Maximus, however, the further back we go in time, the further we get away from the archetype, from the cause: the Old Testament is "shadow," the New Testament is "image" and the "state of things to come" is truth. In other words, the archetype, the cause of "what is accomplished in the synaxis," lies in the future. *The Eucharist is the result of the Kingdom that is to come.* The Kingdom that is to come, a future event (the state of things to come), being the *cause* of the Eucharist, gives it its true *being*.[20]

The symbol or Sacrament or icon belongs to and *participates in* both the eternal and the temporal. But the symbol does not overcome the differences or quench the thirst for participation in the spiritual reality that is symbolized. Quite the contrary. The symbol serves to heighten and intensify the desire for fullness of communion with God.[21] And since the divine reality and the divine action are inherently mysterious and of boundless depth there is no limit to the potential growth of this hunger—or of the delight in its satisfaction.[22] Indeed, paradoxically those whose thirst is satisfied *grow* in thirst, but are not disquieted by this. Both the thirst and its satisfaction are delightful. As Schmemann has it, faith lives and grows, not by curiosity, but by thirst.[23] And the believer joins in worship to have that faith—and that thirst—satisfied in the confirmation of the possibility of communion with the Kingdom and with the God who is its Lord.

---

19. Zizioulas, "Eucharist and Kingdom, I," 6. Cf. Plass, "Transcendent Time in Maximus," 259–77; also Plass, "Timeless Time in Neo-Platonism," 1ff.

20. Zizioulas, "Eucharist and Kingdom, I," 7. See *Scholion on EH* 3.3.2, PG 4:137d.

21. Cf. John of the Cross, *Dark Night* II.5.

22. This theme, termed by him either "joy" or "*Sehnsucht*," is key in the worldview of C.S. Lewis, the "central story of my life" (Lewis, *Surprised by Joy*, 20); see also Lewis, *Pilgrim's Regress*; "Weight of Glory." For analysis see Kilby, *Christian World of C. S. Lewis*, 187, 200–203; Duriez, *Lewis Handbook*, 96–100; Hooper, *Lewis: A Companion and Guide*, 577.

23. Cf. Schmemann, *Eucharist*, 46; also McIntosh, *Mystical Theology*, 201–5.

Parousia: The Personal Divine Presence

For Schmemann the Kingdom of God is "the content of Christian faith—the goal, the meaning and the content of Christian life."[24] Christian life is life in communion with God, and involves knowledge of God. So Schmemann writes, "The Kingdom of God is unity with God, the source of all life, indeed it is life itself."[25] This is the life for which man was created. It is towards this life that the whole of Old Testament history was directed. But, says Schmemann—and it is a crucial point—"for those who have believed in it and accepted it, the Kingdom *is already here and now*, more obvious than any of the "realities" surrounding us."[26]

Personhood is the key. The sacrament is concerned with the personal presence and action of God. It demands in return a personal response. This world and above all liturgy is the place of transforming encounter with Christ. Orthodox tradition has come to insist that the icon and the sacrament function always *personally*.[27] It is important to explore this further.

Presence as Sacramental

Zizioulas writes:

> The symbolism in the Liturgy is not that of a parable or allegory. It is the symbolism of an *icon* as that is understood by the Fathers of the Church, meaning participation in the *ontological content* of the prototype. And the prototype ... is the Kingdom which is to come, and our ultimate reconciliation and union with God when we are incorporated into Christ.[28]

He explains, "[the] whole notion of icon depends quite literally on the notion of person, and on the distinction between person and nature. . . . Thus [with the icon] we can have a *personal* presence without having a *natural* presence."[29] Notice the link made by Zizioulas between *kingdom* and *person*. The Kingdom cannot be understood other than in personalist terms.

In support of the contention that the icon is a medium of *personal* presence Zizioulas quotes Theodore the Studite: "When anyone is depicted

24. Schmemann, *Eucharist*, 40.

25. Schmemann *Eucharist*, 40.

26. Schmemann, *Eucharist*, 41f.

27. Zizioulas, "Symbolism and Realism," 3–17.

28. Zizioulas, "Eucharist and Kingdom, I" 11.

29. Zizioulas, "Symbolism and Realism," 10; cf. Meyendorff, *Christ in Eastern Christian Thought*, 173–92, esp. 190–91.

in an image, it is not the nature but the hypostasis that is depicted . . . . The icon of Christ is nothing other than Christ, apart, of course, from the difference in essence."[30] It is expressly the person who is present and revealed in and through the icon.

Zizioulas explains:

> [I]conic symbolism in the Liturgy is . . . a matter of personal presence and not of natural presence, nature participates in it only in a secondary way and to the degree that it is hypostasized in the person. Thus place, time, matter, colour, speech, smell, hearing, etc. are used in symbolism: not . . . as the source of the symbol—the sources are always personal and historical-eschatological—but as borrowings to express the personal presence.[31]

Meyendorff makes much the same point:

> [E]ncounter with the Word's hypostasis is the real aim of icon-veneration, and this encounter can and must happen through the intermediary of a material image, a witness to the historical reality of the incarnation and of the deification with which *our* human nature has been glorified in Christ.[32]

The matter is crucial. All material creation, all of that which belongs to time and history—these are the context in which human beings live and can learn about God; but they can serve additionally as settings for *encounter* with God, personally, person to person. As such they function according to the divine freedom, in dependence upon the divine will. According to the worldview outlined in Section I, the fundamental reality from which creation has its origin (and in relation to which it continues to exist) is the divine life, which is the life of the divine *persons*. The entire spatio-temporal realm exists in relation to the divine persons, and is to be seen as a divine gift. Where, however, the created realm is assumed to be autonomous and

---

30. Zizioulas, "Symbolism and Realism," 10. *Antirrheticus*, 3.1 (34), PG99.405b; cf. 3.3–7 (14), PG99.424–25); cf John Damascene, *Orth. Faith*, 4, PG94:1004a. This issue became a focus of concern in the iconoclastic controversy, where the matter was related to the Chalcedonian distinction between person and nature. See Ouspensky, *Theology of the Icon*, I, 125–27, cf. 153; cf. Lossky, *Vision of God*, 112: "It is the hypostasis of the Incarnate Word, and not his divine or human nature which is represented in icons of Christ." Lossky refers to Athanasius the Sinaite, who in discussing the angels of the children who "behold the face of God" (Matt 18:10) explains that it is "not nature which sees nature but person who sees person," PG89:132 (Lossky, *Vision of God*, 111). See also "Canons on Iconography," in Bigham, *Image of God the Father*, 109–155 (esp. 117–28); also Evdokimov, *Art of the Icon*, 213–17.

31. Zizioulas, "Symbolism and Realism," 11.

32. Meyendorff, *Christ in Eastern Christian Thought*, 191.

self-existing, it will also be supposed that this natural order is to be manipulated and managed and used essentially for ends and purposes of man's own devising, which are bound to be less than personal—for personhood is defined in relationship to the divine persons and their divine will. To manipulate or manage the created order in disregard of the divine purpose (or the divine *persons*) is to tend towards magic or idolatry.

Personal Presence and Transforming Encounter

After describing (uncontroversially) how the icon brings together three "primary themes" in Orthodox Christian faith—"the reality of the incarnation, the intrinsic goodness of the material creation and the dignity of the human person as fashioned in God's image."[33] Kallistos Ware explains:

> There is, however, one final point, the most important point of all . . . . The icon changes us; it makes us different. Between ourselves and the icon there is, as it were, a two-way movement; we . . . offer veneration; the icon . . . offers sanctifying grace. . . . As a means of grace, conveying sanctifying power, the icon alters our consciousness and our spiritual state. It communicates *theosis* . . . . Without ceasing to be created, we participate through the icon in divine light and glory.[34]

This is crucial. We have seen Heschel suggest that "the secret of being is the eternal within time."[35] With Christ that statement takes on new meaning. "He [Christ] is the image [*eikōn*] of the living God" (Col 1:15; cf. 2 Cor 4:4.), and through encounter with Christ, "we, seeing the glory of the Lord . . . , are being transformed into the same image [*eikōn*], from one degree of glory to another" (2 Cor 3:18). The encounter between Christ and the disciple is inherently personal: Christ comes as *who* he is, not just as what he is; and his coming calls for a personal response, a response that will demand—and can enable—the transformation of the disciple.

Importantly, while *theosis* is the ultimate goal and purpose of Christ's presence, the icon can assist at every stage of the spiritual journey: although their "highest" purpose is to function as vehicles of personal encounter, they can also function didactically.

---

33. Ware, "Praying with Icons," 163.
34. Ware, "Praying with Icons," 148.
35. Heschel, *Sabbath*, 101.

Illustration through Anecdote

Many examples might be cited of people claiming that icons have exerted a profound influence on their lives, both pre-eminent saints like Seraphim and Silouan and more "ordinary" people too.[36] Anthony Bloom tells of a priest who in a Russian church "with a well-known wonder-working icon of Our Lady" became "deeply conscious of her active participation in the service," of a "power originating from the icon that filled the church with prayer."[37]

> Suddenly he felt that the Mother of God in the icon was com-pelling him to pray, directing his prayers, shaping his mind. . . . It was almost a physical presence, there was a person standing there, compelling a response.[38]

In a lecture given at St Basil's House, London, in 1973 Mother Maria recalled an event that occurred in the chapel there some twenty-two years earlier. During the Good Friday watch, while praying before the epi-taphion (a "shroud" bearing the image of the body of Christ), she saw "as it were, Christ, face to face, in the infinite stillness of the tomb."[39] She also mentioned another incident in the same chapel: "I prayed to the Mother of God, and . . . she was there, she was present. It was . . . as if she came out of the Ikon. I can see it now." Here, as in the previous incident, she "knew the *gap* bridged once more, from heaven to earth; the *gap* which . . . we cannot bridge."[40]

She explains:

> Any minute an Ikon can live, or, rather, our eyes be opened. The Ikons are a reminder of our blindness. They tell us that there

---

36. It is recorded that when Seraphim was a ten-year-old child (and still known by his baptismal name, Prokhor) he suffered a life-threatening illness. He was healed after being presented before an icon of the Theotokos. Years later, when ministering as deacon, he "saw our Lord Jesus Christ, appearing in dazzling glory and surrounded by the heavenly hosts." This figure blessed the clergy and people and then "stepped into his icon, by the Royal Door still surrounded by the angelic escort." This happened during the Liturgy on "Great and Holy [i.e., Maundy] Thursday," Zander, *Seraphim of Sarov*, 1f., 9f.; cf. Moore, *Seraphim of Sarov*, 23f.; 65f. Silouan's first experience of the "living Christ" came one evening early in his monastic career when he saw Christ "beside" his ikon, to the right of the Royal Doors. Sophrony, *Saint Silouan*, 26.

37. Bloom, *Living Prayer*, 69.

38. Bloom, *Living Prayer*, 69.

39. Gysi, *Orthodox Potential*, 137.

40. Gysi, *Orthodox Potential*, 139.

would be worlds to see, if our capacity could perceive . . . them.
. . . For an instant I saw the Ikon alive . . . .[41]

She goes on to say that the gift she received in this seeing was not simply an awareness that Christ and the saints were always with her, whether she could see them or not, but the realization that her life's work was to go by the way of faith. The seeing and the not seeing become, as it were, one thing.[42] This she relates directly to the fact that "Truth . . . is not a system of thought . . . ." For "Truth is a *person*," and the search for truth is "the search for the person of Christ . . . , whether we will accept it or not; and it is not at our command."[43] She continues: "Truth is the Mystery of the person of Christ; and, because it is a person, the Mystery is inseparably linked with the event: the event of the encounter."[44] She seeks to elucidate the relationship between this mystery and the icon:

> This oneness of Mystery and event is held firm in the Ikon. The Ikon holds us within the expectancy and the virtuality of the encounter. Any moment it might burst forth into flaming reality.[45]

Subsequently she discusses the relationship between time and eternity.

> The End-point pervades our liturgical days . . . . Christ stands silent and high in Judgement. History and Eternity cross. Past present and future converge at that point. . . . Whatever history holds towards the Judgement is therefore *today*. *Today* Christ is born; *today* he is baptised, transfigured, crucified, risen, ascended . . . .[46]

Everything centers on the mystery of presence, the loving presence of Christ. Perception changes: "Real is now, not what we touch with our hands. Real is what is according to the Judgement of Christ . . . ."[47] And the encounter with Christ expands: "The realism of Truth as a Person stretches into the Communion of Saints. It forces us to open our heart at the inmost center of Love. We are not allowed to contract . . . ." We are taken, she says, into meeting other people "in the Truth, in the reality of each," by which I take her to mean that we are to meet and know one another "in Christ," seeing others as he sees

41. Gysi, *Orthodox Potential*, 139. Zeleski, *Encounter with a Desert Mother*, 66.
42. Gysi, *Orthodox Potential*, 140f.
43. Gysi, *Orthodox Potential*, 141f.
44. Gysi, *Orthodox Potential*, 142.
45. Gysi, *Orthodox Potential*, 142.
46. Gysi, *Orthodox Potential*, 142.
47. Gysi, *Orthodox Potential*, 145.

them and as he would have them be. She includes the cautionary note: "Christ did warn us that we would find him in people, never in ideas."[48]

"The Gospel events have an eternal value, and explicitly said it is presence. It was past and yet [is] never past . . . being Christ himself: being revelation in the ultimate sense."[49] It is in connection with this that Zaleski understands Mother Maria's insistence upon the fact that while truth cannot be taught it can be encountered.[50]

Mother Maria concludes her essay "Potential of Orthodox Thinking" with the proposal that Orthodoxy may have no greater contribution to healing the skepticism and confusion characteristic of this age than its "acute sense of person."[51] Perhaps, more generally, the Church as a whole is called today to help the world rediscover the meaning of personhood.

Nothing in what I have said about the sacramental, mystical function of icons should be taken as implying that they do not also function didactically, even decoratively. They can indeed help to teach about the historical events by which the work of redemption was accomplished and can "illustrate" the doctrines of the faith. But this is never their primary purpose. Icons "mention" earthly events and phenomena only insofar as those events and phenomena belong to the life of the Kingdom. When icons depict events in the life of Christ, they reveal the eternal and abiding dimension of what was accomplished in those events. This is one of the things that distinguishes icons of the crucifixion (say) from non-iconic representations of Christ on the cross. The latter speak principally of Christ's physical sufferings in historical time; the former of the eternal and abiding dimension of Christ's passion. Again, every icon of a saint depicts that saint not just as a creature of flesh and blood, but also as he or she now exists *in Christ*. The primary reference of an icon is not the past but the End. "[I]conic representation is not simply historical, but eschatological."[52]

The source of the transforming action of the icon is the person of the transtemporal Christ. *All* icons are icons, in some sense, of the eschatological Christ. And they all have their unity in him. Again, the life of the End is "one life" and the grace of the End, though rich and diverse and although a multitude of saints now participate in that life it is not, as a consequence, fragmented. Christ and the saints share one life, such that there is no

---

48. Gysi, *Orthodox Potential*, 145.

49. Gysi, *Fool*, 90.

50. Cf. Zeleski, *Encounter with a Desert Mother*, 60f.

51. Gysi, *Orthodox Potential*, 150.

52. Zizioulas, "Symbolism and Realism," 11. Also Ouspensky, *Theology of the Icon* I, 76; cf. Bigham, *Image of God the Father*, 165–84.

"distance" or separation between those who share that life, just as there is no distance between the divine persons. Of the saints Gillet writes: "Their sanctity is but an aspect, a shining ray of the holiness of Christ"; so, in the liturgical commemoration of the saints "[we] celebrate that aspect of our Lord which is specially evidenced by the saint . . . and enter (for our profit) into the relationship of prayer which unites that saint to Christ." Just as "the feasts of our Lord in a mysterious way renew the events of his life, so the feasts of the saints make their lives, their merits, their deaths mysteriously actual. . . . [T]he liturgical year has but one . . . object, Jesus Christ, whether we contemplate him directly, or . . . through the members of his body."[53]

I close this chapter with words from Mother Maria:

> The Church gives us the training of the reality of presence, of the Saints, of the Cross, of the Person of Christ, of the Person of the Holy Spirit, inside the living and real Tradition, a Tradition, not of the past, not of the future, but of the Tradition today, a double movement of Time and Eternity: the Mystery of Christ, true God and true man.[54]

---

53. Gillet, *Year of Grace*, 2.
54. Gysi, *Realism*, 19. See also Gysi, *Orthodox Potential*, 115–35.

22

Time as Iconographic and the Days of the Week as Temporal Icons

The Scope of the Re-Creative Divine Action

In the work of the incarnation, everything that belongs to the created realm was gathered into the life of the divine-human Son and brought back into fullness of right relationship to the Father. Because of its new-found relationship to the eschatological Son, everything that belongs to the created realm is now able to function sacramentally and be Spirit-bearing. Creation is restored to its original purpose: it becomes again a context for a transforming, creative encounter between God and man. Importantly, Christ's willingness to share human suffering means that all sufferings can be used creatively. Nothing in all creation—not the disorders caused by sin, or even death itself—need separate anyone from Christ (cf. Rom 8:37–39).

For this present study, four aspects of Christ's saving, re-creative work are especially significant.

i) All that happens in *history* (all *events*) now take place in relationship to the eschatological Christ. Consequently, all events can be sacramental. This is most particularly true of the sacramental events that are part of the life of the Church—baptism, marriage, the eucharistic celebration, etc. Everyone willing to be in relationship to the eschatological Christ will discover that all the events of his life are means for growth into the relationships of the End, even tribulation and suffering.

ii) All *relationships* now exist within the Son's self-forgetful, loving relationship by the Spirit to the Father, and can therefore function sacramentally. This applies to all human relationships, but it applies, most significantly, to relationships within the Christian community. Importantly, not only can there be sacramental relationship between the senior members of the Christian community (the spiritual elders) and the juniors, imaging the relationship between Father and Son, but the community can incarnate the divinely intended relationship between creation and the divine. The Church is called not only to be Christ's priestly presence in the world—calling down the Father's blessing and ministering the Father's love; it is called also to reveal or actualize (indeed, to incarnate) creation's right response to the divine initiative.[1]

iii) All *matter* is redeemed and brought into relationship to the glorified body of the eschatological Christ; therefore material objects can function sacramentally. This potential is fully realized in the consecrated eucharistic gifts, the water of baptism, the oil of chrism, relics, and icons, for example; but this sacramental, epiphanic function is not confined to them.

iv) All of *time*, including all *temporal cycles* now belong to the eschatological Christ and so can function sacramentally. Christ lived within the natural temporal cycles that are part of human life (the day and cycle of the seasons), and he made use of the liturgical cycles observed in the Jewish practice of his day, particularly the week and the year.

Everything belonging to the spatio-temporal realm can, therefore, in Christ, function sacramentally. But by the divine will, certain elements in the Church's life are especially appointed to function in this way. These include (i) the Sacraments, Daily Offices, and "occasional offices"—funerals, the consecration of church buildings and altars, the blessing of vestments, icons, etc.; (ii) the hierarchical relationships proper to the Church: between the clergy and the general community, within marriage and family life, within monastic life (of spiritual father or mother to disciple, etc.); (iii) relics and consecrated objects, including icons, etc.; and (iv) certain liturgical cycles, notably the day, week, year. All of these—they all belong in some sense to the "covenanted occasions of encounter" mentioned above—have been appointed to help reveal the nature and character of the Son's presence in the world and so help make this world a more effective context for human growth. (All, of course are open to abuse; none will function effectively unless it is functioning *personally*.)

Further Steps towards an Iconographic Theology of Time

Lev Gillet's handbook on the Orthodox liturgical calendar contains insights that help elucidate the understanding of the use of time I have sought to

---

1. To do this it may be necessary for the Church to learn what means for it to be *bride of Christ* and *nurturing mother of growing Christians*. More generally, the Church may need to enter into a deeper understanding of many images from the Scriptures and early Church tradition.

expound.[2] His concern is pastoral rather than scholarly,[3] but his opening chapter contains a beautiful account of the character and purpose of the liturgical year. He acknowledges that the liturgical year functions as a calendar, educational tool, framework for prayer, and a "magnificent lyric poem," but sees it as essentially none of these.

> The liturgy is a body of sacred "signs" that, in the thought and desire of the Church, have a present effect. Each liturgical feast renews and in some sense actualizes the event of which it is the symbol; it takes this event out of the past and makes it immediate; it offers us the appropriate grace, it becomes an "effectual sign," and we experience this efficacy to the extent that we bring to it a corresponding inclination of our soul.[4]

But even this is not enough:

> The liturgical year is, for us, a special means of union with Christ. . . . [E]very Eucharist unites us intimately with Christ . . . But, in the liturgical year, we are called to relive the whole life of Christ. . . . The liturgical year forms Christ in us, from his birth to the full stature of the perfect man.[5]

The liturgical year offers "great spiritual opportunities":

> It provides a frame and support for Christian piety; it gives it a style that is sober and objective; it maintains a body of unity among believers. And above all, it communicates an inspiration, it transmits a life.[6]

He warns:

> One should however beware of excessive "liturgicalism" that would seek to enclose prayer in ritual frames. The liturgical way is not the only way. Saints and mystics have sometimes reduced outward forms to a minimum; solitaries have done without them altogether. Liturgical life is not an end in itself; it is but a means—amongst other means—of reaching the Kingdom of God . . . . Our taking part in the liturgical year is empty and illusory if it is not matched by an inner cycle, and if the events

2. Gillet, *Year of Grace*. The work is concerned particularly with the Byzantine Rite.

3. Gillet, *Year of Grace*, viif.

4. Gillet, *Year of Grace*, 1f.

5. Gillet,, *Year of Grace*, 2.

6. Gillet, *Year of Grace*, 2.

of Christ's life that each feast represented do not find themselves mysteriously renewed in our soul.[7]

Gillet concludes by reiterating themes from his introduction—and pertinent to my concerns. The year ends—and restarts. Gillet asks, "If the fullness has been reached, why come back to the starting point?" He answers, "The human condition is such that we are not able to remain permanently in a maximum state. We need to learn again the first elements of what we think we know." "Then," he adds, "there are our sins." We return through repentance. Gillet continues with the profound insight:

> We would be mistaken if we identified the fullness of the liturgical year with its glorious end. The mystery of liturgical time is the mystery of time itself: time "distorts," and makes the eternal divine reality imperfect, multiple and successive. In God, there is but one moment, in which everything is included. . . . The fullness of the liturgical year is to be thought of qualitatively and not quantitatively; it is achieved if, on any day whatever of the liturgical year . . . we are capable of grasping . . . Christ as a whole . . . . Each feast, and even each day of the year thus becomes the fullness of the whole liturgical cycle. This cycle never repeats itself; each one of its aspects reflects the inexhaustible depth and fullness of Christ, and, as a result, becomes new for us to the extent that we understand it better. The liturgical year is a prism that receives the light of Christ and splits it into different colours. Christ is the year.[8]

What he says of the year, can be applied to the week; and the advantage of making good use of the week is that the cycle repeats so regularly that—like the Sabbath of the Jews—it gives frequent opportunities to enjoy and enter into God's goodness.

Liturgical seasons and festal days can perhaps, then, be seen as *temporal icons,* icons made, not of wood and paint, but of time. Perhaps, as temporal icons, the days of the week can be seen standing within the temporal iconostasis of the week as a whole, and also within the yet larger (architectural) structure of the liturgical year. Everything has its ultimate reference in the eschatological Christ; but each contributory element bears the grace of some particular aspect of the divine-human Christ in his relationship to the Father. The glorified Christ, containing within himself the whole scope of

---

7. Gillet, *Year of Grace*, 2. "[N]o more than the Eucharist is the liturgical year a mere remembering. Through its celebration Christ makes himself present," Crichton, "A Theology of Worship," 27.

8. Gillet, *Year of Grace*, 245f.

the work of the incarnation, makes it possible for icons to be painted. And it is this same glorified Christ—Alpha and Omega, Beginning and End—who makes possible the Church's liturgy of time.

Whoever stands before an icon is standing in the transforming presence of Christ. Whoever celebrates a liturgical event stands within the transforming grace belonging to that day or season. An icon is not raw nature, but nature (wood, paint, etc.) sanctified through a human work performed in dependence upon God. Similarly, events in liturgical time— say particular feast days—offer effective vehicles for encounter with the eschatological Christ insofar as, under divine guidance, they have appropriate order and structure.

Iconographic canons stipulate which elements each icon should include for each festal day—the number and arrangement of the figures, their dress, etc.[9] Use of abstract "symbolic" elements to depict divine persons or portray the saints is anathema to Orthodox iconographic tradition. In an Orthodox church each icon exists in relation both to the other icons in the building and to the structure of the building itself. Kallistos Ware describes the church building as "one great icon."[10] Where the iconographic tradition is healthy it can help to direct and inspire a sacramentalist or iconographic understanding of all that belongs to creation—all nature and all that humankind produces.

We have seen Heschel speak of a Jewish "architecture of time."[11] The task of the liturgist parallels that of the iconographer and church architect.[12] The liturgist is not only responsible for individual services or for elements within them (hymns or canticles, prayers, etc.) but also for the overall liturgical structure—Schmemann's Ordo. The liturgical life of the Church is essentially, not a sequence of separate services, but "one long liturgy," with everything inter-acting, inter-linked, working together. Where this is being realized—a monastery or residential community is perhaps the most likely place—the way opens for the whole of life, hour by hour, day by day, week by week, to become one long liturgy. The iconographic

9. See, e.g., Bigham, *Heroes of the Icon*, 59–61; see also *Painter's Manual of Dynoysius of Fourna* (trans P. Hetherington).

10. Ware, *TSS*, 198. Cf. Ouspensky, *Theology of the Icon* (vol. I), 17–33; Ouspensky, *Theology of the Icon* (vol. II), 275–85.

11. Above, 143.

12. Perhaps also the priesthood of all believers is realized and manifested not only through the members of the community making right use of the material circumstances of their life or of mundane inter-personal relationships, but also through their right use of the *times* and *opportunities* which their life together in Christ presents. The temporal cycles and patterns provide the setting for the liturgy of life.

or sacramental aspect of (say) a feast day or liturgical season can extend beyond the church building. Celebratory meals, extra-liturgical readings, the way the home is decorated, even the clothes that are worn—such things can contribute to the sacramentality of the feast or season. They too can mediate the grace proper to the season and play a part in Christian mystagogy. They belong to what is sometimes termed "the liturgy after the Liturgy."[13] They extend what has happened in church into the rest of life. Such things as the pastoral ministry of the Church to the poor and needy belongs also to this extra-Liturgical liturgy.

The liturgical conventions, canons, and customs governing the Church's use of time—both liturgically and extra-liturgically—resemble the iconographic conventions and canons. But adherence to the canons does not, by iself, produce great icons; inspiration and insight into the mysteries of the End are also needed. The same holds true for the liturgy and liturgical renewal.[14]

I began this study with an account of developments in St Patrick's Hove. I mentioned that the parish use floor-standing icons to mark out the sanctuary area (fig. 5). Since the worship is "in the round" there is no place for an ordinary iconostasis—even if it were thought desirable to have one. Something I proposed some time ago, however, was the use (in addition to the floor-standing icons) of what I termed a "hanging icon-screen." This would be a large rectangular box, about a meter high. It would be open top and bottom, and be suspended some two and a half meters above the altar. To mark the area of the limits of the sanctuary, the most holy area, this "box" would extend beyond the altar by about two meters at the front and the back and at the two sides. (See fig. 6.) All in all, it would measure perhaps 8m front and back and 5m each side. Inside and out it would be covered with large icons. The inside would carry icons of the saints and angels, orientated towards either a large Christ Pantocrator or a large Trinity icon in the center on the

13. e.g., Ware, "Time for the Lord to Act," 21–22.

14. Here I should mention comments of Boris Bobrinskoy (*Mystery of the Trinity*, 148–50) which I encountered only after developing the ideas set out above. They indicate that the iconographic theology of time which I have sought to develop does not stand outside of the traditional Church thought, even if it has never been developed in quite the way I have attempted. Bobrinskoy discusses "how the mystery of Christ unfolds in the liturgy of time, that is, in the annual, weekly or daily . . . cycles" (150). He speaks of the sanctification of the "natural rhythm" of the day and year, and of the "revealed rhythm" of the week (which he terms the "Hebdomad"). He sees this entire work as involving "the *anamnēsis* . . . and the invocation of Christ" and emphasizes the "transparency of liturgical time to the unifying presence of God" (150). Of the week he states, "During the centuries of liturgical elaboration in Byzantium, the liturgical week, centerd around Sunday . . ., has acquired an ecclesiological structure that makes of it a true icon on the mystery of Christ and his Church" (151). He does not develop the idea.

eastern side. I have suggested that on the outside of the four corners would be icons of the four evangelists; these icons could be placed diagonally, across the angle of each corner, so as to be addressing the four "corners" of the world. Across the front of the screen there would be a series of icons relating the paschal mystery. Center-front would be a large crucifix. To either side would be a series of four icons; these, reading from left to right, would be: the Crucifixion, Deposition, Harrowing of Hell, and the Visit of the Myrrh-bearing Women to the Empty Tomb. This sequence would "proclaim" the great saving work accomplished by Christ, but would also indicate that entry to the sanctuary (i.e., the heavenly place) is through the paschal mystery. On the three other outside surfaces there could be icons of the great feasts: nativity, transfiguration, etc., with perhaps some scenes from the Old Testament—all proclaiming the unfolding work of man's redemption.

This screen has never been built. (Much to my regret and disappointment.) I mention it here because the screen and the pattern of the week can be seen as complementary. The screen, in "pictorial" icons, does what the pattern of the week does in temporal ones. Importantly, just as the liturgical week stands as complement to the liturgical year, so the paschal cycle on the icon screen is complemented by the other icons on the screen and by iconographic elements elsewhere in the church. Furthermore, both the icon-screen and the various temporal liturgical patterns should be seen as standing alongside and complementing a whole range of activities belonging to the community's life: its liturgies, its shared meals, its ministry to needy, etc. All these different elements can properly be seen as sacramental. Together they could help enable the life of the community to function mystagogically—as all Christian community life should. For together all these different elements constitute a *spatio-temporal environment* in which Christian discipleship can flourish. The pattern of the week could have a part to play in this, not as an end in itself or as the key to all the rest, but as one element in what would be an all-embracing, multi-faceted (mystagogic and sacramentalized) pattern of life.

In and of itself, however, neither this nor any spatio-temporal "environment" can guarantee growth. Something else is needed.

We come full circle. I began this work reporting that at the beginning of the twentieth century Fr William Sirr looked for the recovery and deepening of the Church's life of prayer, and did so because he saw that religion as such—however sophisticated, however refined—is never enough: it cannot guarantee spiritual growth. Indeed, I also quoted Schmemann as saying that, at heart, Christianity is not really a religion at all, but something of a different order: the mystery of a new life opened up, a life within which men and women share already, even now, here on earth, in the definitive relationship of the divine Son to the Father by the Spirit. No pattern of Church life can, in and of itself, ensure that people come to share that life. And no one can share in this life except through his or her personal response to the divine initiative.

As I said at the opening of this work, since the goal of Christian life is the shared life and relationships of the Kingdom, so the way into that goal will be through learning to participate in the shared life and relationships of Christian community. Any such "environment," therefore, as the one which the pattern of the week and the "hanging" icon-screen might help to constitute will only be effective if it becomes an environment of personal encounter with God and with the other members of the community—i.e., of encounter in and through the Holy Spirit. That is why I believe Christian educational theory needs to be grounded in an adequate anthropology. In earlier chapters (esp. ch. 4) I explored the idea that all humanity is united (by the Holy Spirit) at the level of the heart, such that one person's spiritual response to God will exert a drawing effect on others (but without ever depriving anyone of his freedom or removing the need for him to make a personal response of his own). This being so, insofar as some members of the worshipping community are making a spiritual response to God's initiative, then they will be making it easier for others to enter into the mystery of new life which God has opened up. The relationships that exist within the community can themselves become sacramental—or iconographic.

Perhaps the educational ministry of the Church can be expected to go forward most effectively where, in a whole range of ways, the life of the Church is becoming "iconographic": in its use of the spatio-temporal order, in its relationship to the wider world, and in a whole range of other ways too—most especially in its internal relationships. Where this is happening, the Church will be enabling the participation of the Christian community in the new order of relationships which God wills for it, so that, both individually and collectively, the members of the community will find themselves within (i.e., on the "inside") of the Son's relationship to the Father, so as also to be standing *as creatures* within that relationship which God wills for all creation. In other words, they will find themselves to be sharing the divine life while yet being creatures, and at the same time, becoming the embodiment (the incarnation or realization) of redeemed creation.

Prospect: The Pattern of the Week and Contemporary Pastoral Needs

In conclusion I would like to draw attention to observations about the needs of the contemporary world made by Alasdair MacIntyre at the end of his celebrated work, *After Virtue*.

> It is always dangerous to draw to precise parallels between one historical period and another; and among the most misleading of such parallels are those which have been drawn between our own age . . . and the epoch in which the Roman empire declined into the Dark Ages. Nonetheless certain parallels there are. A crucial turning point in that earlier history occurred when men and women of goodwill turned aside from the task of shoring up the Roman *imperium* . . . . What they set themselves to achieve instead—often not recognizing fully what they were doing—was the construction of new forms of community within which the moral life could be sustained so that both morality and civility might survive the coming age of barbarism and darkness. If my account of our moral condition is correct, we ought also to conclude that for some time now we have reached that turning point. What matters at this stage is the construction of local forms of community within which civility and the intellectual and moral life can be sustained through the new dark ages which are already upon us. . . . This time however the barbarians are not waiting beyond the frontiers; they have already been governing us for quite some time. And it is our lack of consciousness of this that constitutes part of our predicament. We are waiting not for a Godot, but for another—doubtless very different—St Benedict.[15]

When composing his Rule Benedict drew on the work of many others; and his work provided exactly the kind of framework that I have identified in this present work as necessary for personal growth. And while MacIntyre is right to suggest that it is only within *communities* that "intellectual and moral" life can be sustained, the argument can also be taken further, and the claim can made that it is only within community that anyone can discover his or her true nature and purpose, or, more specifically, that the gift of personhood can be realized. Benedict's Rule provided a framework for growth because it both ensured a certain stability within

---

15. MacIntyre, *After Virtue*, 263. Milis is among those who have questioned how influential the Benedictine tradition was in mediaeval culture (Milis, *Angelic Monks*, passim, esp. 152). But historians generally see the Benedictine influence as monumental.

the life of the monastic community while yet also keeping the community open to the transforming presence and action of God. This latter it did in part through providing a context in which those more mature in their discipleship (Abbot, spiritual father, senior brethren) could offer *spiritual* support to their more junior brethren. This practical, personal support was assumed by Benedict. Indirectly the pattern established by Benedict also provided stability for society at large—and kept it open to God too.

If, as many suppose, we are living today through a time of spiritual crisis—"Having constructed a society of unprecedented sophistication, convenience, and prosperity, nobody can remember what it was supposed to be for"[16]—then it ought also to be acknowledged that this is an era in which the Church is re-discovering (or even uncovering) many forgotten or unused gifts. Among them might be numbered the resurgence of interest in the Trinitarian theology, the renewed interest in the iconographic tradition, the burgeoning theological concern with personhood and the recovery of interest in the Church's Jewish origins. Of especial importance is the renewed contact between the Churches of East and West. (We should not forget that recent scholarly work has meant that we also now have both better knowledge of early Christian tradition than any earlier generation and that we have access to an unprecedented collection of early, mediaeval, and pre-modern Christian writings in reliable editions. Christians today can be well-informed in a way never before possible.) Contact with people of other faiths has also given new insight into God's ways with the world. So have insights from the physical, biological, and human sciences. There remains much to be done; but there are also many blessings. Can they be seen as having emerged providentially, so as to equip the Church for the task ahead of it?

The new Benedict awaited by the world might, then, draw on or make use of many of the things I have listed. But perhaps he or she may also make use of the pattern of the week. The pattern of the week can help give shape and direction to a community's life and thereby to help it become an effective context for Christian growth. In particular the pattern of the week might help keep life orientated towards the paschal mystery, helping it to live both "into" and "out of "that mystery. Moreover, if the paschal mystery is absolute in the way that I have been suggesting, then it can be expected that where any Christian community is being drawn into the paschal mystery, its life will impact positively on the wider society of which that community is a part. The pattern of the week can help the life of a community to function mystagogically. It consists of a series

---

16. Clifford Longley, in Sacks, *Faith in the Future*, x.

of "covenanted occasions of encounter," through engagement with which people's lives can be changed. Through the *use* of the pattern of the week— the theory alone is not enough—people may encounter God and one another in the mystery of the cross and resurrection, there to find fulfillment in the eternal love, the divine energy, which, flowing forth from the divine persons, bestows fullness of personhood on all those willing to receive and cooperate with it. Love calls forth love.

Conclusion

In Part One I set out a personalist understanding of Christian education. I grounded this in a personalist ontology. My argument was rooted in the traditional belief that man is made in the divine image. I suggested that what defines the divine persons as personal is the self-forgetful love existing between them, and that consequently, what defines man as personal is the call to live by self-forgetful love, coupled with his potential to do so. I argued that self-forgetful love is always paschal: a person has life in proportion to his or her willingness to lose or give life in order that others might live. I proposed that the educational ministry of the Church must look to enabling human persons to realize their potential to live by self-forgetful love.

I argued that the life and work of the incarnate divine Son sets the agenda for Christian education. During the time of the incarnation a work was going on: step by step the Son was bringing his created humanity into fullness of conformity with his eternal divinity. By the end of that work, that is, after his passion and glorification, the Son had realized within his adopted humanity the relationship with the Father which he had always known in his eternal divinity. The Christian is called to share the life of the glorified Son; but to do that the Christian must be willing to recapitulate the Son's way of growth—or, rather, must be willing to allow the Son to recapitulate within him (or her) the way of growth which he himself first accomplished in his own adopted humanity. (For all is grace and the Christian is called to share the life of the Son not to copy it.) I argued that such participation is only possible because the glorified eschatological Son is always "coming forth" from the Father not only to reveal himself as the End and goal of all human life and to invite human persons into communion with himself but to offer the grace to respond to that invitation. But no one can share the Son's life except insofar as that person is willing to allow himself or herself to be conformed to the Son. (In that sense man's ultimate salvation lies in his own hands.) And because the Son lives in self-forgetful, paschal relationship both to the Father and to all that belongs to the created realm, that means no one can either share the Son's life or enter into the life of the Kingdom except insofar as he or she is willing to be gathered into the paschal mystery. It is only insofar as someone has learnt to participate in the paschal mystery that he or she is "equipped" or "fitted" to share the life of the Kingdom.

On the foundation of this theologically based anthropology I argued that the educational ministry of the Church must look to help people appropriate the life which God is offering—or in other words, to help them learn to live within the paschal mystery. I argued that the result of Christ's redemptive work is that all of life, even its trials and disappointments, can be used creatively, that is for growth in knowledge of and participation in the paschal mystery. (Thanksgiving is the key.) I also suggested that it belongs to the vocation of the Church to engage its members in activities which together constitute what I termed a series of "covenanted occasions of encounter." For God has not only called the Church to engage in certain activities but has also promised to be present and active whenever it does—with the implicit promise that his action will always be directed towards the renewal and regeneration both of the individual Christian and of the communities to which he or she belongs.

In Part Two I explored the idea that the Church might so use the seven-day week as to facilitate personal growth. I suggested that the week can be seen as providing a series of opportunities for the Church to enter ever more deeply into the paschal mystery and all that belongs to Christ's death and resurrection. For it can help the Christian community both to learn to make creative use of suffering and also to enter into the celebration of God's goodness and of the essential goodness of all creation. I outlined the history of the seven-day week and argued that within the divine dispensation or economy the week—essentially a Jewish invention—always looked to this purpose. The Sabbath, the heart of the Jewish week, is a day for celebrating truths fundamental to the paschal mystery: the unfailing goodness of God and created humanity's total dependence upon him. My account of the history of the week offers no original data about Jewish or Christian practice, but I believe that my interpretation of the available data contains original insights. I added no new pieces to the puzzle of how the early Church used the seven-day week, but I believe that have re-arranged the existing pieces in an original way. And I believe that not only is the new image which emerges coherent, but that within this new image many of its component parts take on a new significance. Indeed, I believe that within this new structure the original (or essential) meaning of certain components may have emerged.

Also original are my practical suggestions about the way in which the Church might now find it useful to enrich its weekly patterns of life and worship. I outline the weekly pattern adopted in two Anglican communities: CSWG and St Patrick's, Hove. This pattern is intended to open up the paschal mystery in ways that will enable the worshipping community to participate in that mystery more fully. It also serves to build up the corporate life of the worshipping community, giving that life shape and direction. I made these suggestions because my study of the Jewish background to the Christian week makes it clear that the value of the week for the Jews—and I take it that this is what God himself intended—lay in the *practical observance* of the week, rather than in the contemplation of the theory or theology which underlies it. It will be through sharing in the Church's celebration of the week, rather than through pondering on its meaning, that people will enter into a deeper knowledge of the God who has given them the week—and who is active on their behalf when they are doing what he invites them to do.

In my final chapters I developed an original "iconographic" approach to the Christian understanding of time. I argued the work of the incarnation can be seen as having opened the way for a sacramentalized use of all that belongs to the created realm: space, time matter, relationships. Space and matter can function sacramentally, so as to reveal the life of the Kingdom and to invite and facilitate participation in that life. The Church can use such things as painted icons and sacred space—church buildings, for example—to establish a context or environment in which people can both learn about Christ and the Kingdom and, moreover, can encounter him and his saints face to face. I argued that in a parallel way various temporal cycles can function as vehicles of personal encounter between God and the Church. The right use of such things as the daily, weekly, and annual cycles can enable them to reveal something of the End towards which all human life is directed, and moreover, can make that life present here on earth—and do so in ways that make it possible for people to respond to what is revealed, so that they can begin, even now, to participate in the new order of relationships which constitute the Kingdom. In this connection, however, I also stressed that although the Church can establish patterns of life, or an "environment," which will function sacramentally, these patterns do not function automatically or by magic. They will only function effectively wherever the relationships within the community are becoming sacramentalized; that is, where the leaders and teachers of the community are not only offering teaching and instruction, but are offering personal support to those in their care. In other words, they will function effectively where self-forgetful, paschal relationships are being established within the community.

Finally, I suggest ways in which the use of the pattern of the week might help equip and prepare the Church to address some of the pastoral challenges which confront it today, in particular, questions about the ultimate foundation for social and moral behavior here on earth. The work ends rather as it began, with the claim that the person (whether human or divine) has ultimate value; and that the mature person always desires the good of others, and indeed, is willing to labor and suffer in order that others might know fullness of life.

In summary, then, I have argued that the Church's educational ministry must be directed towards enabling people to participate in that transcendent life which the work of Christ has opened up to them. Baptism introduces the Christian into the eschatological life of Christ, but the Christian is called to appropriate that life. He or she must make it his or her own. The Church is called to establish patterns of life (and orders of relationship) that will help the Christian do this, and I have made a case for believing that the seven-day week might have much more of a part to play here than has generally been recognized.

Postscript and Update

THIS WORK BEGAN TO take form in the 1980s. The main body of the text was submitted as a PhD these in 2002. In the Prologue (above, 1–16) the story of St Patrick's and of CSWG's involvement in the parish, as of 2002 is recorded. After that things soon began to change, and sadly, not in what many saw as a positive direction. CSWG left Hove in 2003, the whole community gathering again at Crawley Down. Fr Alan Sharpe resigned from his post as Vicar of St Patricks' in 2008. Already, some time before that, as part of a pastoral review, the diocese had proposed closing St Patrick's as a parish church. The basic argument was that Brighton and Hove were over-supplied with Anglican churches, and that for all the good work going on at St Patrick's, both in liturgical renewal and in ministry among the homeless, the parish was not financially viable. There is no denying that although attendance at weekday parish worship was generally very good, the Sundays congregation was never large, indeed never large enough for the parish to be financially self-sustaining.

It was widely assumed, therefore, that after Fr Alan's departure the parish would be closed. But late in 2009 John Hind, the then Bishop of Chichester, asked me if I would consider becoming parish priest. Not without misgivings (and against the advice of many) I took on this challenge. I remained parish priest for the next five years.[1]

In 2114 the diocese, by then under the direction of Bishop Marttin Warner and in financial crisis, decided it was time to close St Patrick's. The closure of several other parishes was also announced or under discussion at this time.

For many of those closely involved with St Patrick's—who year after year had made praiseworthy efforts to maintain the rich patterns of worship and to continue ministry among the marginalized and care-worn— the closure came as a heavy blow. Nevertheless, the practical good-sense of the decision could not be doubted. Such a vast building was proving

---

1. I took on the post part-time. Throughout my years in the parish my energies were divided, since I was also working two or three days a week as a hospital chaplain.

impossibly expensive to maintain, and fine though the central area of the church was for worship, the building as a whole offered few facilities for group meetings or community events and wasn't suitable for easy adaptation. There were other problems too. It didn't help that the church was hidden away in a side street, with no provision for nearby car parking. It was also something of a problem that the church was dedicated to St Patrick: casual visitors, newcomers to the area, and even long-term local residents almost invariably assumed the church to be Roman Catholic, and believed that as such it was not the place for them.

Significantly, too, those very factors which made the area so much in need of Christian witness—such as high levels of deprivation and social isolation, and abnormally low levels of social cohesion, coupled with extraordinarily high levels of transience—these were the self-same factors which also made it a very difficult place to build a worshipping community.

Sad it was, though, that a place and so full of promise could not fulfill that promise. Many of those who had been part of the community, whether long-term parishioners, visiting clergy, occasional visitors, or ordinands on placement, recognized it as a place, with a powerful "atmosphere of grace." One visitor, a man with wide experience of Christian liturgy, both at home and abroad, and especially n the Middle East, said that it took him a while to identify what exactly was so special, so compelling about the worship at St Patrick's. Eventually, he said, he realized that this specialness lay in the coming together of a powerful sense of the transcendent with a strong sense of welcome, warmth and mutual appreciation within the gathered community. One committed member of the community summed up what perhaps many felt: "I've never known anywhere quite like it." I myself may be biased—of course I am—but although I am aware that grace abounds throughout the Church and that God is powerfully active in many forms of worship, I, hand on heart, would want to say something very similar.

Figures and Tables

Figures 1–6

Color versions of all these images are available
on the website: LivingInThe8thDay.co.uk.

Tables 1–4

Figure 1: Icon of the Weekly Cycle

Dionisji School, Beginning of Sixteenth Century
Tret'jakov Gallery, Moscow[1]

1. For the image search "Icon hexameron" on Wikimedia Commons. This search will also bring up other Hexameron icons. Artistically, these other icons are for less impressive and theologically they are wayward, with the Father depicted as an old man, etc. (Wikimedia accessed July 2017.)

In the upper part of the work a series of individual image represent the seven days of the week. The themes for the days are those long-established in the Russian Church. Here the sequence runs from the top left: first is a resurrection icon, the Descent into Hell, representing Sunday; the Holy Angels are commemorated on Monday; John the Baptist on Tuesday (here John baptizes the crowds); Mary Mother of God is commemorated on Wednesday; the Apostles on Thursday (here represented by the footwashing); Friday's theme is the cross. The focus of the whole icon is the central "Sabbath of the Saints." In the anonymous text of *The School of Moscow* (1987) it is stated: "Saturday is represented by Christ in glory, surrounded by the Mother of God, St John the Baptist, and the archangels; all are enwrapped in white clothes, including the Precursor who has exchanged his garments of camel-skin for a white cloak.[2] The Sabbath is thus presented as the ultimate goal of human life, where all is fulfilled and transfigured. So it is that in the lower register of the icon ten niches contain group-icons of various orders of saints: male and female martyrs, patriarchs, prophets, ascetics, etc. All is gathered into the final Sabbath of Christ, a Sabbath, which, though implicit in the new creation of the resurrection (and baptism), is only fully realized or actualized when people have appropriated the grace proper to that life.

2. School of Moscow, 26.

Figure 2: "God Rested on the Sabbath Day"

Mid-Sixteenth Century, Pskov School,
Cathedral of the Annunciation, Kremlin (detail).

The icon of which this is a detail is itself part of a larger work that depicts the entire sweep of divine history and "the complete drama of the human's call to holiness."[3] In this detail God is depicted as resting on the seventh day, surrounded by the angelic host. Below him are depicted episodes from the biblical creation stories, including the creation and fall of man. On either side of him are icons of Christ as God's angelic messenger and of Christ crucified. Much of the imagery is non-traditional or unorthodox. Ouspensky explains that in 1772 the Holy Synod of the Russian Church prohibited various forms of religious image, among them, those in which God is show as an elderly man, exhausted by his labors and now "reclining on cushions."[4]

3. Vinci, in Zajcev and Vinci, *Icons and Holiness*, 50, cf. 52.

4. Ouspensky, *Theology of the Icon*, vol. II, 416, n.16; cf. Bigham, *Image of God the Father*, 145. See also *The Complete Collection of the Decisions of the Department of the Orthodox Confession*, vol.2, 293–5 (in Russian). For similar imaged to figure 2 search "Icon God rested" on Wikimedia Commons. (Wikimedia accessed July 2017.)

Figure 3: CSWG, Chapel of Mary and the Angels, Monastery of the Holy Trinity, Crawley Down

Icons of the Incarnation (left) and Christ the Word (right) mark out the sanctuary area. Behind the altar, as focus of the worship, is Rublev's Trinity icon. A hanging crucifix (not visible in this photo) marks the gateway to the sanctuary. The Eucharist is celebrated Eastward-facing with the community gathered in the sanctuary, to either side of the celebrant and deacon, but not between them and the Trinity icon.

Figure 4: CSWG Chapel of Mary and the Angels, Monastery of Christ the Saviour, Hove.

The wall paintings by Russian iconographer Joanna Reitlinger were on loan from the Fellowship of St Alban and St Sergius. The icons in the sanctuary depict the heavenly worship of the saints and angels. Here the focus of the worship is Christ enthroned in glory. In the chapel, largely for practical reasons, the crucifix hangs in the sanctuary, rather than at the gateway of this area. Nevertheless, it still serves to link heaven and earth.

Figure 5: Layout of the Worship Area at St Patrick's Hove.

The worship area was re-ordered in 1986. Icons mark out the sanctuary area. At the offering of the Eucharistic Prayer (and at the intercessions for of the daily Offices) the congregation gathers with the celebrant at the altar. This serves to involve the whole community in the offering of the worship and helps to demonstrate that the responsibility for the worship lies with the whole community (and not just with the priest). The worship is Westward-facing. (note that the central area is carpeted.)

(There is much to be said for an Eastward-facing liturgy. Where the celebrant is Westward-facing—and so facing the people—very easily

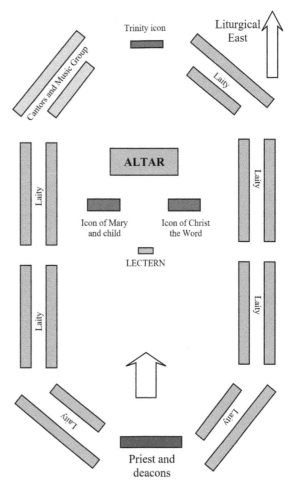

When there is only a small congregation they sit at the western end of the worship area. The cantor or music groups will then also sit nearer to this end of the church.

the Eucharistic Prayer can become a dialogue merely between the celebrant and the people. Where the priest is Eastward-facing, and especially where the community is gathered around him and is also looking East, it is more obvious that the Eucharist is a dialogue between the whole gathered community and God, with the celebrant leading the community in its offering, but not substituting for the community.)

Figure 6: The layout at St Patrick's 2015

Figure 7: Sketch of the Proposed Icon Screen for St Patrick's

A sketch of the hanging icon screen proposed for the sanctuary area at St Patrick's. it would serve to mark out the sanctuary area and is coordinated with floor-standing icons of the Incarnation) i.e., infant Christ and Theotokos) and Christ the Word. At the Eastern end of of the inner surface of the icon screen, and as focus of worship is an icon of Christ in glory. Around the rest of the inner surface are the saints ("a great cloud of witnesses," Heb

12:1), all orientated towards the Christ figure. Across the four inner corners are icons of angels and archangels.

Obliquely, angled across the outer corners are icons of the four evangelists. The rest of the outer surface is covered with icons depicting the saving events in and through which Christ's work was accomplished and man's redemption won. Most importantly, across the front of the screen the paschal mystery is presented. A large crucifix is central. To the left are icons of the Crucifixion and Deposition; to the right, icons of the Decent and of the myrrh-bearing woman at the empty tomb.

(As an extra I envisaged see large bowls of incense burning on metre-high stands below each corner of the screen, giving the effect, so I'd hope, of pillars of incense holding up the screen or of the heavenly and earthly realms being linked (cf. Rev 5:8; 8:3–4).

Table 1: Weekday Themes: Examples from Early, Mediaeval and Orthodox Tradition

	Jewish Tradition	First Christian Generations	Didaché[1]	(Some) Desert Monastic Traditions[2]	Traditional Eastern Orthodoxy[3]
Sun		Resurrection/Eucharist	Resurrection/Eucharist	Resurrection/Eucharist (fellowship day)	Resurrection
Mon				Solitary day	Angelic Host
Tues	Fast			Solitary day	John Baptist
Wed		Fast	Fast	Solitary day	Mary
Thu	Fast			Solitary day	Apostles
Fri		Fast	Fast	Solitary day	Holy Cross

1. Jungmann, *Pastoral Liturgy*, 252–54; cf. Turtullian, *Fasting* 10 (CSEL20:287).

2. See 205–6 above.

3. Bobrinsky, *Trinity*, 151; Dalmais, *LMD* 46 (1956) 65ff.; Jungmann, *Pastoral Liturgy*, 260, n.10.

Table 2: Weekday Themes: Examples from Mediaeval Latin and Modern Roman Practice

	Alcuin: 1⁴ (8th century) Trinity and holiness	Alcuin: 2⁵ (8th century) Theme: sin & sanctification	St Thierry[6] (late 9th century) God and his saints	Medieval Latin Practice[7] (after 1000)	Honorius Augustodunensis[8] (?12 cent.) Themes in the psalms of Nocturns	Ludwig Barbo[9] (15th cent.) Themes for private meditation.	Roman Catholic Eucharistic Themes 1570–1955[10]
Sun	The Trinity	The Gifts of the Spirit	Trinity, Holy Wisdom, Mary	Trinity (Father)	Incarnation/Resurrection	God's goodness	Trinity, or commonly, theme for week of year
Mon	For sinners	Tears	St Michael	Trinity (Son/Wisdom)	Baptism of Christ	Man's Fall	Holy Trinity
Tue	The Angels	Sinful thoughts	St John	Trinity (Holy Spirit)	Birth of Christ	Birth of Christ	The Angels
Wed	Holy Wisdom	Humility	St Peter	No settled or generally accepted theme	Betrayal by Judas	Jesus' flight to Egypt and public ministry	Apostles (from 1920, also Joseph, Peter, and Paul
Thu	Love (caritas)	The temptations of the flesh	St Stephen	No decided theme (Gethsemane for meditation)	Eucharist/Arrest	Persecution of Christ, and Eucharist.	1604 also Holy Eucharist; since 1935 also Christ's priesthood)
Fri	Holy Cross	Tribulation	Holy Cross	Holy Cross	Death on the Cross	Passion	The Cross (from 1604 also the Passion)
Sat	Mary	Mary	Theodoric (patron)	Mary	Burial	Descent, Resurrection, Ascension	Mary

4. Jungmann, *Pastoral Liturgy*, 254ff.

5. Jungmann, *Pastoral Liturgy*, 255.

6. Jungmann, *Pastoral Liturgy*, 260.

7. Jungmann, *Pastoral Liturgy*, 258–59.

8. Jungmann, *Pastoral Liturgy*, 265–70 (see PL172:640–42).

9. Jungmann, *Pastoral Liturgy*, 267–68. Cf Jungmann, *Pastoral Liturgy*, 268–72.

10. Jungmann, *Pastoral Liturgy*, 251–52. After 1955 all the days lost their themes except for Saturday, which remained a commemoration of Mary.

Table 3: Weekday Themes: Modern Examples

	Fr Jean-Claude Tromas[11]	Taizé[12]	Jerusalem Community, St Gervaise, Paris[13]	CCP[14]
Sun	Resurrection/ Beginnings	Resurrection	Resurrection	Resurrection
Mon	Trinity		"Desert Day"—spent outside of Paris in quiet and prayer	Pentecost
Tue	Holy Spirit			Advent
Wed	Christ Incarnate			Christmas
Thu	Apostles/Eucharist/ Gethsemane			Eucharist
Fri	Passion and Cross	After Evening Prayer: prayer around an icon of the cross	Eucharist and Vigil before the Sacrament	Passion
Sat	Mary/Tomb/Church	Vigil of the Resurrection with celebration of the Light of the Resurrection	As week day, save for evening vigil	Saints/Kingdom

11. As in CSWG 1978 (Mattins).

12. See "Times of prayers at Taizé, www.taize.fr/en_article70.html. Accessed July 2017.

13. Peers, "Schools of Prayer," 8–11 (cf. 28 n.28; see also Pingault, *Renouveau de L'Eglise*, 138–9.

14. *CCP* 1992.

Table 4: Weekly Observance, CSWG and St Patrick's

	CSWG Crawley Down	CSWG Hove (the monastic community joins the parish community for worship from Thursday to Sunday)	St Patrick's Hove (Figures in brackets indicate the number of people attending)
Sun	**Beginnings: Creation, Resurrection, Pentecost** Matins: 5–6am; Lauds: 7–7.45am Euch: 11am–12.30pm; EP:5.30–6.30pm	**Beginnings: Creation, Resurrection, Pentecost** Matins: 5–6am; Lauds: 7–7.45am Euch: 11am–12.30pm (60–80), EP:5.30–6.30pm	**Beginnings: Creation, Resurrection, Pentecost** MP: 9–9.20am (10–20) Euch: 10.30–12noon (60–80) EP: 5–7pm (20–50)
Mon	**Angels** Matins: 5–6am; Lauds: 7–7.45am EP: 6.30–7pm: Euch: 7–8pm	**Angels** Matins: 5–6am; Lauds: 7–7.45am EP: 6.30pm; Euch: 7–7.45pm	**No theme** MP: 8–8.30am (10); EP: 6.30 Euch: 7–7.40pm (20)
Tue	**John Baptist** Matins: 5–6am; Lauds: 7–7.45am EP: 6.30–7pm: Euch: 7–8pm	**John Baptist** Matins: 5–6am; Lauds: 7–7.45am EP: 6.30pm; Euch: 7–7.45pm	**No theme** MP: 8–8.30am (10); Euch: 10.30–11.40am EP: 6.30pm (15)
Wed	**Mary** Matins: 5–6am; Lauds: 7–7.45am EP: 6.30–7pm: Euch: 7–8pm	**Mary** Matins: 5–6am; Lauds: 7–7.45am EP: 6.30pm; Euch: 7–7.45pm; EP:5.30–6.30pm	**No theme** MP: 8–8.30am (10); EP: 6.30 Euch: 7–7.40pm (20)

	CSWG Crawley Down	CSWG Hove (the monastic community joins the parish community for worship from Thursday to Sunday)	St Patrick's Hove (Figures in brackets indicate the numbers of people attending)
Thu	**Apostles** Matins: 5–6am; Lauds: 7–7.45am EP: 6.30–7pm: Euch: 7–8pm Gethsemane	**Apostles** Matins: 5–6am; Lauds: 7–7.45am EP: 6.30; Euch: 7–7.45pm Teaching and vigil: 7.40–9pm	**Morning: No theme;** **Evening theme: Eucharist** MP: 8–8.30am (10) EP: 6.30pm; Euch: 7–7.40pm (20) Teaching and Vigil: 7.40–9pm (20)
Fri	**Passion** Matins: 5–6am; Lauds 7–7.45am Pre-Sanct: 5–6.30pm	**Passion** Vigil: 7–8am; MP 8–8.30am Pre-Sanct 6.30–7.15 pm (followed by simple shared 'breaking of the fast' 7.15–7.45	**Passion** Vigil: 7–8am (10); MP: 8am (12) Pre-Sanct: 6.30–7.15pm (25) followed by simple shared 'breaking of the fast' 7.15–7.45
Sat	Mary/Tomb/Church	**Sabbath: Rest and Vigil** MP: 9am; Euch: 12noon, followed by shared meal. EP and Vigil 6.30–8pm	**Sabbath: Rest & Vigil** MP 9am (10) Euch: 12noon, followed by meal (20) EP and Vigil 6.30–8pm (10)

Website Links

The website (LivingInThe8thDay.co.uk) offers pdf versons of leaflets and service booklets produced in connection with this book.

Please note, this downloadable material was produced in the early 1990s for the community at St Patrick's, Hove. Some elements in the pattern at St Patrick's (Benediction on Sunday evening, for example) would not be acceptable (or particularly desirable) elsewhere.

"The Pattern of the Week": Leaflets from St Patrick's. This comprises as set of six three-fold leaflets with a wrap-round cover.

An introductory leaflet outlines the thinking behind the pattern of the week. There are separate leaflets for Sunday and the days from Thursday to Saturday, while a single leaflet covers the period from Monday to Thursday morning. The leaflets share a common format: the front-cover introduces the theme; inside, that theme is developed and something said about the worship, prayer and other activities which will be going on in church and in the parish rooms; suggestions are also made about ways in which the theme of the day can be taken up in the home.

Liturgy Booklet: The Eucharistic rite, St Patrick's

Liturgy Booklet: The Pre-Sanctified Rite, St Patrick's

Bibliography

Abraham, W. J. *The Logic of Evangelism*. London: Hodder and Stoughton, 1989.

Albrektson, B. *History and the Gods*. Lund: Gleerup, 1967.

Aldred, Cyril. *Akhenaten*. London: Abacus, 1972.

Alfeyev, Hilarion. *The Spiritual World of Isaac the Syrian*. Kalamazoo, MI: Cistercian, 2000.

Allison, Dale C. *The New Moses, a Matthean Typology*. Edinburgh: T. & T. Clark, 1993.

Allison, C. FitzSimons. *The Cruelty of Heresy*. London: SPCK, 1994.

Allchin, A. M. *Participation in God: A Forgotten Strand in Anglican Tradition*. London, DLT, 1988.

Allman, J. J. *Prophétism Sacramental*. Neuchâtel: Delachaux et Niestlé, 1964.

Andreasen, Niels-Erik A. *The Old Testament Sabbath: A Tradition-Historical Investigation*. Missoula, MT: Society of Biblical Literature, 1972.

Annas, Julia. "Epicurus' Philosophy of Mind." In *Companions to Ancient Thought 2: Psychology*, edited by Stephen Everson, 84–101. Cambridge: Cambridge University Press, 1991.

Anon. *School of Moscow*. Milan: La Casa di Matriona, 1987.

———. *The Way of a Pilgrim*. Translated by H. Bacovcin. New York: Doubleday, 1992.

Anscombe, G. E. M. *Collected Philosophical Papers* II. Cambridge: Cambridge University Press, 1982.

Anson, Peter F. *The Call of the Cloister*. London: SPCK, 1955.

Aristotle. *The Compete Works of Aristotle: The Revised Oxford Translation*. Edited by. J. Barnes. Oxford: Oxford University Press, 1984.

Armitage, Nicholas. "Knowing and Unknowing in Orthodox Spirituality." *Sobornost* 22:1 (2000) 7–20.

Astley, Jeff. *The Philosophy of Christian Religious Education*. Birmingham, AL: Religious Education Press, 1994.

Atkins, Peter. "Purposeless People." In *Persons and Personality: A Contemporary Enquiry*, edited by A. R. Peacock and G. Gillet, 12–32. Oxford: Blackwell, 1987.

Aveni, Anthony. *Empires of Time: Clocks, Calendars, and Cultures*. 1990. Reprint. London: Taurus Parke, 2000.

Aves, John. "Persons in Relation: John Macmurray." In *Persons, Divine and Human: King's College Essays in Theological Anthropology*, edited by Christoph Schwöbel and Colin E. Gunton, 120–37. Edinburgh: T. & T. Clark, 1991.

Bacchiocchi, S. *From Sabbath to Sunday: A Historical Investigation of the Rise of Sunday Observance in Early Christianity*. Rome: Pontifical Gregorian University Press, 1977.

Bacher, W. "Ein Name des Sonntags im Talmud." *ZNW* 6 (1905) 202.

Bacovcin, H, trans. *The Way of a Pilgrim*. New York: Doubleday, 1992.

Baillie, John. *Our Knowledge of God*. London: Oxford University Press, 1939.

Ball, Bryan W. *The Seventh-Day Men: Sabbatarians and Sabbatarianism in England and Wales 1600–1800*. Oxford: Clarendon, 1994.

Balthasar, Hans Urs von. *Cordula oder der Ernstfall*. Eisiedeln: Herder, 1967.

———. *Katholisch: Aspekte des Mysteriums*. Einsiedeln: : Herder, 1975.

———. *Kosmische Liturgie, Maximus der Benkenner*. Frieburg in Brisgau: Herder, 1941.

———. *Liturgie cosmique, Maxime le Confesseur*. 1941. Reprint. Paris: Aubier, 1947.

———. *Man in History*. London: Sheed and Ward, 1968.

———. *Mysterium Paschale: The Mystery of Easter*. Translated by Aidan Nichols. Edinburgh: T. & T. Clark, 1990.

———. *Theodramatik, 2: Die Personen des Spiels, part 1: Der Mensche in Gott*. Einseiedeln: Johannes Verlag, 1976 (= *Theo-Drama: Theological Dramatic Theory, 2: The Dramatis Personae: Man in God*. Translated by Graham Harrison. San Francisco: Ignatius, 1993.)

———. "Theologie and Heiligkeit." *Wort and Wahrheit* 3 (1948) 881–96.

———. "Theology and Holiness." In *Explorations in Theology*, Vol. 1: *The Word Made Flesh*. San Francisco: Ignatius, 1989.

Balthasar, Hans Urs von, and Adrienne von Speyr. *Kreuz and Hölle. Part 2: Die Auftragshöllen*. Einsiedeln: Johannes Verlag, 1972.

Banks, Emil. *Deification in Eastern Orthodoxy: An Evaluation and Critique of the Theology of Dumitru Staniloae*. Paternoster Theological Monographs. Carlisle, UK: Paternoster, 1999.

Banks, R. *Jesus and the Law in the Synoptic Tradition*. Cambridge: Cambridge University Press, 1975.

Barnes, Jonathan. *Aristotle*. Oxford: Oxford University Press, 1992.

———. *Early Greek Philosophy*. Harmondsworth, UK: Penguin, 1987.

Barker, Margaret. *The Great High Priest: The Temple Roots of Christian Liturgy*. Edinburgh: T. & T. Clark, 2003.

———. *Temple Mysticism: An Introduction*. London: SPCK, 2011.

———. *Temple Theology: An Introduction*. London: SPCK, 2004.

Barr, James. *Biblical Words for Time*. London: SCM, 1962.

———. *Escaping from Fundamentalism*. London: SCM, 1980.

———. *The Semantics of Biblical Language*. 1961. Reprint. London: SCM, 1987.

Barth, Karl. *Church Dogmatics*, Vol. I, Part 2. Translated by G. T. Thomson and Harold Knight. Edinburgh: T. & T. Clark, 1956.

Barton, Stephen C. "Community." In *Dictionary of Biblical Interpretation*, edited by R. J. Coggins and J. L. Holden, 134–38. London: SCM, 1990.

———. "The Communal Dimension of Earliest Christianity: A Critical Survey of the Field." *JTS* NS 43.2 (1992) 399–427.

Baukham, R. J. "The Lord's Day." In *From Sabbath to Lord's Day: A Biblical, Historical and Theological Investigation*, edited by D. A. Carson, 221–50. Grand Rapids: Zondervan, 1982.

———. "Sabbath and Sunday in the Protestant Tradition." In *From Sabbath to Lord's Day: A Biblical, Historical and Theological Investigation*, edited by D. A. Carson, 311–41. Grand Rapids: Zondervan, 1982.

————. "Sabbath and Sunday Rest in the Medieval Church." In *From Sabbath to Lord's Day: A Biblical, Historical and Theological Investigation*, edited by D. A. Carson, 299–309. Grand Rapids: Zondervan, 1982.

————. "Sabbath and Sunday Rest in the Post-Apostolic Church." In *From Sabbath to Lord's Day: A Biblical, Historical and Theological Investigation*, edited by D. A. Carson, 251–98. Grand Rapids: Zondervan, 1982.

Bebawi, George. "Eastern Orthodox Worship." In *Foundation Documents of the Faith*. Edited by C. Rodd, 111–24. Edinburgh: T. & T. Clark, 1987.

Bebbington, David. *Patterns in History, A Christian Perspective of Historical Thought*. 1979. Reprint. Leicester, UK: Apollos, 1990.

Beckwith, R. T. "The Jewish Background to Christian Worship." In *The Study of Liturgy*, edited by C. Jones et al., 39–50. London: SPCK, 1978.

Beckwith, R. T., and W. Stott. "The Day, its Divisions and Its Limits, in Biblical Thought." *Evangelical Quaterly* 43 (1971) 218–27.

————. *This is the Day: The Biblical Doctrine of the Christian Sunday in Its Jewish and Early Christian Setting*. London: Marshall, Morgan and Scott, 1978

Behr, John, trans. Irenaeus, *Apostolic Preaching*. Crestwood, NY: SVS Press, 1997.

Behr-Sigel, E. *Lev Gillet: A Monk of the Eastern Church*. Translated by Helen Wright. London: Fellowship of St Alban and St Sergius, 1999.

Benoit, Pierre. "L'Ascension." *Revue Biblique* 56 (1949) 161–203.

Berger, Peter; Brigitte Berger, and Hansfried Kellner. *The Homeless Mind: Modernization and Consciousness*. New York: Random, 1973.

Berlin, Isaiah. *Two Concepts of Liberty*. Oxford: Clarendon, 1958.

Berrin, Susan, ed. *Celebrating the New Moon: A Rosh Chodesh Anthology*. Northvale, NJ: Aronson, 1996.

Bickerman, E. J. *Chronology of the Ancient World*. 1968. Reprint. London: Thames and Hudson, 1980.

Bigham, Stephen. *Heroes of the Icon*. Torrance, CA: Oakwood, no date.

————. *The Image of God the Father in Orthodox Theology and Iconography, and Other Studies*. Torrance, CA: Oakwood, 1995.

Bishop, Hugh. *The Easter Drama*. London, Hodder and Stoughton, 1958.

————. *The Passion Drama*. London: Hodder and Stoughton, 1956.

Bishop, J. G. "The Anglican Tradition." In *A Manual for Holy Week*, edited by C. P. M. Jones, 43–54. London: SPCK, 1967.

Blue, Lionel. *Bedside Manna*. London: Gollancz, 1992.

Bloom, Anthony. *Living Prayer*. London: DLT, 1966.

Bobrinskoy, Boris. *The Mystery of the Trinity: Trinitarian Experience and Vision in the Biblical and Patristic Tradition*. Crestwood, NY: SVS Press, 1999.

————. "Worship and the Ascension of Christ." *SVSQ* 3:4 (1959) 108–35.

Bonhoeffer, Dietrich. *Ethics*. Edited by Eberhard Bethge; translated by Neville Horton Smith. London: SCM, 1955.

Bonner, G. "Augustine's Conception of Deification." *JThS* 37 (1986) 369–86.

Boojamra, J. L. *Foundations in Orthodox Christian Education*. Crestwood, NY: SVS Press, 1989.

————. "Socialization as a Historical Model for Christian Integration." *SVSTQ* 25 (1981) 219–39.

————. "The Role of Family and Community in Religious Development." In *Perspectives on Orthodox Education: Report of the Orthodox Education Consultation for Rural/*

Developing Areas, edited by Constance J. Tarasar. Syosset, 59–73. New York: Syndesmos & Department of Religious Education of the Orthodox Church in America, 1983.

Boorstein, Daniel J. *The Discoverers*. New York: Random House, 1983.

Bourdeaux, Michael. *Risen Indeed: Lessons in Faith from the USSR*. London: DLT, 1983.

Boros, Ladislaus. *The Moment of Truth: Mysterium Mortis*. London: Search, 1973 (German text 1962).

Botte, B. "Les dénominations du dimanche dans la tradition chrétienne." *Le dimanche: Lex Orandi* 39 (1965) 7–28.

Bouché-Leclercq, A. *L'astrologie grecque*. Paris: Leroux, 1899.

Bouteneff, Vera. *Father Arseny, 1893–1973: Priest, Prisoner, Spiritual Father*. 1994. Reprint. Crestwood, NY: SVS Press, 1998.

Bouyer, Louis. *The Christian Mystery, from Pagan Myth to Christian Mysticism*. Edinburgh: T. & T. Clark, 1990.

———. *Eucharist: Theology and Spirituality of the Eucharistic Prayer*. Translated by Charles Underhill Quinn. Notre Dame, IN: University of Notre Dame Press, 1968.

———. *History of Christian Spirituality*, Vol. I. Translated by Mary Perkins Ryan. London: Burns and Oats, 1963. (French text 1960).

———. *Introduction to Spirituality*. Translated by Mary Perkins Ryan. London: DLT, 1961.

———. *Life and Liturgy*. London: Sheed and Ward, 1956. (First issued as *Liturgical Piety*, 1955; French text 1954.)

———. *Newman, His Life and Spirituality*. London: Burns and Oats, 1958.

———. *The Paschal Mysery*. London: George Allen and Unwin, 1951. (Translated from the first French edition of 1947.)

———. *Rite and Man*. London: Burns and Oats, 1963.

Bowne, B. P. *Personalism*. Boston: Houghton, Mifflin, 1908.

Bradshw, Paul F. *Daily Prayer in the Early Church*. London: SPCK (Alcuin Club), 1981.

Braine, David. *The Human Person: Animal and Spirit*. Notre Dame, IN: University of Notre Dame Press, 1992.

Braun, Moshe A. *The Jewish Holy Days, Their Spiritual Significance*. Northvale, NJ: Aronson, 1996.

Breasted, James Henry. "Ikhnaton, the Religious Revolutionary." In *Cambridge Ancient History* II, 109–30. Cambridge: Cambridge University Press, 1924.

Bria, Ion. *The Liturgy after the Liturgy, Mission and Witness from an Orthodox Perspective*. Geneva: WCC, 1996.

Brightman, E. S. *The Problem of God*. New York: Abingdon, 1930.

Brown, Hunter, ed. *Images of the Human: The Philosophy of the Human Person in a Religious Context*. Chicago: Loyola, 1995.

Brown, Raymond E. (S.S). *An Adult Christ at Christmas. Essays on the Three Biblical Christmas Stories*. Collegeville, MN: Liturgical, 1977.

———. *The Birth of the Messiah: A Commentary on the Infancy Narratives in Matthew and Luke*. New York: Doubleday, 1977.

———. *The Critical Meaning of the Bible*. London: Chapman, 1982.

———. "The Date of the Last Supper" *BiTod* (1964) 727–33.

———. *The Death of the Messiah, from Gethsemane to the Grave: A Commentary on the Passion Narratives in the Four Gospels*. 2 vols. London: Chapman, 1994.

————. *The Gospel According to John (I–XII)*. The Anchor Yale Bible Commentaries. New Haven, CT: Yale University Press, 1966.

————. "Not Jewish Christianity and Gentile Christianity, But Types of Jewish/Gentile Christianity." *CBQ* 45 (1983) 74–79.

————. "NT Background for the Concept of Local Church." *Proceedings of the Catholic Theological Society of America* 36 (1981) 1–14.

Brueton, D. *Many Moons*. New York: Prentice Hall, 1991.

Buber, Martin. *I and Thou*. Translated by Ronald Gregor Smith. 2nd ed. Edinburgh: T. & T. Clark, 1958. (German text 1923.)

————. *The Knowledge of Man*. Edited by M. Friedman. New York: Harper & Row, 1965.

————. *Moses*. 1946. Reprint. New York: Harper, 1958.

Bunge, Gabriel. *The Rublev Trinity*. New York: SVS Press, 2007.

Bugnini, Annibale. *The Reform of the Liturgy 1948–1975*. Collegeville, MN: Liturgical, 1990.

Bunnin, Nicholas, ed. *The Blackwell Companion to Philosophy*. Oxford: Blackwell, 1996.

Burgess, Stanley M. *The Holy Spirit: Eastern Christian Tradition*. Peabody, MA: Hendrickson, 1989.

————. *The Holy Spirit: Medieval Roman Catholic and Reformation Traditions*. Peabody, MA: Hendrickson, 1997.

Burkhardt, Jacob. *The Civilization of the Renaissance in Italy*, Vol. 1. 1878. Reprint. New York: Harper, 1958.

Butterfield, Herbert. *Christianity and History*. London: Bell, 1949.

Cabié, Robert. *The Church at Prayer*, Vol. 2: *The Eucharist*. Translated by Matthew J. O'Connell. London: Chapman, 1986.

Cain, Kathleen. *Luna: Myth and Mystery*. Boulder: Johnson, 1991.

Cairns, D. *The Image of God in Man*. London: SCM, 1953.

Callenwaert, C. *Sacris erudiri*. Steenbrügge: Abbatia S. Petri de Aldenburgo, 1940.

Camelot, Th. "The Theology of the Image of God." *Journal of Philosophical and Theological Sciences* 40 (1956) 443–71.

Cannon, W. W. "The Weekly Sabbath." *ZAW* 49 (1931) 325–27.

Cappuyns, M. "Liturgie et théologie." In *Le vrai visage de la Liturgie, Cours et conférences des semaines liturgiques*, 175–209. Louvain: Abbeye de Mont César, 1938.

Carpenter, Humphry. *The Inklings*. London: HarperCollins, 1997.

Carrington, Philip. *The Primitive Christian Calendar: A Study in the Making of the Marcan Gospel*. Cambridge: Cambridge University Press, 1952.

Carroll, John. *Humaninsm: The Wreck of Western Culture*. London: Fontana, 1993.

Carson, D. A., ed. *From Sabbath to Lord's Day: A Biblical, Historical and Theological Investigation*. Grand Rapids: Zondervan, 1982.

Carson, D. A. "Jesus and the Sabbath in the Four Gospels." In *From Sabbath to Lord's Day*, edited by D. A. Carson, 57–97. Grand Rapids: Zondervan, 1982.

Cassidy, Sheila. "Towards a Theology of Hospice Care." In *Light from the Dark Valley: Reflections on Suffering and Dying*. London: DLT, 1994.

Cassim, Quassim. "Reductionism and First-Person Thinking." In *Reduction, Explanation, and Realism*, edited by David Charles and Kathleen Lennon, 361–80. Oxford: Clarendon, 1992.

Catherine Louise, Sr., SSM. "The Planting of the Lord: The History of the Society of St Margaret in England, Scotland and the USA, 1855–1995." Published privately, 1995.

Causse, Antonin. *Les pauvres d'Israël.* Strasbourg: Librerie Istra, 1922.

Chifflot, Th. G. "Le Christ et le Temps." *LMD* 13 (1952) 26–49.

Charles, R. H., ed. *The Apocrypha and Pseudoepigraphia of the Old Testament in English.* 1913. Reprint. Oxford: Clarendon, 1977–78.

Childs, Brevard S. *Biblical Theology in Crisis.* Philadelphia: Westminster, 1970.

———. *Memory and Tradition in Israel.* Studies in Biblical Theology 37. Naperville, IL: A. R. Allenson, no date.

Chrysostomos, Bishop of Etna (California). "Comments on the Late Fathers Alexander Schmemann and John Meyendorff, a Reply to Mr. Ognian Ranchev." No pages. Online http://orthodoxinfo.com/phronema/commentsschmey.aspx. (Accessed July 2017.)

———. "Orthodox People Apart." *Orthodox Tradition* 9.1 (1992) 25–26.

———. "Protopresbyter Georges *Florovsky.*" *Orthodox Tradition* 11.2 (1994) 28–29.

Clément, Olivier. *The Roots of Christian Mysticism.* London: New City, 1993. (Original French text, 1982.)

———. *The Spirit of Solzhenitsyn.* Translated by Sarah Fawcett and Paul Burns. London: Search, 1976.

———. *Transfigurer le Temps.* Neuchâtel: Les Presses de Taizé, 1959.

Cobb, P. G. "The History of the Christian Year." In *The Study of Liturgy,* edited by Chesslyn Jones et al., 403–19. London: SPCK, 1978.

Collingwood, R. G. *The Idea of Nature.* Oxford: Oxford University Press, 1945.

Colson, F. H. *The Week: An Essay on the Origin and Development of the Seven-day Cycle.* Cambridge: Cambridge University Press, 1926.

Congar, Yves M. J. *I Believe in the Holy Spirit,* Vol. 3. Translated by David Smith. 1980. Reprint. London: Chapman, 1983.

Coniaris, Anthony M. *Sacred Symbols that Speak,* Vol. II. Minneapolis: Light and Life, 1987.

Cooper, John W. *Body, Soul and Life Everlasting.* 1989. Reprint. Grand Rapids: Eerdmans, 2000.

Corcoran, Kevin, ed. *Soul, Body and Survival: Essays on the Metaphysics of the Human Person.* Ithaca, NY: Cornell University Press, 2001.

Cornford, F. M. *From Religion to Philosophy: A Study in the Origins of Western Speculation.* 1912. Reprint. Hassocks, UK: Harvester, 1980.

Cottingham, John. *Descartes.* Oxford: Blackwell, 1986.

Cotton, P. *From Sabbath to Sunday.* Bethlehem, PA: Times, 1933.

Crichton, J. D. *The Liturgy of Holy Week.* London: Goodlife-Neale, 1971.

———. *The Living Christ.* London: Collins, 1988.

———. "A Theology of Worship." In *The Study of Liturgy,* edited by Cheslyn Jones et al., 1–29. London: SPCK, 1978.

Crisp R., and M. Slote, eds. *Virtue Ethics.* Oxford: Oxford University Press, 1997.

Crouzel, H. *Théologie de l'image de Dieu chez Origène.* Paris: Aubier, 1956.

The Community of the Servants of the Will of God, Fr. Gregory. *CSWG Office of Matins to Conclude the Night Vigil* (adapted from Jean-Claude Tromas OFM Cap., *Office de l'Ermitage St Fançois*). Crawley Down, UK: CSWG, 1978.

————. *The Divine Office in the Renewal of the Christian Life*, Fr. Gregory CSWG. Crawley Down, Sussex: CSWG, 1979.

————. *Fr. Gilbert Shaw (1886–1967), A Memoir*. Crawley Down, UK: CSWG, 2001.

————. *Introducing CSWG: An Application of Monastic Theology to the Formation of an Anglican Contemplative Community for Men*. 1979. Rev. ed. Crawley Down, UK: CSWG, 1986. (The undisclosed author is Fr. Gregory CSWG.)

————. *A Manual of Eucharistic Living: Being the Rule of the Associates of the Community of the Servants of the Will of God*. Crawley Down, UK: CSWG, 1984. (Undisclosed author Fr. Gregory CSWG.)

————. *Monastic Rule: Community of the Servants of the Will of God*. Crawley Down, UK: CSWG, revision of 1972.

————. *The Prophetic View of the Monastic Life* (Incorporating CSWG, Community Report: Year of Assessment 1978). Crawley Down, UK: CSWG, 1983. (Undisclosed author Fr. Gregory CSWG.)

————. *St. Patrick's, How it All Began* (including the sermon preached by Bishop Eric Kemp at the inauguration of the Monastery of Christ the Saviour). CSWG: Crawley Down, UK: CSWG, 1995.

Cullman, Oscar. *Christ and Time: The Primitive Christian Conception of Time and History*. Philadelphia: Westminster, 1950.

Cuming, G. J. *A History of Anglican Liturgy*. London: Macmillan, 1969.

Curtis, Geoffrey. *William of Glasshampton: Friar, Monk, Solitary*. 1947. Reprint. London: SPCK, 1978.

Dale, Anthony. *Fashionable Brighton 1820–1860*. London: Oriel, 1947.

Dalmais, H. "Le dimache dans la liturgie byzantine." *LMD* 46 (1956) 60–67.

Danby, Herbert, trans. *The Mishnah: Translated from the Hebrew with Introduction and Brief Explanatory Notes*. Oxford: Oxford University Press, 1933.

————. *Tractate Sanhedrin, Mishna and Tosefta*. New York: Macmillan, 1919.

Dancy, Jonathan, ed. *Reading Parfit*. Oxford: Blackwell, 1997.

Daniélou, Jean. *The Bible and the Liturgy*. Notre Dame, IN: University of Notre Dame Press, 1964. (French text, 1956.)

Daniélou, Jean, and Henri Marrou. *Christian Centuries*, Vol. 1. London: DLT, 1964.

Davidsion, Donald. "Mental Events." In *Essays on Actions and Events*, 207–24. Oxford: Clarendon Press, 1971.

Davis, Charles. "Ghetto or Desert: Liturgy in a cultural Dilemma." *SL* 7.2–3 (1970) 10–27.

Davies, W. D, and Dale C. Allison. *The Gospel According to Saint Matthew*, Vol. 1. Edinburgh: T. & T. Clark, 1988.

Davies, J. *The Caroline Captivity of the Church*. Oxford: Oxford Historical Monographs, 1992.

Dawn, Marva J. *Keeping the Sabbath Wholly*. Grand Rapids: Eerdmans, 1989.

de Bruyne, D., OSB, "L'Origine des processions de la chandeleur et des rogations à propos d'un sermon inédit." *RBén.* 34 (1922) 14–26.

de Lacey, Douglas R. "The Sabbath/Sunday Question in the Pauline Corpus." In *From Sabbath to Lord's Day: A Biblical, Historical and Theological Investigation*, edited by D. A. Carson, 221–50. Grand Rapids: Zondervan, 1982.

De-la-Noy, Michael. *The Church of England: A Portrait*. London: Simon & Schuster, 1993.

de Lubac, Henri., SJ, *Catholicisme: les aspects sociaux du dogma*. Translated by L. C. Sheppard and E. Englund. 1950. Reprint. London: Burns and Oates, 1962. (Later reissued as *Catholicism: Christ and the Common Destiny of Man*. San Francisco: Ignatius, 1988.)

Dicken, E. W. Trueman. *The Crucible of Love*. London: DLT, 1963.

Dix, Gregory. *The Shape of the Liturgy*. Westminster: Dacre, 1945.

———. *The Treatise on the Apostolic Tradition of St Hippolytus of Rome*. 1937. Rev. ed. Corrections by Henry Chadwick. London: SPCK, 1968.

Dobbelaere, K. "Trend Report: Secularisation: A Multi-Dimensional Concept." *Current Sociology* 29.2 (1981) 3–153.

Dollimore, Jonathan. *Death, Desire and Loss in Western Culture*. Harmondsworth, UK: Penguin, 1999.

Donahue, C. "The Agapé of the Hermits of Scété." *Studia Monastica* 1 (1959) 97–114.

Dove, John, SJ. *Strange Vagabond of God: The Story of John Bradburne*. 1983. Reprint. Dublin: Poolbeg, 1990.

Doze, André. *Joseph, Gardien du Shabbat*. Nouan-Le-Fuzelier: Éditions des Béatitudes, 1993.

Dressler, Harold H. P. "The Sabbath in the Old Testament." In *From Sabbath to Lord's Day: A Biblical, Historical and Theological Investigation*, edited by D. A. Carson, 21–41. Grand Rapids: Zondervan, 1982.

Dugmore, C. W. *The Influence of the Synagogue on the Divine Office*. Oxford: Oxford University Press, 1944.

Dumaine, H. "Dimanche." *DACL* 4:858–994.

Duncan, David Ewing. *The Calendar*. London: Forht Estate, 1998.

Dunn, J. D. G. *The Christ and the Spirit*. Grand Rapids: Eerdmans, 1998.

———."Jesus Tradition in Paul." 1994. In *The Christ and the Spirit*, 169–89. Grand Rapids: Eerdmans, 1998.

———. "Paul's Understanding of the Death of Jesus as Sacrifice." 1991. In *The Christ and the Spirit*, 190–211. Grand Rapids: Eerdmans, 1998.

Dupré, Louis. *The Common Life: The Origins of Trinitarian Mysticism and Its Development by Jan Ruusbroec*. New York: Crossroads, 1984.

Duriez, Colin. *C. S. Lewis Handbook*. Eastbourne, UK: Monarch, 1990.

Eccles, John. *How the Self Controls Its Brain*. Berlin: Springer-Verlag, 1994.

Eccles, John, and Friedrich Beck. "Quantum Aspects of Brain Activity and the Role of Consciousness." *Proceedings of the National Academy of Science* 89 (1992) 357–61.

Eccles, John, and Karl Popper. *The Self and Its Brain*. Berlin: Springer-Verlag, 1977.

Edson, M. *Loved into Life: An Eight Day Biblical Journey*. London. Marshall Pickering, 1993.

Elchaninov, Alexander. *Diary of a Russian Priest*. Translated by Helen Iswolsky; edited by Kallistos Timothy Ware. London: Faber and Faber, 1967.

Eliade, M. *A History of Religious Ideas*, I. Translated by Willard R. Trask. Chicago: University of Chicago Press, 1979.

Ellard, G. *Master Alcuin, Liturgist*. Chicago: Loyola University Press, 1956.

Elliger, Karl. *Leviticus*. HAT 4. Tübingen: Mohr, 1966.

Engel, Diana R. *The Hebrew Concept of Time and the Effect on the Development of the Sabbath*. Washington, DC: University of America Press, 1976.

Evans, G. R. *Philosophy and Theology in the Middle Ages*. London: Routledge, 1993.

Evans, Richard J. *In Defence of History*. London: Granta, 1997.

Evdokimov, Paul. *The Art of the Icon: A Theology of Beauty*. Translated by Steven Bigham. Redondo Beach, CA: Oakwood, 1990. (French text, 1972.)

————. "St Seraphim of Sarov: Icon of Orthodox Spirituality." *Ecumenical Review*, 15.3 (1963) 264–70.

Everson, Stephen, ed. *Companions to Ancient Thought 2: Psychology*. Cambridge: Cambridge University Press, 1991.

Fackenheim, Emil L. *To Mend the World: Foundations of Future Jewish Thought*. New York: Schocken, 1982.

Fagerberg, David W. *What Is Liturgical Theology: A Study in Methodology*. New York: Pueblo, 1992.

Farrer, Austin. *The Brink of Mystery*. Edited by Charles C. Conti. London: SPCK, 1976.

————. *A Rebirth of Images: The Making of John's Apocalypse*. London: Dacre, 1949.

Faulkener, Hazel. "St Patrick's." In *Hove Encyclopedia; Brunswick Town*, edited by July Middleton. Hove, UK: printed for author, date not known.

Faulkner, Hazel, and Judy Middleton. *St Patrick's Church, Hove—A History*. Published privately, c. 1980.

Feldman, Louis H., and Reinhold, Meyer, eds. *Jewish Life and Thought among Greeks and Romans: Primary Readings*. Edinburgh: T. & T. Clark, 1996.

Ferguson, Everett. *Backgrounds of Early Christianity*. 2nd ed. Grand Rapids: Eerdmans, 1993.

Filaret, Metropolitan (Archbishop of Chernigov). *Istorichesky obzor pesnopistzev i pesnopenii Grecheskoy Tserkv*. Historical Survey of Hymnographers and Hymns of the Greek Church. Chernigov, 1864.

Filson, Floyd V. *"Yesterday": A Study of Hebrews in the Light of Chapter 13*. London: SCM, 1967.

Fisch, Thomas, ed. *Liturgy and Tradition: Theological Reflections of Alexander Schmemann*. Crestwood, NY: SVS Press, 1990.

Flew, Anthony, ed. *Body, Mind, and Death*. New York: Macmillan, 1964.

Florensky, Pavel. *The Pillar and the Ground of the Truth*. Translated by Boris Jakim. Princeton, NJ: Princeton University Press, 1997. (Russian text 1914.)

Florovsky, Georges. *Creation and Redemption*, Vol. 3 in Florovky's Collected Works. Belmont, MA: Norland, 1976.

————. "Lamb of God." *SJT* 4.1 (1951) 13–28.

————. "*Sobornost:* The Catholicity of the Church." In *The Church of God*, edited by Eric Mascall, 51–74. London: SPCK, 1934.

Fordor, Jerry A. *Psychological Explanation*. New York: Random House, 1968.

Fowler, J. W., Karl Ernst Nipkow, and Friedrich Schweitze, eds. *Stages of Faith and Religious Development: Implications for Church, Education and Society*. London: SCM, 1992.

Francis, Leslie. "Theology and Education: A Research Perspective." *SJT* 32.1 (1979) 61–70.

Francis, Leslie, and Adrian Thatcher, eds. *Christian Perspectives for Education: A Reader in the Theology of Education*. Leominster, UK: Fowler Wright, 1990.

Fancke, J. *Van Sabbath naar Zondag*. Amsterdam: Uitgeverij Ton Bolland, 1973.

Franz, A. *Die Messe im deutchen Mittelalter*. Frieburg: Herder, 1902.

Freeman, P. *The Principles of the Divine Office*, Vol. 1, *"Morning and Evening Prayer."* London: Parker, 1893.

Frend, W. H. C. *Martyrdom and Persecution in the Early Church.* Oxford: Blackwell, 1965.

———. *The Rise of Christianity.* London: DLT, 1984.

Fergusson, Everett. *Backgrounds of Early Christianity.* 2nd ed. Grand Rapids: Eerdmans, 1993.

———. "Sabbath or Sunday? A Review Article." *Restoration Quarterly* 23 (1980) 172–81.

Gavin, F. *The Jewish Antecedents of the Christian Sacraments.* London: SPCK, 1928.

Gill, Christopher. "Is There a Concept of Person in Greek Philosophy?" In *Companions to Ancient Thought 2: Psychology*, edited by Stephen Everson, 166–93. Cambridge: Cambridge University Press, 1991.

Gillard, Jean. "Dimanche." *DS* 3:948–82.

Gillet, Lev. *Communion in the Messiah.* London: Lutterworth, 1942.

———. *The Year of Grace of the Lord.* (Published under the pseudonym "A Monk of the Eastern Church.") Translated by D. Cowen. Oxford: Mowbrays, 1980. (French text, 1971.)

Gilson, Étienne. *Being and Some Philosophers.* 2nd ed. Toronto: Pontifical Institute of Medieval Studies, 1952.

Ginzberg, Louis. *The Legends of the Jews*, Vol. 3. Translated by Paul Radin. Philadelphia: Jewish Publication Society of America, 1947. (German text in seven volumes, 1909–38.)

Goldenberg, Robert. "The Jewish Sabbath in the Roman World up to the Time of Constantine the Great." *ANRW* II, 19.1, 414–47.

Goodman, M. D. "Legal Puzzles." In *A Tribute to Geza Vermes: Essays on Jewish and Christian Literature and History*, edited by Philip R. Davies and Richard T. White, 227–46. Sheffield, UK: JSOT, 1990.

Goricheva, Tatiana. *Talking about God is Dangerous.* Translated by John Bowden. London: SCM, 1986. (German text, 1984.)

Goudoever, J. van. *Biblical Calendars.* 2nd ed. Leiden: Brill, 1961.

Grayeff, Felix. *Aristotle and His School.* London: Duckworth, 1974.

Greer, Rowan A., trans. and ed. *Origen: An Exhortation to Martyrdom, Prayer, and Selected Works.* London: SPCK, 1979.

Greenacre, Roger, and Jeremy Haselock. *The Sacrament of Easter.* 2nd ed. Leominster, UK: Gracewing, 1989.

Greenberg, Blu. *How to Run a Traditional Jewish Household.* New York: Simon and Schuster, 1983.

Greenfield, Susan. *The Human Brain.* London: Phoenix, 1997.

———. "Soul, Brain, Mind." In *From Soul to Self*, edited by M. James C. Crabbe, 108–25. London: Routledge, 1999.

Gross, J. *La divinisation du chrétien d'après les Pères grecs.* Paris: Lecoffre, 1938.

Guillaumont, Antoine. "Les sens du noms du coeur dans l'antiquité." *Études Carmélitaines* 29 (1950) 41–81.

Guiver, George. *Company of Voices: Daily Prayer and the People of God.* London: SPCK, 1988.

Gunstone, J. T. A. *The Feast of Pentecost.* Studies in Christian Worship 8. London: Faith, 1967.

Gunton, Colin E. "Trinity, Ontology and Anthropology: Towards a Renewal of the Doctrine of *Imago Dei.*" In *Persons Human and Divine: King's College Essays in*

Theological Anthropology, edited by Colin Gunton and Christoph Schwöbel, 47–61. Edinburgh: T. & T. Clark, 1991.

———. *Yesterday and Today.* London: DLT, 1983.

Gustafson, James M. "The Church: A Community of Moral Discourse." In *The Church as Moral Decision-Maker,* 83–95. Philadelphia: Pilgrim, 1970.

Guthrie, W. C. K. *The Greek Philosophers from Thales to Aristotle.* London: Methuen, 1950.

———. *History of Greek Philosophy,* Vol. I. Cambridge: Cambridge University Press, 1962.

Gysi, Lydia (Mother Maria of Normanby). *The Fool and Other Writings.* Edited by Sister Thekla. Normanby, UK: Greek Orthodox Monastery of the Assumption, 1980.

———. *Hidden Treasure.* Normanby, UK: Greek Orthodox Monastery of the Assumption, 1972.

———. *The Jesus Prayer.* Normanby, UK: Greek Orthodox Monastery of the Assumption, 1980.

———. *The Realism of the Orthodox Faith,* Normanby, UK: Greek Orthodox Monastery of the Assumption, 1975.

Gysi, Lydia (Mother Maria of Normanby), Sister Thekla, and Sister Katherine. *Orthodox Potential.* Newport Pagnal, UK: Library of Orthodox Thinking, 1973.

Ha-am, Ahad (Asher Hirsch Ginzberg). *Al Parashat Derachim* ("At the Crossroads"), 3 vols. 1895. Reprint. Berlin: Judischer Verlag, 1922.

Hacking, R. D. *Such a Long Journey: A Biography of Gilber Shaw, Priest.* London: Mowbray, 1988.

Haitch, Russell. "Alexander Schmemann." http://www.talbot.edu/ce20/educators/orthodox/alexander_schmemann/. (Accessed July 2017.)

Hamlyn, D. W. *Metaphysics.* Cambridge: Cambridge University Press, 1984.

Hardinge, Leslie. *The Celtic Church in Britain.* London: SPCK, 1972.

Hare, J. C. "On the Names of the Days of the Week." In *Philological Museum* I. Cambridge: Printed for J. Smith for Deightons, 1832.

Harrison, Vera. "Perichoresis in the Greek Fathers." *SVTQ* 35 (1991) 35–65.

Hartman, E. *Aristotelian Investigation: Substance, Body and Soul.* Princeton: Princeton University Press, 1977.

Harton, F. P. *The Elements of the Spiritual Life: A Study in Ascetical Theology.* London: SPCK, 1957.

Hausherr, Irénée. *Philautie: De la tendresse pour soi à la charité, selon Maxime le Confesseur.* Orientalia Christiana Analecta 137. Rome: Edizioni Orientalia Christiana, 1952.

Haskell, Thomas L. "Objectivity is Not Neutrality: Rhetoric and Practice in Peter Novick's *That Noble Dream.*" *History and Theory* 29 (1990) 129–57.

Hasker, William. *The Emergent Self.* Cornell, NY: Cornell University Press, 1999.

Hauerwas, Stanley. *A Community of Character: Towards a Constructive Christian Social Ethic.* Notre Dame, IN: University of Notre Dame Press, 1981.

Hebblethwaite, Brian. "Time and Eternity and Life after Death." *Heythrop Journal* 20 (1979) 57–62.

Heinzer, F., and C. von Schönborn, eds. *Maximus Confessor (Actes du Symposium sur Maxime le Confesseur, Fribourg, 2–5 September 1980).* Fribourg: Éditions Universitaires, 1982.

Heller, Agnes. *Ethics of Personality.* London: Blackwell, 1996.

Hengel, Martin. *Judaism and Hellenism*. Translated by John Bowden. Two volumes in one (pages numbered independently: a = text, b = notes). London: SCM, 1974. (German text, 1973).

Herwegen, I. *Antike, Germanentum und Christentum*. Salzburg: Anton Pustet Verlag, 1932.

———. *Kirche und Selle. Die Seelenhaltung des Mysterienkultes und ihr Wandel in Mittelalter*. Münster in Westfal: Aschendorff, 1926.

Heschel, Abraham Joshua. *God in Search of Man*. Philadelphia: Jewish Publication Society, 1959.

———. *Man Is Not Alone*. New York: Farrar, Straus, & Young, 1951.

———. *The Sabbath: Its Meaning for Modern Man*. 1951. Reprint. New York: Noonday, 1991.

Hessey, James Augustus. *Sunday: Its Origin, History and Present Obligation*. The Bampton Lectures for 1860. London: Murray, 1866.

Hetherington, P., trans. *The Painter's Manual (of Dionysius of Fourna)*. Torrance, CA: Oakwood, 1989.

Hicks, R. D. *Aristotle, de Anima*. Cambridge: Cambridge University Press, 1907.

Hierotheos Vlachos (Metropolitan of Nafpaktos). *Orthodox Psychotherapy*. 3rd ed. Translated by Esther Williams. Levadia, Greece: Birth of the Theotokos Monastery, 1997.

Hodgkins, William. *Sunday: Christian and Social Significance*. London: Independent, 1960.

Holland, Bernard, ed. *Friedrich von Hügel: Selected Letters, 1896-1924*. 1927. Reprint. London: Dent, 1972.

Hooper, Walter. *C. S. Lewis: A Companion and Guide*. London: Fount, 1996.

Hope, Fr. Colin (CSWG). "True Vision with Praise." In *Panel of Monastic Musicians: Bulletin*, Advent 1991.

Hopko, Thomas. *The Lenten Spring*. Crestwood, NY: SVS Press, 1983.

———. *Monastic Elder and Parish Priest*. Crestwood, NY: SVS Press, nd. (pub. ref.: TH795A).

———. *Two "No's" and One "Yes": A Sermon in Memory of Father Alexander Schmemann*. SVTQ 28.1 (1984) 45–48. Reprinted: OTS 21 (1993) OTS 21 (1993).

Horgan, John. *The End of Science*. London: Little, Brown, 1996.

———. *The Undiscovered Mind: How the Brain Defies Explanation*. London: Weidenfeld and Nicolson, 1999.

Horner, G., ed. *The Statutes of the Apostles, or, Canones ecclesiastici*; I. London: Williams and Norgate, 1904.

Horsfall, Tony. *Working from a Place of Rest*. London: Bible Reading Fellowship, 2010.

Howison, G. H. *The Limits of Evolution*. 2nd ed. New York: MacMillan, 1905.

Huber, H. *Geist und Buchstabe der Sonntagsruhe*. Salzburg: Müller, 1958.

Hügel, Fiedrich von. *The Mystical Element of Religion as Studied in Catherine of Genoa and Her Friends*, 2 vols. London: Dent, 1908.

Hunter Blair, Peter. *The World of Bede*. London: Secker and Warburg, 1970.

Illingworth, R. J. *Personality—Human and Divine, Being the Bampton Lectures for 1894*. London: Macmillan, 1894.

Ingold, Tim. "Humanity and Animality." In *Companion Encyclopedia of Anthropology*, edited by T. Ingold, 14–32. London: Routledge, 1994.

Inwagen, Peter von. *God, Knowledge and Mystery.* Cornell: Cornell University Press, 1995.

Irwin, Terence. "Aristotle's Philosophy of Mind." In *Companions to Ancient Throught 2*, edited by Stephen Everson, 56–83, Cambridge: Cambridge University Press, 1991.

———. *Classical Philosophy.* Oxford: Oxford University Press, 1999.

———. *Classical Thought.* Oxford: Oxford University Press, 1987.

Jacobson, B. S. *The Sabbath Service: An Exposition of Its Structure, Contents, Language and Ideas.* Translated by Leonard Oschry. Tel Aviv: Sinai, 1981.

Jaffe, Nina. *Tales for the Seventh Day: A Collection of Sabbath Stories.* New York: Scholastic, 2000.

Jaubert, Annie. *La date de la cène.* Etudes bibliques. Paris: Gabalda, 1957.

Jenkins, David E. *The Glory of Man.* London: SCM, 1967.

———. *What is Man?* London: SCM, 1970.

Jeremias, J. *The Eucharistic Words of Jesus.* Translated by Norman Perrin. London: SCM, 1966. (From the German 3rd ed., 1964).

Jervell, Jacob. *Theology of the Acts of the Apostles.* Cambridge: Cambridge University Press, 1996.

Jewett, Paul K. *The Lord's Day: A Theological Guide to the Christian Day of Worship.* Grand Rapids: Eerdmans, 1971.

Johnson, A. R. *The One and the Many in the Israelite Conception of God.* Cardiff: University of Cardiff Press, 1942.

Jones, C. P. M., ed. *A Manual for Holy Week.* London: SPCK, 1967.

Jones, Cheslyn, Geoffrey Wainwright, Edward Yarnold (SJ), eds. *The Study of Liturgy.* London: SPCK, 1978.

Jones, Peter. *Ancient and Modern.* London: Duckworth, 1999.

Josipovici, Gabriel. *The Book of God: A Response to the Bible.* New Haven, CT: Yale University Press, 1988.

Jounel, Pierre. "Sunday and the Week." In *The Church at Prayer*, Vol. 4: *The Liturgy and Time*, edited by A. G. Martimort et al.; translated by Matthew J. O'Connell, 9–29. London: Chapman, 1986.

Joyce, Paul. "The Individual and the Community." In *Beginning Old Testament Study*, rev. ed., edited by John William Rogerson, 77–93. London: SPCK, 1998.

Jungmann J. A., SJ, "Beginnt die Christliche Woche mit Sonntag?" *ZKT* 55 (1931) 605–21

———. "Der liturgische Wochenzyklus." *ZKT* 9 (1957) 51–57.

———. *The Meaning of Sunday.* Translated by Clifford Howell, S.J. London: Challoner, 1961.

———. *Missarum Sollemnia* I. Wein: Herder, 1949.

———. *Pastoral Liturgy.* Translated by Ronald Walls. 1960. Reprint. London: Chaloner, 1962.

———. *The Place of Christ in Liturgical Prayer.* 2nd ed. Translated by A. Peeler. New York: Alba House, 1965.

Jurgens, William A. *The Faith of the Early Fathers*, Vol. 1. Collegeville, MN: Liturgical, 1970.

Kalaushofer, Alex. "Taylor-made Selves." *TMP* 12 (2000) 37–40.

Kant, Immanuel. *Groundwork of the Metaphysics of Morals* (1785), translated by H. J. Paton as *The Moral Law.* London: Hutchinson, 1956.

Kaplan, Aryeh. *Sabbath: Day of Eternity.* 2nd ed. New York: National Conference of Synagogue Youth/Union of Orthodox Jewish Congregations of America, 1982.

Katz, Elihu, et al. *The Secularization of Leisure: Culture and Communication in Israel.* London: Faber & Faber, 1976.

Katz, David S. *Sabbath and Sectarianism in Seventeenth-Century England.* Leiden: Brill, 1988.

Kavanagh, Aiden, et al. *Made, Not Born.* Notre Dame, IN: University of Notre Dame Press, 1976.

Keble, John. *Letters of Spiritual Counsel.* Oxford: Parker, 1870.

——, ed. *Works of that Learned and Divine, Mr Richard Hooker,* Vol. 1. Oxford: Clarendon, 1888.

Kelly, J. N. D. *Early Christian Doctrines.* 5th ed. London: Black, 1977.

Kerr, Fergus. *Theology After Wittgenstein.* Oxford: Blackwell, 1986.

Kohmiakov, A. S. *The Church is One.* 1864. Reprint. London: SPCK, 1948.

Kierkegaard, Søren. "The Ancient Tragical Motif as Reflected in the Modern." In *Either/Or,* translated by David F. Swenson and Lillian Marvin Swenson; revised by Howard A. Johnson. Princeton, NJ: Princeton University Press, 1971.

Kilby, Clyde. *The Christian World of C. S. Lewis.* Abingdon: Marcham, 1965.

Kiprian, Archimandrite. *Evkharistiya* (The Eucharist). Paris: YMCA, 1947.

Klaus, A. *Ursprung und Verbreitung der Driefaltigkeitmesse.* Werl: Franziskus-Dr., 1938.

Klawans, Jonathan. "Was Jesus' Last Supper a Seder?" *Bible Review,* October 2001, 24–33, 47.

Koenig, Adrio. *The Eclipse of Christ in Eschatology.* Grand Rapids: Eerdmans, 1997.

Kolektiv avtorov (= various). *Complete Collection of Decisions and Orders by the Office of the Orthodox Confession of the Russian Empire. November 6, 1796–March 11, 1801* (Russian edition, 2015). no loc: Book-on-Demand, ltd., 2015.

Kraabel, A. T. "Paganism and Judaism: The Sardis Evidence." In *Paganisme, Judaïsme, Christianisme: Influences et affrontements dans le monde antique. Melanges offerts à Marcel Simon,* edited by André Benoit et al., 13–34. Paris: Boccard, 1978.

Kraft, R. A. "Some Notes on Sabbath Observance in Early Christianity." *Andrews University Seminary Studies* 3.1 (1965) 18–33.

Krovocheine, Basil. "The Ascetical and Theological Teaching of Gregory Palamas." *ECQ* 4 (1938) 1–67.

Küng, Hans. *On Being a Christian.* London: Collins, 1977.

Ladd, George Eldon. *Jesus and the Kingdom.* Waco, TX: Word, 1964.

Laffont, R., ed. *Le Jour du Seigneur.* Paris: F-X le Roux, 1948.

Langford, Glenn. "The Concept of Education." In *New Essays in Philosophy of Education,* edited by Glen Langford and D. J. O'Connor, eds., 3–32. London: RKP, 1973.

——. *Philosophy and Education.* London: Macmillan, 1968.

——. "Reply to Adrian Thatcher." *JPE* 14.1 (1980) 129–36.

L'Arche. "Charter of the Communities of L'Arche." Reprinted in *An Ark for the Poor,* 117–20. London: Chapman, 1995.

Lash, Nicholas. "Friday, Saturday, Sunday" (The Aquinas Lecture given at Blackfriars 29 January 1990). *New Blackfriars* 29 (1990) 109–19.

——. *Theology on Dover Beach.* London: Darton, Longman and Todd, 1979.

Law, William. *A Serious Call to a Devout and Holy Life.* 1728. Reprint. London: Dent, 1967.

Lawson-Tancred, H., ed. *Aristotle, De Anima (On the Soul)*. Harmondsworth, UK: Penguin, 1986.

Leclercq, H. "La dévotion médiévale envers le crucifié." *LMD* 75 (1963) 119–32.

———. "Jours de la Semaine." *DACL* VII.2:2741–2.

Le Déaut, Roger. "Judaisme." *DS* 8:1517–18.

Lee, F. N. *The Covenental Sabbath*. London: Lord's Day Observance Society, 1969.

Leenhardt, F. J. *Le sacrement de la sante cène*. Neuchatel: Delachaux and Niestlé, 1948.

Lefebvre, M-T Louis. *Abbé Huvelin, Apostle of Paris*. Dublin: Clonmore and Reynolds, 1967.

Leon, H. J. *The Jews of Ancient Rome*. Philadelphia: Jewish Publication Society of America, 1961.

Leslau, Wolf. *Falascha Anthology*. 1951. New Haven, CT: Yale University Press 1987.

Lewy H, and J. Lewy. "The Origin of the Week in the Oldest West Asiatic Calendar." *HUCA* 17 (1942–43) 1–152.

Lewis, C. S. *The Allegory of Love*. 1936. Reprint. London: Oxford University Press, 1975.

———. *George Macdonald: An Anthology*. 1946. Reprint. London: Collins, 1983.

———. *Great Divorce*. London: Bles, 1946.

———. *Miracles*. 1960. Reprint. London: Fontana, 1967.

———. *Out of the Silent Planet*. London: Bodly Head, 1938.

———. *Pilgrim's Regress*. 1935. Reprint. London: Bles, 1943.

———. *A Preface to Paradise Lost*. 1942. Reprint. London: Oxford University Press, 1960.

———. *Surprised by Joy*. London: Bles, 1955.

———. "Weight of Glory." Reprinted in *Transpostion and Other Essays*. London: Bles, 1949.

Lewis, H. D. *The Elusive Mind*. London: Allen and Unwin, 1969.

Liddon, Henry Parry. *Life of Edward Bouverie Pusey*. London: Longmans, 1893–97.

Ligier, L. "From the Last Supper to the Eucharist." In *New Liturgy*, edited by Lancelot C. Sheppard, 113–25. London: DLT, 1970.

Ligier, L. "The Origins of the Eucharistic Prayer: from the Last Supper to the Eucharist." *SL* 9 (1973) 176–85.

Lincoln, Andrew T. "Sabbath, Rest, and Eschatology in the New Testament." In *From Sabbath to Lord's Day: A Biblical, Historical and Theological Investigation*, edited by D. A. Carson, 197–220. Grand Rapids: Zondervan, 1982.

———. "From Sabbath to Lord's Day: A Biblical Perspective." In *From Sabbath to Lord's Day: A Biblical, Historical and Theological Investigation*, edited by D. A. Carson, 343–412. Grand Rapids: Zondervan, 1982.

Longridge, W. H., ed. *Further Letters of Richard Meux Benson, Student of Christ Church, Founder and First Superior of the Society of St. John the Evangelist*. London: Mowbray, 1920.

Löser, Werner. *Im Geiste des Origenes: Hans Urs von Balthasar als Interpret der Theologies der Kirchenväte*. Frankfurt: Knecht, 1976.

Lossky, Vladimir. *In the Image and Likeness of God*. London: Mowbray, 1975. (French text 1967.)

———. *The Mystical Theology of the Eastern Church*. Cambridge: James Clarke, 1957. (French text 1944.)

———. *The Vision of God*. Translated by Ashleigh Moorhouse. London: Faith, 1963.

Lot-Borodine, M. *La Déification de l'homme selon la doctrine des pères grecs*. Paris: Cerf, 1970.

Louth, Andrew. "Manhood into God." In *Essays Catholic and Radical*, edited by K. Leech and R. D. Williams, 70–80. London: Bowerdean 1983.

———. *Maximus the Confessor*. London: Routledge, 1996.

———. *Modern Orthodox Thinkers*. London: SPCK, 2015.

———. *Theology and Spirituality*. Oxford: SLG Press, 1976.

———. *The Wilderness of God*. London: DLT, 1991.

Lovibond, Sabina. "Plato's Theory of Mind." In *Companions to Ancient Thought 2: Psychology*, edited by Stephen Everson, 35–55. Cambridge: Cambridge University Press, 1991.

Lowes, John Livingston. *Geoffrey Chaucer*. London: Oxford University Press, 1934.

Lucas, J. R. *The Freedom of the Will*. Oxford: Oxford University Press, 1970.

Luneau, A. *L'histoire du salut chez les Pères de l'Eglise. La doctrine des âges du monde*. Theologie historique, Vol. 2. Paris: Editions Beauchesne, 1964.

Lycan, W. G. *Consciousness*. Cambridge: MIT Press, 1987.

Maas, Wilhelm. *Gott und die Hölle: Studien zum Descendus Christi*. Einsiedelm: Johanes Verlag, 1979.

McArthur, A. A. *The Evolution of the Christian Year*. London: SCM, 1953.

McCasland, S. V. "The Origin of the Lord's Day." *JBL* 49 (1930) 65–82.

McClendon, James Wm. Jr., and Brad J. Kallenberg. "Ludwig Wittgenstein: A Christian in Philosophy." *SJT* 51.2 (1998) 131–61.

Macdonald, George. "The Child in the Midst." *Unspoken Sermons* Series I, Sermon 1. London: Straham, 1867.

———. *Unspoken Sermons*, Third Series (1889). Available at http://www.ccel.org/ccel/macdonald/unspoken3.pdf. Accessed July 2017.

McGuckin, J. A. *The Transfiguration of Christ in Scripture and Tradition*. Studies in the Bible and Early Christianity, 9: Lewiston, NY: Mellen, 1986.

McIntosh, Mark A. *Mystical Theology: The Integrity of Spirituality and Theology*. Oxford: Blackwell, 1998.

McIntyre, John. *The Christian Doctrine of History*. Edinburgh: Oliver and Boyd, 1957.

MacIntyre, Alasdair. *After Virtue: A Study in Moral Theory*. 2nd ed. London: Duckworth, 1985.

———. *Three Rival Versions of Moral Enquiry*. London: Duckworth, 1990.

———. *Whose Justice? Which Rationality?* London: Duckworth, 1988.

Mackinnon, D. M. "Aristotle's Conception of Substance." In *New Essays on Plato and Aristotle*, edited by Renford Bambrough, 97–119. London: Routledge and Kegan Paul, 1965.

Macquarrie, John. *Mary for All Christians*. London: Collins, 1991.

———. *Twentieth-Century Religious Thought*. 2nd ed. London: SCM, 1971.

Macmurray, John. *Persons in Relationship*. 1961. Reprint. London: Faber, 1995.

———. *The Self as Agent*. 1957. Reprint. London: Faber, 1995.

Maguire, Henry. *The Icons of their Bodies: Saints and the Images in Byzantium*. Princeton, NJ: Princeton University Press, 1996.

Maimonides, Moses. *The Guide for the Perplexed*. Translated by M. Friedländer. New York: Dutton, 1910.

Mantzaridis, Georgios I. *The Deification of Man: St Gregory Palamas and the Orthodox Tradition*. Translated by Liadain Sherrard. Crestwood, NY: SVS Press, 1984.

————. *Orthodox Spiritual Life*. Brookline, MA: Holy Cross Orthodox Press, 1994.

Manzarides, Georgios I. (=Mantzaridis Georgios I.). *Time and Man*. South Canaan, PA: St Tikhon's Seminary Press, 1996.

Markus, Robert. *The End of Ancient Christianity*. 1990. Reprint. Cambridge: Cambridge University Press, 1999.

Marechal, Joseph. *The Psychology of the Mystics*. London: Burns, Oates & Washbourne, 1927.

Mareschi, Giovanni. *La histologia di Hans Urs von Balthasar: La figura di Gesù Cristo espressione visibile di Dio*. Rome: Università Gregoriana Editrice, 1977.

Mateos, J. "The Origins of the Divine Office." *Worship* 41 (1967) 477–85.

Marthaler, Berard. "Socialization as a Model for Catechesis." In *Foundations of Religious Education*, edited by Patraic O'Hare, 64–92. New York: Paulist, 1978.

Marthaler, Berard L. "The Date of Easter, Anno Domini, and Other Calendar Considerations: Chronology or Eschatology?" *Worship* 73 (1999) 194–211.

Martimort, A. G., I. H. Dalmais, and P. Jounel. *The Church at Prayer*, vol. 4: *The Liturgy and Time*. Translated by Matthew J. O'Connell. London: Chapman, 1986.

Maritain, Jacques. *The Person and the Common Good*. Translated by J. J. Fitzgerald. 1946. Reprint. Notre Dame, IN: University of Notre Dame Press, 1966.

Martin, David. *A General Theory of Secularization*. Oxford: Blackwell, 1978.

Marrou, Henri I. *A History of Education in Antiquity*. Translated by George Lambe. New York: Sheed and Ward, 1956.

Mascall, E. L., ed. *The Church of God*. London: SPCK, 1934.

————. *The Openness of Being*. London: DLT, 1971.

————. *Words and Images: A Study in the Possibility of Religious Discourse*. London: DLT, 1957.

Matthew the Poor (Mattá al-Miskin). *The Communion of Love*. Crestwood, NY: 1984.

Maurice, F. D. *Doctrine of Sacrifice Deduced from the Scriptures*. London: Macmillan, 1893.

May, Gerhard. *Creatio ex Nihilo, the Doctrine of "Creation out of Nothing" in Early Christian Thought*. Translated by A. S. Worall. Edinburgh: T. & T. Clark, 1994. (German text, 1976.)

Meeks, Wayne. *The First Urban Christians*. New Haven, CT: Yale University Press, 1983.

————. *The Moral World of the First Christians*. London: SPCK, 1987.

Mercenier, P. F., and F. Paris. *La Prière des Eglises de rite Byzantine*, II/1. Amey-sur-Meuse: Chevetogne, 1939.

Mersch, E. *Le Corps Mystique du Christ, Etudes de Théologie Historique*. Louvain: Museum Lessianum, 1933.

Meyendorff, John. *Byzantine Theology: Historical Trends and Doctrinal Themes*. Oxford: Mowbray, 1974.

————. *Christ in Eastern Christian Thought*. 1975. Reprint. Crestwood, NY: SVS Press, 1987.

————. "A Life Worth Living." *SVTQ* 28.1 (1988) 3–10.

————. *Marriage, An Orthodox Perspective*. Crestwood, NY: SVS Press, 1970.

————. *A Study of Gregory Palamas*. London: Faith, 1964. (French text, 1959.)

————. "The Synthesis of Faith and Practice: The Time of Holy Saturday." In *Orthodox Synthesis, the Unity of Theological Thought*, edited by Joseph J. Allen, 51–63. Crestwood, NY: SVS Press, 1981.

————. "Theosis in the Eastern Christian Tradition." SCMCS III, 470–76.

Michels, Agnes Kirsopp. *The Calendar of the Roman Republic*. Westport, CT: Greenwood, 1967.

Middleton, Judy. *Brunswick Town*. Private publication, 2001.

———. *Hove Encyclopedia*. Private publication, 2000–.

Milis, Ludo. *Angelic Monks and Earthly Men*. Woodbridge, UK: Boydell, 1992.

Millgram, Abraham E., ed. *Sabbath: The Day of Delight*. Philadelphia: Jewish Publication Society of America, 1944.

Minns, Denis (OP). *Irenaeus*. London: Chapman, 1994.

Mitchell, Basil. "Reflections on C. S. Lewis, Apologetics and the Moral Tradition." In *A Christian for All Christians*, edited by Andrew Walker and J. Patrick, 7–26. London: Hodder and Stoughton, 1990.

Moberly, R. C. *Atonement and Personality*. London: John Murray, 1901.

Moltmann, Jürgen. *God in Creation*. London: SCM, 1985.

Montefiore, Hugh W. *The Epistle to the Hebrews*. London: Black, 1964.

Moore, Achimandrite Lazarus, trans. *John Climacus: The Ladder of Divine Ascent*. London: Faber & Faber, 1959.

Moore, Achimandrite Lazarus. *St Seraphim of Sarov*. Blanco, TX: New Sarov, 1994.

Moore, G. F. *Judaism*. 3 vols. Cambridge: Harvard University Press, 1927.

Morgan, Robert. "Biblical Theology." In *Dictionary of Biblical Interpretation*, edited by R. J. Coggins and J. L. Houlden, 86–89. London: SCM, 1990.

Morris, Brian. *Anthropological Studies of Religion*. Cambridge: Cambridge University Press, 1987.

———. *Anthropology of the Self*. London: Pluto, 1994.

———. *Western Conceptions of the Individual*. Oxford: Berg, 1991.

Morris, Colin. *The Discovery of the Individual: 1050–1200*. London: Harper and Row, 1972.

Mounier, E. *A Personalist Manifesto*. Translated by monks of St John's Abbey. London: Longmans, 1938. (French text 1936.)

Murdoch, Iris. *The Sovereignty of Good*. London: Routledge and Kegan Paul, 1970.

Mursell, Gordon. *The Story of Spirituality: Two Thousand Years from East to West*. London: Lion, 2001.

Muckle, J. T. "The Doctrine of St. Gregory of Nyssa on Man as the Image of God." *Mediaeval Studies* 7 (1945) 55–84.

Musther, John. "'Exploration into God': An Examination." In *Orthodoxy and the Death of God*, edited by A. M. Allchin, 57–77. London: Fellowship of St Alban and St Sergius, 1971.

Nellas, Panayiotis. *Deification in Christ: Orthodox Perspectives on the Nature of the Human Person*. Translated by Norman Russell. Crestwood, NY: SVS Press, 1987.

Neusner, Jacob. *A History of the Jews in Babylonia*. 5 vols. Leiden: Brill, 1966–70.

———. *The Mishna*. New Haven, CT: Yale University Press, 1988.

Newbigin, L. *The Other Side of 84*. London: BBC Publications, 1983.

Newman, L. I. *Hasidic Anthology*, 2nd ed. New York: Schocken Books, 1963.

———. *Talmudic Anthology: Tales and Teachings of the Rabbis*. New York: Behrman House, 1945.

Newman, John Henry. *The Idea of a University, defined and illustrated in nine discourses delivered to the Catholics of Dublin in occasional lectures and essays addressed to the members of the Catholic University*. 1852. Edited by Martin J. Svaglic. Notre Dame, IN: Notre Dame Press, 1980.

Nichols, Aidan. *Theology in the Russian Diaspora. Church, Fathers, Eucharist in Nikolai Afansèv, 1893-1966.* Cambridge: Cambridge University Press, 1989.

————. *Light from the East.* London: Sheed & Ward, 1995.

Nicholson, Kelly. *Body and Soul, the Transcendence of Materialism.* London: Routledge, 1997.

Nillson, N. M. P. *Primitive Time Reckoning.* Lund: Gleerup, 1920.

Nowell, Irene. "Purity of Heart in the Old Testament." In *Purity of Heart in Early Ascetic and Monastic Literature: Essays in Honour of Juana Raasch, OSB,* edited by Harriet Luckman, 17-30. Collegeville, MN: Liturgical, 1999.

O'Brian, Thomas Charles, ed. *Documents on the Liturgy, 1963-1979—Conciliar, Papal, and Curial Texts.* International Commission on English in the Liturgy. Collegeville, MN: Liturgical, c. 1982.

O'Donnell, J. *Hans Urs von Balthasar.* London: Chapman, 1992.

Oesterley, W. O. E. *The Jewish Background of the Christian Liturgy.* Oxford: Oxford University Press, 1925.

Osborne, Basil (Bishop Basil [Osborne] of Segeivo). *The Light of Christ: Sermons for the Great Fast.* Witney, UK: St. Stephen's Press, 1992.

————. "Living in the Future." In *Living Orthodoxy in the Modern World,* edited by Andrew Walker and Costa Carras, 23-36. London: SPCK, 1996.

Ouspensky, Leonid. *Theology of the Icon,* Vol. I. Translated by Anthony Gythiel. Crestwood, NY: SVS Press, 1978.

————. *Theology of the Icon,* Vol. II. Translated by Anthony Gythiel. Crestwood, NY: SVS Press, 1992.

Ouspensky, Leonid, and Vladimir Lossky. *The Meaning of Icons.* 1952. Reprint. Crestwood, NY: SVS Press, 1982.

Pahn, P. C. *Eternity in Time—A Study of Karl Rahner's Eschatology.* Selinsgrove, PA: Susquehanna University Press, 1988.

Parfit, Derek. *Reasons and Persons.* Oxford: Clarendon, 1984.

Parker, Richard A. "The Calendars and Chronology." In *The Legacy of Egypt,* edited by J. R. Harris, 13-26. Oxford: Clarendon, 1971.

Parker Kenneth L. *The English Sabbath: A Study of Doctrine and Discipline from the Reformation to the Civil War.* Cambridge: Cambridge University Press, 1988.

Parry, Abbot, OSB, *The Rule of St Benedict.* Leominster, UK: Gracewing, 1990.

Paton, H. J., trans. *The Moral Law.* A translation of I. Kant, *Groundwork of the Metaphysics of Morals* (1785). London: Hutchinson, 1956.

Peacock, A. R., and G. Gillet, eds. *Persons and Personality: A Contemporary Enquiry.* Oxford: Blackwell, 1987.

Peers, Richard. "Schools of Prayer: The Renewal of the Liturgy of the Hours in Three Monasteries." BA diss., University of Southampton, 1993.

Pelikan, J. *Christianity and Classical Culture.* New Haven, CT: Yale University Press, 1993.

Perrin, Norman. *Jesus and the Language of the Kingdom.* Philadelphia: Fortress, 1976.

Philaret of Moscow, *Oraisons funèbres, homélies et discours.* French translation by A. de Stourdza, Paris: Cherbuliez Librarire, 1849.

Philip, Abraham. "Theology of the Anaphora of St James." In *A Study on the Malankara Mar Thoma Church Liturgy,* edited by M.V. Abraham et al. Manganam, Kottayam, India: Thomas Mar Athanasius Orientation Centre, 1993.

Pickering, W. S. F. "Anglo-Catholicism: Some Sociological Observations." In *Tradition Renewed: The Oxford Movement Conference Papers*, edited by Geoffrey Rowell, 153–72. Allison Park, PA: Pickwick, 1986.

Pingault, P. *Renouveau de L'Eglise: Les Communautés Nouvelles*. Tournai: Le Sarment/ Feyard, 1989.

Plantinga, Alvin. *Does God Have a Nature?* Milwaukee: Marquette University Press, 1980.

Plass, Paul. "Timeless Time in Neo-Platonism." *The Modern Schoolman* 55 (1977) 1–59.

———. "Transcendent Time in Maximus the Confessor." *The Thomist* (1980) 259–77.

Plekon, Michael. "The Church, the Eucharist and the Kingdom: Towards an Assessment of Alexander Schmemann's Theological Legacy." *SVTQ* 40 (1996) 119–43.

———. "Review Essay: Russian Theology and Theologians Revisited." *SVTQ* 45 (2001) 409–19.

Pole, J. *Au Coeur des Villes*. Paris: Éditions Saint-Paul, 1987.

Pomazansky, Michael. "The Liturgical Theology of Father A. Schmemann." Reprinted in *Selected Essays by Michael Pomazansky*, 82–102. Jordanville, NY: Holy Trinity Monastery, 1996. http://orthodoxinfo.com/phronema/pom_lit.aspx. Accessed July 2017.

Porter, H. B. *Sunday: The Day of Light*. Greenwich, CT: Seabury, 1960.

Prejean, Helen. *Dead Men Walking*. New York: Random House, 1993.

———. "Giving in to Life." *The Plough Reader*, Summer 2001, 16–18.

Prestige, G. L. *God in Patristic Thought*. 1937. Reprint. London: SPCK, 1964.

———. "*Perichōréō* and *perichōrēsis'* in the Fathers." *JTS* 29 (1928) 242–52.

Putnam, Hilary. *Representation and Reality*. Cambridge: MIT, 1988.

Rad, Gerhard von. "There Remains Still a Rest for the People of God." In *The Problems of the Hexateuch and Other Essays*, translated by E. W. Trueman Dicken, 94–102. Edinburgh: Oliver and Boyd, 1966. (German text 1958.)

Rahner, Karl. *On the Theology of Death. Questiones Disputatae*, 2. 2nd ed. London: Burns and Oates, 1965.

———. *Teaching of the Catholic Church*. New York: Alba House, 1975.

———. *The Trinity*. Translated by J. Donceel. London: Burns & Oats, 1969.

Raitt; J., Bernard McGinn, John Meyendorff, eds. *Christian Spirituality: High Middle Ages and Reformation*. London: Routledge and Kegan Paul, 1987.

Ramsey, Michael. *Jesus and the Living Past*. Oxford: Oxford University Press, 1980.

Ratzinger, Joseph. "Abschied vom Teufel." In *Dogma und Verkündigung*, Donauwörth: Erick Wewel Verlag, 1973, 225–34. English translation "Farewell to the Devil." In *Dogma and Preaching: Applying Christian Doctrine to Daily Life*, translated (from the 4th ed.) by Michael J. Miller and Matthew O'Connell; edited by Michael J. Miller, 197–205. San Francisco CA: Ignatius, 2011.

Regan, F. A. *Dies dominica and Dies solis: The Beginning of the Lord's Day in Christian Antiquity*. Washington, DC: Catholic University of America Press 1961.

Regan, P. "Pneumatological and Eschatological Aspects of Liturgical Celebration." *Worship* 51 (1977) 346–47.

Regnault, Lucien. *The Day to Day Life of the Desert Fathers in Fourth-Century Egypt*. Translated by Étienne Poirier Jr. Petersham, MA: St Bede's, 1999.

Régnon, Théodore de. *Etudes de théologie positive sur la Sante Trinité*, 4 vols. Paris: Victor Retaux, vols I and II, 1892; II and IV, 1898. Reprinted London: Forgotten Books, 2017.

Richards, E. G. *Mapping Time: The Calendar and Its History*. Oxford: Oxford University Press, 1998.

Ricoeur, Paul. "The Model of the Text: Meaningful Action Considered as Text." In *Hermeneutics and the Human Sciences*, edited and translated by J. B. Thompson, 197–221. Cambridge: Cambridge University Press, 1981.

Riesenfeld, H. "Sabbat et jour du Seigneur." In *NT Essays. Studies in Memory of T. W. Manson*, edited by Angus J. B. Higgins, 210–18. Manchester: Manchester University Press: 1959.

Riley, H. M. 1974, *Christian Initiation*. Washington, DC: The Catholic University of America, 1974.

Rist, J. M. *Eros and Psyche: Studies in Plato, Plotinus and Origen*. Toronto: University of Toronto Press, 1964.

Robinson, Gnana. *The Origin and Development of the Old Testament Sabbath: A Comprehensive Exegetical Approach*. New York: Lang, 1988.

Robinson, H. Wheeler. *The Christian Experience of the Holy Spirit*. 1928. Reprint. London: Collins Fontana 1980.

———. "The Hebrew Conception of Corporate Personality." In *Werden und Wesen des Alten Testaments*, edited by Paul Volz, Friederich Stummer, and Johannes, 49–62. Hempel Beiheft zur Zeitschrift fur die Alttestamentliche Wissenschaft 66. 1936. Rev. ed. *Corporate Personality in Ancient Israel*. Philadelphia: Fortress, 1980.

Rodd, Cyril S. *Foundation Documents of the Faith*. Edinburgh: T. & T. Clark, 1987.

Rogerson, John William. "The Hebrew Conception of Corporate Personality." *JTS* 21 (1970) 1–16.

Royall, Arthur. *Gilbert Shaw and The Sidney*. http://www.royall.co.uk/royall/gilbert-shaw-sidney.htm, May 2000. (Accessed July 2017.)

Rordorf, Willy. "Sabbath." In *EECh* 748.

———. *Sabbat et Dimanche dans l'Eglise ancienne*. Translated by E. Visinand, and W. Nussbaum. Neuchâtel: Delachaux et Niestlé Éditeurs, 1972.

———. "Sunday: The Fulness of Christian Liturgical Time." *SL* 14 (1982) 90–96.

———. *Sunday: The History of the Day of Rest and Worship in the Earliest Centuries of the Church*. SCM: London, 1968. (German text, 1962.)

Rorty, Richard. *Truth and Progress: Philosophical Papers*, Vol. 3. Cambridge: Cambridge University Press, 1998.

Roscher, W. H. *Die enneadischen und hebdomadischen Fristen und Wochen der ältesten Griechen*. Leipzig: Teubner, 1903.

Rousseau, Olivier. *The Progress of the Liturgy*. Westminster, MD: Newman, 1951.

Rowell, Geoffrey. *The Vision Glorious: Themes and Personalities of the Catholic Revival in Anglicanism*. Oxford: Oxford University Press, 1983.

Rowland, C. "A Summary of Sabbath Observance in Judaism at the Beginning of the Christian Era." In *From Sabbath to Lord's Day: A Biblical, Historical and Theological Investigation*, edited by D. A. Carson, 43–55. Grand Rapids: Zondervan, 1982.

Russell, D. S. *Between the Testaments*. London: SCM, 1960.

———. *From Early Judaism to Early Church*. London: SCM, 1986.

Russell, Norman, trans. *The Lives of the Desert Fathers: The History of the Monks of Egypt*. Kalamazoo, MI: Cistercian, 1981.

Ryle, Gilbert. *Concept of Mind*. London: Hutchinson, 1949.

Sacks, Jonathan. *Faith in the Future*. London: DLT, 1995.

Saggs, W. H. F. *The Encounter with the Divine in Mesopotamia and Israel.* London: Athlone, 1978.

Salardini, Anthony J. *Matthew's Christian-Jewish Community.* Chicago: Chicago University Press, 1994.

Sampson, Philip, Vinay Samuel, and Chris Sugden, eds. *Faith and Modernity.* Oxford: Regnum, 1994.

Sanders, E. P. *Paul and Palestinian Judaism.* London: SCM, 1977.

Sarna, Nahum M. *Exodus: Shemot: The Traditional Hebrew Text with the New Jewish Publications Society Translation.* Philadelphia: Jewish Publications Society, 1991.

———. *Exploring Exodus: The Heritage of Biblical Israel.* New York: Shocken, 1986.

———. *Genesis: Be-Reshit: The Traditional Hebrew Text with New Jewish Publications Society Translation.* Philadelphia: Jewish Publications Society, 1994.

———. *Understanding Genesis.* 1966. Reprint. Shocken: NY, 1970.

Saward, John. *The Mysteries of March.* London: Collins, 1990.

———. *Perfect Fools. Folly for Christ's Sake in Catholic and Orthodox Spirituality.* Oxford: Oxford University Press, 1980.

Saxby, Harold. "The Time-Scheme in the Gospel of John." *Expository Times* 14.1 (1992) 9–13.

Sayre, Patricia. "Personalism." In *A Companion to Philosophy of Religion,* edited by Philip L. Quinn and Charles Taliaferro, 151–58. Oxford: Blackwell, 1997.

Seters, J. van. *In Search of History.* New Haven, CT: Yale University Press, 1983.

Schoedel, William R. *Ignatius of Antioch.* Philadelphia: Fortress, 1985.

Schmemann, Alexander. "Address to the Convention of the Antiochian Archdiocese of North America," *Sourozh* 15 (1983) 23–27.

———. *The Celebration of Faith: I Believe.* Sermons, Vol. 1. Translated by John J. Jillions. Crestwood, NY: SVS Press, 1991.

———. *Church, World and Mission.* Crestwood, NY: SVS Press, 1979.

———. *The Eucharist, Sacrament of the Kingdom.* Crestwood, NY: SVS Press, 1988.

———. "Final Sermon." In *The Orthodox Church,* 20.2 (1984). http://www.schmemann. org/byhim/thankyoulord.html. (Accessed July 2017.)

———. *For the Life of the World: Sacraments and Orthodoxy.* 1965. Reprint. Crestwood, NY: SVS Press, 1988.

———. *Great Lent.* 1969. Reprint. Crestwood, NY: SVS Press, 1974.

———. *The Historical Road of Eastern Orthodoxy.* Translated by Lydia W. Kesich. London: Harvill, 1963.

———. "Holy Things for the Holy: Some Remarks on Receiving Holy Communion," printed as an appendix in Schmemann, *Great Lent* (1974 ed.), 107–33.

———. *Holy Week: A Liturgical Explanation for the Days of Holy Week.* 1971. Reprint. New York: OCA, 1979.

———. *Introduction to Liturgical Theology,* 2nd ed. Translated by Ashleigh Moorhouse. London: Faith, 1975. (Russian text 1960.)

———. *The Journals of Father Alexander Schmemann, 1973–1983* Translated and edited by Julia Schmemann. Crestwood, NY: SVS Press, 2000.

———. "Liturgical Theology: Its Tasks and Method." *SVTQ* 1.4 (1957) 16–27.

———. *Liturgy and Life: Lectures and Essays on Christian Development through Liturgical Experience.* New York: Department of Religious Education, Orthodox Church in America, 1974.

————. "Liturgy and Theology," *The Greek Orthodox Theological Review* 17 (1972) 86–100. (Reprinted in Schmemann, *Liturgy and Tradition*, 49–68.)

————. *Liturgy and Tradition*. Edited by Thomas Fisch. Crestwood, NY: SVS Press, 1990.

————. "The Problems of the Orthodox Church in America: II. The Liturgical Problem," *SVTQ* 8.4 (1964) 166–85.

————. "The Problems of the Orthodox Church in America: III. The Spiritual Problem," *SVTQ* 9.4 (1965) 175–86.

————. "Two 'Nos' and One 'Yes'." *SVTQ* 28.1 (1984) 45–48.

School of Moscow. Milan: La Casa di Matriona, 1987. (Anon.)

Schreiber, V. G. *Gemeinschaften des Mittelalters*. Munster: Regensburg, 1948.

Schroeder, Paul. "Suffering towards Personhood: John Zizioulas and Fyodor Dostoevsky in Conversation on Freedom and the Human Person." *SVTQ* 45.3 (2001) 243–64.

Schultz, Hans-Joachim. *The Byzantine Liturgy: Symbolic Structure and Faith Expression*. Translated by M. J. O'Connell. New York: Pueblo, 1986.

Schürer, Emil. "Die siebentägige Woche in Gebrauch der christlichen Kirche der ersten Jahrhunderte." *ZNW* 6 (1905) 1–66.

————. *History of the Jewish People in the Age of Jesus Christ (175bc–ad135)*. Translated by Géza Vermès and Fergus Millar; organizing editor Matthew Black. 2 vols. Rev. ed. Edinburgh: T. & T. Clark, Vol. I, 1973, and Vol. II, 1979.

Schwöbel, Christoph, and Colin E. Gunton, eds. *Persons Human and Divine: King's College Essays in Theological Anthropology*. Edinburgh: T. & T. Clark, 1991.

Schwöbel, Christoph. "Human Being as Relational Being: Twelve Theses for a Christian Anthropology." In *Persons Human and Divine*, 141–65. Edinburgh: T. & T. Clark, 1991.

Scorer, P. "Alexander Schmemann (1921–83)." Sobornost 6.2 (1984) 64–68.

Searle, John. *Mind, Language and Society: Philosophy in the Real World*. London: Weidenfeld and Nicholson, 1999.

Searle, M. "The Journey of Conversion." *Worship* 54 (1980) 35–55.

————. "Liturgy as Metaphor." *Worship* 55 (1981) 98–120.

Seters, J. van. *In Search of History*. New Haven, CT: Yale University Press, 1983.

Sharf, Andrew, "The Eighth Day of the Week." In *Kathegetria: Essays Presented to Joan Hussey*, edited by J. Chrysostomides, 27–50. Porphyrogenitus, 1988.

Shaw, Gilbert. "Father William S.D.C. of Glasshampton." *Sobornost* (old series) 6.5 (1967) 324–32.

Shepherd, Massey Hamilton, ed. *The Eucharist and Liturgical Renewal*. Oxford: Oxford University Press, 1960.

Sheppard, L. ed. *The New Liturgy*. London: DLT, 1970.

Sheredega, Natalya. "Andrei Rublev: Image of the Holy Trinity." *Tretyakov Magazine*, 3.40, 2013, article 2. http://www.tretyakovgallerymagazine.com/articles/%E2%84%963-2013-40/andrei-rublev-image-holy-trinity. (Accessed July 2017.)

Sherwood, Dom Polycarp (OSB). *The Earlier Ambigua of Saint Maximus the Confessor and His Refutation of Origenism*. Rome: Herder, 1955.

————. ed., *St. Maximus the Confessor: The Ascetic Life. The Four Centuries on Charity*. ACW 21. London: Longmans, 1955.

Shoumantoff, Alex, *The Mountain of Names: A History of the Human Family*. 1985. Reprint. New York: Kondasha, 1995.

Simon, M. *Versus Israel: A Study in the Relations Between Christians and Jews in the Roman Empire (135–425)*. Oxford: Oxford University Press, 1986.

Singer, S. trans., *The Authorized Daily Prayer Book of the United Hebrew Congregation of the British Commonwealth of Nations*. 1890. 2nd ed. London: Eyre & Spottiswoode, 1962.

Sirr, Fr William, SDC. *Whatchman, What of the Night?* Published anonymously. London: Mowbray, 1935.

Sittser, Gerald L. *A Grace Disguised: How the Soul Grows through Loss*. London: Hodder and Stoughton, 1996.

Smallwood, E. Mary. *The Jews under Roman Rule, from Pompey to Diocletian*. Leiden: Brill, 1981.

Solberg, Winton U. *Redeem the Time: The Puritan Sabbath in Early America*. Cambridge: Harvard University Press, 1977.

Solzhenitsyn, Alexander. *The Gulag Arcipelago* 2 (Parts III–IV). Translated by Thomas P. Whitney. London: Collins/Fontana, 1975.

Sophrony (Sakarov), Archimandrite. *His Life is Mine*. Oxford: Mowbray, 1977.

———. *On Prayer*. Tolleshunt Knights, UK: Stavropegic Monastery of St John the Baptist, 1996.

———. *Saint Silouan the Athonite*. Tolleshunt Knights, UK: Stavropegic Monastery of St John the Baptist, 1991.

———. "The Unity of the Church in the Image of the Trinity: Orthodox Doctrine of the Trinity as the Basis of the Doctrine of the Church." This undated cyclostyled text corresponds to the French text: "Unité de l'église à l'image de la Sainte Trinité: Triadologue Orthodoxe comme principe de l'ecclésiologie." In *La félicité de connaître la voie*, 11–55. Genève; Labor et Fides, 1988.

———. *Wisdom from Mount Athos*. Oxford: Mowbray, 1974.

Sorabji, Richard. "Soul and Self in Ancient Philosophy." In *From Soul to Self*, edited by M. James C. Crabbe, 8–32. London: Routledge, 1999.

———. *Time, Creation and the Continuum*. London: Duckworth, 1983.

Spalding, A. W. *Origin and History of the Seventh-day Adventists*. 4 vols. Washington, DC, 1961–62.

Spink, Katherine. *Mother Teresa*. London: HarperCollins, 1997.

SSM: Sister Gabriel and Sisters of St Margaret's Convent. *Doing the Impossible, A Short Sketch of St Margaret's Convent East Grinstead 1855–1980*. Published privately, 1984.

Stacey, David. *The Pauline View of Man*. London: Macmillan, 1956.

Stambaugh, John, and David Balch. *The Social World of the First Christians*. London: SPCK, 1986.

Staniloae, Dumitru. *Eternity and Time*. Oxford: SLG Press, 2001.

———. *The Experience of God*, Vol. 1: *Revelation and Knowledge of God*. Translated and edited by Ioan Ionita and Robert Barringer. Brookline, MA: Holy Cross Orthodox Press, 1994.

———. *The Experience of God*, Vol. 2: *The World: Creation and Deification*. Translated and edited by Ioan Ionita and Robert Barringer. Brookline, MA: Holy Cross Orthodox Press, 2000.

———. *The Victory of the Cross*. Oxford: Fairacres, 1970.

Statman, Daniel, ed. *Virtue Ethics: A Critical Reader*. Edinburgh: Edinburgh University Press, 1997.

Stein, M. *Greek and Latin Authors on Jews and Judaism*, Vol. 1: *From Heroditus to Plutarch*. Jerusalem: Israel Academy of Sciences and Humanities, 1976.

Stern, H. *Le calendrier de 354*. Institut Français de Beyrouth, Bibliothèque archeologique et historique 55; Paris: Geuthner, 1953.

Stevens, Richard, ed. *Understadning the Self*. London: Sage, 1996.

Stramara, Daniel F. Jr. "Gregory of Nyssa's Terminology for Trinitarian Perichoresis." *Vigiliae Christianae* 52.3 (1998) 257–63.

Strawson, P. F. *Individuals: An Essay in Descriptive Metaphysics*. 1959. Reprint. London: Methune, 1964.

Storkey, Elaine. "Modernity and Anthropology." In *Faith and Modernity*, edited by P. Sampson et al., 136–50, Oxford: Regnum, 1994.

Sunday Missal 1975. *The Sunday Missal*. London: Collins, 1975.

Swartley, Willard M. *Slavery, Sabbath, War and Women: Case Issues in Biblical Interpretation*. Scottdale, PA: Herald, 1983.

Swinburne, Richard. "Body and Soul." In *The Mind-Body Problem*, edited by Richard Warner and Tadeusz Szubka, 311–16. Oxford: Blackwell, 1984.

———. *The Evolution of the Soul*. Oxford: Clarendon, 1986.

Taft, Robert (SJ). "Historicism Revisited." In *Liturgical Time: Papers Read at the 1981 Congress of Societas Liturgica*, edited by W. Vos and G. Wainwright. Rotterdam: Liturgical Ecumenical Centre Trust, 1982 = *SL* 14 (1982) 97–109.

———. *The Liturgy of the Hours in East and West*. Collegeville, MN: Liturgical, 1986.

———. "The Liturgical Year: Studies, Prospects, Reflections." *Worship*, 1981, 2–23.

———. *Problems in Liturgical Understanding*. Washington, DC: Pastoral, 1984.

Talley, Thomas J. "The Eucharistic Prayer of the Ancient Church According to Recent Research: Results and Reflections." *SL* 11 (1976) 138–58.

———. *The Origins of the Liturgical Year*. New York: Pueblo, 1986.

———. *Worship: Reforming Tradition*. Washington, DC: Pastoral, 1990.

Taylor, Charles. *A Secular Age*. Cambridge: Harvard University Press, 2007.

———. *Sources of the Self: The Making of the Modern Identity*. Cambridge: Cambridge University Press, 1989.

Thatcher, Adrian. "Christian Theism and the Concept of a Person." In *Persons and Personality: A Contemporary Enquiry*, edited by A. R. Peacock and G. Gillet, 180–90. Oxford: Blackwell, 1987.

———. "Education and the Concept of a Person." *JPE* 14.1 (1980) 117–29.

———. "Learning to Become Persons—A Theological Approach to Educational Aims." *SJT* 36 (1983) 521–33.

———. "The Recovery of Christian Education." In *Christian Perspectives for Education: a Reader in the Theology of Education*, edited by L. J. Francis and A. Thatcher, 273–81. Leominster, UK: Fowler Wright, 1990.

———. *Truly a Person, Truly God*. London: SPCK, 1990.

Thekla, Sister, ed. *Mother Maria, Her Life in Letters*. London: DLT, 1979.

Thibaut, J-B. *Ordre des Offices de la Semaine Sainte à Jérusalem du IVe au Xe siècle*. Paris: Maison de la Bonne Presse, 1926.

Thorndike, Herbert. *The Theological Works of Herbert Thorndike, 1598–1672*, Vol. 5, Oxford: Parker, 1854. https://archive.org/details/thetheologicalwo05thoruoft. (Accessed July 2017.)

Thornton, L. S. *Richard Hooker: A Study of His Theology*. London, SPCK, 1924.

Thunberg, L. *Man and the Cosmos*. Crestwood, NY: SVS Press, 1985.

————. *Microcosm and Mediator: The Theological Anthropology of Maximus the Confessor*. Lund: Gleerup, 1965.

Thurian, M. *The Eucharistic Memorial*, Part I, The Old Testament. London: Lutterworth, 1960.

————. *The Eucharistic Memorial*, Part II, The New Testament. London: Lutterworth, 1961.

Tillich, Paul. *Systematic Theology*, Vol. 3. Welwyn, UK: Nisbet , 1964.

Tkachuk, John."Love from Knowledge: An Introduction to Father Pavel Florensky." *SVTQ* 45 (2001) 329–42.

Trianosky, Gegory Velazco y. "What Is Virtue Ethics?" In *Virtue Ethic*, edited by Daniel Statman, 42–55. Edinburgh: Edinburgh University Press, 1997.

Trochu, Francis. *The Curé d'Ars, Jean-Marie-Baptiste Vianney (1786–1859)*. 2nd ed. Translated by Buckfast Abbey. 1930. Reprint. London: Burns and Oates, 1977.

Trubetskoi, Eugene N. *Icons: Theology in Color*. Translated by Getrude Vakar. New York: St. Vladimir Press, 1973.(Russian text, 1915–16.)

Tugwell, Simon. *The Apostolic Fathers*. London: Chapman, 1989.

Turner, Max. M. B. "The Sabbath, Sunday and the Law in the Pauline Epistles." In *From Sabbath to Lord's Day*, edited by D. A. Carson, 99-157. Grand Rapids: Zondervan, 1982.

Tyrer, J. W. *Historical Survey of Holy Week: Its Services and Ceremonial*. Alcuin Club Collections xxix. Oxford: Oxford University Press, 1932.

Unesco. *Cultures and Time* (no editor named). Paris: Unesco, 1976.

Uspensky, Nicholas. *The Evening Worship of the Orthodox Church*. Translated by Paul Lazor. Crestwood, NY: SVS Press, 1985.

Vandenbroucke, F. "La dévotion au crucifié à la fin du moyen âge." *LMD* 75 (1963) 133–43.

Veilleux, Armand, trans. *The Life of Saint Pachomius*, Kalamazoo, MI: Cistercian, 1980.

Verhey, Allen. *The Great Reversal: Ethics and the New Testament*. Grand Rapids: Eerdmans, 1984.

Vermes, Pamela. *Buber*. London: Weidenfiled & Nicholson, 1988.

Vlachos, Metropolitan Hierotheos S. of Nafpaktos. *Orthodox Psychotherapy*. 3rd ed. Levadia, Greece: Birth of the Theotokos Monastery, 1997.

Vogel, C. J. de. *Philosophia I, Studies in Greek Philosophy*. Philosophical Texts and Studies 19, I. Assen: VanGorcum, 1970.

Vogel, C. *Introducion aux sources de l'histoire du culte chrétien au moyen âge*. Spoletto: Centro italiano di studi sull'alto medioevo, 1966.

————. *Medieval Liturgy: An Introduction to the Sources*. Translated by Niels Rasmussen and William Storey. Washington, DC: Pastoral, 1986.

Vos, Wiebe, and Geoffrey Wainwright, eds. *Liturgical Time: Papers Read at the 1981 Congress of Societas Liturgca*. Rotterdam: Liturgical Ecumenical Center Trust, 1982.

Vriezen, Theodorus Christiaan. *The Religion of Ancient Israel*. Translated Hubert Hoskins. Philadelphia: Westminster, 1967.

Wainwright, Geoffrey. "The Baptismal Eucharist before Nicea: An Essay in Liturgical History." *SL* 4 (1965) 9–36.

————. *Christian Initiation*. London: Lutterworth, 1970.

————. *Doxology: The Praise of God in Worship, Doctrine and Life: A Systematic Theology*. London: Epworth, 1980.

————. *Eucharist and Eschatology*. 2nd ed. London: Epworth, 1978.

————. "The Rites and Ceremonies of Christian Initiation." *SL* 10 (1974) 2–24.

————. "Sacramental Time." In *Liturgical Time: Papers Read at the 1981 Congress of Societas Liturgca*, edited by Wiebe Vos and Geoffrey Wainwright, 135–46: Rotterdam: Liturgical Ecumenical Center Trust, 1982.

Walker, Andrew G. "The Concept of a Person in Social Science: Possibilities for a Theological Anthropology." In *Forgotten Trinity*, Vol. 3: *A Selection of Papers Presented to the BCC Commission on Trinitarian Doctrine Today*, edited by Alasdair I. C. Heron, 137–57. London: BCC/CCBI, 1991.

————. *Enemy Territory: The Christian Struggle for the Modern World*. London: Hodder & Stoughton, 1987.

Walker, Andrew G.. and James Patrick, eds. *A Christian for All Christians*. London: Hodder and Stoughton, 1990.

Ward, Benedicta. *The Sayings of the Desert Fathers*. Kalamazoo, MI: Cistercian, 1975.

Ward, Heather. *The Gift of Self*. London: DLT, 1990.

————. *Giving Yourself Away*. Nottingham, UK: Grove, 1988.

Ward, Keith. *In Defence of the Soul*. 1992. Reprint. Oxford: One World, 1998.

Ware, Kallistos. "The Fool in Christ as Prophet and Apostle." *Sobornost* 6.2 (1984) 6–28.

————. "The Meaning of the Great Fast." In *The Lenten Triodion*, translated by Kallistos Ware and Mother Mary, 13–68. London: Faber, 1984.

————. "'It is time for the Lord to act': The 'Divine Liturgy as Heaven on Earth." *Sobornost* 23.1 (2001) 7–22.

————. "Praying with the Body: The Hesychast Method and Non-Christian Parallels." *Sobornost* 14.2 (1992) 6–35.

————. "Praying with Icons." In *One in 2000, Towards Catholic–Orthodox Unity*, edited by J. McPartlan, 141–68. Slough, UK: St Paul's, 1993.

————. "The Soul in Greek Christianity." In *From Soul to Self*, edited by M. James C. Crabbe, 49–69. London: Routledge, 1999.

Ware, Kallistos, and Mother Mary, trans. *The Festal Menaion*. London: Faber, 1969.

————. *The Lenten Triodion*. London: Faber, 1978.

Webb, C. C. J. *God and Personality: Being the Gifford Lectures delivered in the University of Alberdeen in the Years 1918 and 1919. First Course*. London: Allen, 1920.

Webster, Derek. "A Spiritual Dimension for Education?" In *Christian Perspectives for Education: A Reader in the Theology of Education*, edited by Leslie Francis and Adrian Thatcher, 355–64. Leominster, UK: Fowler Wright, 1990.

Webster, H. *Rest Days: A Sociological Study*. New York: Macmillan, 1916.

Weinandy, Thomas G. *In the Likeness of Sinful Flesh*. Edinburgh: T. & T. Clark, 1993.

Wensink, A. J., trans. *Mystic Treatises by Isaac of Nineveh*. 1923. Reprint. Wiesbaden: Sändig, 1969.

Wernle, Paul. *Beginnings of Christinaity*, Vol. 1. Translated by G. A. Biermann. Edited by W. D. Morrison. London: Williams, 1903.

Westerhoff, John H. (III). *Will Our Children Have Faith?* New York: Seabury, 1976.

Westermann, W. L. *The Slave Systems of Greek and Roman Antiquity*. Philadelphia: American Philosophical Society, 1955.

White, James F. *Roman Catholic Worship: Trent to Today*. New York: Paulist, 1995.

Wiedemann, T. *Greek and Roman Slavery; A Sourcebook*. Baltimore: John Hopkins University Press, 1981.

Wigley, John. *The Rise and Fall of the Victorian Sunday*. Manchester: Manchester University Press, 1980.

Williams, Rowan. "Balthasar and Rahner." In *The Analogy of Beauty: The Theology of Hans Urs von Balthasar*, edited by John Riches, 11–34. Edinburgh: T. & T. Clark, 1986.

Williams, Esther. *The Heart of Salvation: The Life and Teachings of Saint Theophan the Recluse*. Translated and edited by Robin Amis. Newbury, MA: Praxis Institute Press, n.d. (c. 1990).

Wilson, Daniel. *The Divine Authority and Perpetual Obligation of the Lord's Day*. London: Thynne, 1913. (From sermons delivered in 1827 and 1830.)

Wilson, John. *Approach to Moral Education*. Oxford: Farmington Trust, 1967.

———. *Education in Religion and the Emotions*. London: Heinemann, 1971.

Williams, Barrie. *The Franciscan Revival*. London: DLT, 1982.

Williams, Charles. *The Descent of the Dove*. London: Religious Book Club, 1939.

Williams, R. D. "The Theology of Personhood." *Sobornost* 6.6 (1972) 415–30.

Wittgenstein, Ludwig. *Culture and Value*. 2nd ed. Translated by Peter Winch. Oxford: Blackwell, 1980.

———. *Philosophical Investigations*. Translated by G. E. M. Anscombe. 1953. Reprint. Oxford: Blackwell, 1972.

Wolff, H. W. *Anthropology of the Old Testament*. Translated by M. Kohl. Philadelphia: Fortress, 1974.

Wright, N. T. *The New Testament and the People of God*. London: SPCK, 1992.

———. *Jesus and the Victory of God*. London: SPCK, 1996.

Wright, Tom, and Marcus Borg. *The Meaning of Jesus*. London: SPCK, 2012.

Yannaras, Christos. *The Freedom of Morality*. Translated by Elizabeth Brier. Crestwood, NY: SVS Press, 1984.

Yarnold, Edward. *Time for God*. London: Collins, 1994.

Yang, Yong-Eui. *Jesus and the Sabbath in Matthew's Gospel*. Sheffield, UK: Sheffield Academic Press, 1997.

Zander, Valentine. *St Seraphim of Sarov*. London: SPCK, 1975.

Zajcev, Boris, and Anna Vinci. *Icons and Holiness*. Rome: La Casa di Matriona, 1991.

Zeleski, Irma. *Encounter with a Desert Mother (Mother Maria Gysi)*. Toronto: Peregina, 1997.

Zerubavel, Eviatar. *The Seven Day Circle, the History and Meaning of the Week*. London: Collier Macmillan, 1985.

Zimmerli, W. *Mose 1–11*. Zürich: Zwingli-Verlag, 1943.

Zizioulas, J. D. *Being as Communion: Studies in Personhood and the Church*. Crestwood, NY: SVS Press, 1985.

———. "The Early Christian Community." SCMCS I, 23–43.

———. "The Eucharist and the Kingdom of God" (Part I). *Sourozh* 58 (1994) 1–12.

———. "The Eucharist and the Kingdom of God" (Part II) *Sourozh* 59 (1995) 22–38.

———. "Human Capacity and Human Incapacity: A Theological Exploration of Personhood." *SJT* 28 (1975) 401–48.

———. "On Being a Person: Towards an Ontology of Personhood." In *Persons Human and Divine: King's College Essays in Theological Anthropology*, edited by C. Schwöbel and C. Gunton, 33–46. Edinburgh: T. & T. Clark, 1991.

———. "Symbolism and Realism in Orthodox Worship." *Sourozh* 79 (2000) 3–17.

Zolotov, Andrei. "East-West Church and Ministry Report." http://www.eastwestreport. org/articles/ew06304.htm (Accessed July 2017.) And see "Ecumenical News International Bulletin," no. 11. June 1998, 16–17.

For the following ancient and pre-modern sources I use the title abbreviations and text numbering found in the following editions:

Albo, Joseph. *Book of Principles*, Vol. 3, tr. Isaac Husik. Philadelphia: Jewish Publication Society of America: 1930.

Aristotle. *The Compete Works of Aristotle: The Revised Oxford Translation*. Edited by J. Barnes. Oxford: Oxford University Press, 1984.

Descartes, René. *The Philosophical Writings of René Descartes*. Edited and translated by John Cottingham, Robert Stoothoff, Dugald Murdoch, and Anthony Kenny. 3 vols. Cambridge: Cambridge University Press, 1984–91.

Maimonides, Moses. *The Guide for the Perplexed*. Translated from the Arabic by M. Friedländer. New York: Dutton, 1910.

Plato. *Plato, The Collected Dialogues, including Letters*. Edited by Edith Hamilton and Huntington Cairns. Princeton NJ: Princeton University Press, 1963.

Abbreviations for Titles of Patristic Sources

Athanasius

Arians.	*Orations against the Arians*
Epist. heortast.	*Festal Letters*
Inc.	*On the Incarnation of the Logos*

Augustine

Ps	*Expostion of the Psalms*
Trin.	*On the Trinity*

Basil

Moral Rules	*Moral Rules*, Fathers of the Church, series 9.
Nativity	*On the Nativity of Christ*, PG 31
HS	*On the Holy Spirit*

Benedict of Nursia

Rule	*Monastic Rule*

Clement Alex. (Clement of Alexandria)

Str.	*Stromata (Miscellanies)*

Dionysisus: Psuedo-Dionysius the Areopagite

    Myst.   *On Mystical Theology*

Ephrem of Syria

    Serm.   *Sermons*

Epiphanius

    De fid.   *Exposition of the Faith*
    Haer.   *Against Eighty Heresies*

Eusebius

    EH   *Ecclesiastic History*
    Vita Const.   *Life of Constantine*

Epiphanius of Salamis

    De fide.   *Expositon of the Faith*
    Haer.   *Against Eighty Heresies*

Gregory Nazianzen

    De nov. Dom   *On the Divine Names*
    Or.   *Orations*

Gregory of Nyssa

    Eun.   *Against Eunomius*
    Not Three Gods *That there are Not Three Gods*
    On Man   *On the Making of Man (De hominis opificio)*
    Soul   *Dialogue on the Soul and Resurrection*

Gregory Palamas

    Triads   *Triads in Defense of the Holy Hesychasts*

Hippolytus

    Dan.   *Exposition of Daniel*
    AT   *Apostolic Tradition*

Irenaeus

    Proof   *Proof of the Apostolic Preaching*

    AH   *Adversus Haereses*

Isaac of Syria

    Treaties   *Mystic Treaties by Isaac of Nineveh* from Bedjan's Syriac text by A. J. Wensinck (Amsterdam, 1923).

    Homilies   *The Ascetical Homilies.* Boston: The Holy Transfiguration Monastery, 1984.

John Cassian

    Inst.   *Institutes*

    Conf.   *Conferences*

John Damascene

    Orth. Faith   *The Orthodox Faith*

    Transfig.   *First Discourse on the Transfiguration*

John Moscus

    Patum spiritale   *The Meadow*

Justin

    Dial.   *Dialogue*

Maximus

    Amb.   *Book of Ambiguities*

    Cent.Car.   *Centuries on Love*

    Cent.Theo   *Centuries on Theology*

    Cent.Var.   *Centuries on Various Topics*

    Myst.   *Mystagogy*

    Schol.   *Scholia on the "Ecclesiastical Hierarchy" of Dionysius the Areopagite* (PG 4).

    Thal.   *Questions to Thalassius on the Scriptures*

Nicholas Cabasilas

    Life   *The Life in Christ*

Origen of Alexandria

> *Joh.*   *Commentary on the Gospel of John*

Palladius

> *HL*   *Lausiac History*

Socrates Scolasitcus

> *EH*   *Ecclesiastical History*

Sozomen

> *EH*   *Ecclesiastical History*

Tertullian

> *Cor.*   *On the Crown (De corona)*
> *Prayer*   *On Prayer*
> *Fasting*   *On Fasting*